MCAT Course Book

Printed in the United States of America

Second Printing, 2017

ISBN 978-1-944935-10-8

Next Step Test Preparation, LLC
4256 N Ravenswood Ave
Suite 207
Chicago, IL 60613

www.nextstepmcat.com

ABOUT THE AUTHORS

Bryan Schnedeker is Next Step Test Prep's Vice President for MCAT Tutoring and Content. He manages all of our MCAT instructors nationally and counsels hundreds of students when they begin our tutoring process. He has been teaching and tutoring MCAT students since 2001 (starting at one of the big prep course companies before joining our team). He has attended medical school and law school and scored a 44 on the old MCAT, a 525 on the new MCAT, and a 180 on the LSAT. Bryan has worked with thousands of MCAT students over the years and specializes in helping students looking to achieve elite scores.

Dr. Anthony Lafond is Next Step's MCAT Content Director. He has been teaching and tutoring MCAT students for over a decade. He earned his MD and PhD degrees from UMDNJ—New Jersey Medical School with a focus on rehabilitative medicine. Dr. Lafond believes that both rehabilitative medicine and MCAT education hinge on the same core principle: crafting an approach that puts the unique needs of the individual foremost.

To find out about MCAT tutoring or working directly with Anthony or Bryan, visit our website: http://nextsteptestprep.com/mcat

Updates may be found here:
http://nextsteptestprep.com/mcat-materials-change-log/

If you have any feedback for us about this book please contact us at mcat@nextsteptestprep.com

Version: 2018-01-01

This page left intentionally blank.

TABLE OF CONTENTS

INTRODUCTION

Hello and welcome to Next Step's MCAT Course Book. In this book you will find hundreds of practice questions, dozens of practice passages and tons of MCAT strategy and MCAT content to help raise your score on Test Day.

This book will take you through the 20 lessons that comprise Next Step's online MCAT class. While you can download individual lesson PDFs from your online course website, or follow along with the lessons by simply watching the slides on the screen, we strongly recommend you always have this book open in front of you during lessons. Having a single book that has all of your notes and practice work will make later review much easier.

The key to mastering the MCAT (and getting the most out of your course!) involves taking a step-by-step approach. Start by watching the orientation video presented when you first log on to your MCAT home page at nextstepmcat.com. Then use the study plan generator to craft a study plan customized to your calendar and your needs. Finally, take the half-length Next Step MCAT diagnostic test to get a sense of your starting point. We also recommend that you follow up your MCAT diagnostic with our science content diagnostic to analyze your content strengths and weaknesses. While the science content diagnostic is optional, it provides valuable feedback.

Once you've gotten all of that groundwork out of the way, you can dive into your prep by starting Lesson 1.

Everyone here at Next Step would like to wish you the best of luck with your prep!

Thank you,

Bryan Schnedeker
Vice President for MCAT Content
Next Step Test Preparation, LLC

STOP! READ THIS FIRST!

How to Use This Book

This book is a companion to the online videos for Next Step's MCAT course. It does not contain answers and explanations—or even an answer key. For this book to be of use, you must be a Next Step class student and be using it to follow along your Next Step MCAT classes.

The class sessions have been designed to be a mix of the three things needed for Test Day success—content review, question practice, and passage practice. While the class sessions do cover all of the high-yield strategies and content that you will need, this book is not complete prep by itself; you will get no value out of simply reading through this book without the accompanying videos.

Every single class session has homework to be completed before the class, using your other Next Step MCAT books (notably the MCAT Content Review series and the Strategy and Practice series). To get the most out of the class lessons, you should keep up with the homework to be completed before and after each session.

Given the volume of homework to do, class lessons should be spaced out on a one-to-three times per week schedule. While it is possible to go through class lessons every other day (or even every day), working on such a compressed time scale will make it tough to do enough homework to get the most out of your prep.

Finally, you should take advantage of one of Next Step's unique class feature: live group office hours. Next Step conducts live office hours several times a week, giving you access to the most experienced MCAT teachers in the world—the ones that wrote your course! The live group office hours are conducted by teachers with the highest possible qualifications—years of experience, a 98th+ percentile score on the real MCAT, and experience writing and editing the Next Step course materials. If you find that you have a question that isn't answered by the books or videos, the group office hours let you get your questions answered.

Before diving into the lessons, be sure to complete the following preliminary steps:

1. Watch the orientation video the first time you log in at nextstepmcat.com
2. Complete the half-length Next Step MCAT Diagnostic Test
3. (optional) Complete the Science Content Diagnostic Test
4. Use the online Study Plan tool to set up your study calendar

LESSON 1

Introduction to MCAT Strategy

To Do Before Lesson 1

- ☐ Watch the Orientation Video for your online syllabus
- ☐ Set up your online Study Plan (found by clicking the "Study Plan" tab at the top of your nextstepmcat.com home page)
- ☐ Take the MCAT Diagnostic half-length exam under TIMED conditions
- ☐ Visit the AAMC website to review MCAT procedures and timelines

In Lesson 1

About the MCAT
Test Day: When, What to Bring
Question Types: Science
Reading the Passage: Science
Question Types: CARS
Reading the Passage: CARS
Strategies: Timing and Studying
The Next Step Class and Resources
Study Plan Building

To Do After Lesson 1

- ☐ Take the MCAT Diagnostic Exam under TIMED conditions (if not already done)
    - Review the Diagnostic Exam
- ☐ Read Verbal and Quantitative Chapters 1 and 2
- ☐ Read Chemistry and Organic Chemistry Chapter 1
    - Complete the practice passages in these chapters

About the MCAT

1. Exam Structure

- 8 AM start
- Same section order, different passage order

2. Exam Dates

- January, March–September

3. MCAT Scoring and Score Reports

- Focus on percentile rather than scaled number

4. Test Day: What to Bring

- In the room with you vs. in your locker

Sections on the MCAT

Chemical and Physical Foundations: 95 min, 44 passage-based questions, 15 discrete questions

Critical Analysis and Reasoning Skills: 90 min, 53 passage-based questions

Biological and Biochemical Foundations: 95 min, 44 passage-based questions, 15 discrete questions

Psychological and Social Foundations: 95 min, 44 passage-based questions, 15 discrete questions

Exam Structure

Test Section	Topics Tested	# of Questions	Time
Tutorial *(optional)*	-	-	10 minutes
1. Chemical and Physical Foundations of Biological Systems	Chemistry (30%) Biochemistry (25%) Physics (25%) Organic Chemistry (15%) Biology (5%)	59	95 minutes
Break *(optional)*	-	-	10 minutes
2. Critical Analysis and Reasoning Skills	No outside knowledge needed. No natural science passages. All you need to answer the questions is in the passage. (500-600 words per passage).	53	90 minutes
LUNCH Break *(optional)*	-	-	30 minutes
3. Biological and Biochemical Foundations of Living Systems	Biology (65%) Biochemistry (25%) Chemistry (5%) Organic Chemistry (5%)	59	95 minutes
Break *(optional)*	-	-	10 minutes
4. Psychological, Social, and Biological Foundations of Behavior	Psychology (65%) Sociology (35%) Biology (5%)	59	95 minutes
Test Time	-	-	6 hours, 15 minutes
Total "Seated" Time (approx.)	-	-	7 hours, 30 minutes

Exam Dates for 2018

Admin Date	Score Release
January 19-20	February 23
January 25	February 27
March 24	May 1
April 6	May 8
April 20-21	May 22
May 5	June 5
May 18-19	June 19
May 24	June 26
June 1-2	July 3
June 16	July 17
June 29-30	July 31
July 7	August 7
July 20-21	August 21
July 24	August 23
August 3-4	September 5
August 9-10	September 11
August 18	September 18
Aug 31 - Sept 1	October 2
September 8	October 9
September 18-19	October 23

Choosing Your Test Date

MCAT Scoring and Score Reports

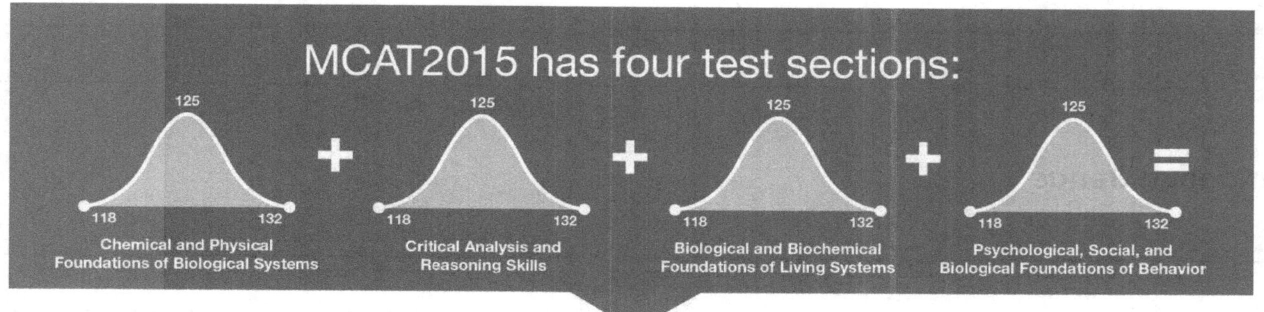

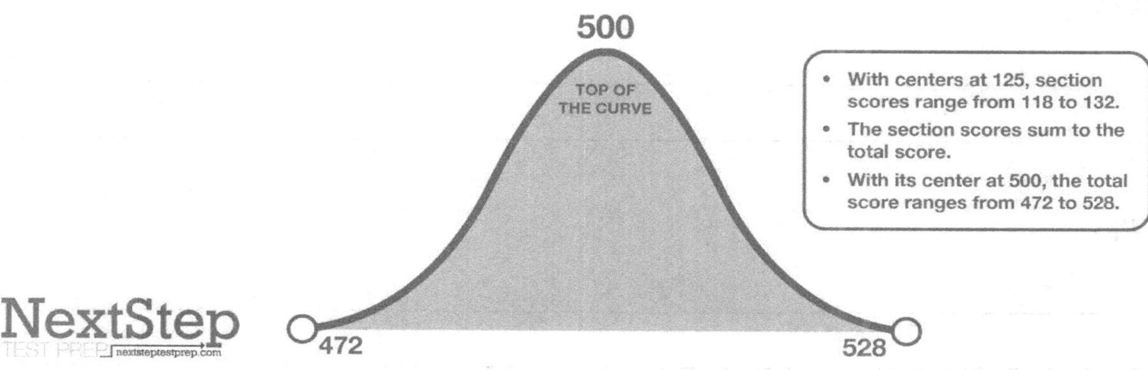

MCAT Score Report Exam taken on 05/30/2015

Section	Score	Confidence Band[1]	Percentile Rank of Score[2]	Score Profile[3]
Chemical and Physical Foundations of Biological Systems	125	124 ◆ 126	50%	118 125 132
Critical Analysis and Reasoning Skills	127	126 ◆ 128	75%	118 125 132
Biological and Biochemical Foundations of Living Systems	130	129 ◆ 131	97%	118 125 132
Psychological, Social, and Biological Foundations of Behavior	124	123 ◆ 125	45%	118 125 132
MCAT Total Score	**506**	**504 ◆ 508**	**76%**	

Notes:

[1]Test scores, like other measurements, are not perfectly precise. The confidence bands around test scores mark the ranges in which the test taker's true scores likely lie. The diamond shapes and shading indicate that the test taker's true score is more likely to be in the center of the confidence bands than at the ends.

[2]The percentile ranks of scores are the percentages of test takers who received the same score or lower scores.

[3]For the four sections, the score profile shows a test taker's strengths and weaknesses.

Percentile Ranks

____

____

Confidence Bands

____

____

Scaled Score

____

____

Score Profile

____

____

My score goal is ______________________.

Test Day: What to Bring

In the room with you:

____

____

In your locker:

____

____

- You can bring food and drink (not refrigerated!)
- Aspirin
- Tissues
- Your purse/wallet/phone (off!!)

How the MCAT Tests Us

Question Format

Passage-based and Conceptual Questions

Emphasis on Critical Thinking

What is on the Current MCAT

Content

Integration of Sciences

Research Design and Statistical Methods

Strategy

Question Types: Science

	Task	Example
Skill 1		
Skill 2		
Skill 3		
Skill 4		

READING THE PASSAGE Science

First, the conjugation is performed in solution by mixing antibodies with an excess of azide-modified oligonucleotides. The resulting mix containing antibody-DNA conjugates and remaining free antibodies and oligonucleotides is incubated, and the products are immobilized on agarose beads. After washes to remove unconjugated antibodies, the captured antibody-DNA conjugates along with unconjugated oligonucleotides are both released by enzymatic cleavage using the restriction enzyme MlyI that cleaves at the border of the complementary region (Figure 2. between the capture and conjugate oligonucleotides to release single-stranded DNA-coupled conjugates. The eluate was then captured on protein G beads and washes were conducted to remove any free oligonucleotides having no antibodies attached. Finally, purified conjugates were eluted from the protein G beads by lowering the pH.

What to look out for:

____

____

Why vs. How

____

____

Takeaway:

____

____

My Notes:

____

____

____

EXAMPLE

Interpreting Scientific Figures

# of MIB1 positive cells	56±3.2	143±5.7	110±16.7
Injury	+	+	+
anti-monocyte antibody	+	-	+
TGFβ agonist	-	-	+

11±1.1	42±3.7	10±2.1	
+	+	+	Injury
+	-	+	TGFBR1 antagonist
-	-	+	TGFBR2 antagonist

What to look out for:

Takeaway:

My Notes:

Strategy

Question Types: CARS

	Task	Example
Skill 1		
Skill 2		
Skill 3		

READING THE PASSAGE **CARS**

While the central otherworldly concerns of the Taoist religion have led some commentators to assert that Taoism is a "religion without religious texts", nothing could be further from the truth. The key texts of Taoism may lack the same coherence and historicity of the Talmud or the Qur'an, but there are nonetheless various works that have profound influence, and no small authority among nearly all Taoist sects.

What to look out for:

____

____

Takeaway:

____

____

My Notes:

____

READING THE PASSAGE CARS

It goes without saying that the Tao Te Ching is the central work of all Taoist religion. Despite two and a half millennia of debate over its origins, authorship, and date of origin, it remains the foundational work of Taoist philosophy and a central component of Taoist ritual. So important is this work that even commentaries on it (themselves many hundreds of years old) have become important religious texts themselves.

What to look out for:

Takeaway:

My Notes:

Next Step MCAT Section Strategy: Science

1. Order of questions
2. Timing cheat sheet
3. Micro-breaks
4. The review screen

Order of questions

With the **one question at a time** format of the exam, the strategy of skipping and/or saving passages for later will not be efficient. In the sciences you should budget ≈ 8 minutes per passage and question set. Reading the passage should take about ≈ 3-4 minutes, with ≈ 5 minutes for the questions.

- Discrete questions first
- Passages in order

Method 1 (Sciences):

Item Complete	Time Remaining
Discrete questions	80 minutes
Passages 1-2	64 minutes
Passages 3-4	48 minutes
Passages 5-6	32 minutes
Passages 7-8	16 minutes
Passages 9-10	0 minutes

Pros:

____

____

____

Cons:

____

____

____

Method 2 (Sciences):

Do the section in order, checking the clock every 2-3 passages. Use 1 min per discrete Q, 8 min/passage average.

Pros:

____

____

____

Cons:

____

____

____

Next Step MCAT Section Strategy: CARS

With the **one question at a time** format of the exam, the strategy of skipping and/or saving passages for later will not be efficient.

In CARS you have 10 minutes per passage. You want to check your pace every 2-3 passages.

You should spend 3-4 minutes reading, and 6-7 minutes answering the questions. Spend more time where the points are.

Item Complete	Time Remaining
Passages 1-2	70 minutes
Passages 3-4	50 minutes
Passages 5-6	30 minutes
Passages 7-8	10 minutes
Passages 9	0 minutes

Strategy

Timing Cheat Sheet

As you get used to your timing strategies, you can quickly create this crib sheet as you start each section to remind you of your timing until you internalize your own ideal pacing.

Science

CARS

Skipping passages

Micro-breaks

- Your brain will take breaks whether you want it to or not
- Take control of the breaks
- Every single passage
- Every second passage
- Every third passage

The review screen

- Navigate quickly to discrete sets in method 1.
- "Review Incomplete"
- "Review Marked"

Which method do you think will suit you best?

What is the best way to determine your ideal strategy?

What are the potential problems with skipping around the section?

Strategy

Next Step MCAT Question Strategy

Attacking the Question

Read
Read the Q stem

Rephrase
Put the task in your own words so you are sure you know what it means.

Research
Research the passage or your own knowledge (depending on the section, question type) and come up with a framework for your answer.

Respond
Choose the answer that is best supported by your research and satisfies the question stem.

EXAMPLE

Each of the following structures develop from the mesoderm EXCEPT:

I. lining of trachea
II. erythrocytes
III. myocardium

A. I only
B. I and II only
C. II and III only
D. I, II and III

Learning MCAT Content

1. Study groups
2. Lessons Learned Journal
3. Study sheets
4. Mnemonics
5. Spaced repetition

1. Study groups

- Group of 3, class members
- Meet once a week
- Each person has homework—2 passages
- Homework:
    i. Prep the passage: highlighting, note-taking, analyzing the diagram
    ii. Prep the questions: answer them, read the "hints", develop explanations
    iii. Come up with at least three "lessons learned" from each passage
- Have one group representative that will email the group.
    i. Date, time, location, attendance for meeting
    ii. Which passages were reviewed?
    iii. Summary of all the "lessons learned"

2. Lessons Learned Journal

- Start a Word document to record all of your Lessons Learned Journal
- What is a "Lesson Learned"?
    i. Key concept or mnemonic you forgot
    ii. Strategy note
    iii. Anything you want to do (or not do!) on Test Day
- After completing: any practice passages, practice questions in your MCAT books
- Review the entire LLJ at the end of each week
- Will be anywhere from 25—125 pages by the time you are done

3. Study sheets

- Avoid passive methods!
- A single page to summarize an important concept area (e.g. Hb binding curve)
- You should make a study sheet each week to share with your study group

Study Sheet Example: Solubility Rules

NO_3^-	All soluble	Fe_2O_3	Insoluble
SO_4^{2-}	Soluble ***except Hg, Pb, Ca, Sr, Ba***	SrS, $Sr(OH)_2$	Soluble
CaS, $Ca(OH)_2$	Soluble	CH_3COO^-	All soluble
NH_4^+	All soluble	$(NH_4)_2S$	Soluble
Metal oxides	Insoluble ***except alkali, Ca, Sr, Ba***	BaS, $Ba(OH)_2$	Soluble
ClO_4^-	All soluble	Ag^+	Insoluble except NO_3^-, ClO_4^-, CH_3COO^-
Na^+	All soluble	CO_3^{2-}	Insoluble except w. alkali or ammonium
S^{2-}	Insoluble ***except w. alkali, alk earth or ammonium***	$Pb(OH)_4$	Insoluble
Pb^{2+}, Pb^{4+}	Insoluble except NO_3^-, ClO_4^-, CH_3COO^-	PO_4^{3-}	Insoluble except w. alkali or ammonium
K^+	All soluble	Hg_2S	Insoluble
$Ba(NO_3)_2$	Soluble	$Ca(CrO_4)_2$	Soluble
$SrSO_4$	Insoluble	Ag_2NO_3	Soluble
Li^+	All soluble	$CaCO_3$	Insoluble
CH_3COONa	Soluble	OH^-	Insoluble except w. alkali, alk earth or ammonium
Acetate	All soluble	Li_2S	Soluble
Halogens	Soluble ***except Ag, Hg, Pb***	Hg_2^{2+}, Hg^{2+}	Insoluble except NO_3^-, ClO_4^-, CH_3COO^-

Solubility Rules: Level 1

NO_3^-		Fe_2O_3	Insoluble
SO_4^{2-}		SrS, $Sr(OH)_2$	Soluble
CaS, $Ca(OH)_2$		CH_3COO^-	
NH_4^+		$(NH_4)_2S$	
Metal oxides	Insoluble ***except alkali, Ca, Sr, Ba***	BaS, $Ba(OH)_2$	Soluble
ClO_4^-	All soluble	Ag^+	Insoluble except NO_3^-, ClO_4^-, CH_3COO^-
Na^+	All soluble	CO_3^{2-}	Insoluble except w. alkali or ammonium
S^{2-}	Insoluble ***except w. alkali, alk earth or ammonium***	$Pb(OH)_4$	Insoluble
Pb^{2+}, Pb^{4+}	Insoluble except NO_3^-, ClO_4^-, CH_3COO^-	PO_4^{3-}	Insoluble except w. alkali or ammonium
K^+	All soluble	Hg_2S	
$Ba(NO_3)_2$	Soluble	$Ca(CrO_4)_2$	
$SrSO_4$	Insoluble	Ag_2NO_3	Soluble
Li^+		$CaCO_3$	Insoluble
CH_3COONa	Soluble	OH^-	
Acetate		Li_2S	Soluble
Halogens		Hg_2^{2+}, Hg^{2+}	Insoluble except NO_3^-, ClO_4^-, CH_3COO^-

Solubility Rules: Level 2

NO_3^-		Fe_2O_3	
SO_4^{2-}		SrS, $Sr(OH)_2$	Soluble
CaS, $Ca(OH)_2$		CH_3COO^-	
NH_4^+		$(NH_4)_2S$	
Metal oxides	Insoluble ***except alkali, Ca, Sr, Ba***	BaS, $Ba(OH)_2$	Soluble
ClO_4^-	All soluble	Ag^+	
Na^+	All soluble	CO_3^{2-}	
S^{2-}		$Pb(OH)_4$	Insoluble
Pb^{2+}, Pb^{4+}	Insoluble except NO_3^-, ClO_4^-, CH_3COO^-	PO_4^{3-}	Insoluble except w. alkali or ammonium
K^+		Hg_2S	
$Ba(NO_3)_2$		$Ca(CrO_4)_2$	
$SrSO_4$		Ag_2NO_3	
Li^+		$CaCO_3$	
CH_3COONa	Soluble	OH^-	
Acetate		Li_2S	Soluble
Halogens		Hg_2^{2+}, Hg^{2+}	

Solubility Rules: Level 3

NO_3^-		Fe_2O_3	
SO_4^{2-}		SrS, $Sr(OH)_2$	
CaS, $Ca(OH)_2$		CH_3COO^-	
NH_4^+		$(NH_4)_2S$	
Metal oxides		BaS, $Ba(OH)_2$	
ClO_4^-		Ag^+	
Na^+		CO_3^{2-}	
S^{2-}		$Pb(OH)_4$	
Pb^{2+}, Pb^{4+}		PO_4^{3-}	
K^+		Hg_2S	
$Ba(NO_3)_2$		$Ca(CrO_4)_2$	
$SrSO_4$		Ag_2NO_3	
Li^+		$CaCO_3$	
CH_3COONa		OH^-	
Acetate		Li_2S	
Halogens		Hg_2^{2+}, Hg^{2+}	

4. Mnemonics

- Good ones are outrageous, naughty, or related to people you know (or all 3!)
- Can be visual, auditory, kinesthetic
- You should create a new mnemonic every other week

EXAMPLES

The classification hierarchy for living things:

The 7 elements that are diatomic gases at standard conditions:

Or memorize it phonetically

EXAMPLE

Or memorize information visually:

1 H 1.008																	2 He 4.00
3 Li 6.94	4 Be 9.01											5 B 10.81	6 C 12.01	7 N 14.01	8 O 16.00	9 F 19.00	10 Ne 20.18
11 Na 22.99	12 Mg 24.31											13 Al 26.98	14 Si 28.09	15 P 30.97	16 S 32.07	17 Cl 35.45	18 Ar 39.95
19 K 39.10	20 Ca 40.08	21 Sc 44.96	22 Ti 47.88	23 V 50.94	24 Cr 52.00	25 Mn 54.94	26 Fe 55.85	27 Co 58.93	28 Ni 58.69	29 Cu 63.55	30 Zn 65.39	31 Ga 69.72	32 Ge 72.61	33 As 74.92	34 Se 78.96	35 Br 79.90	36 Kr 83.80
37 Rb 85.47	38 Sr 87.62	39 Y 88.91	40 Zr 91.22	41 Nb 92.91	42 Mo 95.94	43 Tc (98)	44 Ru 101.1	45 Rh 102.9	46 Pd 106.4	47 Ag 107.9	48 Cd 112.4	49 In 114.8	50 Sn 118.71	51 Sb 121.75	52 Te 127.60	53 I 126.90	54 Xe 131.29

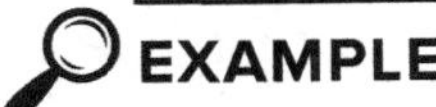

EXAMPLE

How the right hand rule works for $F = qvB\sin\theta$:

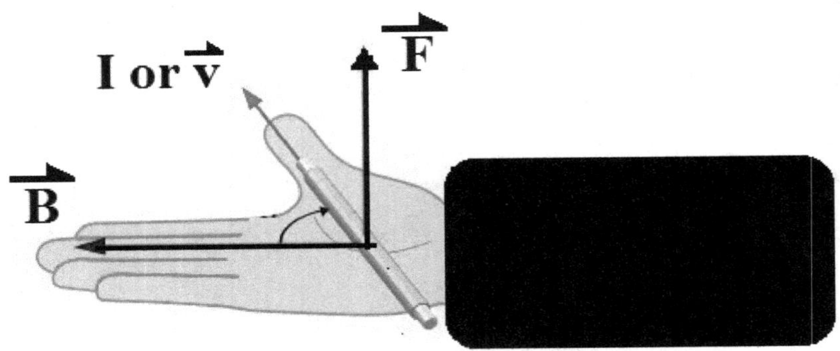

5. Spaced repetition

- To learn things you ***must*** do two things: ______________ and ______________.

EXAMPLE

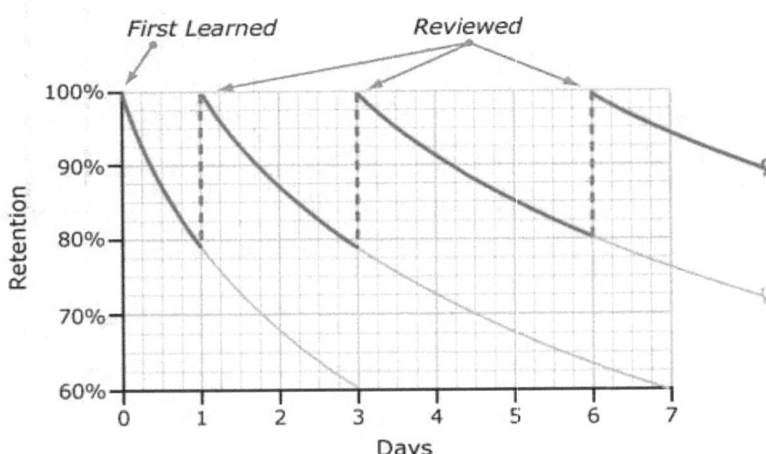

- When you do the questions at the end of the chapter come back and review them:
  i. At the very end of the day
  ii. The next day
  iii. The next week

The Next Step MCAT Class

This class will be a mix of several learning methods and MCAT practice types proven to help improve your score in the most efficient way possible.

1. Strategy Discussion
2. Passage Practice
3. Content Review
4. Content Practice Questions

1. Strategy Discussion

- Strategies for attacking the passages
- Strategies for managing stress
- Strategies for how to study effectively

2. Passage Practice

- Two or more passages in every class
- Frequent CARS practice. Everyone's favorite!

3. Content Review

- Not simply a lecture
- You will be expected to have read the content in advance
- Discussion of particular aspects that are confusing
- Study Sheet and Worksheet exercises in this book

4. Content Practice Questions

- Reviewing science principles is not enough!
- Content will be applied by practicing questions
- Done in the style of MCAT discrete questions

Your Available Resources

Content review

Content practice

Passage practice

Timing/Pacing practice

Endurance practice

AAMC materials

Free materials

Books: MCAT Review series

Books: Additional Practice series

Online: QBank

Make Your Study Calendar

Days per week

How long?

Where?

What resources?

Milestones

Study groups

Yes Dr. ______________________________ it *is* worth it.

To Do After Lesson 1

- ☐ Take the MCAT Diagnostic Exam under TIMED conditions (if not already done)
    - Review the Diagnostic Exam
- ☐ Read Verbal and Quantitative Chapters 1 and 2
- ☐ Read Chemistry and Organic Chemistry Chapter 1
    - Complete the practice passages in these chapters

Critical Analysis and Reasoning Skills

LESSON 2

To Do Before Lesson 2

- ☐ Take the MCAT Diagnostic Exam under TIMED conditions (if not already done)
  - Review the Diagnostic Exam
- ☐ Read Verbal and Quantitative Chapters 1 and 2
- ☐ Read Chemistry and Organic Chemistry Chapter 1
  - Complete the practice passages in these chapters

In Lesson 2

Effective Reading in CARS
CARS Skill 1: Understanding the Passage
Analyzing Opinions and Arguments
CARS Skill 2: Understanding Opinions and Arguments
CARS Skill 3: Opinions and Arguments and New Information
Timed Practice Passage
Lessons Learned Journal

To Do After Lesson 2

- ☐ Read and complete Verbal and Quantitative Reasoning Chapters 3 and 4
  - Determine the correct CARS reading strategy for you
- ☐ Read Physics Chapters 1 and 2
- ☐ Read Chemistry and Organic Chemistry Chapters 2 and 3
- ☐ Read Biology Chapters 1 and 2

Effective Reading in CARS

Key Terms—

Opinions—

Contrast—

Cause and Effect—

This page left intentionally blank.

Effective Reading Exercise—Passage 1

Sir John Lubbock's ties to Darwin are exceedingly easy to trace: not only was he a member of the "X Club," a dining club of scientific gentleman who banded together to support and defend Darwin's theories after the 1859 publication of *The Origin of Species*, but he was a close personal friend of the older scientist; he grew up near Darwin's Down House and received comments on several of his works from him before publication. Yet, as George Stocking argues, it is appropriate to consider the bulk of Victorian anthropologists (or, to be historically accurate, ethnologists), "Darwinistic" if not "Darwinian." By this, Stocking means that while many of the theories espoused in the anthropology of the day might not have been "explicit or directly implied in *The Origin*," there were a range of "metaphysical, moral, or ideological notions deriving from other sources that were intermingled with Darwinism," including the raising of "new questions which had not been relevant in other contexts." Thus Victorian anthropology can be linked to a new approach to science fueled by, if not entirely cohesive with, Darwin's ideas.

The Darwinistic elements of approaches such as Lubbock's are most obvious in terms of two seemingly contradictory claims about human culture: the uniformity of cultural development and the idea that natural selection created favored groups. Like other social evolutionists of his time, Lubbock rejected the notion that all human groups began at an advanced level of civilization (exemplified, for proponents of the devolution theory, by Western European men), but certain "savage" groups "unlearned" that high level of civilization. Instead, proponents of an evolutionary anthropology argued for a progressive sequence of development. As Sir Edward Tyler, one of Lubbock's contemporaries, wrote,

> . . . the condition of culture among the various societies of mankind . . . is a subject apt for the study of laws of human thought and action. On the one hand, the uniformity which so largely pervades civilization may be ascribed, in great measure, to the uniform action of uniform causes; while on the other hand its various grades may be regarded as stages of development or evolution, each the outcome of previous history, and about to do its proper part in shaping the history of the future."

Lubbock's own particular contribution to this theory included his coining of the terms "Paleolithic" and "Neolithic" in his examinations of the characteristics of particular stages of development and arguing that contemporary "primitive" cultures represented European man's prehistoric state.

Yet despite an insistence that all groups theoretically move through the same stages, Lubbock, as did many of his cohorts, saw the modern-day existence of "primitive" cultures as evidence of their evolutionary unfitness. While Europeans had advanced through the stages of civilization, he argued, the groups that had not failed to do so because they lacked fitness. While humans shared a general physical fitness, variation existed in mental fitness to develop and, Lubbock wrote, "the great principle of natural selection . . . in man affects the mind and has little influence on the body." In arguing thusly, Bruce Trigger argues, Lubbock introduced an element of biological fitness to utilize culture. "What was new," writes Trigger, "was Lubbock's . . . insistence that, as a result of natural selection, human groups had become different from each other, not only culturally, but also in their biological capacities to utilize culture."

[Adapted from "Lubbock and Darwin" by R. Grubbs]

Passage taken from the Next Step online QBank - CARS Passages

¶ 1

¶ 2

¶ 3

¶ 4

Main idea:

Effective Reading Exercise

The CARS section requires you to focus more on ideas and arguments rather than facts. Think about the following questions and determine if your reading strategy allows you to answer or research your answer for these questions efficiently.

The author quotes Tyler in order to:

____

____

Based on the key terms noted, where in the passage might you find the information needed to answer this question?

____

____

How would you summarize Lubbock's opinion on human development?

____

____

What are the types of fitness discussed in the passage?

____

____

What effect did the *Origin of Species* have on anthropology?

____

____

This page left intentionally blank.

Question Practice—Critical Reading Payoff

Sir John Lubbock's ties to Darwin are exceedingly easy to trace: not only was he a member of the "X Club," a dining club of scientific gentleman who banded together to support and defend Darwin's theories after the 1859 publication of *The Origin of Species*, but he was a close personal friend of the older scientist; he grew up near Darwin's Down House and received comments on several of his works from him before publication. Yet, as George Stocking argues, it is appropriate to consider the bulk of Victorian anthropologists (or, to be historically accurate, ethnologists), "Darwinistic" if not "Darwinian." By this, Stocking means that while many of the theories espoused in the anthropology of the day might not have been "explicit or directly implied in *The Origin*," there were a range of "metaphysical, moral, or ideological notions deriving from other sources that were intermingled with Darwinism," including the raising of "new questions which had not been relevant in other contexts." Thus Victorian anthropology can be linked to a new approach to science fueled by, if not entirely cohesive with, Darwin's ideas.

The Darwinistic elements of approaches such as Lubbock's are most obvious in terms of two seemingly contradictory claims about human culture: the uniformity of cultural development and the idea that natural selection created favored groups. Like other social evolutionists of his time, Lubbock rejected the notion that all human groups began at an advanced level of civilization (exemplified, for proponents of the devolution theory, by Western European men), but certain "savage" groups "unlearned" that high level of civilization. Instead, proponents of an evolutionary anthropology argued for a progressive sequence of development. As Sir Edward Tyler, one of Lubbock's contemporaries, wrote,

> . . . the condition of culture among the various societies of mankind . . . is a subject apt for the study of laws of human thought and action. On the one hand, the uniformity which so largely pervades civilization may be ascribed, in great measure, to the uniform action of uniform causes; while on the other hand its various grades may be regarded as stages of development or evolution, each the outcome of previous history, and about to do its proper part in shaping the history of the future."

Lubbock's own particular contribution to this theory included his coining of the terms "Paleolithic" and "Neolithic" in his examinations of the characteristics of particular stages of development and arguing that contemporary "primitive" cultures represented European man's prehistoric state.

Yet despite an insistence that all groups theoretically move through the same stages, Lubbock, as did many of his cohorts, saw the modern-day existence of "primitive" cultures as evidence of their evolutionary unfitness. While Europeans had advanced through the stages of civilization, he argued, the groups that had not failed to do so because they lacked fitness. While humans shared a general physical fitness, variation existed in mental fitness to develop and, Lubbock wrote, "the great principle of natural selection . . . in man affects the mind and has little influence on the body." In arguing thusly, Bruce Trigger argues, Lubbock introduced an element of biological fitness to utilize culture. "What was new," writes Trigger, "was Lubbock's . . . insistence that, as a result of natural selection, human groups had become different from each other, not only culturally, but also in their biological capacities to utilize culture."

[Adapted from "Lubbock and Darwin" by R. Grubbs]

Passage taken from the Next Step online QBank - CARS Passages

1. Based on the passage, proponents of the devolution theory believed that:
   A. uniform natural laws indicate the likeliness of the entropy of social structures.
   B. cultural development only occurred in groups with the proper mental fitness.
   C. Western Europeans inevitably decline from the heights of their cultural evolution.
   D. it was possible for a group to move backwards through stages of civilization.

2. Which of the following conclusions about Lubbock's beliefs about natural selection can be inferred from the passage?
   A. He believed that it was more likely to operate somatically than psychologically in humans.
   B. He believed that it was more likely to operate psychologically than somatically in humans.
   C. He had severe doubts as to whether natural selection's precepts applied to humans.
   D. He argued that it was the sole factor that led to variation between human groups.

3. The author quotes Tyler in order to:
   A. highlight Lubbock's insistence that human groups had varying amounts of cultural fitness.
   B. argue that uniformitarian views served to illustrate and defend Darwin's views.
   C. explain the origin of terms such as "Paleolithic" and "Neolithic".
   D. demonstrate that many Victorian anthropologists linked laws of species and human development.

4. All of the following approaches might be termed "Darwinistic" EXCEPT:
   A. one that insisted that human evolution did not occur through natural selection, as claimed in The Origin.
   B. one based on the writings of Herbert Spencer, a Victorian who espoused evolutionary ideas.
   C. an ethnology text that raised questions about the fitness of various groups to evolve culturally.
   D. an article that applied the moral questions raised in The Origin to religious questions of the time period.

CARS Skill 1: Understanding the Passage

Skill 1: Foundations of comprehension

- Understanding the structure of a passage
- Identifying the main idea of a passage

Skill 1 questions will comprise 30% of all CARS questions (≈15 questions)

The main idea should correctly summarize the author's reason for writing passage and, if applicable, the tone with which the ideas are presented by the author.

What is the main idea for practice passage 1?

____

____

How does the author support the comparison between Lubbock and Darwin?

____

____

Main idea questions will appear in the CARS section, but there will not be many. More importantly, having a good grasp of the main idea will minimize your chances of being tempted by a clever wrong answer by keeping you focused on the goal of the passage.

CARS Skill 2: Understanding Opinions & Arguments

Skill 2: Reasoning within the text

- Understand and reason about the opinions and arguments in a passage
- Identify the different parts of the arguments and their relationships to each other
- Recognize the meanings of opinions made by the author and others if applicable

Skill 2 questions will comprise 30% of all CARS questions (≈16 questions)

5. Based on the passage, with which of the following stances would Lubbock be most likely to agree?
   A. The metaphysical and moral elements of Darwin's theories proved far more useful to anthropologists than the physical aspects of his ideas.
   B. Neolithic humans proved to be more affected by natural selection than those of Paleolithic times.
   C. Human civilization has evolved through recognizable stages, but certain groups do not have the biological fitness to develop culturally.
   D. Most human cultures began at advanced stages of civilization but struggled under natural forces.

What can you look for while reading to help identify opinions in CARS passages?

____

____

What are some common opinion sources the testmakers will include in CARS passages?

____

____

CARS Skill 3: Opinions and Arguments and New Information

Skill 3: Reasoning beyond the text

- Incorporate new information to determine its effect on the passage opinions and arguments.
- Use the passage opinions and arguments in new situations.

Skill 3 questions will comprise 40% of all CARS questions (≈22 questions)

6. Suppose that a Victorian textbook on ethnology was discovered that focused on what it termed "primitive" cultures. This would most lend credence to the passage's claim that:

   A. members of the X Club had been successful in disseminating Darwin's theories.
   B. anthropologists such as Lubbock understood some cultures to be representative of the prehistoric stages of development.
   C. Paleolithic and Neolithic stages were actually far more advanced than earlier anthropologists had given them credit for.
   D. anthropology corrected many of the misapprehensions of ethnology.

7. Based on the passage, which of the following models of human development would Lubbock find likely?

   A. A culture begins with simple tools, evolves physically to develop more complex devices, and ultimately rises to a high level of civilization.
   B. A culture bypasses the Paleolithic stage, evolves mentally to develop more complex devices, and ultimately rises to a high level of civilization.
   C. A culture begins with simple tools, evolves mentally to develop more complex devices, and ultimately falls from its previous high level of civilization.
   D. A culture begins with simple tools, evolves mentally to develop more complex devices, and ultimately rises to a high level of civilization.

This page left intentionally blank.

MCAT Practice Passage 2

In Hopi Indian culture, the house belongs to the woman. She literally builds it, and she is the head of the family, but the men help with the lifting of timbers, and now-a-days often lay up the masonry if desired; the woman is still the plasterer. The ancestral home is very dear to the Hopi heart, men, women, and children alike.

The women bring water, clay, and earth, and mix a mud mortar, which is used sparingly between layers of stone. Walls are from eight to eighteen inches thick and seven or eight feet high, above which rafters or poles are placed and smaller poles crosswise above these, then willows or reeds closely laid, and above all reeds or grass holding a spread of mud plaster. When thoroughly dry, a layer of earth is added and carefully packed down. All this is done by the women, as well as the plastering of the inside walls and the making of the plaster floors.

Now the women proceed to plaster the interior, to which, when it is dry, a coat of white gypsum is applied (all with strokes of the bare hands), giving the room a clean, fresh appearance. In one corner of the room is built a fireplace and chimney, the latter often extended above the roof by piling bottomless jars one upon the other, a quaint touch, reminding one of the picturesque chimney pots of England. The roofs are finished flat and lived upon as in Mediterranean countries, particularly in the case of one-story structures built against two-story buildings, the roof of the low building making the porch or roof-garden for the second-story room lying immediately adjacent.

Formerly, the house was practically bare of furniture save for the fireplace and an occasional stool, but the majority of the Hopi have taken kindly to American small iron cook stoves, simple tables and chairs, and some of them have iron bedsteads. Even now, however, there are many homes, perhaps they are still in the majority, where the family sits in the middle of the floor and eats from a common bowl and sleeps on a pile of comfortable sheep skins, rolled up when not in use.

In the granary, which is usually a low back room, the ears of corn are often sorted by color and laid up in neat piles, red, yellow, white, blue, black, and mottled, a Hopi study in corn color. Strings of native peppers add to the colorful ensemble.

[Adapted from The Unwritten Literature of the Hopi, by Hattie Greene Lockett, 1933.]

¶1:

¶2:

¶3:

¶4:

¶5:

Main idea:

Passage taken from the Next Step online QBank - CARS Passages

8. Which of the following best describes the author's attitude to Hopi living conditions?
   A. Simple, clean and attractive
   B. Crude and somewhat garish, but functional
   C. Charmingly backwards
   D. Aesthetically attractive and seductively opulent

9. Which of the following titles most accurately describes this passage?
   A. How to Construct a Traditional Hopi House
   B. Hopi Architecture, Then and Now
   C. The Hopi House and its Social Implications
   D. An Overview of the Traditional Hopi Home

10. Which of the following home-building tasks is, according to the passage, often assigned to men?
    A. Laying and attaching of timbers
    B. Plastering
    C. Masonry
    D. Application of gypsum

11. According to the passage, until recently, Hopi homes normally did NOT include:
    A. any furniture, even the smallest stool.
    B. a gypsum coating.
    C. timber building materials.
    D. iron-made furnishings.

12. The passage implies that male children of a family:
    A. will live outdoors, as the house is for women only.
    B. gain their adult home only by marrying a woman.
    C. are able to inherit their ancestral home only if they are eldest, not automatically.
    D. are responsible for the day-to-day upkeep and structural integrity of their home as children.

Overview of Opinions and Arguments in CARS Passages

Effective analysis of the opinions and arguments in CARS passages will require reading for and identifying:

- Authors' or others' point of view
- Awareness of the passage purpose

Consider the following statement:

A hospital is given 500 vials of a new drug, 220 of which are designated to be preserved for other studies, and 280 of which are to be used for experimentation to test the drug's efficacy. In 5 years, the 280 vials are used, and the hospital is still unsure of the drug's efficacy, and the drug requires more testing. The 220 vials that are to be preserved are on the table. The study ran over budget two years ago and has been dipping into the hospital's general operating funds to continue. Other researchers at the NIH have produced promising results using a close analogue of the drug.

What differing purposes would this person or group address? What might their thesis be? What evidence would be most effective in achieving their purpose?

The scientist who is in charge of completing the drug study

The drug company that developed the new drug and earmarked the 220 vials for additional studies

The hospital's financial administrators

The other researchers at the NIH

Overview of Opinions and Arguments in CARS Passages

EXAMPLE

There are several components of opinions and arguments the MCAT will ask you to understand. Here is an example:

> The consumption of walnuts reduces the levels of cholesterol and triglycerides in the blood and hence helps reduce the risk of vascular disease. A group of male subjects eating 1 oz. of walnuts each day for 6 months showed a 16 percent reduction in cholesterol and a 10 percent reduction in triglycerides. Over the same period a second group of similar subjects who consumed no nuts showed only a 2 percent reduction in cholesterol and a 4 percent reduction in triglycerides

Conclusion—The proposition reached from the premises and evidence of an argument or opinion.

___

Examples/Support—The stated evidence or data used to support the argument or opinion.

___

Premise—The stated or unstated assumptions necessary to formulate the argument or opinion.

___

Deduction—Moving from a stated conclusion to another unstated, yet necessary, conclusion.

___

Timed MCAT CARS Practice Passage

CARS is the one section of the exam where you do not need to study outside content prior to practice. The sooner you get used to the format, outline, style, and timing of the test, the better you will score on your exam.

1. Complete your reading of the passage (4-5 minutes).
   - Write down the main idea of the passage. Also note what you think are the key ideas of each paragraph.
   - Compare your main idea and takeaway points to the explanations when you are done with the questions.
   - Were there any key terms or important opinions you missed? How might you have recognized them?

2. Complete the practice questions on your own (5-6 minutes).
   - Rephrase each question in your own mind after reading it to clarify the task.
   - Research the relevant area(s) of the passage for information related to the task.
   - Respond by choosing the answer that fits your research *and* satisfies the task.
   - If no answer seems obvious, eliminate unsupported answers.

3. Analyze wrong answer choices.
   - What was tempting about the wrong answers?
   - Identify why the correct answer is correct.
   - Explain why the wrong answers should have been eliminated.

This page left intentionally blank.

MCAT Practice Passage

The distinctive features of Millet's art are so marked that the most inexperienced observer easily identifies his work. As a painter of rustic subjects, he is unlike any other artists who have entered the same field. We get at the heart of the matter when we say that Millet derived his art directly from nature. His pictures . . . have a peculiar quality of genuineness beside which all other rustic art seems forced and artificial.

The human side of life touched him most deeply, and in many of his earlier pictures, landscape was secondary. Gradually he grew into the larger conception of a perfect harmony between man and his environment. Henceforth landscape ceased to be a mere setting or background in a figure picture, and became an organic part of the composition. As a critic once wrote of *The Shepherdess*, "the earth and sky, the scene and the actors, all answer one another, all hold together, belong together."

In figure painting Millet sought neither grace nor beauty, but expression. The leading characteristic of his art is strength, and he distrusted the ordinary elements of prettiness as taking something from the total effect he wished to produce. It was always his first aim to make his people look as if they belonged to their station. His was the genuine peasant of field and farm, no imaginary denizen of the poets' Arcady.

While Millet's art is, in its entirety, quite unique, there are certain interesting points of resemblance between his work and that of some older masters. He is akin to Rembrandt both in his indifference to beauty and in his intense love of human nature. Millet's indifference to beauty is the more remarkable because in this he stood alone in his day and generation, while in the northern art of the seventeenth century, of which Rembrandt is an exponent, beauty was never supreme.

As a lover of human nature, Millet's sympathies, though no less intense than Rembrandt's, were less catholic. His range of observation was limited to peasant life, while the Dutch master painted all classes and conditions of men. Yet both alike were profound students of character and regarded expression as the chief element of beauty. Rembrandt, however, sought expression principally in the countenance, and Millet had a fuller understanding of the expressiveness of the entire body.

Millet's instinct for pose was that of a sculptor. Many of the figures for his pictures were first carefully modeled in wax or clay. Transferred to canvas they are drawn in the strong simple outlines of a statue. It is no extravagant flight of fancy which has likened him to Michelangelo. In the strength and seriousness of his conceptions, the bold sweep of his lines, and, above all, in the impression of motion which he conveys, he has much in common with the great Italian master. Like Michelangelo, Millet gives first preference to the dramatic moment when action is imminent.

When Millet represents repose it is as an interval of suspended action, not as the end of completed work. The *Shepherdess* pauses but a moment in her walk and will immediately move on again. The man and woman of *The Angelus* rest only for the prayer and then resume their work. The *Man with the Hoe* snatches but a brief respite from his labors.

To the qualities which are reminiscent of Michelangelo, Millet adds another in which he is allied to the Greeks. This is his tendency towards generalization. It is the typical rather than the individual which he strives to present. "My dream," he once wrote, "is to characterize the type." So his figures, like those of Greek sculpture, reproduce no particular model, but are the general type deduced from the study of many individuals.

[Adapted from Jean Francois Millet, by Estelle M. Hurll]

Passage taken from the Next Step online QBank - CARS Passages

13. An appropriate title for this essay might be:

A. Millet, Rembrandt, and Michelangelo: Painters of the Rustic
B. The Expressive Landscapes of Jean Millet
C. Jean Millet: Expressions of the Genuine
D. The Idealized Peasant: The Works of Jean Millet

14. Which statement best captures the author's description of Millet's portrayal of landscape?

A. In his early works, landscape was an organic part of the composition.
B. Over time, landscape became less background and more important to the overall composition.
C. As Millet's paintings became more sculptural, his landscapes became less important.
D. Because Millet loved human nature, he cared less for the natural world.

15. What does the author most likely mean by the statement that Millet's peasant is "no imaginary denizen of the poet's Arcady"?

A. Rather than invent his subjects, Millet's peasants were actual people the artist knew.
B. Rather than idealize the peasant, Millet aimed to portray his subjects as they actually appeared.
C. Millet preferred to paint peasants because they did not have "ordinary elements of prettiness."
D. Millet's peasants, though not beautiful, were truly poetic.

16. Suppose a previously unknown 19th century painting were discovered. It depicts three figures picking potatoes; they look as if they are statues, posed against an indistinct background. Critics decide that the work is *not* attributed to Millet for all of the following reasons EXCEPT:

A. Millet's paintings exhibited great harmony between figure and background, and this work does not.
B. Millet's subjects, rather than looking posed, seem to be taking a short pause from their activities, while these seem unmoved.
C. A painting with such sculptural qualities would be more likely attributed to Michelangelo than to Millet.
D. Expressiveness of landscape was important to Millet.

17. Which of the following most accurately describes the author's comparison of the work of Millet with that of Rembrandt?

A. Rembrandt's paintings tend to more religious themes than those of Millet.
B. Millet primarily painted peasants, whereas Rembrandt's subjects were more diverse.
C. Millet was less interested in physical beauty than was Rembrandt.
D. While both Rembrandt and Millet were students of character, Rembrandt was more interested in expressions of beauty.

18. The passage attributes which of the following to the works of Millet?

I. An expression of harmony between humans and their surroundings
II. An ability to portray expression in the body and not just the face
III. A tendency to present the typical rather than the individual I only

A. I only
B. I and II only
C. I and III only
D. I, II, and III

19. The author cites which of the following as evidence of Millet's kinship with sculptors such as Michelangelo?

A. The impression of suspended motion in Millet's work
B. Millet's tendency towards generalization
C. The resemblance of Millet's sculptures to Greek models
D. Millet's early works in wax and clay

MCAT Strategy: How to Review CARS Passages

The key to CARS improvement is repetition and learning from mistakes. Do not rush to take another practice passage until you have reviewed and analyzed your most recent performance.

Guidelines for CARS Review:

- Go over EVERY question, including the ones you got wrong and the ones you guessed on, right or wrong.
- Reviewing CARS can take twice as long as completing the timed practice problems.
- Were you able to find question-relevant information in the passage quickly when you needed it?
- Why did you get the question wrong?

Things to note when reviewing your practice CARS passages

___

___

Strategy

Lessons Learned Journal

The Lessons Learned Journal (LLJ) is your way of keeping track of the mistakes and errors you make in the course of your MCAT study.

CARS success is dependent upon finding a reliable and efficient strategy for dealing with the passage and the questions.

What to record on your LLJ:

___

___

Here is an example:

Question #	Type	Topic	Lesson Learned
Diag, Q3	3	Philosophy	Research ALL places in pass. where author opinion comes up

Lessons Learned Journal: Lesson 1 Passages

Date:

Question #	Type	Topic	Lesson Learned

To Do After Lesson 2

- ☐ Read and complete Verbal and Quantitative Reasoning Chapters 3 and 4
  - Determine the correct CARS reading strategy for you
- ☐ Read Physics Chapters 1 and 2
- ☐ Read Chemistry and Organic Chemistry Chapters 2 and 3
- ☐ Read Biology Chapters 1 and 2

LESSON 3

Science Strategy and Chemistry 1

To Do Before Lesson 3

- ☐ Read and complete Verbal and Quantitative Reasoning Chapters 3 and 4
    - Determine the correct CARS reading strategy for you
- ☐ Read Physics Chapters 1 and 2
- ☐ Read Chemistry and Organic Chemistry Chapters 2 and 3
- ☐ Read Biology Chapters 1 and 2

In Lesson 3

Problem-solving Warm-up
Effective Reading in the Sciences
    Review of Chem/Phys Foundations Passage
        Highlighting
        Note-Taking
    Science Skill 1—Science Recall
    Science Skill 2—Scientific Reasoning
Science Skill 3—Scientific Research Design
Science Skill 4—Data Interpretation
Practice: Chemical/Physical Foundations Passage
How to Build your Science Foundation
MCAT Practice Passage

To Do After Lesson 3

- ☐ Read Chemistry and Organic Chemistry Chapters 4 and 5
- ☐ Read Physics Chapters 3 and 4
- ☐ Read Verbal and Quantitative Reasoning Chapters 5 and 6
- ☐ Read Biology Chapters 3 and 4

Problem-solving Warm-up

1. All of the following atomic properties increase across a period EXCEPT:

   A. effective nuclear charge.
   B. atomic radius.
   C. electronegativity.
   D. electron affinity.

2. Which of the following numbers describes the orbital shape for an electron?

   A. Principal quantum number
   B. Angular quantum number
   C. Magnetic quantum number
   D. Spin quantum number

3. Excited electrons lose their extra energy by emitting electromagnetic radiation and, in doing so, fall back into their original and stable energy level. Which of the following electromagnetic emissions would have the greatest energy?

   A. Radio
   B. X-rays
   C. Infrared
   D. Violet light

4. Researchers analyzing the radiation given off by a sample create a filter that arrests the movement of any particle more massive than 1.5 amu. Which of the following decay products will be trapped in their filter?

   A. β particle
   B. α particle
   C. γ particle
   D. Positron

5. The reaction below is carried out at 298 K. If the initial $[CO_2] = 0.75$ M, which of the following MUST be equal to the ΔG of the reaction when the CO_2 concentration has reached 0.375 M?

   $CO_2\,(g) + H_2O\,(l) \rightarrow H_2CO_3\,(aq)$ $\qquad$ $K_{eq} = 3.5 \times 10^2$, $\Delta G° = 40$ kJ/mol

   A. 0 kJ/mol
   B. $-RT \ln (3.5 \times 10^2)$ kJ/mol
   C. $e^{-RT(0.375)}$ kJ/mol
   D. 40 kJ/mol

Effective Reading in the Sciences

Reading science passages on the MCAT means being able to keep track of important (i.e. likely to be tested) information in the passage. You must be able to anticipate, recognize, and understand scientific concepts presented in many different forms.

Type of information	**What to look out for**

Two effective methods of keeping track of key information:

________________________ and ________________________

Strategy

Highlighting vs. Note-taking

Electrospinning is a technique used to produce filters, membranes, and tissue scaffolds for implants. Electrospinning occurs when the electric forces at the surface of a polymer solution overcome the surface tension and cause and electrically charged jet to be ejected. The solvent evaporates as the jet travels in air, leaving behind charged polymer fibers that lay themselves randomly on a metallic electrode (collector). An experiment was performed on three different fibers to determine their mechanical properties. A 10 N initial load and a stress rate of +0.5 N/s were used. Results of the experiment are shown in Figure 2. The Young's modulus was calculated by analyzing the peak stress that the sample was able to endure without deforming.

What to look out for:

____

____

Why vs. how

____

____

Takeaway:

____

____

Highlighting vs. Note-taking

When water that contains dissolved calcium carbonate is warmed, CO_2 is removed from the water as gas. This eventually leads to the formation of calcium carbonate scales. Over time these scales reduce the effective radii of the pipes, leading to flow interruptions.

Magnesium ions can also form precipitates via their reactions with sodium salts of organic acids. The soap's efficacy is reduced by its sequestration by magnesium. Reaction 3 shows the sequestration of the soap molecule by Mg^{2+}.

$$2\ NaC_{10}H_{18}CO_2\ (aq) + Mg^{2+}\ (aq) \rightarrow Mg(C_{10}H_{18}CO_2)_2\ (s) + 2\ Na^{+}\ (aq)$$

Reaction 1

De-scaling agents are often used to clear blocked pipes. These agents are usually acidic compounds that react with the carbonate present in the scale to produce carbon dioxide and a soluble salt.

¶1

¶2

Reaction 1

¶3

Highlighting Method

PROS:

CONS:

What kind of information is worth highlighting in MCAT science passages?

Note-taking Method

PROS:

CONS:

What kind of information is worth summarizing in MCAT science passages?

Discussion: Your Passage Method

What is the goal of any notes you take in MCAT science passages?

____

____

How can you make your notes more efficient?

____

____

Which strategy will work best for YOU in the Sciences?

____

____

What will allow you to determine the ideal strategy for YOUR performance?

____

____

VSEPR Theory and Molecular Shape

Non-bonding Electrons and Bonding Electrons

Electronic vs. Molecular Geometry

EXAMPLE

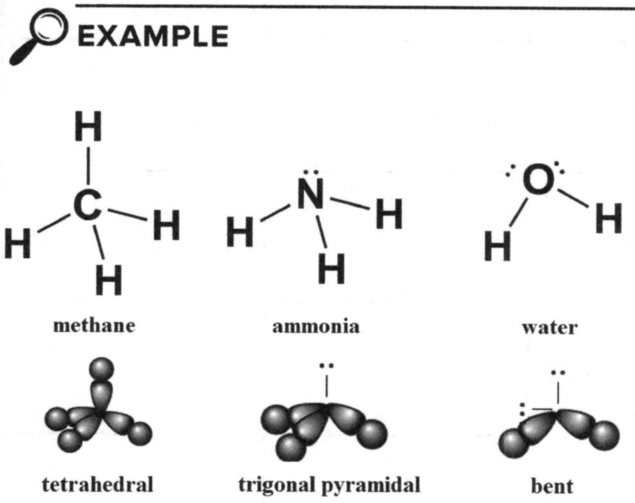

Non-bonding Electrons and Molecular Geometry

VSEPR Theory and Molecular Shape

# of Bonding Groups	# of Lone Pair Electrons	Electronic Geometry	Molecular Geometry	Bond Angle
2	0	linear		
3	0	trigonal planar		
2	1	trigonal planar		
4	0	tetrahedral		
3	1	tetrahedral		
2	2	tetrahedral		
5	0	trigonal bipyramidal		
2	3	trigonal bipyramidal		
6	0	octahedral		
4	2	octahedral		

This type of information lends itself well to active learning via ________________.

VSEPR Theory and Molecular Shape

EXAMPLE

Net molecular dipole depends on:

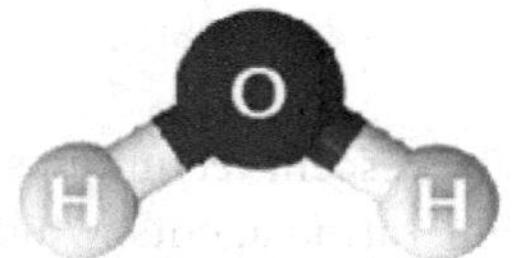

EXAMPLE

Bond Dipole vs. Molecular Dipole

Takeaway: ________________ do not guarantee ________________.

Diagnostic: Chemical and Physical Foundations Passage 1

Oral drug delivery systems are limited by the short gastrointestinal transit time, leading to low bioavailability. Drug delivery systems able to retain the dosage form in the stomach are needed. Research into floating drug delivery systems (FDDS) may satisfy this need.

¶1

FDDS can be approached by either effervescent or non-effervescent techniques. Ideal effervescent techniques achieve floating duration times >16 hours in the stomach. Effervescent FDDS incorporate gas generating agents, which provide buoyancy. Newer research focuses on non-effervescent systems, where the swelling of polymers joined to the drug entraps air within the polymeric matrix, providing buoyancy to the dosage form.

¶2

A study was performed on the antidiabetic sulfonylurea glipizide. The drug and one of three polymers were mixed in a mortar according to the ratios described in Table 1. A drop of water was added, and the mixture was kneaded until a homogenous paste was obtained. The mixture was then placed in an oven at 50 °C for 30 min to remove water. The compound was then compressed into tablets which served as the basis for drug release and buoyancy measurements.

¶3

Drug	Bulk Density	Trial 1	Trial 2	Trial 3
Glipizide	0.2 g/mL	1:1	1:4	1:8
FDDS Polymer		gelucire	B-cyclodextrin	Polaxemer-188
Gelucire	0.6 g/mL			
β-cyclodextrin	0.3 g/mL			
Polaxemer-188	0.1 g/mL			

Table 1 The density of glipizide and the three polymers and the drug to polymer ratio in each trial

Table 1

To test *in vitro* drug release of solid dispersions, the tablets were placed into dissolution vessels containing 900 mL of 0.1 M HCl. Dissolution studies were carried out for one hour, with samples withdrawn at predetermined intervals. Drug concentrations were assayed using HPLC methods. The dissolution experiments were carried out in triplicate and the results for are shown in Figure 1. *In vitro* buoyancy was also tested. Tablets were placed in a vessel containing 500 mL of 0.1 M HCl. The time taken for the tablet to rise to the surface of the dissolution media (floating lag time) and total duration that the tablet remained on the surface (total floating time) were recorded.

¶4

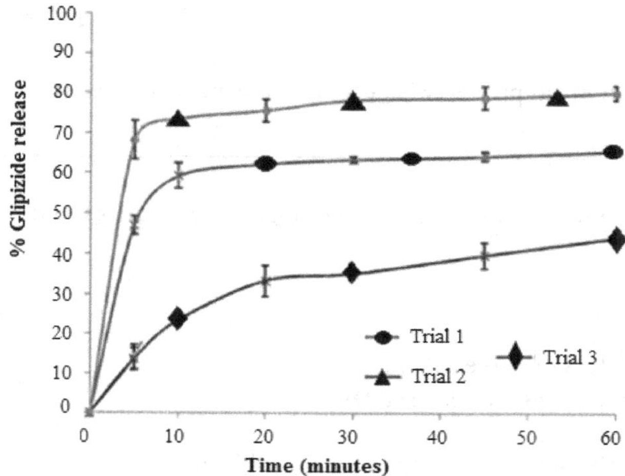

Figure 1 Drug release as a function of time and pill composition

Figure 1

The K_{sp} for glipizide-cyclodextrin in a chyme solution at 37 °C was determined to be 5.8 x 10^{-4}. Increased solubility of drug dispersions may be achieved by wetting via hydrophilic polymers, or polymer size reduction.

(Note: all pills for the above trials have the same volume.)

¶5

MCAT Science Skill 1

Skill 1 questions test your ability to recognize and recall MCAT-relevant science. They will also expect you to be able to relate concepts from chemistry, biology, and physics together. In addition to passage-based questions, many discrete questions will fit into this skill category.

Skill 1 questions will comprise 35% of the Chem/Phys section (20-21 questions).

Tolazamide is an aromatic drug with a similar structure to glipizide. Which of the following is most likely a part of tolazamide?

A. C_6H_5
B. C_6H_6
C. C_6H_8
D. $C_6H_{12}O_6$

A good understanding of what chemical property is needed to answer this question?

Metal cations such as calcium and magnesium are often conjugated with drugs to improve bioavailability. These cations are:

A. weakly electronegative.
B. alkali metals.
C. derived from the atomic loss of two electrons.
D. formed by the reduction of their standard states.

What science content area(s) is this question testing and/or combining?

MCAT Science Skill 2

Skill 2 questions will test your ability to apply scientific principles to problem-solving. They may also ask you to evaluate scientific theories presented in the passage or question. Success on these questions will rely on understanding MCAT science as opposed to simple memorization.

Skill 2 questions will comprise 45% of the Chem/Phys section (26-27 questions).

Which of the following correctly lists the floating lag times for the three trials in increasing order? (note: assume that the mixing of the drug and polymer does not change the density of either component)

A. Trial 1 < Trial 2 < Trial 3
B. Trial 2 < Trial 1 < Trial 3
C. Trial 3 < Trial 2 < Trial 1
D. Trial 2 < Trial 3 < Trial 1

What information is needed to make your scientific prediction?

A student preparing for the experiments inadvertently adds an additional 400 mL of the same acid solution to the dissolution vessel. What will be the new pOH of this solution?

A. 1.0
B. 6.0
C. 11.0
D. 13.0

What are a mathematical formula and chemical principle being tested in this question?

MCAT Science Skill 3

Skill 3 questions will require you to understand and evaluate proper scientific research methods. These questions will emphasize proper medical research. Questions on study design, research biases and ethics of the experiments and studies discussed on the exam fit into this category.

Skill 3 questions will comprise 10% of the Chemical/Physical Foundations section (5-6 questions).

Students conducting experiments on a sample of a new anti-hypertension medication obtain the results shown in the figure below.

EXAMPLE

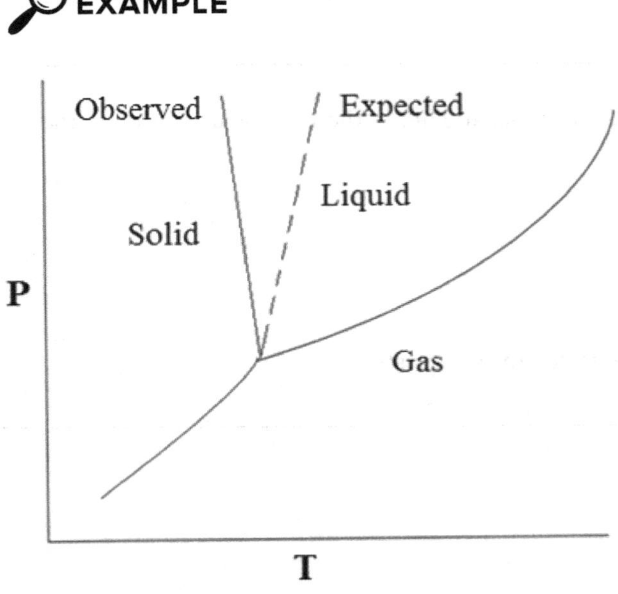

Which of the following errors most accurately explains this discrepancy?

A. The sample was kept at too low a temperature prior to testing.
B. The sample was kept at too high a temperature prior to testing.
C. The sample was incompletely purified from its aqueous suspension.
D. The sample was contaminated with another drug of similar composition.

What aspect of the research design is important to identify when reading?

MCAT Science Skill 4

Skill 4 questions will require you to understand and evaluate the results of scientific research. Some of these questions may ask you to consider the scientific, logical, or statistical conclusions that can be made from the data presented by the experiments and figures in the passage.

Skill 4 questions will comprise 10% of the Chem/Phys section (5-6 questions).

In a town with hard water, house 1 installs a softening system in which the excess Ca^{2+} in the water is removed and slows the buildup of precipitate. House 2 has no such system. Assuming both houses have roughly equal water usage patterns, and the water operates under stable pressure, which of the following graphs depicts the flow rate of tap water in house 1 and in house 2 over time?

EXAMPLE

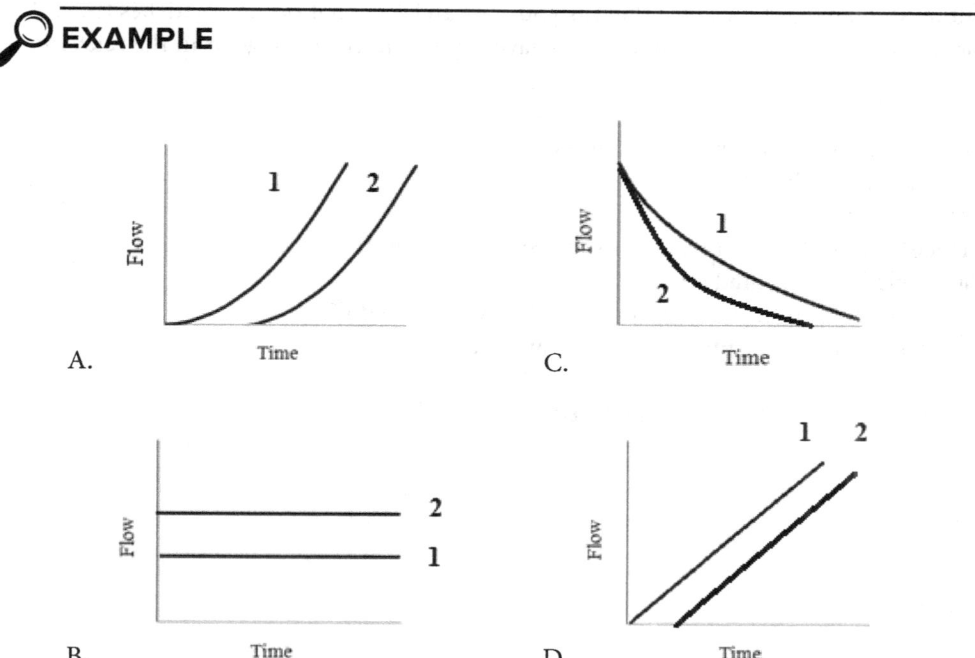

What are the mathematical relationships shown in each figure?

A: __________

B: __________

C: __________

D: __________

Timed MCAT Practice Passage

Mastery of the MCAT sciences is a two-part process. First you must study to understand (not just memorize!) the science content, and then you must study the content actively, and challenge yourself within the context of the exam.

1. Complete your reading of the passage (3-4 minutes)
    - Write down what you believe to be the primary science content underlying the passage.
    - What facts or concepts do you anticipate will be tested? When you are done with the questions determine if you were correct. What passage clues were there to imply related topics that showed up in the questions?
    - Were there any key terms or important scientific relationships you missed?
    - Were you able to draw any conclusions from the data, if presented?

2. Complete the practice questions on your own (4-5 minutes)
    - Rephrase each question in your own mind after reading it to clarify the task.
    - Research the relevant area(s) of the passage or your own knowledge for information related to the task.
    - Respond to the question by choosing the answer that fits your research/calculations *and* satisfies the task.
    - If no answer seems obvious, eliminate answers that fail to have support in the passage or in the relevant science.

3. Analyze your wrong answer choices to the questions you missed.
    - Did you understand the task in the question?
    - What skill type was the question?
    - Did you know the science/formula/concept needed to answer the question?
    - Did you recognize the science being hinted at?
    - Were you able to find information in the passage quickly when you needed it?
    - Were there any necessary scientific concepts you failed to apply to the question?
        - If so, why?
    - If you made a mistake in calculations, have you identified your mistake?

This page left intentionally blank.

Carbon dioxide is a molecular compound with a linear structure and exists primarily in the gas phase under normal temperature and pressure conditions. The solid is often referred to as dry ice, in which the molecular units form a trigonal unit-cell crystal structure, in which the O-C-O angle is essentially 180° and the C=O bond lengths of 1.16 Å are shorter than the C=O bond lengths observed in organic carbonyl compounds (1.23 Å), and only slightly longer than that observed in carbon monoxide (1.13 Å).

The liquid phase does not exist under standard conditions of temperature and pressure, and relatively high pressures are required to condense the gas to the liquid (Figure 1). The properties observed are the result of the weak intermolecular interactions, which stand in stark contrast to the properties of its silicon homolog, silica (SiO_2, which forms a network solid in which each silicon atom is bonded to four oxygen atoms. Supercritical carbon dioxide has received considerable interest as a solvent for the extraction of organic compounds from complex matrices, such as in the preparation of decaffeinated coffee in lieu of using chlorocarbon solvents such as chloroform ($CHCl_3$) or methylene chloride (CH_2Cl_2) The structure of caffeine is shown in Figure 2.

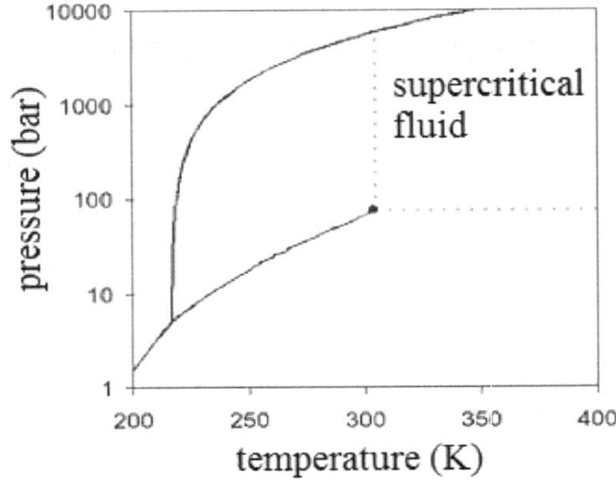

Figure 1 Phase diagram for carbon dioxide, (1.01 bar = 1 atm = 101 kPa)

Figure 2 Structural formula of caffeine

There is considerable debate about the nature of the intermolecular interactions of carbon dioxide under extremely high pressure. Molecular modeling calculations suggest that oxygen lone pairs on neighboring molecules begin to interact with the carbon atoms, causing the O-C-O angle to bend and the intramolecular C=O bonds to lengthen. The significance of this is related to proposals made for the sequestration of carbon dioxide in order to circumvent some of the greenhouse effects that occur when carbon dioxide is released into the atmosphere.

Passage taken from the Next Step online QBank

6. Which of the following is closest to the O-Si-O bond angle in silica?

   A. 90°
   B. 109°
   C. 120°
   D. 180°

7. According to the results of the experiment, CO_2 at 1000 kPa and 100 °C will exist as a:

   A. solid.
   B. liquid.
   C. gas.
   D. supercritical fluid.

8. Which of the following compounds would NOT be extracted to any significant extent by supercritical carbon dioxide?

   A. 1,3,7-Trimethylpurine-2,6-dione
   B. Ammonium nitrate
   C. Methyl salicylate
   D. Benzaldehyde

9. Which of the following would represent the primary intermolecular force in a methylene chloride/caffeine solution?

   A. London dispersion forces
   B. Dipole-dipole interactions
   C. Hydrogen bonding
   D. Ion-dipole interactions

How to Build Your MCAT Science Foundation

Flashcards

Useful for:

Formula Sheets

Useful for:

Units

Useful for:

Content Questions

Useful for:

Discrete Questions

Useful for:

Passage Questions

Useful for:

Strategy

How to "Memorize" Scientific Trends

The MCAT emphasizes integration and testing of relationships. Many times the successful application of a trend depends on the relationships within or between trends, NOT pure memorization.

When learning scientific concepts, focus on the relationship between the variables and how they influence each other. Knowing units will also allow you to properly set up dimensional analysis when needed.

	Units	Relationships
Molarity		
Molality		
Charles' Law		
Boyle's Law		
Ideal Gas Law		
pH		
Freezing Point Depression		
Boiling Point Elevation		

Properties of the Gas Phase

Assumptions of the Kinetic Theory

1. The average kinetic energy of the molecules is proportional to the absolute temperature.
2. Molecules (or atoms) move randomly with a distribution in speeds which does not change.
3. The molecules undergo elastic collisions with other molecules and the walls, but otherwise exert no forces on each other.
4. The total average energy of a gas under isothermal conditions is constant.
5. The volume of the gas molecules is negligible compared to the total volume of the gas.

This leads to a concept of kinetic temperature and to the ideal gas law...

Properties of the Gas Phase

An ideal gas can be characterized by three state variables: absolute pressure (P), volume (V), and absolute temperature (T).

The relationship between them may be deduced from kinetic theory and is called the ideal gas law, which incorporates Boyle's law, Charles' law, as well as Avogadro's principle.

1 mol of an ideal gas @ STP occupies ________________________

STP is ________________________ and ________________________.

Properties of the Gas Phase

The expression for gas pressure developed from kinetic theory relates pressure and volume to the average molecular kinetic energy.

Comparison with the ideal gas law leads to an expression for temperature referred to as the kinetic temperature.

$$PV = nRT \longleftrightarrow PV = 2/3\ N\ [1/2\ mv^2]$$

More commonly expressed via…

(per molecule)

(per mole)

Where k is the Boltzmann constant (no need to memorize)

Content and Practice Item Review

The Rule of 2s

For example:

# of bonding groups	# of lone pair electrons	Electronic Geometry	Molecular Geometry	Bond Angle
2	0			
3	0			
2	1			
4	0			
3	1			
2	2			
5	0			
2	3			
6	0			
4	2			

Content vs. Critical Thinking

Content and Practice Item Review

The 2-pass Method

What

How

Identifying Areas of MCAT Opportunity

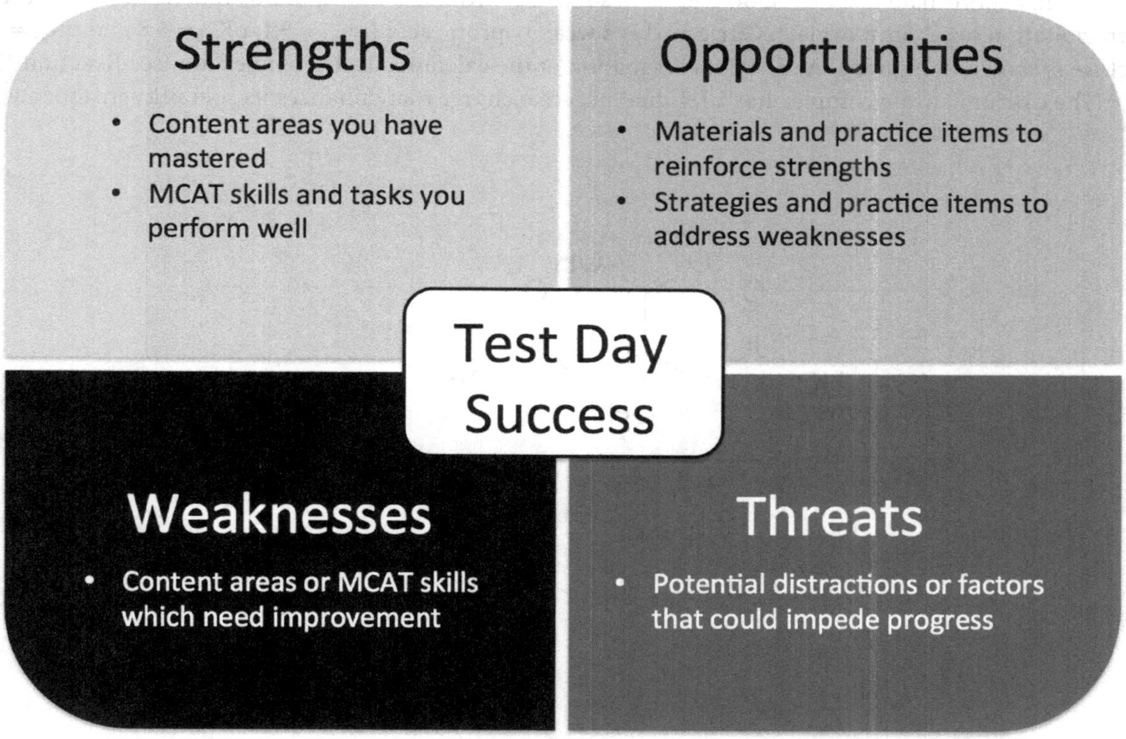

Strengths

- Content areas you have mastered
- MCAT skills and tasks you perform well

Opportunities

- Materials and practice items to reinforce strengths
- Strategies and practice items to address weaknesses

Test Day Success

Weaknesses

- Content areas or MCAT skills which need improvement

Threats

- Potential distractions or factors that could impede progress

S: ______________________________

W: ______________________________

O: ______________________________

T: ______________________________

MCAT Practice Passage

Kidney stones are insoluble aggregate crystals that can form in the urine of certain people. One of the compounds that can contribute to the formation of kidney stones is calcium oxalate (CaC_2O_4, MW = 128.097 g/mol, $K_{sp} = 2.3 \times 10^{-9}$). Oxalic acid is a naturally occurring diprotic acid, ($H_2C_2O_4$, $pK_{a1} = 1.3$ and $pK_{a2} = 4.3$) present in a number of foods, including rhubarb and spinach. Oxalic acid can be produced from oxaloacetate, which plays an important role in the citric acid cycle. Uric acid can also contribute to the formation of kidney stones and can also crystallize in the synovial fluid of the joints, producing inflammation and the painful symptoms associated with gout. In humans, uric acid is the final oxidation product of purine metabolism and like oxalic acid, is a diprotic acid ($H_2C_5H_2N_4O_3$, $pK_{a1} = 5.4$ and $pK_{a2} = 10.3$). Unlike oxalic acid, it is not completely ionized at pH levels typical for urine (pH = 7.13).

If the urine becomes supersaturated, seed crystals can result in the formation of a large mass, or stone, in one of several possible locations, including the bladder, the ureters and the kidneys. Small stones (< 3 mm) are readily passed. However, large stones can cause obstruction and renal colic, or worse. In some cases ultrasound can be used to break up stones and facilitate their passing, however in extreme cases, surgery may be required.

Urine contains a number of natural chelating agents, one of which is citrate. These chelating agents are polydentate ligands (Lewis bases) that coordinate to a metal ion and form soluble coordination compounds that help prevent the nucleation and precipitation of calcium oxalate. Citric acid is a weak triprotic acid ($pK_{a1} = 3.1$, $pK_{a2} = 4.8$ and $pK_{a3} = 6.4$), whose structure is shown in Figure 1. At 37 °C the formation of the calcium citrate complex ion (see Reaction 1) has $K_{eq} = 1.9 \times 10^3$. The calcium citrate complex has a residual negative charge that enhances its solubility in aqueous solution.

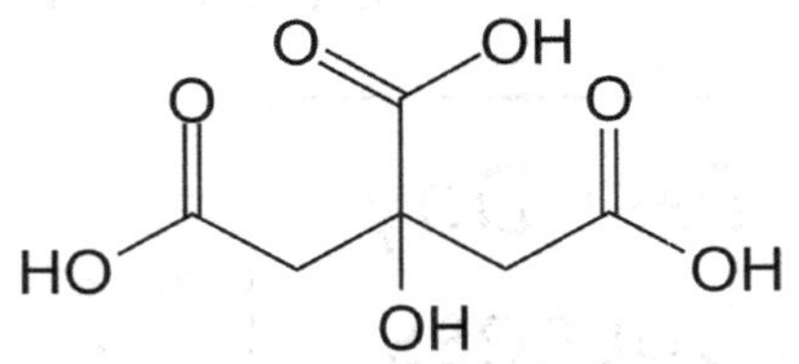

Figure 1 The structure of citric acid ($H_3C_6H_5O_7$)

Reaction 1 $Ca^{2+}(aq) + C_6H_5O_7^{3-}(aq) \rightarrow CaC_6H_5O_7^{1-}(aq)$

Passage taken from the Next Step online QBank

10. Which of the following formulas best represents the predominant form of citric acid in solution when it is dissolved in normal urine?

   A. $C_6H_8O_7$
   B. $C_6H_7O_7^-$
   C. $C_6H_6O_7^{2-}$
   D. $C_6H_5O_7^{3-}$

11. Which of the following temperatures corresponds to the formation of the calcium citrate complex discussed in the passage?

   A. 0 K
   B. 273 K
   C. 310 K
   D. 373 K

12. Based on information in the passage, what is the equilibrium constant for the following reaction?

$$CaC_2O_4\ (s) + C_6H_5O_7^{3-}\ (aq) \longleftrightarrow CaC_6H_5O_7^-\ (aq) + C_2O_4^{2-}\ (aq)$$

   A. 2.3×10^{-7}
   B. 4.4×10^{-6}
   C. 2.3×10^{-5}
   D. 4.4×10^{-4}

13. If equal molar solutions of oxalic acid, uric acid, citric acid, and urea are prepared, which solution will have the lowest pH?

   A. Oxalic acid, because it has the largest K_{a1} value.
   B. Uric acid, because it has the largest pK_{a2} value.
   C. Citric acid, because it is a triprotic acid.
   D. Urea, because it is a basic compound.

14. Which of the following molecules is most likely to produce uric acid (shown below) as a result of metabolism?

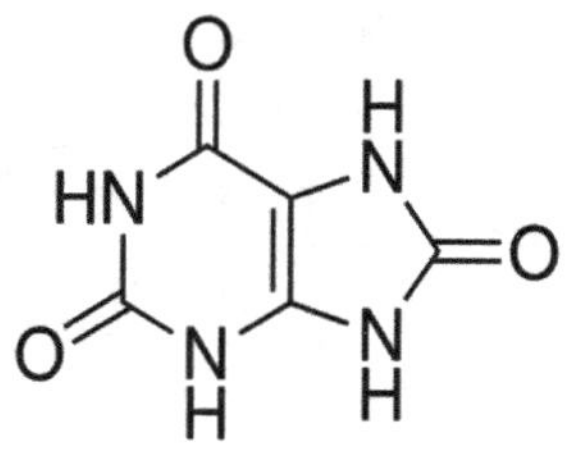

   A. Thymine
   B. Guanine
   C. Cytosine
   D. Glucose

Problem-solving Cooldown

15. The chemical formula of calcium phosphate is:

    A. $Ca(PO_4)$.
    B. $Ca_3(PO_4)$.
    C. $Ca_2(PO_4)_3$.
    D. $Ca_3(PO_4)_2$.

16. Acetic acid dissociates in solution as shown below:

$$CH_3COOH + NaOH \longleftrightarrow CH_3COO^-Na^+ + H_3O^+ \qquad pK_a = 4.8$$

    What is the pH of a 0.10 M solution of sodium acetate?

    A. 2.5
    B. 7.1
    C. 8.9
    D. 12.8

17. Which of the following compounds has the highest boiling point?

    A. CH_4
    B. NH_3
    C. H_2O
    D. HF

To Do After Lesson 3

- [ ] Read Chemistry and Organic Chemistry Chapters 4 and 5
- [ ] Read Physics Chapters 3 and 4
- [ ] Read Verbal and Quantitative Reasoning Chapters 5 and 6
- [ ] Read Biology Chapters 3 and 4

This page left intentionally blank.

LESSON 4

Biology 1

To Do Before Lesson 4

- ☐ Read Chemistry and Organic Chemistry Chapters 4 and 5
- ☐ Read Physics Chapters 3 and 4
- ☐ Read Verbal and Quantitative Reasoning Chapters 5 and 6
- ☐ Read Biology Chapters 3 and 4

In Lesson 4

Problem-solving Warm-up
Enzyme Kinetics
Effective Reading in the Sciences
Cellular Metabolism
Reading MCAT Figures
MCAT Practice Passage
Build your Science Foundation
Transcription and Translation
Problem-solving Cooldown
MCAT Practice Passage

To Do After Lesson 4

- ☐ Read Biochemistry Chapters 1 and 2
- ☐ Read General Chemistry and Organic Chemistry Chapter 6
- ☐ Read Physics Chapters 5 and 6
- ☐ Complete Biology QBank 3: Eukaryotic and Prokaryotic Cells

Problem-solving Warm-up

1. Which of the following would you NOT find in a bacterial cell?

   A. Ribosome
   B. Cell membrane
   C. DNA
   D. Golgi apparatus

2. The molecules used in forming the interior of the eukaryotic cell membrane are synthesized in the:

   A. SER.
   B. RER.
   C. mitochondria.
   D. nucleolus.

3. What will be the net movement of water if the following container is setup with a semi permeable membrane separating the 2 chambers?

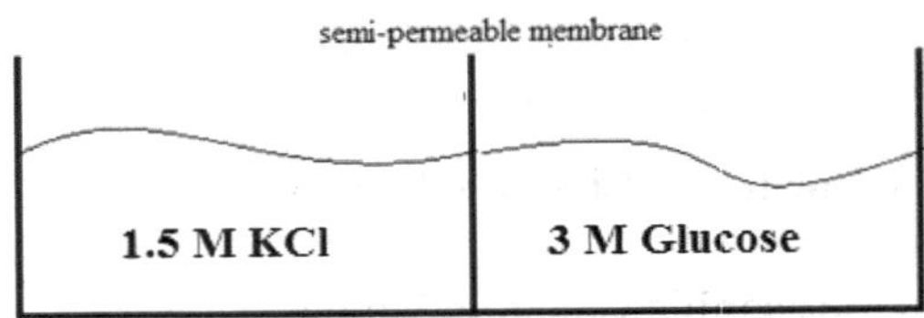

   A. The water will move left.
   B. The water will move right.
   C. The water will not move.
   D. The water will move left, then right.

4. If the membrane in the container was built like a eukaryotic cell membrane which means of glucose transportation would most likely result?

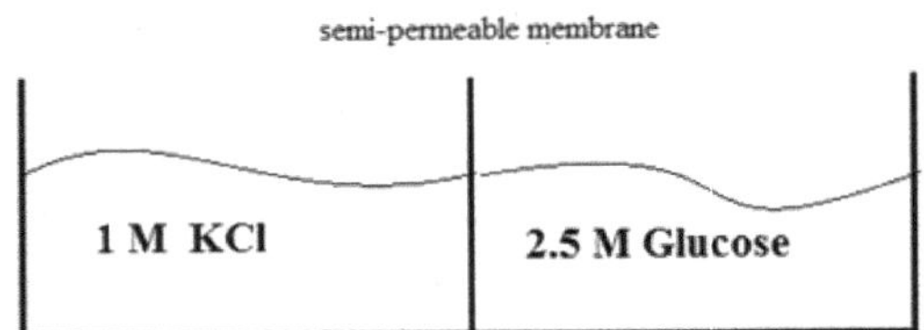

   A. Diffusion of glucose
   B. Active transport of glucose
   C. Secondary active transport of glucose
   D. Facilitated transport of glucose

5. A mutation occurs in a chromosome located in a spermatogonium. After meiosis is complete, how many of the resulting spermatids will be affected?

   A. 1
   B. 2
   C. 3
   D. 4

Enzyme Kinetics

K_m and V_{max}:

Uncompetitive inhibitors:

Competitive inhibitors:

Noncompetitive inhibitors:

K_{cat} and enzyme efficiency

Michaelis-Menten kinetics

Michaelis-Menten Curves

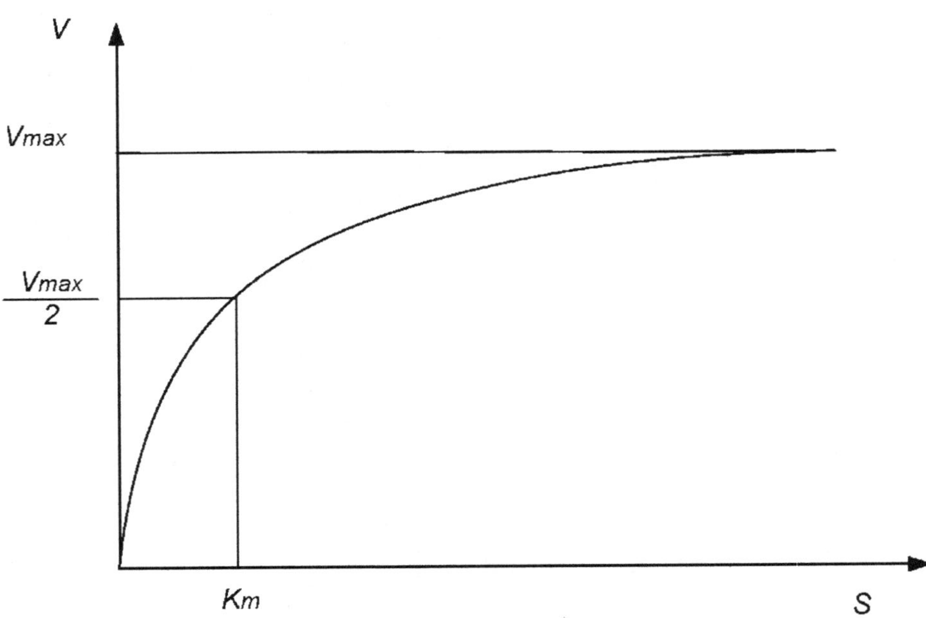

Add in to the plot above the Michaelis-Menten curves for (i) a competitive inhibitor and (ii) a noncompetitive inhibitor.

Lineweaver-Burk Plots

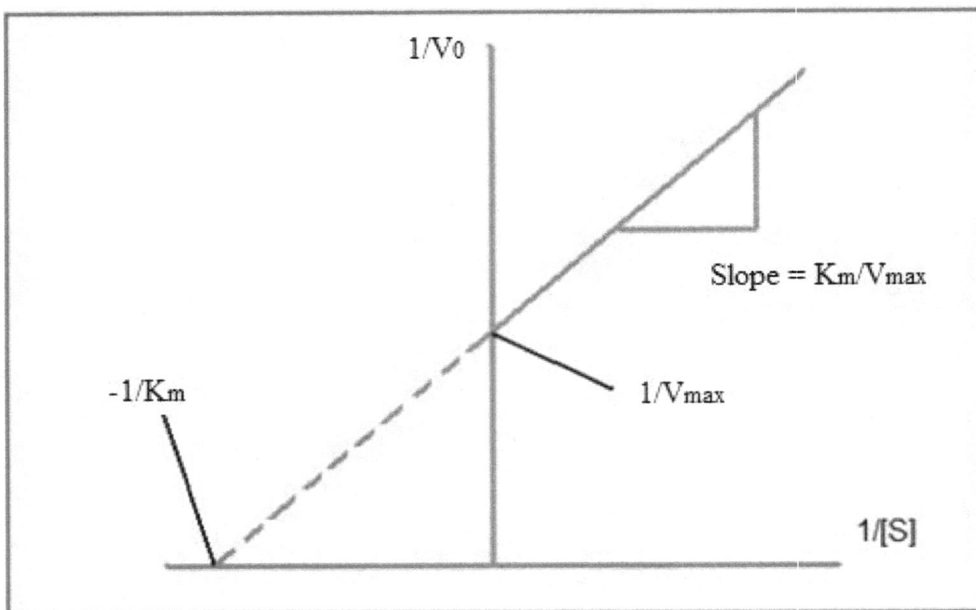

Add in to the plot above the Lineweaver-Burk Plots for (i) a competitive inhibitor, (ii) a noncompetitive inhibitor, and (iii) an uncompetitive inhibitor.

This page left intentionally blank.

Effective Reading in the Sciences

Reading science passages on the MCAT means being able to keep track of important (i.e. likely to be tested) information in the passage. You must be able to anticipate, recognize, and understand scientific concepts presented in many different forms.

Practice Passage

Erythropoiesis is the process by which new red blood cells are created in the body. Typical red blood cells will circulate for about 120 days, after which time they undergo apoptosis. On average there are 2.5 x 10^{13} erythrocytes in circulation in an adult.

The process begins with the secretion of the hormone erythropoietin (EPO) from the kidney. The kidney contains chemoreceptors that react to a drop in O_2 partial pressure in circulating blood. In response to a hypoxic environment, kidney cells produce EPO. In adults, concentrations of EPO range from 30-160 ng/mL.

EPO targets cells in the bone marrow to direct the formation of erythrocyte precursors from hematopoietic stem cells. Once the cell reaches the stage of reticulocyte, it has only to increase production of hemoglobin to become an erythrocyte. The percent of reticulocytes in circulation is a good indicator of the level of new erythrocytes creation. Normally reticulocytes comprise 1% of all red blood cells.

Red blood cell count needs to be carefully regulated so that complications do not arise from having too few or too many red blood cells in circulation at a given time. The fact that EPO binds red blood cells while in circulation means that even in large amounts, EPO will not act unless there is a significant reduction in erythrocyte count. Hepcidin is a peptide hormone that inhibits iron release from macrophages in bone marrow, making it impossible to form the heme group necessary for erythrocyte function. Increased levels of hepcidin therefore coincide with decreased hematocrit. Hepcidin also acts as an inhibitor of ferroportin, which transports iron from the gut into the body.

Passage taken from the Next Step online QBank

6. If a person donates blood on January 1, on which day are they most likely to have elevated amounts of erythropoietin in circulation?

   A. February 6
   B. March 4
   C. May 2
   D. July 1

7. Under which of the following categories does blood fall?

   A. Heart tissue
   B. Lymph tissue
   C. Kidney tissue
   D. Connective tissue

8. Which of the following might result from living at high elevation?

   A. Increased blood viscosity
   B. Greater plasma volume
   C. Reduced hematocrit
   D. Increased hepcidin production

9. Which of the following would most likely cause a reticulocyte count of 0.4%?

   A. Increased ferroportin activity
   B. Decreased hepcidin activity
   C. Internal bleeding
   D. Irradiation of bone marrow

10. According to the information in the passage, what mass of erythropoietin is found in the serum of the average adult?

    A. 25 μg
    B. 50 μg
    C. 100 μg
    D. 200 μg

Cellular Metabolism

Glycolysis

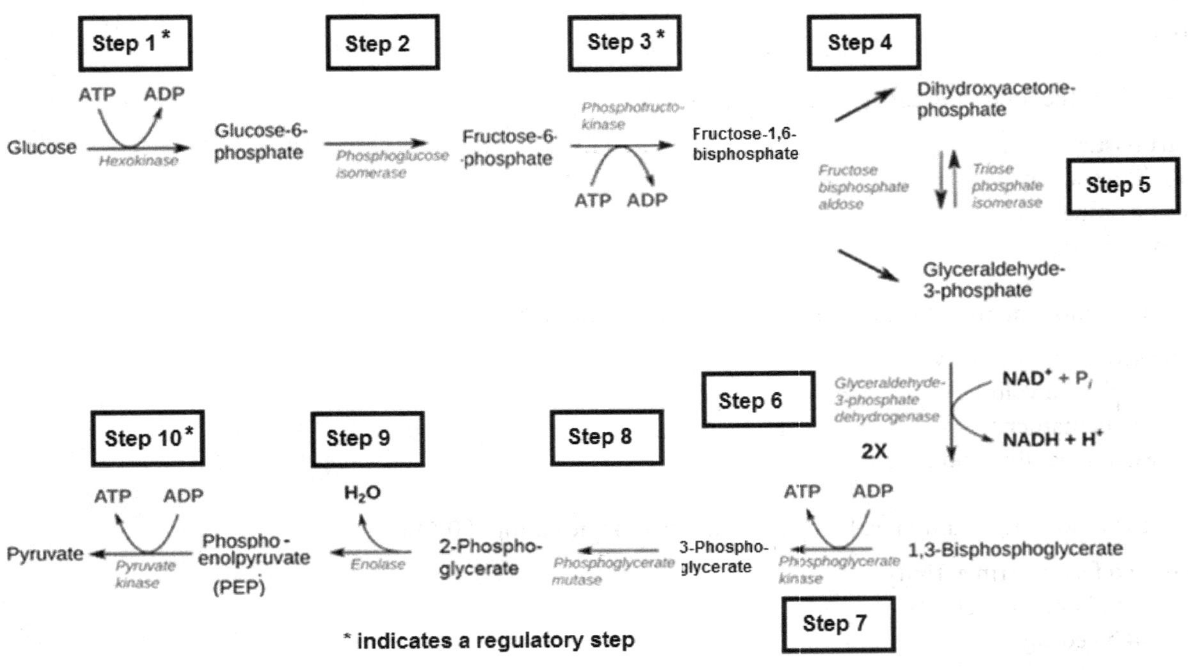

How many net ATP does glycolysis yield?

____

Where in the cell does glycolysis occur?

____

What reaction bridges the gap from glycolysis to the citric acid cycle?

____

Regulation:

____

The Citric Acid Cycle

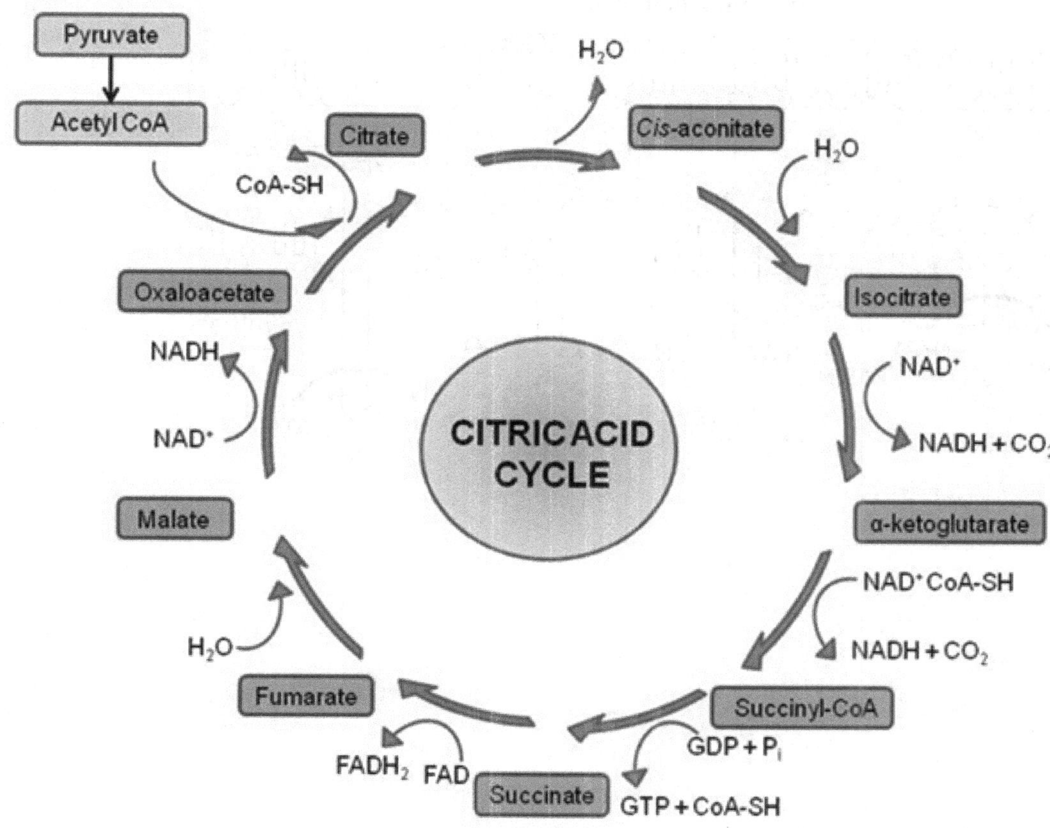

How many TCA cycles result from 1 round of glycolysis? ____________________

What is the net gain of ATP from the TCA cycle? ____________________

Where in the cell does the TCA cycle occur? ____________________

The electrons used in the electron transport chain are produced by the TCA cycle via the reduction of ________________________ and ________________________.

Electron Transport Chain

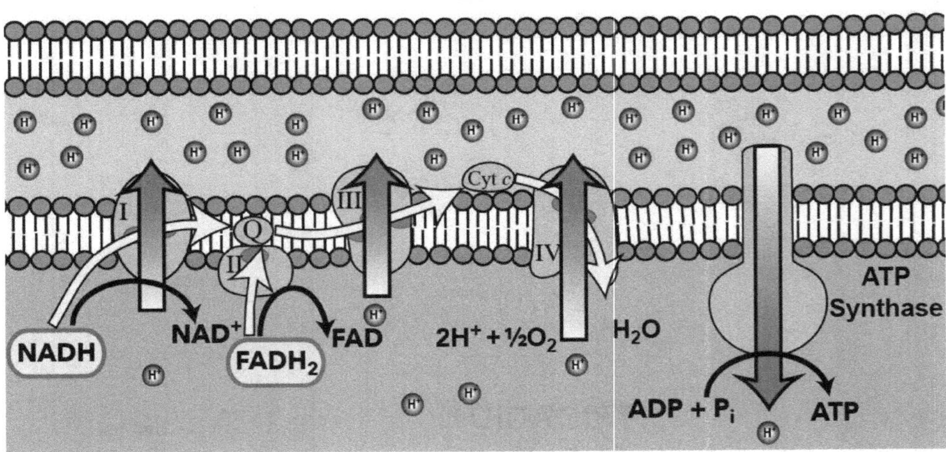

How many net ATP does the ETC yield? ____________________

Where in the cell does the ETC occur? ____________________

What is the final electron acceptor in the ETC? ____________________

Infants have brown fat cells which express a protein that acts to dissipate the proton gradient, yet allows O_2 consumption to continue. What effect might this have on ATP generation? Why might this mechanism have evolved?

____

____

Reading MCAT Figures

1. Science passages—analyzing figures
   - Glance at the figures at the start of the passage then study them as you read.
     - Title, axes, units
     - Extremes, inflection points
     - Trends (positive/negative/none)
     - Intercepts and intersections
     - Error bars
   - Correlate the text with the figure
     - Arguably your single most important job while reading a science passage.
     - What does the text say about the graph?
     - What does the data in the graph reveal about the text?
   - What do figure types tell us about the data the exam might present?

     Bar graph

     Time-series plot

     XY-line graph

     Scatter plot

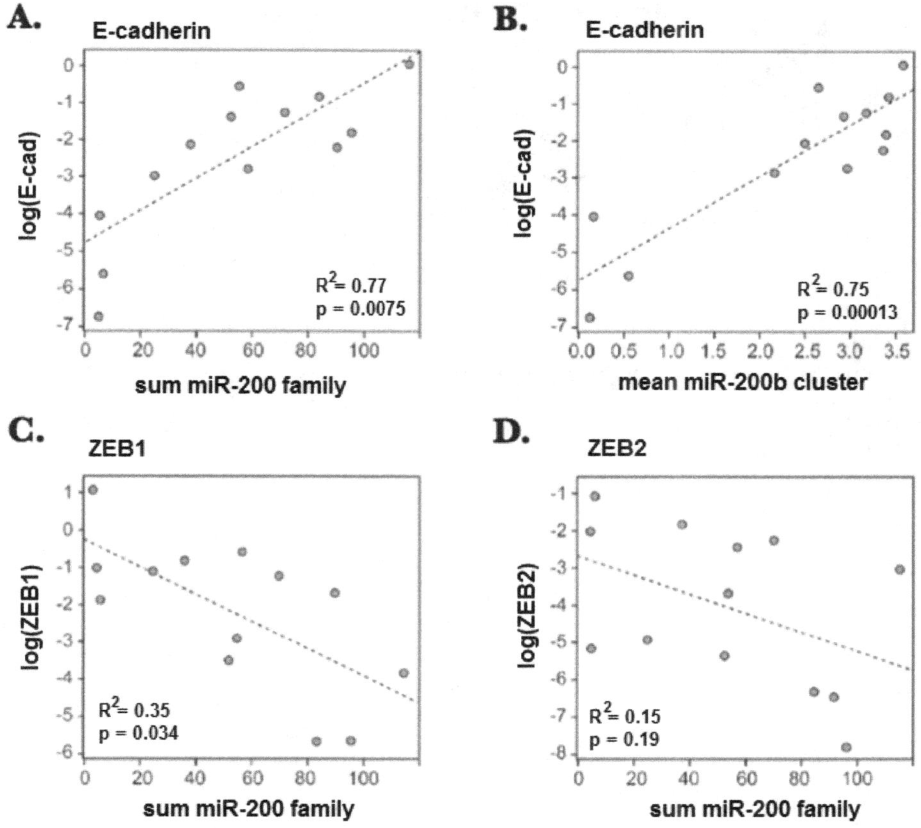

Repeat Count	Disease Status	Age of Onset	Probability of Affected Offspring
< 26	Will not be affected	N/A	None
27-35	Will not be affected	N/A	Elevated, but P << 50%
36-39	May be affected	After 40	50%
40+	Will be affected	Between 25-39; earlier with increased repeat count	50%

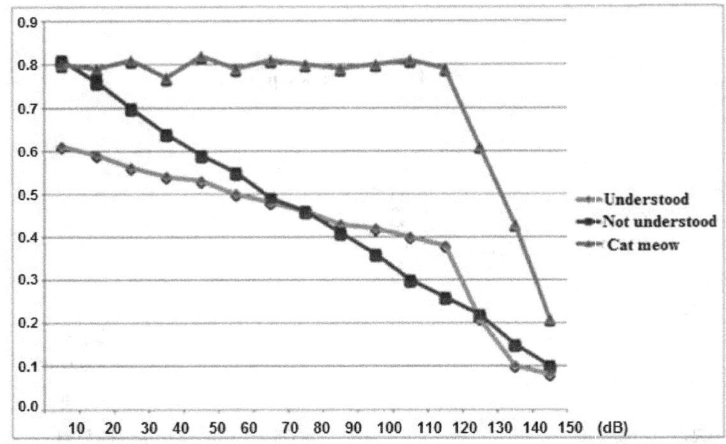

Figure 2 The jnd as a function of intensity for a recording of speech in a language understood by the listener, one not understood by the listener, and a recognizable non-speech sound (a cat's meow)

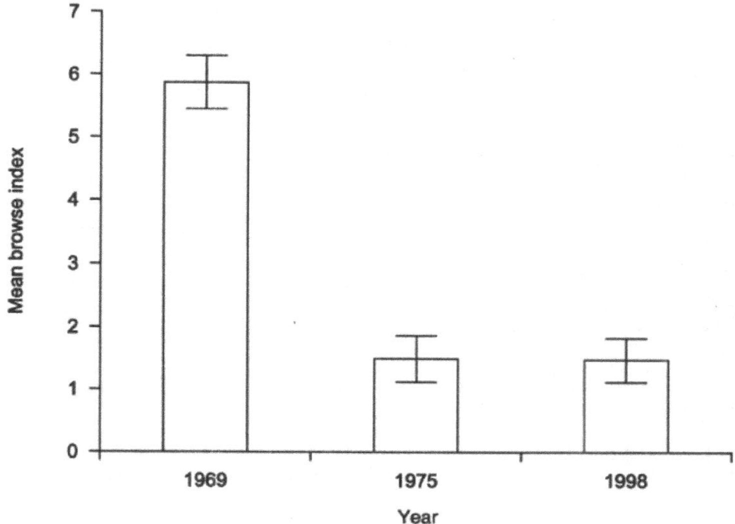

Is there a potential flaw/bias in the figure presented?

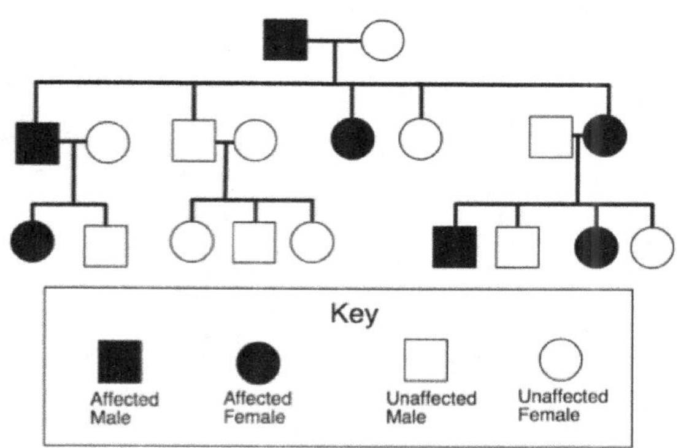

Figure 2 Inheritance of Grave's disease in family X

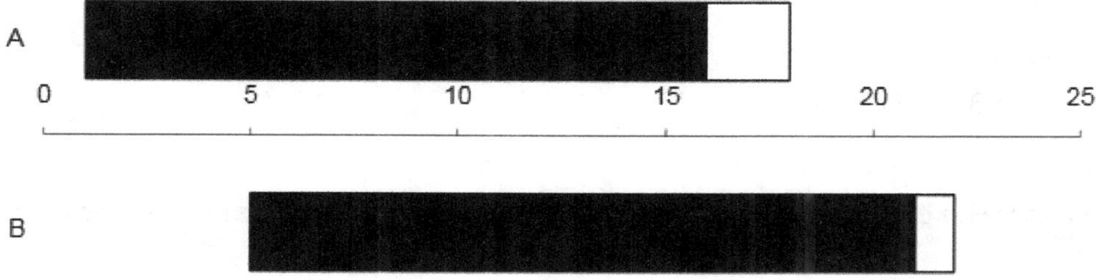

Figure 3 Comparison of solvent distance moved in test strip

Equation 1 $\ln k = \ln A - (E_a/RT)$

Equation 2 $\ln K_{eq} = (\Delta S/R) - (\Delta H/RT)$

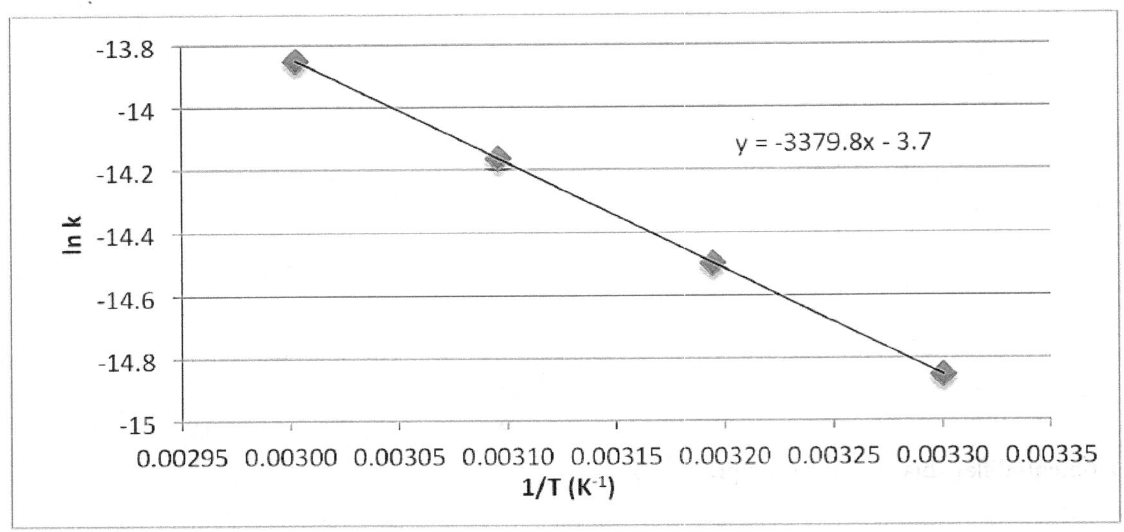

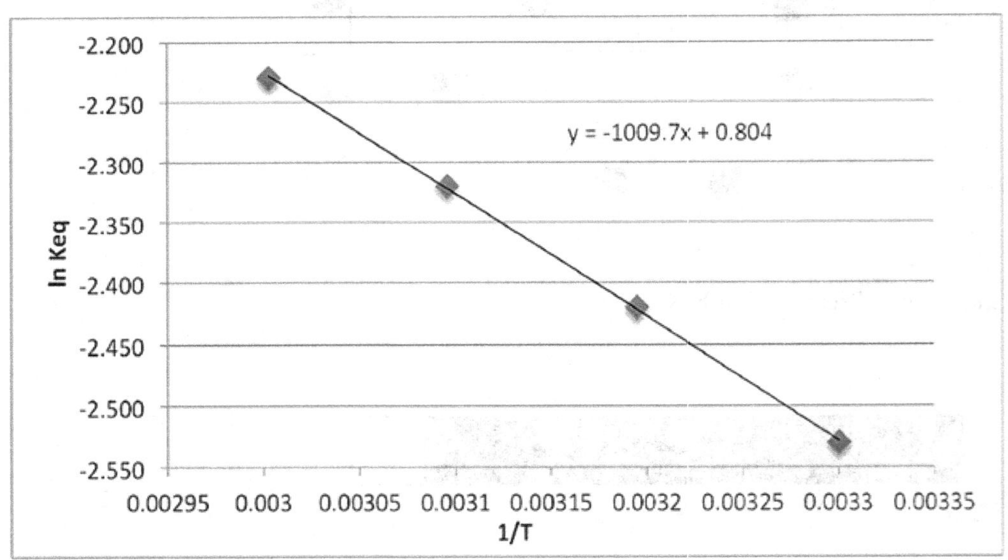

Figure 2 A van't Hoff plot of ln K_{eq} versus 1/T for the hydrolysis of starch catalyzed by amylase

MCAT Figure Analysis Exercise

When preparing for the exam, we want to have all of our skills sharpened. This means working on our data analysis skills.

Use this exercise on practice passages, research papers, or figures from your content review books. By your exam date these thought processes, if mastered, will allow you properly understand data, and this will lead to a higher score.

1. Determine what question is being asked by the experiment reported in the figure.
2. Outline the experiments or studies that generated the results in the figure.
3. Anticipate what the results would look like given different answers to the experimental question.
4. Determine where the positive and negative controls are presented.
5. Determine if the pattern you anticipated is observed and compare your conclusion from observation with the conclusions that has been drawn in the passage.
6. Determine how the results from the experiment reported in a figure contribute to the overall conclusions drawn by the paper (there may be more than one result reported in a figure and more than one conclusion to be drawn from it.).

Timed MCAT Practice Passage

Mastery of the MCAT sciences is a two-part process. First you must study to understand (not just memorize!) the science content, and then you must study the content actively and challenge yourself within the context of the exam

1. Complete your reading of the passage (3-4 minutes).
   - Write down what you believe to be the primary science content underlying the passage.
   - What facts or concepts do you anticipate will be tested? When you are done with the questions determine if you were correct. What passage clues were there to imply related topics that showed up in the questions?
   - Were there any key terms or important scientific relationships you missed?
   - Were you able to draw any conclusions from the data, if presented?

2. Complete the practice questions on your own (4-5 minutes)
   - Rephrase each question in your own mind after reading it to clarify the task.
   - Research the relevant area(s) of the passage or your own knowledge for information related to the task.
   - Respond to the question by choosing the answer that fits your research/calculations *and* satisfies the task.
   - If no answer seems obvious, eliminate answers that fail to have support in the passage or in the relevant science.

3. Analyze your wrong answer choices to the questions you missed.
   - Did you understand the task in the question?
   - What skill type was the question?
   - Did you know the science/formula/concept needed to answer the question?
   - Did you recognize the science being hinted at?
   - Were you able to find information in the passage quickly when you needed it?
   - Were there any necessary scientific concepts you failed to apply to the question?
     - If so, why?
   - If you made a mistake in calculations, have you identified your mistake?

This page left intentionally blank.

Practice Passage

Entry of enveloped viruses into cells can occur by membrane fusion or by endocytosis. Viral envelope proteins attach to receptors on the surface of target cells, triggering fusion with the host cell, uncoating and emptying of the viral contents into the cell. In endocytosis, viral particles are endocytosed by host cell endosomes. Following entry into the host cell, viral particles can be released from the endosomes in a pH-dependent mechanism, most likely because of conformational changes in envelope protein receptors caused by the action of host cell pH-dependent proteases during endosomal acidification.

Particles of human immunodeficiency virus (HIV)—an enveloped virus—produced in the presence of the viral factor Nef are more infectious than particles produced in the absence of this protein. The mechanism underlying this effect is poorly understood. In order to study Nef-mediated infectivity enhancement, HIV particles were engineered to contain envelope protein receptors from CXCR4-dependent (X4. HIV (an uncommon, receptor specific form of HIV which requires the cell surface protein CD4 for viral entry), amphotropic murine leukemia virus (ampho), or the vesicular stomatitis virus (VSV). The infectivity of these engineered particles, as well as that of a HIV particle containing the most common envelope protein, CCR5 (R5., were measured in the presence or absence of Nef. Results are given in Figure 1.

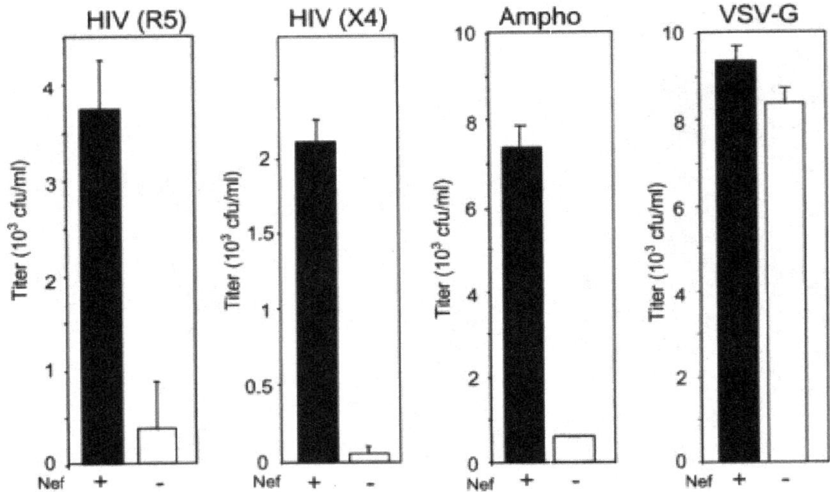

Figure 1 Effect of Nef on infectivity with hybrid viral particles containing various envelope proteins (Note: increased titer count correlates directly with increased viral infectivity; error bars indicate standard deviation)

Passage taken from the Next Step online QBank

To test the hypothesis that Nef-mediated rate enhancement is specific to envelope protein fusion only at neutral pH, the scientists produced Nef$^+$ and Nef$^-$ HIV hybrids with Ebola virus glycoprotein (Ebola-GP), which has recently been shown to facilitate fusion through a low-pH-dependent mechanism. The infectivity of these particles, as well as three previously synthesized hybrids, was tested in the presence or absence of bafilomycin A1, an agent that prevents the acidification of endosomes by blocking the function of the vacuolar H^+ ATPase. Results are shown in Figure 2.

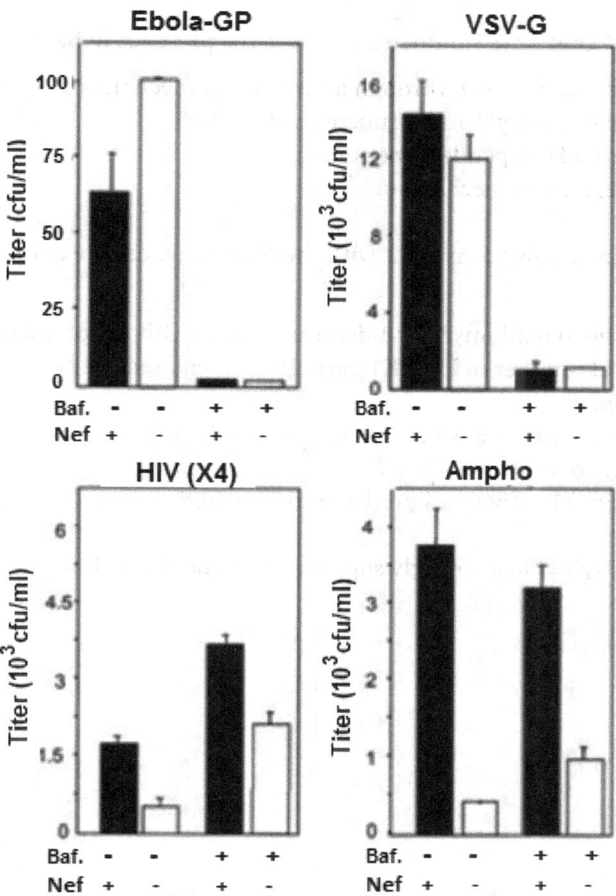

Figure 2 Effect of Nef and bafilomycin A1 (Baf) on infectivity with hybrid viral particles containing various envelope proteins (Note: Black bars indicate Nef+ hybrid, white bars indicate Nef- hybrids; increased titer count correlates directly with increased viral infectivity; error bars indicate standard deviation).

Passage taken from the Next Step online QBank

11. Which of the following would best explain the observed results of pH-dependent activity in Ebo-GP envelope proteins?

   A. Reduced pH causes reduced enzyme activity.
   B. The pH-dependent proteases require Nef to direct construction of infectious conformations.
   C. pH dependent enzymes allow the formation of smaller protein fragments.
   D. The pH-dependent proteases have no effect.

12. The trials shown in Figure 2 that were conducted in the in the presence of bafilomycin A1 suggest that:

   A. all particles tested must enter the cell through a neutral-pH mechanism.
   B. Ebola-Gp and VSV-G entry is a pH-independent mechanism.
   C. X4 and Ampho entry is a pH-dependent mechanism.
   D. VSV-G entry is a pH dependent mechanism.

13. Are the results of HIV-X4 infectivity consistent with the Nef-mediated rate enhancement hypothesis discussed in the passage?

   A. No, because high pH due to bafilomycin A1 decreased the likelihood of infection.
   B. No, because a significant number of HIV-X4 particles that entered the cells failed to survive subsequent endosomal acidification.
   C. Yes, Nef+ particles containing HIV X4 envelope proteins display approximately equal infectivity with or without bafilomycin A1 treatment.
   D. Yes, because bafilomycin A1 activity allowed a more productive route of entry to the virus.

14. The experiments on Nef activity most strongly support the theory that viral efficiency is mediated by Nef in which viral hybrids?

   I. CCR5
   II. CXCR-4
   III. Ampho
   IV. VSV

   A. II only
   B. IV only
   C. I, II and III only
   D. I, II, III and IV

EXAMPLE

Recall and Recognition in Biology Worksheet Exercise

Mitosis vs. Meiosis

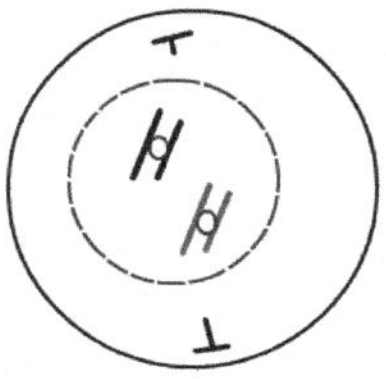

Before mitosis:
- DNA replicates during S phase

Prophase:
- Chromatin condenses into chromosomes
- Centrioles form and spindle fibers form
- Nuclear envelope breaks down

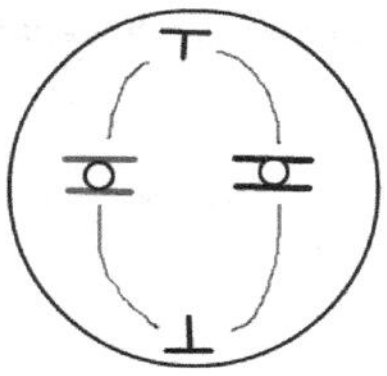

Metaphase:
- Chromosomes line up on metaphase plate
- Centrioles are attached to spindle fibers

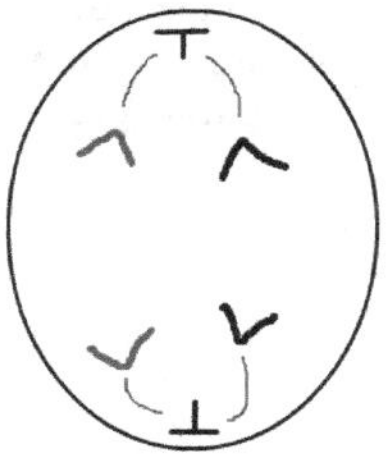

Anaphase:
- Centromeres split
- Sister chromatids are pulled apart

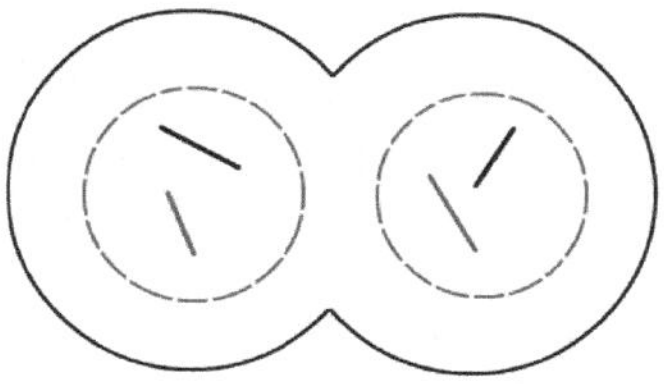

Telophase:
- Cell membrane pinches in half
- Nuclear envelopes reform
- 2 identical daughters produced

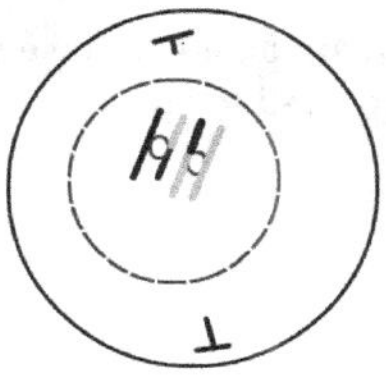

Before meiosis:
- DNA replicates during S phase

Prophase I:
- Chromatin condenses into chromosomes
- Centrioles form and spindle fibers form
- Nuclear envelope breaks down
- Chiasmata form tetrads and crossing over

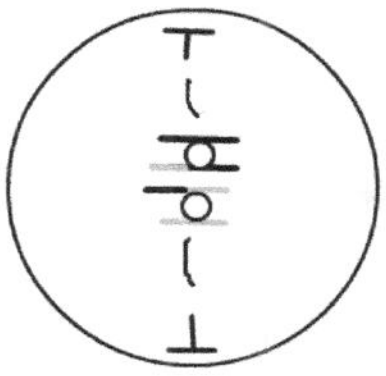

Metaphase I:
- Chromosomes pairs line up on metaphase plate
- Centrioles are attached to spindle fibers

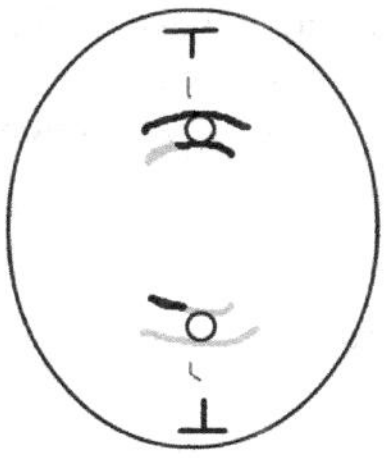

Anaphase I:
- Homologous pairs are pulled apart

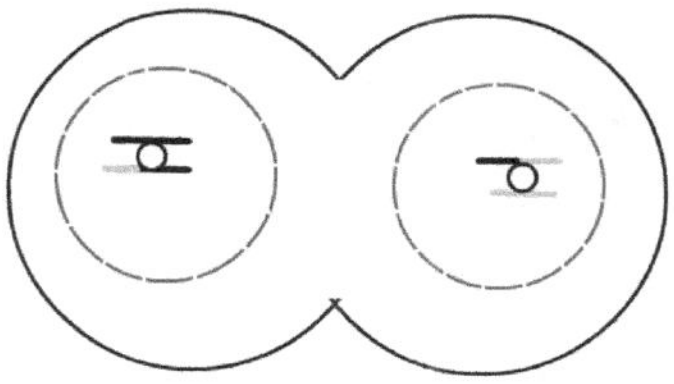

Telophase:
- Cell membrane pinches in half
- Nuclear envelopes reform
- 2 haploid daughters produced

Mitosis vs. Meiosis Worksheet—Level 1

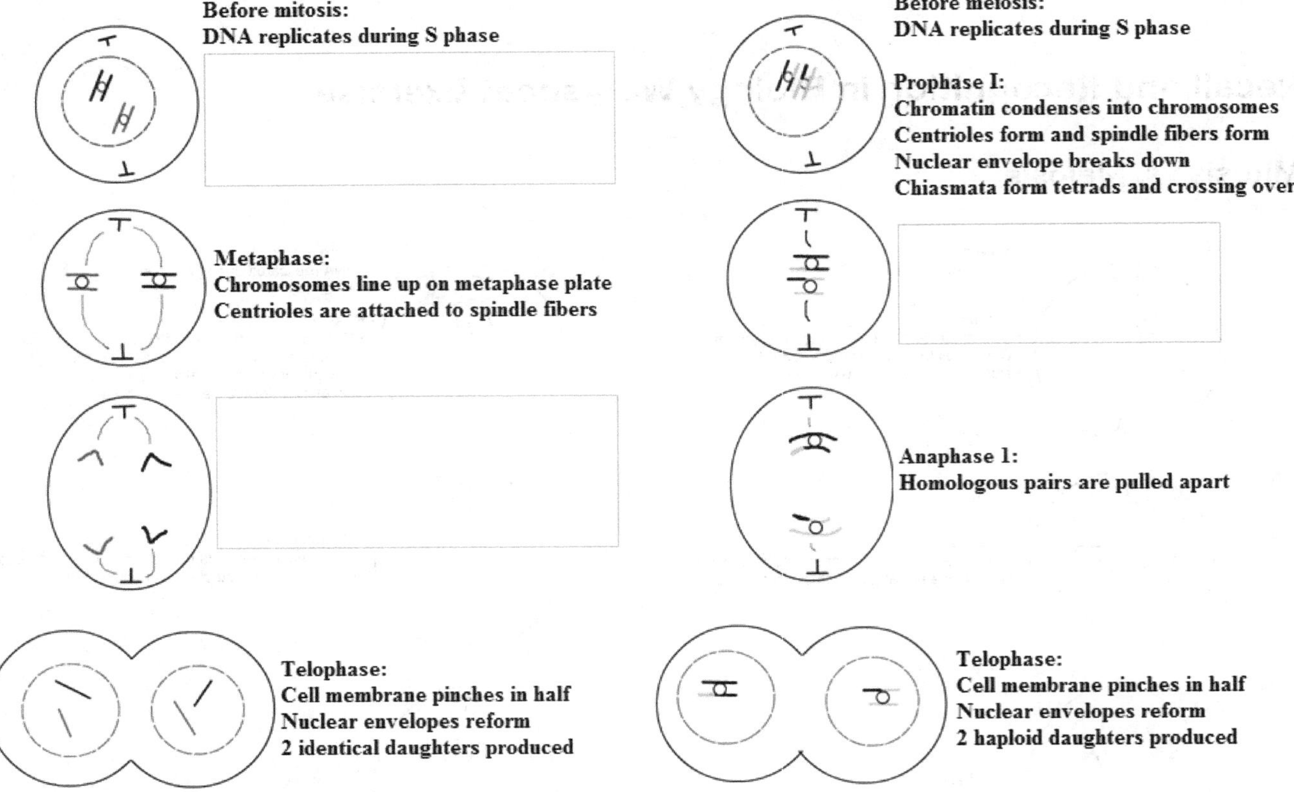

Mitosis vs. Meiosis Worksheet—Level 2

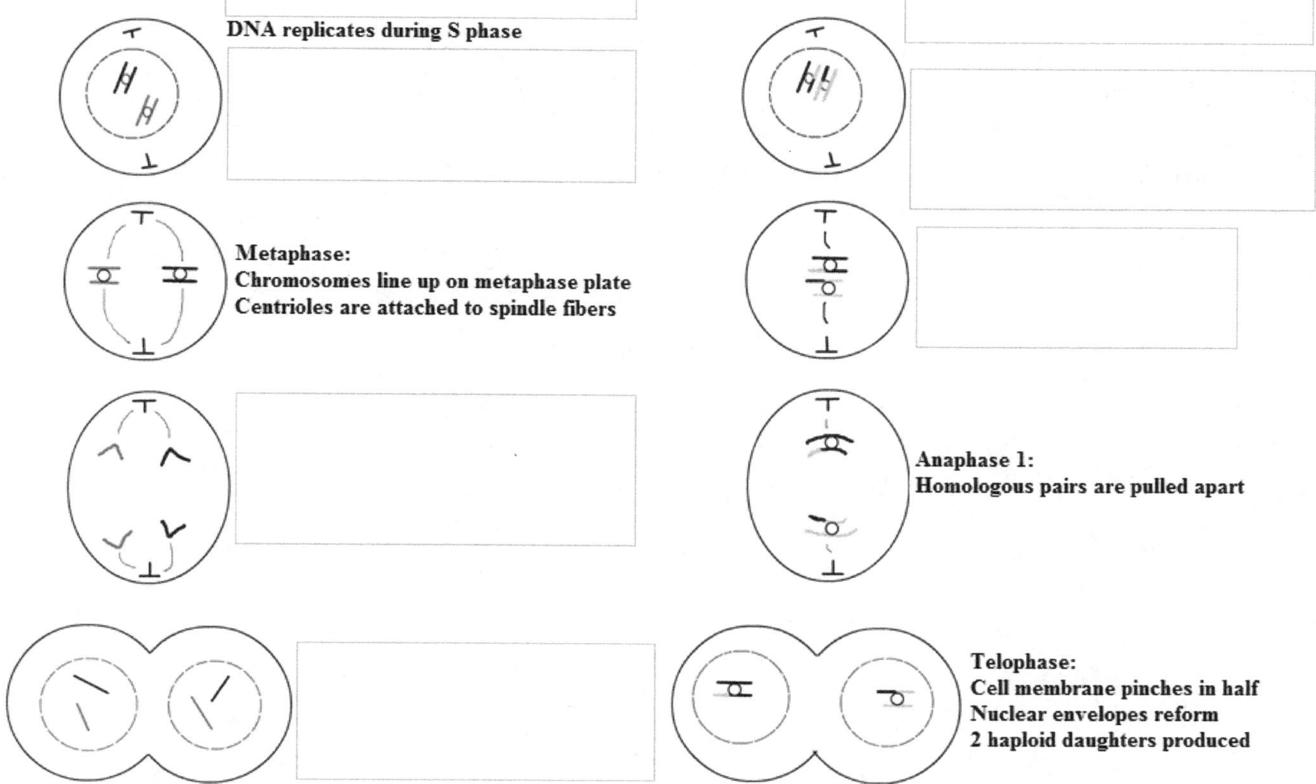

Mitosis vs. Meiosis Worksheet—Level 3

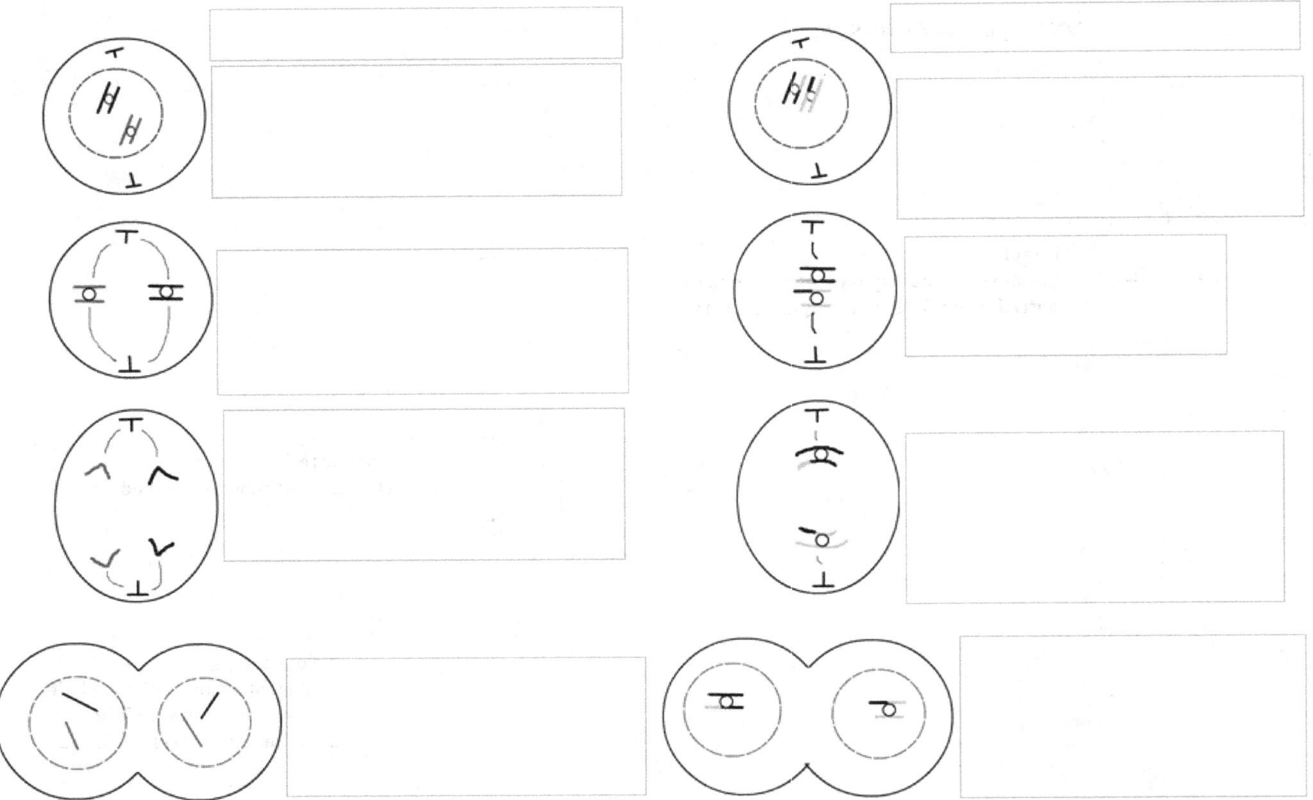

DNA Replication

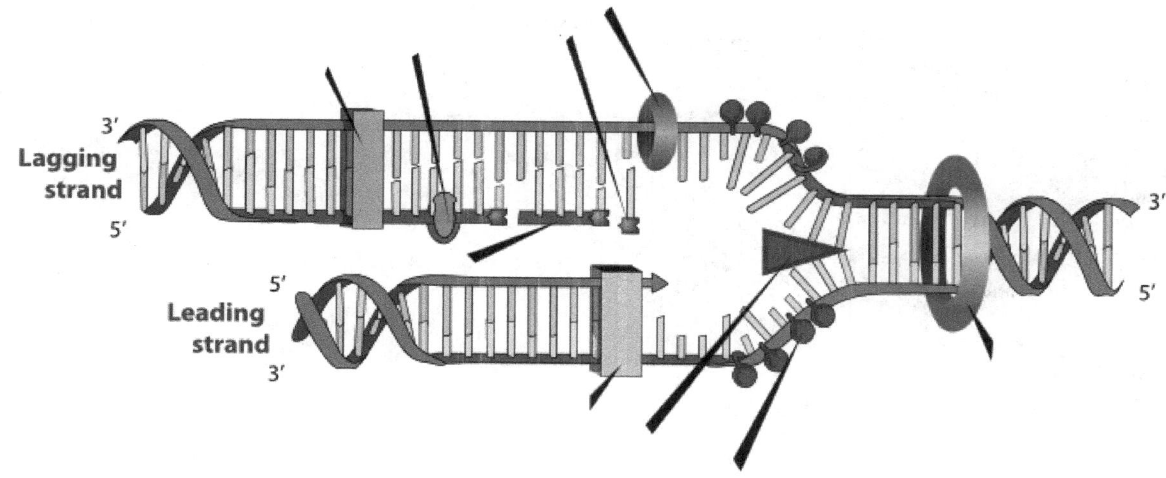

DNA polymerase (base pairing)

DNA ligase, helicase, primase

Topoisomerase

Leading strand vs. lagging strand

Okazaki fragment

RNA primer

SSBs

Transcription

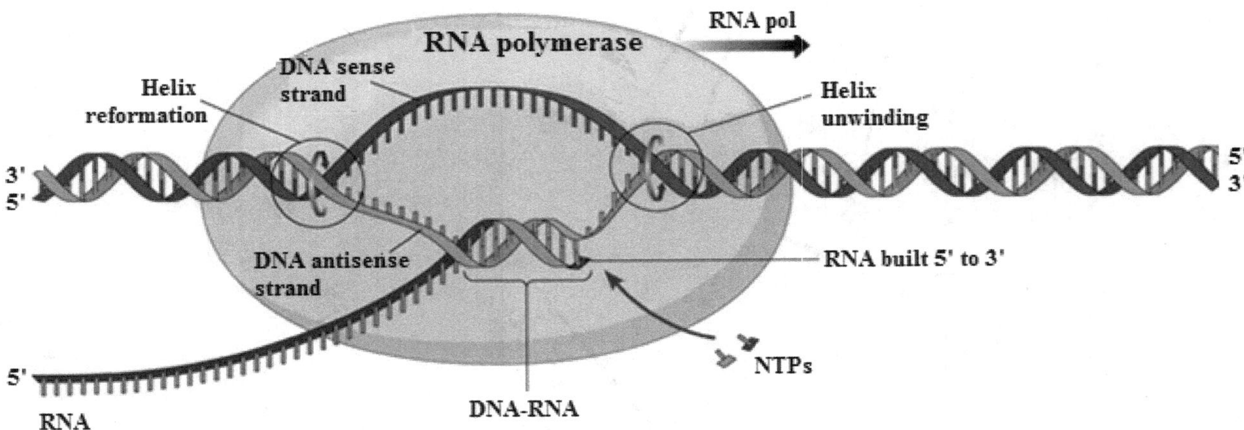

DNA vs. RNA

Prokaryotic vs. eukaryotic transcription

Initiation

Termination

Post-transcriptional modifications

Translation

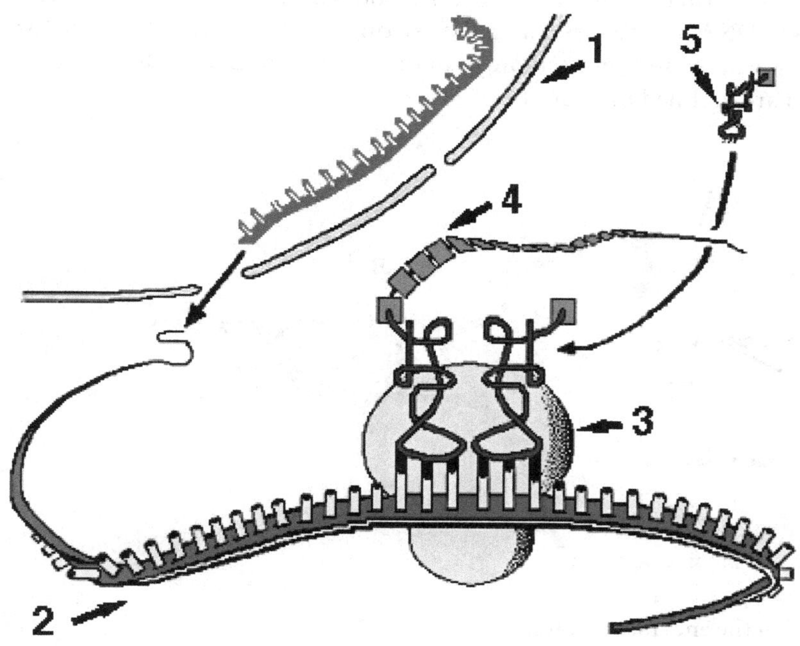

1:

2:

3:

4:

5:

Initiation

Elongation

Termination

Codons and mutation types

MCAT Practice Passage

A DNA polymerase is an enzyme that catalyzes the formation of a strand of nucleotides based on a DNA template. During the S phase of the cell cycle, two copies of DNA polymerase act on the existing genetic material to create two new copies. The process of DNA replication however, requires much more than the presence of DNA polymerase. The many enzymes involved and their function are outlined in figure 1.

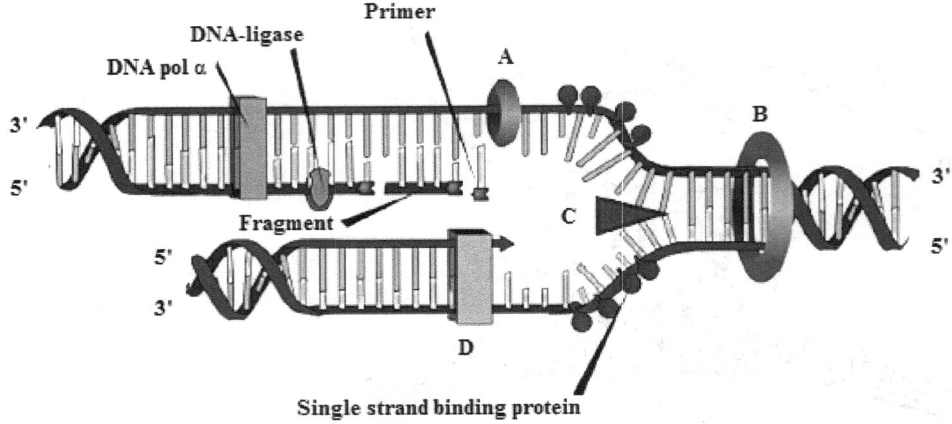

Figure 1 A schematic of DNA replication with all of the enzymes involved

The function of DNA polymerase is simply to read a single strand of DNA and add the correct nucleotide to complement the template. DNA polymerase can only add new nucleotides to the 3' end of the strand being synthesized. DNA polymerases make about one mistake per billion nucleotides added. Most DNA polymerases have the built in ability to recognize and correct these mistakes when they occur. When mistakes occur, the offending base is cleaved out of the strand by enzymes and DNA polymerase will add the correct base. After this, DNA ligase connects the loose ends.

DNA ligase catalyzes the joining together of two DNA strands by forming a phosphodiester bond between the two strands. DNA ligase first binds an AMP molecule to a lysine residue in its structure. This AMP is attacked by the 5' phosphate group between the nucleotides, transferring the AMP to the phosphate group. The addition of the AMP to the 5' phosphate makes the phosphorous atom more susceptible to attack by the 3' OH group of the next nucleotide. The attack results in the release of AMP and H2O and the formation of a phosphodiester bond.

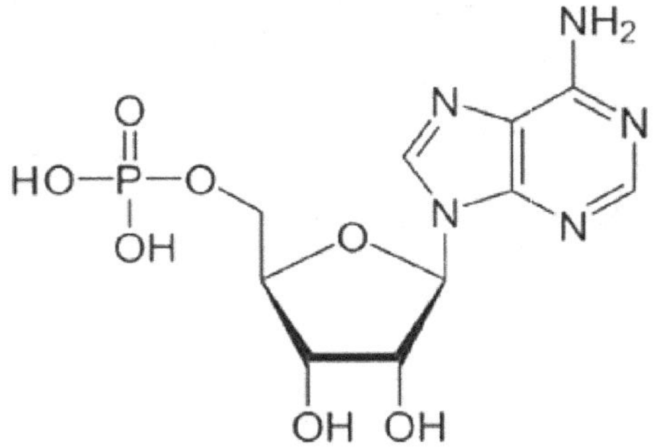

Figure 2 AMP

Passage taken from the Next Step Biology review book, Chapter 3

15. If there are 6 billion base pairs in a diploid cell, how many errors will occur on average during DNA replication in that cell?

    A. 3
    B. 6
    C. 9
    D. 12

16. If the following DNA strand is being opened and replicated from right to left, which strand will be the lagging strand?

```
5' AGTCTCCGGATTAACGATGC 3'
   ||||||||||||||||||||
3' TCAGAGGCCTAATTGCTACG 5'
```

    A. The top strand will be the lagging strand because DNA polymerase will be adding nucleotides in the 3’ direction from left to right on the top strand.
    B. The top strand will be the lagging strand because DNA polymerase will be adding nucleotides in the 3’ direction from right to left on the top strand.
    C. The bottom strand will be the lagging strand because DNA polymerase will be adding nucleotides in the 3’ direction from left to right on the bottom strand.
    D. The bottom strand will be the lagging strand because DNA polymerase will be adding nucleotides in the 3’ direction from right to left on the bottom strand.

17. Which of the following represents the bond formation between adjacent nucleotides being joined by DNA ligase?

    A. 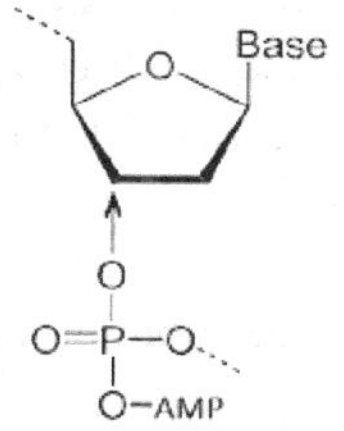
    Base
    O
    O=P—O
    O—AMP

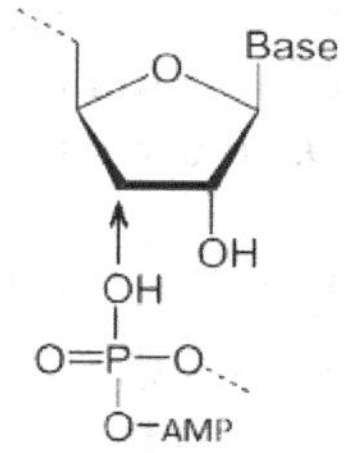

    B.
    Base
    OH OH
    OH
    O=P—O
    O—AMP

    C.
    Base
    OH
    OH
    O=P—O
    O—AMP

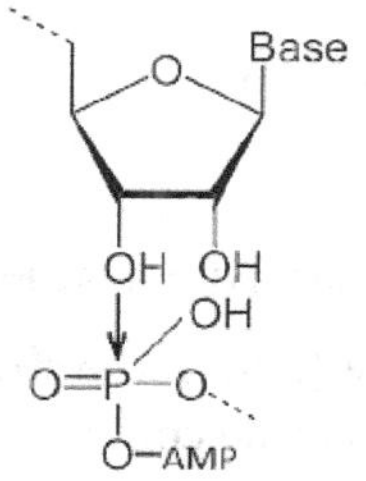

    D.
    Base
    OH
    OH
    O=P—O
    O—AMP

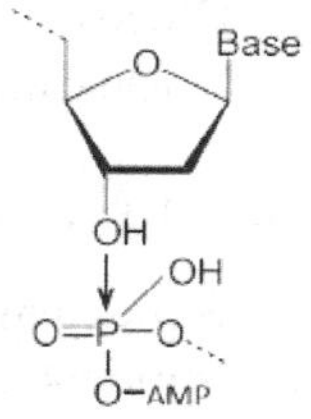

18. Which of the following labeled items in Figure 1 is an RNA polymerase which catalyzes the synthesis of short RNA segments complementary to the template strand?

    A. A
    B. B
    C. C
    D. D

19. Which of the following best describes the effect of addition of AMP to a phosphate group?

    A. AMP is electron-donating and contributes to the phosphate’s nucleophilic affinity.
    B. AMP is electron-donating and contributes to the phosphorus atom’selectrophilic nature.
    C. AMP is electron-withdrawing.
    D. AMP is electron-donating and contributes to the phosphorus atom’s electronegativity.

Problem-solving Cooldown

20. Which of the following is true of mitosis?

    A. Homologous pairs line up along the metaphase plate during metaphase.
    B. Genetic recombination occurs during prophase.
    C. Microfilaments separate sister chromatids during anaphase.
    D. It occurs only in germ cells.

21. Which of the following is NOT a biological monomer?

    A. Amino acid
    B. Nucleotide
    C. Glucose
    D. Nucleic acid

22. Since dsDNA is a highly charged polyanion, its resistance to heat denaturation:

    A. is independent of the weight of the strands.
    B. is independent of nucleotide content.
    C. increases in the presence of salts.
    D. does not depend on hydrophobic interactions.

23. Which pyrimidine base contains an amino group at carbon 4?

    A. Uracil
    B. Adenine
    C. Thymine
    D. Cytosine

24. If ribose or 2-deoxyribose is added to a nitrogen base, the resulting compound is called a:

    A. nucleoside.
    B. nucleotide.
    C. nucleic acid.
    D. peptide.

To Do After Lesson 4

- [ ] Read Biochemistry Chapters 1 and 2
- [ ] Read General Chemistry and Organic Chemistry Chapter 6
- [ ] Read Physics Chapters 5 and 6
- [ ] Complete Biology QBank 3: Eukaryotic and Prokaryotic Cells

This page left intentionally blank.

LESSON 5

Physics 1

To Do Before Lesson 5

- ☐ Read Biochemistry Chapters 1 and 2
- ☐ Read General Chemistry and Organic Chemistry Chapter 6
- ☐ Read Physics Chapters 5 and 6
- ☐ Complete Biology QBank 3: Eukaryotic and Prokaryotic Cells

In Lesson 5

Problem-solving Warm-up
Mastering Equations
Translational Motion & Newtonian Mechanics
Effective Reading in the Sciences
MCAT Practice Passage
Biomechanics
Training Your Physics Recall
MCAT Practice Passage
Problem-solving Cooldown
Test-like Thinking: CARS Practice Passage

To Do After Lesson 5

- ☐ Read Physics Chapters 7 and 8
- ☐ Read Verbal and Quantitative Reasoning Chapters 7 and 8
- ☐ Read General Chemistry and Organic Chemistry Chapter 7
- ☐ Complete Physics QBank 1: Motion, Force, and Work

Problem-solving Warm-up

1. A block is pushed from rest with force, F_{app}, until it reaches velocity, v. The surface has coefficients of static friction and kinetic friction that are greater than 0. Which of the following conditions must be met?

   A. $\Delta KE_{obj} > W_{friction}$
   B. The coefficient of static friction is less than the coefficient of kinetic friction
   C. The work done by F_{app} is greater than the work done by friction
   D. $\Delta KE_{obj} < W_{friction}$

2. Using a block and tackle system with 5 ropes and a 50 kg load, what length of rope and what force would a person need to use to lift the load 1 meter?

   A. 5 meters, 100 N
   B. 1 meter, 500 N
   C. 10 meters, 500 N
   D. 1 meter, 250 N

3. The human forearm is an example of what kind of lever?

   A. Class 1 lever, with a mechanical advantage greater than 1
   B. Class 2 lever, with a mechanical advantage greater than 1
   C. Class 2 lever, with a mechanical advantage less than 1
   D. Class 3 lever, with a mechanical advantage less than 1

4. What is the net work done by a person when lifting a 10 kg object from the ground and holding it motionless 1.5 m above the ground for 75 seconds?

   A. 150 J
   B. 2 W
   C. 0 J
   D. 150 N

5. Which of the following scenarios has non-conservative forces at work?

   A. Lifting an object with an ideal lever
   B. An object sliding down a frictionless inclined plane
   C. A (+) charge placed next to another (+) charge
   D. Turbulent blood flow in the aorta

How to "Memorize" Equations

The MCAT emphasizes integration and testing of relationships. Many times the successful use of a formula or equation will depend on the relationships in the equation, not calculation.

When learning equations, focus on: ____

and ____.

Keeping track of ________________ will allow you to derive a needed equation in a pinch.

	Equation	Units	Relationships
Gravitational Force			
Electrostatic Force			
Kinetic Energy			
Potential Energy			
Mechanical Work			

Free Body Diagrams

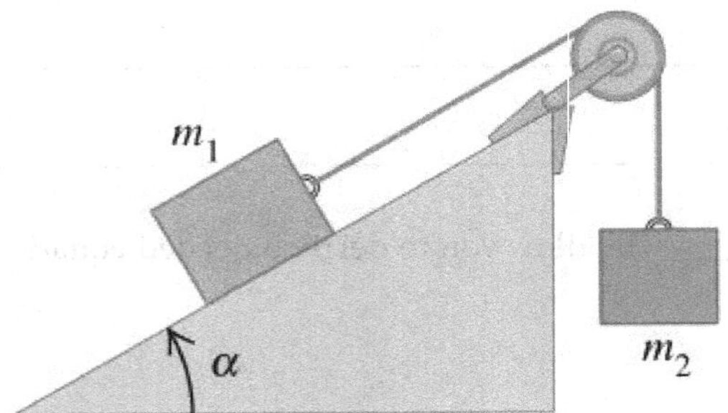

Which forces on the block are conservative? Which are non-conservative?

How does the force of static friction change as the angle increases?

How does the force pulling m_1 down the plane change as the angle decreases?

Why does pushing m_1 up the incline NOT violate the work-energy theorem?

Kinematics Force and Energy—Recall Exercise

Trig Functions:

Angle	Sin	Cos
0	0	$\sqrt{4}/2$
30	$\sqrt{1}/2$	$\sqrt{3}/2$
45	$\sqrt{2}/2$	$\sqrt{2}/2$
60	$\sqrt{3}/2$	$\sqrt{1}/2$
90	$\sqrt{4}/2$	0
180	0	−1

Kinematic Equations:

$v_f =$ $V_0 + at$

$d =$ $V_0t + (1/2)at^2$

$v_f^2 =$ $V_0^2 + 2ad$

$d =$ $[(V_1+V_2)/2]t$

Projectile Motion:

$v_o \sin\theta =$ $\sqrt{(2gh)}$

$v_o \cos\theta =$ constant

$v_o \sin\theta =$ V_{yi}

v_y @ max h = 0 m/s

$a_x =$ 0 m/s²

$a_y =$ −10 m/s²

Force:

$F =$ ma

$F_g =$ $\frac{GMm}{r^2}$

Angular Frequency of a spring = $\omega = \sqrt{\frac{K}{m}}$

Hooke's Law = $(F = -kx)$

Mechanical Advantage = $\frac{F_{out}}{F_{in}}$

Efficiency = $\frac{W_{out}}{W_{in}}$

$F_{spring} = -k\Delta x$

$F_f = \mu F_n$

$\tau = rF\sin\theta$

Energy Equations:

$E_K = KE = \frac{1}{2}mv^2$

$P = \frac{W}{T} = \frac{\text{Work}}{\text{Time}}$

$W_{net} = \Delta KE$

$W = Fd\cos\theta$

$E_{spring} = (\frac{1}{2})kx^2$

$PE_{grav} = mgh$

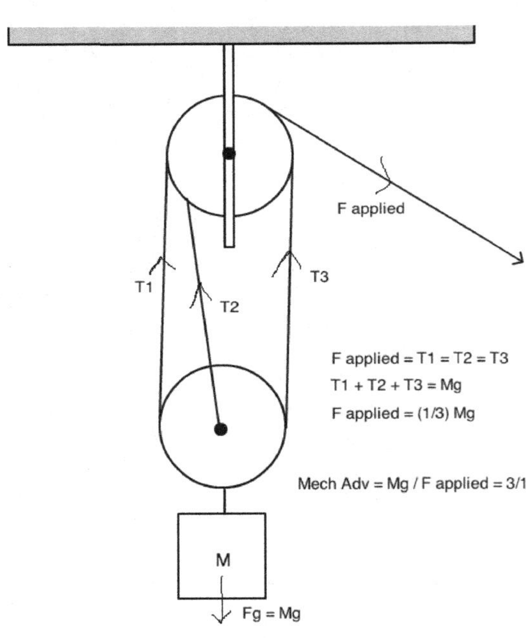

This page left intentionally blank.

Effective Reading in the Sciences

Reading science passages on the MCAT means being able to keep track of important (i.e. likely to be tested) information in the passage. You must be able to anticipate, recognize, and understand scientific concepts presented in many different forms.

Students in a biophysics class used the experimental setup shown in Figure 1 to simulate a human arm. The apparatus consisted of a horizontal beam having a length (L) of 0.50 m and a mass (Mbeam) of 2.0 kg, was attached to a frictionless hinge, which was also attached to a vertically oriented beam having a frictionless wheel at the top.

A massless string was initially attached in the middle of the horizontal beam at a distance from the center of the pivot point of the hinge. The string was draped over the wheel and then attached to a standard brass mass (M1.. The angle formed between the string and the horizontal beam was 60°. A second standard 1.0 kg brass mass ($M_{2.}$ was then attached at the end of the horizontal beam. The weight of M1 was adjusted until the two beams once again formed a right angle.

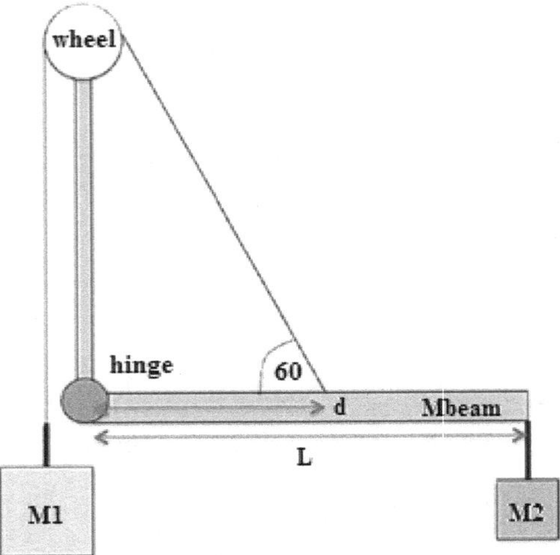

Figure 1 Simulation of human arm. (Note: sin 30° = cos 60°= 0.5, sin 60° = cos 30° = 0.866, tan 30° = 0.577, tan 60° = 1.732. Drawing not to scale)

Passage taken from the Next Step Physics review book, Chapter 2

6. When the system in the passage is at equilibrium, what is the length of the string between where it is attached to the horizontal beam and the point where it comes in contact with the wheel?

   A. 0.3 m
   B. 0.5 m
   C. 0.7 m
   D. 1.0 m

7. What is the mass of the brass weight hanging from the end of the string if the system is at equilibrium?

   A. 2.3 kg
   B. 3.0 kg
   C. 4.6 kg
   D. 6.0 kg

8. If the string is cut, what happen to mass 2?

   A. It will undergo translation and rotation.
   B. It will undergo translation but not rotation.
   C. It will undergo rotation but not translation.
   D. It will undergo neither translation nor rotation.

9. According to figure 1, when the arm flexes to lift a load, which of the following CANNOT be true?

   A. The work done on the load and the work done by the biceps are equal.
   B. The force generated by the bicep is greater than the weight of the load.
   C. The force effort is applied on the opposite side of the fulcrum from the weight of the load.
   D. The load moves a greater distance than the bicep force.

10. The force of mass 2 in the experiment approximates the actions of which anatomical part of the human body?

    A. Ligaments
    B. Triceps
    C. Humerus
    D. Radius

Biomechanics

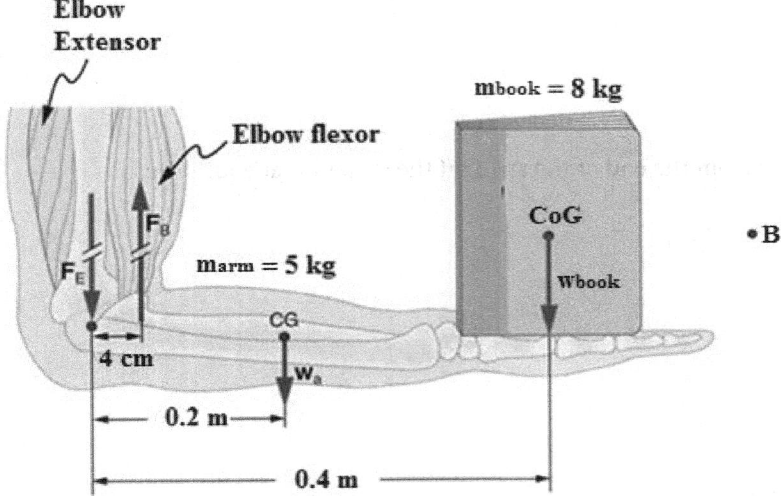

τ=0

Calculate the force the biceps muscle must exert to hold the forearm and its load as shown.

FB=r₂Wa + r₃Wb = r₁FB   FB = (r₂Wa+r₃Wb)/r₁ = [(0.2m)(5kg)(10m/s²) + (0.4m)(8kg)(10m/s²)] / 0.04m

= 1050N

If point B represents the center of mass of the book, what would the free body diagram look like?

FB ↑ · Wa ↓ · Wb ↓ · Fe ↓

What is the ratio of the force exerted by the bicep to the weight supported by the muscle?

1050N/130N   arm + load = 130N   Fb/(Wa+Wb) = 8 = 1050/130

What would happen to the torque on the elbow if the book were held closer to the elbow?

τ = rF sinθ   Torque would decrease

If most muscles are attached to bones via tendons close to joints, what does this do to their mechanical advantage?

mechanical advantage <1

What does this say about F_{output} vs. F_{input}?

input force > output force

The elbow can be modeled as a Class 3 lever. What kind of lever is the ankle? The skull? Second class Load is in the middle

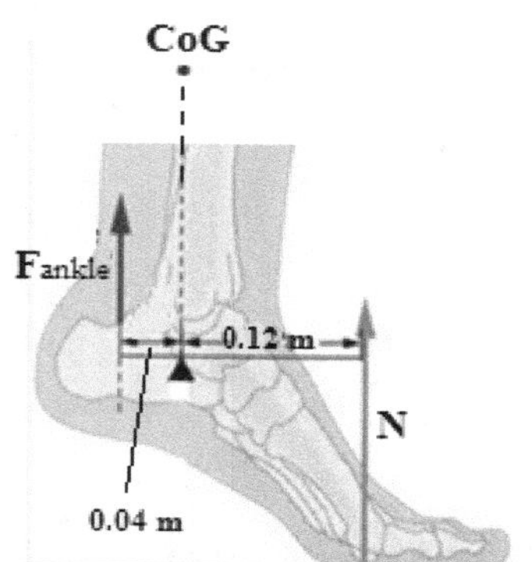

Torque = 0.12m x 75kg x 10m/s2 = 90Nm

A 75-kg ballet dancer stands on his toes by exerting an upward force through the Achilles tendon. What is the force in the Achilles tendon if he stands on one foot (Note: assume the forces are at right angles to the lever arm)?

F = 90/0.04 = 2250N

What is the force at the pivot of the ankle?

3000N Total F on joint = (Ftendon + weight 2250 + 750)

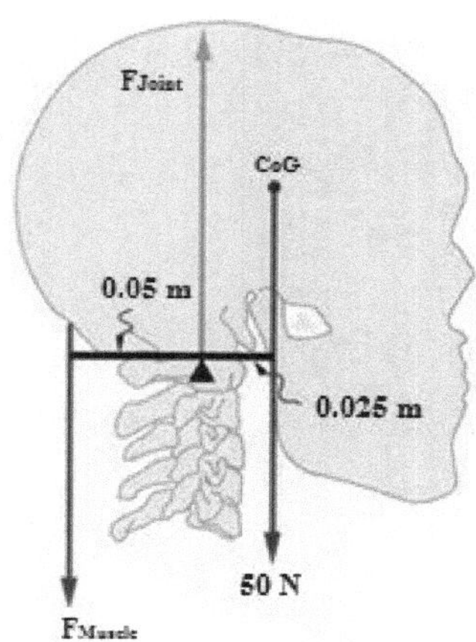

First class Lever - Fulcrum in the middle

What happens to your head if you fall asleep in class?

head will fall foreward

Why must this occur?

Center of gravity of skull is forward from joint

What must be true of the neck muscles when you are awake?

must exert a force (by muscles) when awake to keep the head erect

EXAMPLE

Kinematics Force and Energy: Worksheet Exercise Level 1

Trig Functions:

$\cos 90° = \sin 0° = 0$

$\cos 60° = \sin 30° =$ √1/2

$\cos 45° = \sin 45° = \sqrt{2}/2$

$\cos 30° = \sin 60° = \sqrt{3}/2$

$\cos 0° = \sin 90° =$ √4/2

Kinematic Equations:

$v_f =$ $v_0 + at$

$d = v_o t + (1/2)at^2$

$v_f^2 =$ $v_0^2 + 2ad$

$d =$ $\left(\frac{v_1 + v_2}{2}\right) \cdot t$

Projectile Motion:

$v_o \sin\theta = \sqrt{(2gh)}$

$v_o \cos\theta =$ Constant

$v_o \sin\theta = v_{yi}$

v_y @ max h = 0 m/s

$a_x =$ 0 m/s²

$a_y = -10 \text{ m/s}^2$

Force Equations:

$F =$ ma

$F_g = GMm/r^2$

Mechanical Advantage: Fout / Fin

Efficiency: Wout / Win

$F = -k\Delta x$

$F_f =$ μF_N

$\tau = rF\sin\theta$

Energy Equations:

$KE =$ $\frac{1}{2}mv^2$

$P = W/t$

$W_{net} =$ ΔKE

$W = Fd\cos\theta$

$PE_{spring} =$ mgh

$PE_g = mgh$

$\Delta TE = \Delta KE + \Delta PE$

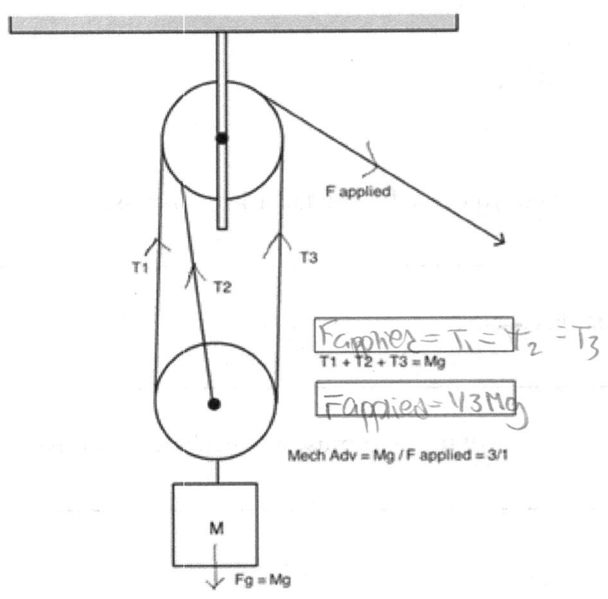

EXAMPLE

Kinematics Force and Energy: Worksheet Exercise Level 2

Trig Functions:

cos 90° = sin 0° = 0

cos 60° = sin 30° = $\sqrt{1}/2$

cos 45° = sin 45° = $\sqrt{2}/2$

cos 30° = sin 60° = $\sqrt{3}/2$

cos 0° = sin 90° = $\sqrt{4}/2$

Kinematic Equations:

$v_f = v_0 + at$

$d = v_o t + (1/2)at^2$

$v_f^2 = v_0^2 + 2ad$

$d = \left[\frac{(v_1 + v_2)}{2}\right] \cdot t$

Projectile Motion:

$v_o \sin\theta = \sqrt{(2gh)}$

$v_o \cos\theta =$ constant

$v_o \sin\theta = v_{yi}$

v_y @ max h = 0 m/s

$a_x = 0\ m/s^2$

$a_y = -10\ m/s^2$

Force Equations:

$F = ma$

$F_g = GMm / r^2$

Mechanical Advantage: F_{out}/F_{in}

Efficiency: W_{out}/W_{in}

$F = -k\Delta x$

$F_f = \mu F_N$

$\tau = rF\sin\theta$

Energy Equations:

$KE = \frac{1}{2}mv^2$

$P = W/t$

$W_{net} = \Delta KE$

$W = Fd\cos\theta$

$PE_{spring} = mgh$

PE_{grav} $\Delta KE + \Delta PE$

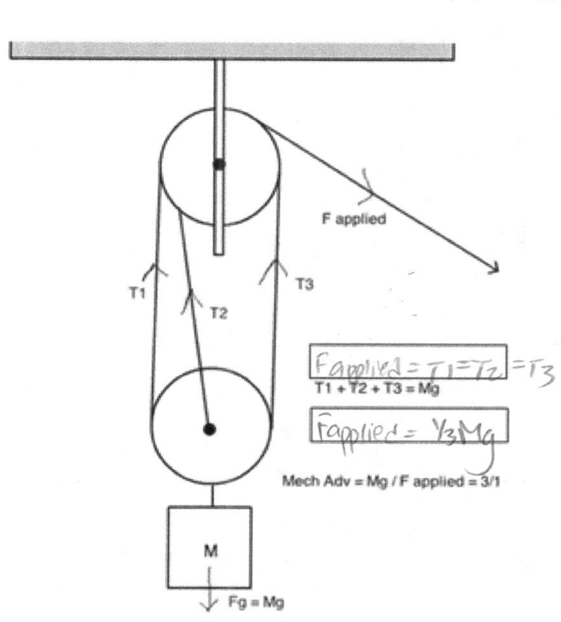

EXAMPLE

Kinematics Force and Energy: Worksheet Exercise Level 3

__Trig Functions__:

cos 90° = sin 0° = 0

cos 60° = sin 30° = $\sqrt{1}/2$

cos 45° = sin 45° = $\sqrt{2}/2$

cos 30° = sin 60° = $\sqrt{3}/2$

cos 0° = sin 90° = $\sqrt{4}/2$

__Kinematic Equations__:

v_f = $V_0 + at$

d = $\frac{(V_1+V_2)}{2} \cdot t$

v_f^2 = $V_0^2 + 2ad$

d = $V_0 t + \frac{1}{2} at^2$

__Projectile Motion__:

$v_o\sin\theta$ = $\sqrt{(2gh)}$

$v_o\cos\theta$ = Constant

$v_o\sin\theta$ = V_{yi}

v_y @ max h = 0 m/s

a_x = 0 m/s²

a_y = −10 m/s²

__Force Equations__:

F = ma

F_g = $\frac{GMm}{r^2}$

Mechanical Advantage: Fout/Fin

Efficiency: Wout/Win

F = $-k\Delta x$
spring

F_f = μF_N

τ = $rF\sin\theta$

__Energy Equations__:

E_k = $\frac{1}{2}mv^2$

P = W/T

W_{net} = ΔKE

W = $Fd\cos\theta$

E_{spring} = $(\frac{1}{2})kx^2$

E_{grav} = mgh

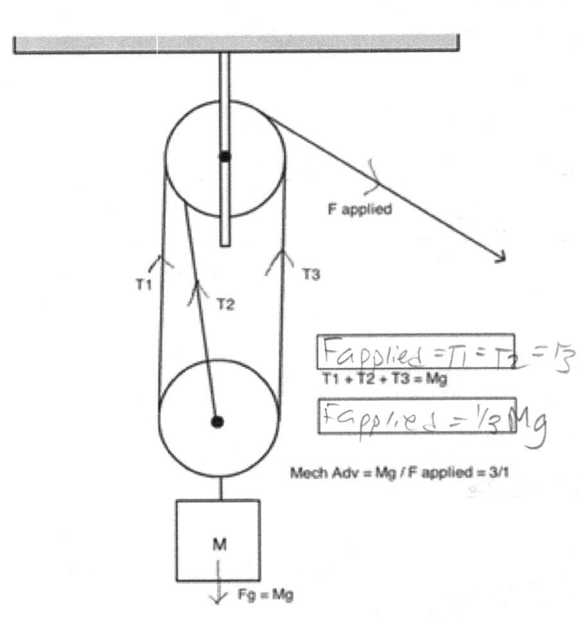

Timed MCAT Practice Passage

Mastery of the MCAT sciences is a two-part process. First you must study to understand (not just memorize!) the science content, and then you must study the content actively and challenge yourself within the context of the exam.

1. Complete your reading of the passage (≈ 3 minutes).
   - Write down what you believe to be the primary science content underlying the passage.
   - What facts or concepts do you anticipate to be tested? When you are done with the questions determine if you were correct. What passage clues were there to imply related topics that showed up in the questions?
   - Were there any key terms or important scientific relationships you missed?
   - Were you able to draw any conclusions from the data, if presented?

2. Complete the practice questions on your own (4-5 minutes)
   - Rephrase each question in your own mind after reading it to clarify the task.
   - Research the relevant area(s) of the passage or your own knowledge for information related to the task.
   - Respond to the question by choosing the answer that fits your research/calculations *and* satisfies the task.
   - If no answer seems obvious, eliminate answers that fail to have support in the passage or in the relevant science.

3. Analyze the questions.
   - Did you understand the task in the question?
   - What skill type was the question?
   - Did you know the science/formula/concept needed to answer the question?
   - Did you recognize the science being hinted at?
   - Were you able to find information in the passage quickly when you needed it?
   - Were there any necessary scientific concepts you failed to apply to the question?
     - If so, why?
   - If you made a mistake in calculations, have you identified your mistake?

Drag, also known as fluid resistance or air resistance, is defined as a force that acts perpendicularly to the motion of an object as it travels through a surrounding fluid. Unlike many other resistive forces, such as dry friction, drag is unique in that it is dependent upon velocity. As velocity increases, so does drag. This is because drag results from the collision of the object with the individual molecules that are present within the fluid. An object travelling faster through the fluid will collide with more molecules per unit time and therefore experience greater drag.

This property of fluids also explains the phenomenon of terminal velocity when an object is in free fall. As the velocity of a skydiver increases, the drag force also gradually increases while the gravitational force remains the same.

The force of drag can be calculated using Equation 1, where F_D is the force of drag, ρ is the density of the fluid the object is travelling through, A is the surface area of the object, C_D is the coefficient of drag related to the shape of the object, and v is the velocity of the object.

$$F_D = \frac{1}{2}\rho A C_D v^2$$

Equation 1 The force of drag formula

Figure 1 shows the results of an experiment where velocity trajectories were recorded for the same parachutist from three different heights.

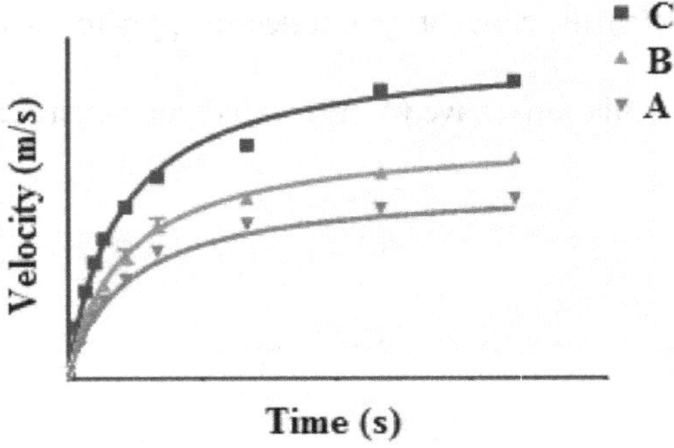

Figure 1 Velocities of parachutist

11. Once a skydiver has reached terminal velocity, which of the following accurately illustrates Newton's 3rd Law?

A. The gravitational force of the Earth on the skydiver and the drag force exerted on the skydiver by the air
B. The normal force of the skydiver on the air and the normal force of the air on the skydiver
C. The drag force on the skydiver by the air and the drag force on the air by the skydiver
D. The gravitational force that the Earth exerts on the skydiver and the gravitational force that the skydiver exerts on the Earth

12. The point at which a skydiver that has reached terminal velocity is most accurately described as:

A. dynamic equilibrium.
B. static equilibrium.
C. dynamic disequilibrium.
D. static disequilibrium.

13. Which of the following represents terminal velocity?

A. $\sqrt{[\rho C_D/2F_D]}$
B. $\sqrt{[2m/C_D]}$
C. $\sqrt{[2mg/\rho AC_D]}$
D. $\sqrt{[A\rho/2mC_D]}$

14. Assuming the jumper used the same body position for each jump, which of the falls shown in Figure 1 most likely occurred at the lowest altitude?

A. Free fall A
B. Free fall B
C. Free fall C
D. They all occurred at the same height

15. A skydiver falling in a horizontal position with their arms out has reached terminal velocity. If they reposition to a vertical position and pull in their arms, how would their terminal velocity change?

A. The terminal velocity will be zero
B. The terminal velocity will decrease
C. The terminal velocity will not change
D. The terminal velocity will increase

Problem-solving Cooldown

16. A 2 kg object is dropped from the top of a 300 m building. After 3 seconds, what is its kinetic energy?

    A. 300 J
    B. 600 J
    C. 900 J
    D. 1800 J

17. What is the ratio of initial gravitational potential energy to final gravitational potential energy if a 40 kg object resting 10m above the ground is taken and placed 60 meters above the ground on the moon ($g_{moon} \approx 1/6\ g_{earth}$)?

    A. 1:6
    B. 1:1
    C. 2:1
    D. 6:1

18. What happens to the electrical potential energy of charge +Q as it is moved closer to charge -Q?

    A. It increases.
    B. It decreases.
    C. It increases then decreases.
    D. It decreases then increases.

19. A 50 kg object is dropped from a height of 20 m. What is its final velocity just before it hits the ground?

    A. 2 m/s
    B. 20 m/s
    C. 200 m/s
    D. There is not enough information to determine the answer

20. What is the energy required to operate a 1000 W bulb for 1 hour?

    A. 3.6 kJ
    B. 1000 kJ
    C. 3.6 MJ
    D. 36 MJ

This page left intentionally blank.

Test-Like Thinking: CARS Practice Passage

The roots of journalism lie in two very distinct camps: first, with the brute attempt to control the flow of information and thereby cudgel the public into acceptance of the elite's version of events; second, with the attempt only to entertain, to bring "news" in the forms of stories and songs from distant places sung by traveling entertainers who thought only to provide diversion for their audiences. As literacy became widespread through the 19th century, the modern form of the newspaper emerged, although it would take until well into the 20th century for a system of professional journalistic ethics to emerge. By the middle of the 20th century, journalism had evolved into a respectable profession with its own norms, rules, and mechanisms for the censure of those violating them. Advertising is at the very beginning of this progression.

Advertising can most clearly contribute to the advancement of civilized society not through a further crowding of society's communicative spaces with ever more raucous, shock- and entertainment-driven messages. Instead, advertising must seek to develop a balance between meeting the commercial goals of the advertisers, the informational needs of the consumer, and the professional ethics that all meaningful human occupations should strive for. Due to the increasing sophistications of market research through the 1970's and 80's, we have only come to think of advancement in advertising as mere technical precision that allows advertisers to achieve the commercial goals of their clients with greater and greater success. But mere financial gain and technical mastery do not a profession make.

The notion of a profession arose most distinctly in the case of medicine. In that context, practitioners were expected to provide their patients with information, to have a certain level of technical mastery in their trade, and to make a healthy living while practicing their profession. Doctors were not expected to starve in service of a noble goal; in nearly every society we have studied, those practicing what the society recognizes as "healing arts" have actually been among the richest or most powerful. Thus it is a false dichotomy to oppositionally juxtapose money and professionalism. Yet it is this very dichotomy that leads those in advertising to blithely dismiss any notions of advertising-as-profession as the most naive of assertions. Even worse, much of the public seems to have accepted, if not outright celebrated, the primacy of financial success for all marketplace transactions. The idea that advertising would even begin to truthfully communicate information is seen as a raucous joke. In a recent film, the plot was driven by the simple question, "what if there were no such thing as lying?" and the better part of the film's humor derived from showing advertisements that were simple, straightforward communications of a product's advantages and disadvantages. Rather than appreciate them as representations of what advertising could be, the audience is meant to laugh.

To free ourselves from the bind of a finance-first view of advertising, there must be a fundamental shift in how consumers view advertising. At present, we react with either passive consumption or cynical acceptance of their manipulations. We must instead demonstrate that we value honesty and clear communication by rewarding those businesses that use such tactics, and sharply punishing those that are disingenuous. A single week-long boycott of a company's services would send a clearer message than any political posturing by ineffectual elected officials.

As the bulk of our commercial activity moves online, consumers and advertisers in technologically developed countries are confronted with a new opportunity: either reproduce the same old cycle of technically brilliant manipulations and cynical reactions, or generate a new advertising professionalism that seeks to engage with consumers in an information exchange in the way that a journalist engages with readers, a doctor with patients, or a teacher with students.

[Adapted from, "Ethics in Advertising: Impossible Possibilities" by R. Carriero, 2011.]

Passage taken from the online Next Step QBank

21. The author's argument would be *most* weakened if which of the following were true?

    A. A boycott of a company's products would motivate that company to engage in less truthful and more manipulative advertising practices.
    B. Consumers tend to be happier with purchases when they believe the advertising that motivated them to make the purchase was largely truthful.
    C. Consumers tend to less happy with purchases when they believe the advertising that motivated them to make the purchase was largely truthful.
    D. The roots of medical professionalism are inseparable from its origins as a semi religious field practiced by people who were both doctor and priest.

22. The author makes which of the following assumptions regarding the nature of the advertising business?

    A. Companies that spend a proportionally larger portion of their revenues on advertising will capture most business.
    B. Advertisers have been so successful with past models of raucous shock-driven messaging that they are unlikely to change in the future.
    C. Advertising itself is a profession, much like medicine or journalism or education.
    D. Advertisers are aware of and respond to consumer attitudes about the tone and content of the messages being advertised.

23. The author believes that society will impose pressure on advertisers to change their behavior as a result of:

    A. a paradigm shift in the values that make up a profession.
    B. increased trust in advertisers to express honest opinions.
    C. a failure of journalism to live up to its professional standards.
    D. an increased valuation of candor in communications.

24. As used in the passage, dichotomy (paragraph 3. most nearly means:

    A. the choice to meet two goals at once.
    B. a choice between two mutually exclusive ends.
    C. the placement of two ideas next to each other.
    D. an incorrect assumption regarding an important choice.

25. The author implies that the relationship between financial success and honesty with consumers is:

    A. not without tension, though it is possible to achieve both ends.
    B. one with a long history in the practice of medicine in which medical practitioners have demonstrated that they are mutually incompatible.
    C. a dichotomy, since making money and behaving professionally are incompatible.
    D. is what leads directly to the financial success of the professional.

To Do After Lesson 5

- [ ] Read Physics Chapters 7 and 8
- [ ] Read Verbal and Quantitative Reasoning Chapters 7 and 8
- [ ] Read General Chemistry and Organic Chemistry Chapter 7
- [ ] Complete Physics QBank 1: Motion, Force, and Work

LESSON 6

Organic Chemistry

To Do Before Lesson 6

- ☐ Read Physics Chapters 7 and 8
- ☐ Read Verbal and Quantitative Reasoning Chapters 7 and 8
- ☐ Read General Chemistry and Organic Chemistry Chapter 7
- ☐ Complete Physics QBank 1: Motion, Force, and Work

In Lesson 6

Problem-solving Warm-up
Effective Reading in the Sciences
Diagnosing Isomers
Differentiating Isomers
MCAT Practice Passage
How to Build your Science Foundation
Diagnosing Reactions
Biologically Important Reactions
MCAT Practice Passage
Problem-solving Cooldown

To Do After Lesson 6

- ☐ Read General Chemistry and Organic Chemistry Chapters 9 and 10
- ☐ Read Biology Chapters 5 and 6
- ☐ Read Biochemistry Chapters 3 and 4
- ☐ Complete Organic Chemistry QBank 1: Stereochemistry, Alkanes, and Alcohols

Problem-solving Warm-up

1. Which of the following isomers of butane has the lowest steric strain?

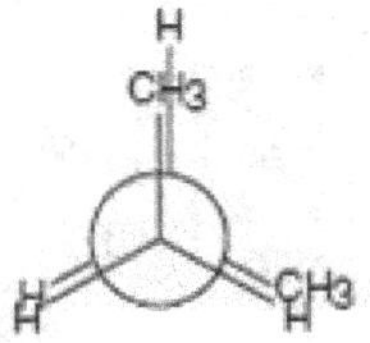

A.

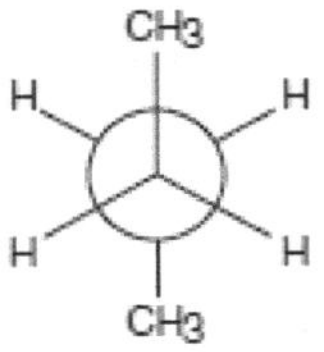

B.

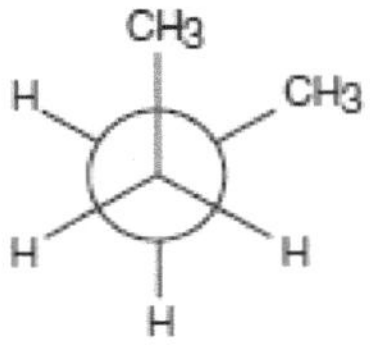

C.

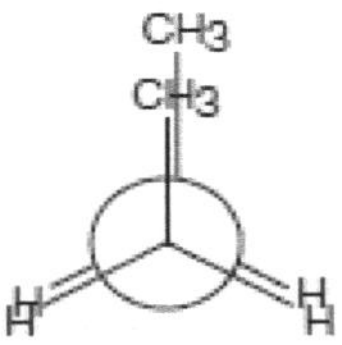

D.

2. The molecules shown below are an example of:

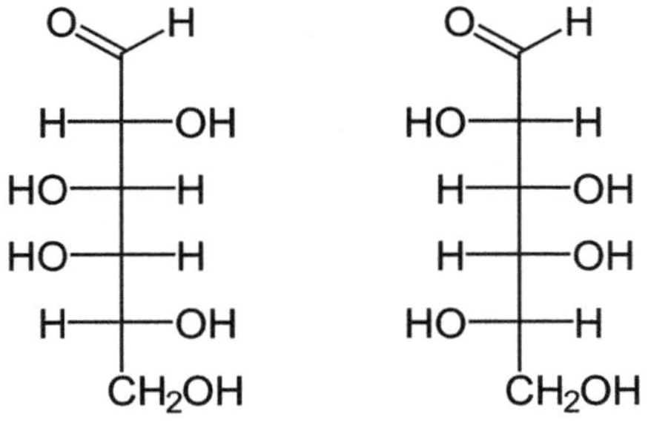

D-Galactose   L-Galactose

A. diastereomers.
B. constitutional isomers.
C. enantiomers.
D. cis/trans isomers.

3. Which of the following compounds is optically inactive?

A.

```
     CH3
H ——+—— Cl
H ——+—— Cl
     CH3
```

B.

```
     CH3
H ——+—— Cl
Cl ——+—— H
     CH3
```

C.

```
     CH3
H ——+—— F
F ——+—— H
     CH3
```

D.

```
     CH3
F ——+—— H
H ——+—— F
     CH3
```

4. What are the expected bond angles on the carbonyl carbon in formaldehyde?

A. 104.5°
B. 107°
C. 109.5°
D. 120°

5. Which of the following molecules has a higher boiling point?

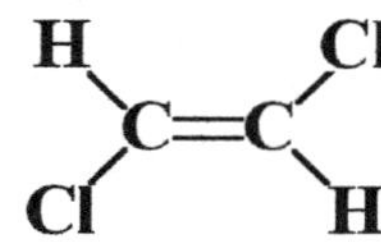

1

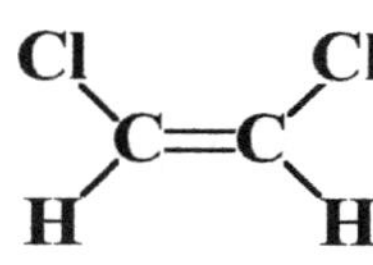

2

A. Molecule 1, due to heavier molecular weight
B. Molecule 2, due to heavier molecular weight
C. Molecule 1, due to a greater molecular dipole
D. Molecule 2, due to a greater molecular dipole

Effective Reading in the Sciences

Reading science passages on the MCAT means being able to keep track of important (i.e. likely to be tested) information in the passage. You must be able to anticipate, recognize, and understand scientific concepts presented in many different forms.

Practice Passage

Aldehydes and ketones are functional groups found in a number of biologically important molecules. The structural formulas for a few examples are shown in Figure 1. The shapes of these molecules play an important role in their function and how they interact with different types of nerve receptors. For example, carvone has two optically active forms that have distinctly different flavor sensations R-carvone is known as oil of spearmint, whereas S-carvone is the oil of caraway seeds.

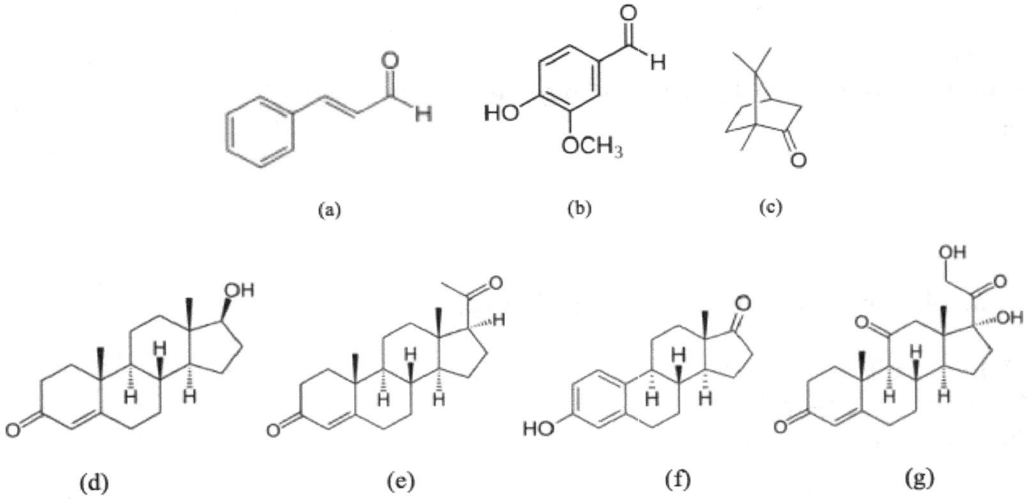

Figure 1 Structural formulas for examples of naturally occurring aldehydes and ketones: (a) cinnamon; (b) vanillin; (c) camphor; (d) testosterone; (e) progesterone; (f) esterone; and (g) cortisone.

Both Benedict's solution and Tollen's solutions are useful reagents to test for aldehydes. In the former, a positive test results when the basic royal blue cupric solution is reduced to form a precipitate of cuprous oxide. A positive test for the latter results when the ammoniacal solution of silver ion is reduced to silver metal.

Passage taken from the Next Step online QBank

6. Which of the following would NOT give a positive Benedict's test?

    I. Cinnamon
    II. Vanillin
    III. Camphor
    IV. Carvone

    A. I and II only
    B. I and III only
    C. II and IV only
    D. III and IV only

7. What are the oxidation numbers of the silver species in the Tollen's test before and after a positive test?

    A. +1 and 0, respectively
    B. +2 and +1, respectively
    C. +3 and +2, respectively
    D. +2 and 0, respectively

8. Which of the following best describes the isomer of 2-methyl-5-(1-methylethenyl)-2 cyclohexanone shown below?

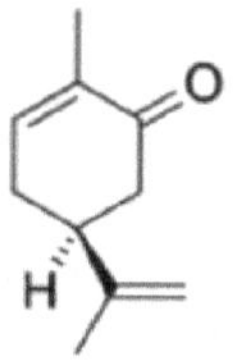

    O
    H

    A. This isomer is R-carvone, which is oil of spearmint.
    B. This isomer is R-carvone, which is oil of caraway.
    C. This isomer is S-carvone, which is oil of spearmint.
    D. This isomer is S-carvone, which is oil of caraway.

9. Which of the following would be most useful in distinguishing propanal from propanone?

    A. Proton NMR spectroscopy
    B. IR spectroscopy
    C. UV-Vis spectroscopy
    D. Rotation of plane-polarized light

10. A typical reaction for enzymes of the COX family is shown below with X representing the substrate.

$$H^+ + O_2 + X\text{—}H + NADPH \rightarrow H_2O + X\text{—}OH + NADP^+$$

    Which of the following correctly describes the action of oxygen?

    A. It serves as an oxidizing agent.
    B. It serves as a reducing agent.
    C. It serves as a catalyst.
    D. It serves as an electrophile.

Strategy

Diagnosing Isomers

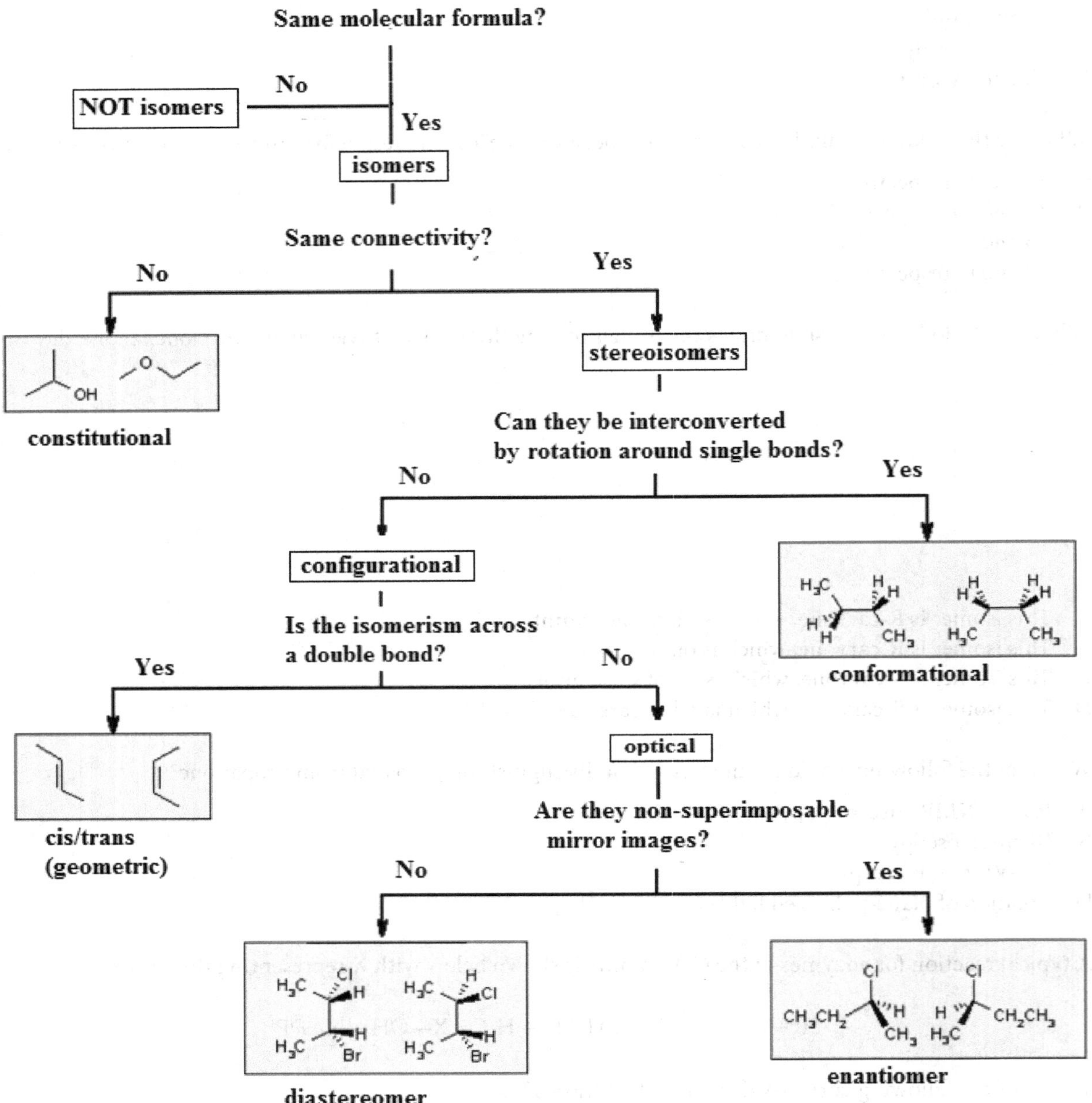

Name the type of isomer shown in each pair

(1)

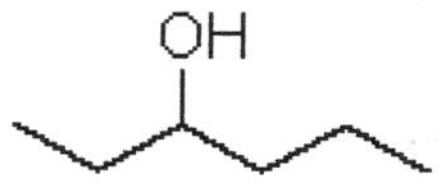

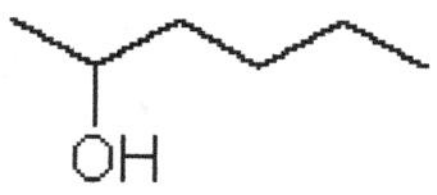

(2)

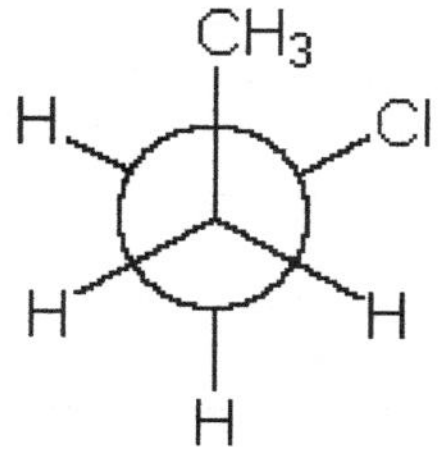

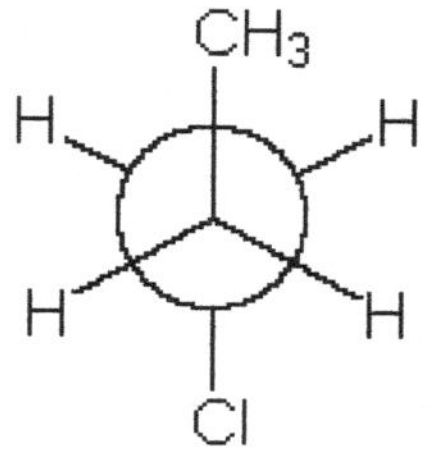

(3)

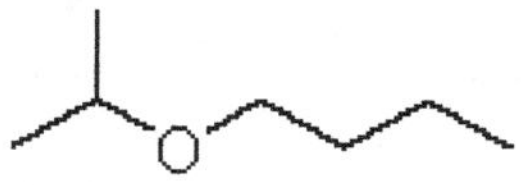

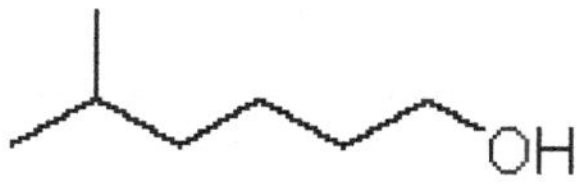

(4)

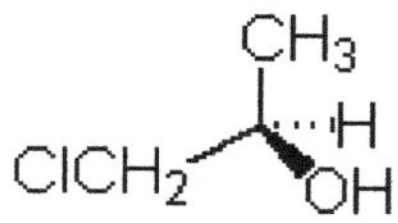

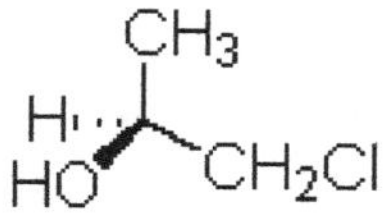

(5)

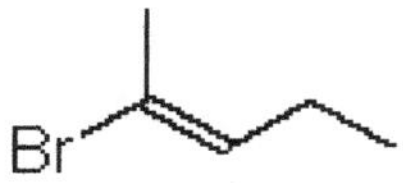

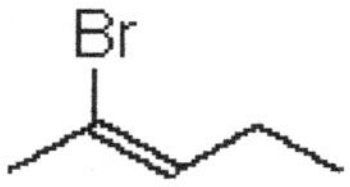

(6)

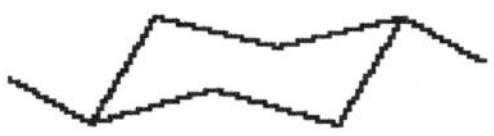

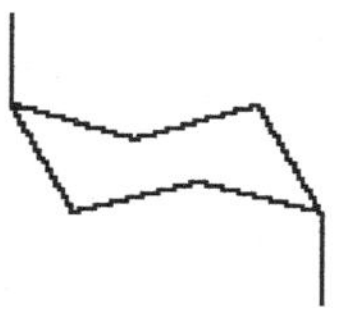

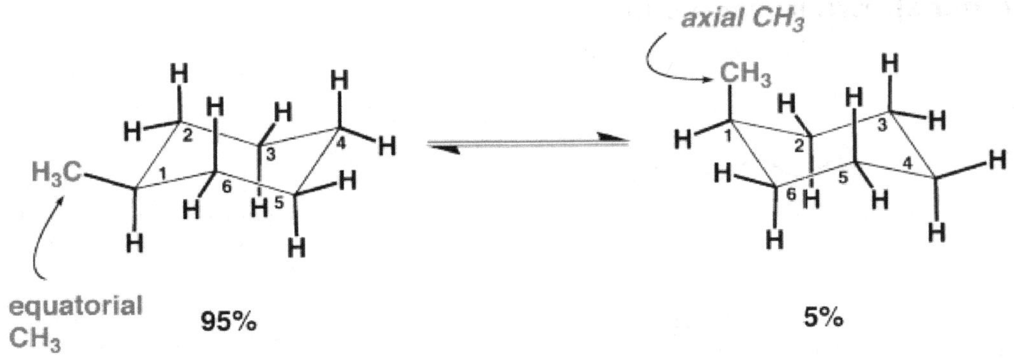

axial CH_3

equatorial CH_3 95%

5%

Which of these conformations is more stable? Why?

What substituent property will change when a ring rearranges to a new conformation? Which property will not?

Draw all possible stereoisomers of $CH_3CHBrCHClCH_3$.

Strategy

Determining Chirality

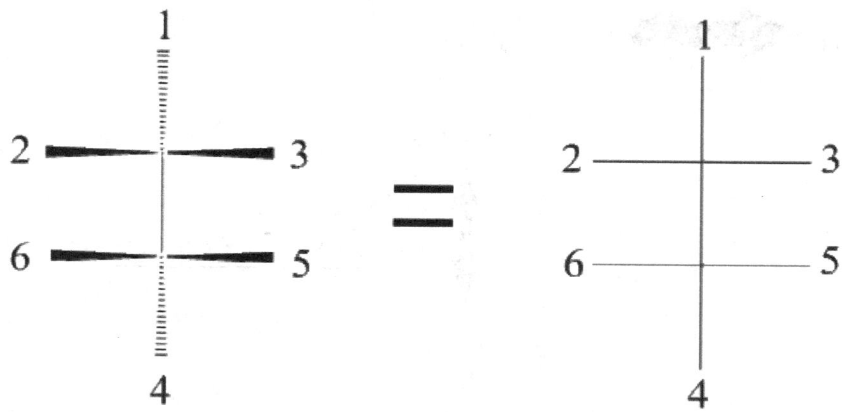

Determining absolute configuration:

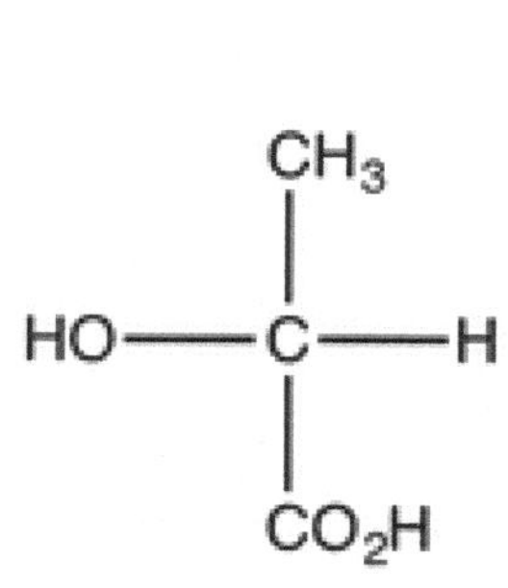

CHO
H—OH
HO—H
H—OH
H—OH
CH_2OH

(counterclockwise but H is horizontal so it is R)

If H or lowest priority group is on a horizontal arm then you must ~~convert~~ invert your answer

This is R

1. Assign priority to the ligand attached to the chiral center (1→4, based on atomic #).
2. Trace the three highest-priority ligands starting with the highest (i.e. 1-2-3).
3. Check the direction of 1-2-3: clockwise = R, counterclockwise = S.
4. If your lowest-priority ligand is pointed towards you (on horizontal) invert answer.

Enantiomers vs. Diastereomers

Flipped all chiral carbons

enantiomers

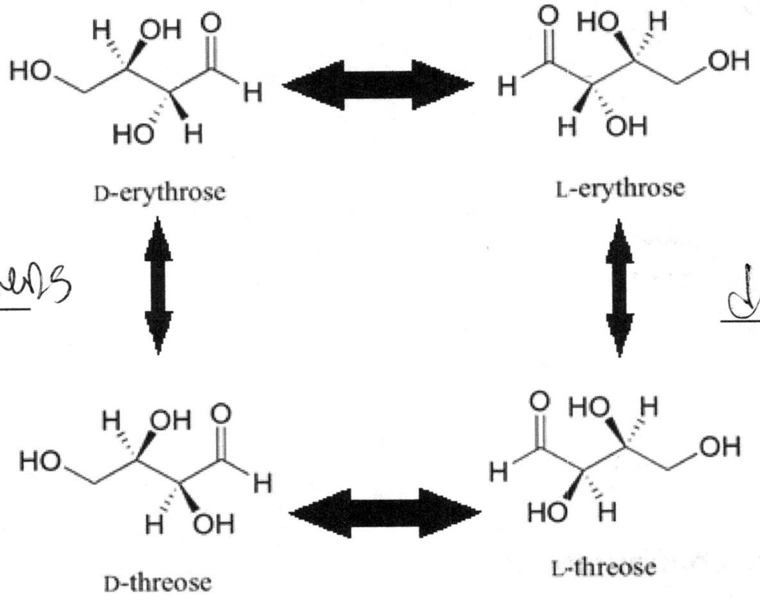

D-erythrose

L-erythrose

diasteriomers

diasteriomers

Flipped only 1 chiral center (less than all)

D-threose

L-threose

enantiomers

Meso Compounds

– not optically active
do not rotate plain polarized light

Determine whether the following molecules are chiral, meso, or achiral but NOT meso.

achiral

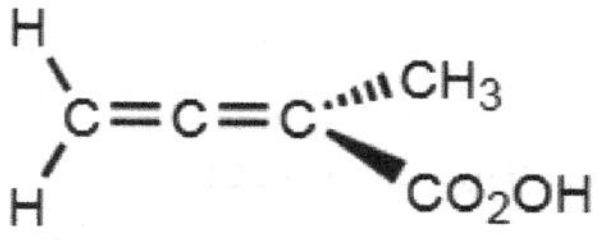

- Chiral centers
– meso

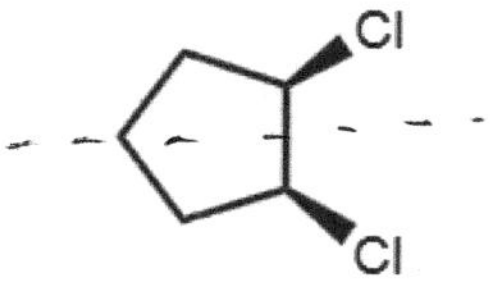

–2 or more chiral centers
- have at least 1 plain of symmetry

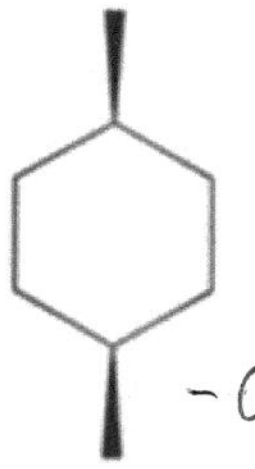

-achiral

meso

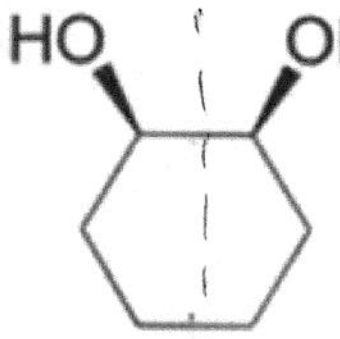

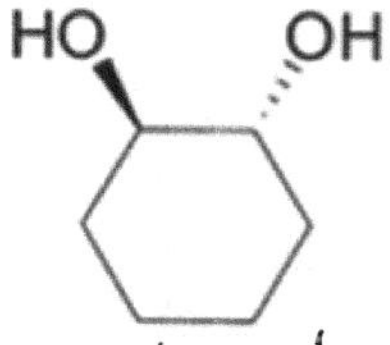

Chiral

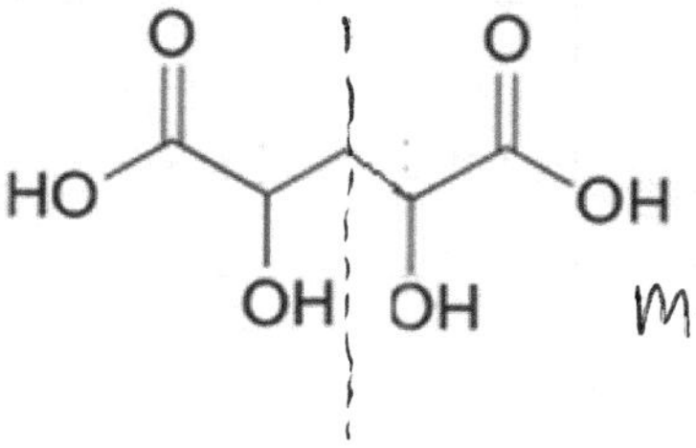

meso

Cis/Trans Isomers

-net molecular dipole
- stronger polarity
- Cis Fatty-acids (Better for you)

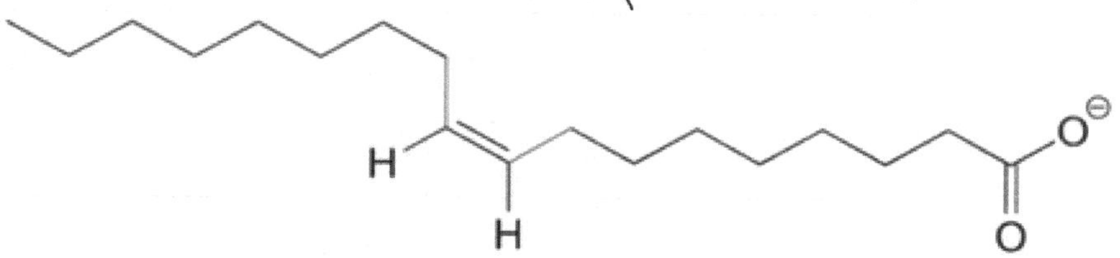

– higher Boiling point

- Trans Fatty acid

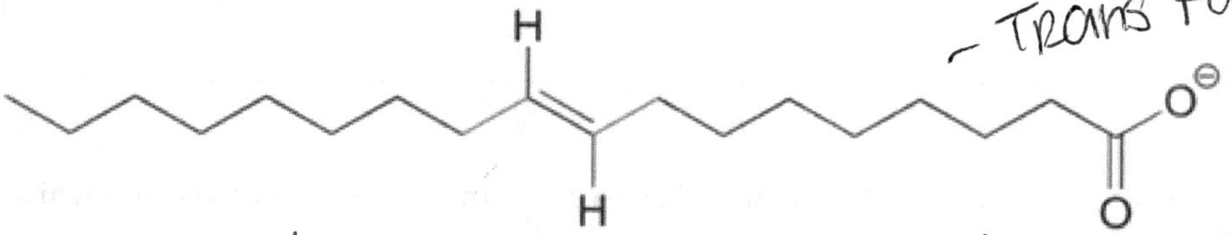

- pack tighter, more stable solid structure

– higher melting point

Which of the two fatty acids above will have the higher melting point? Higher boiling point?

Link to Biology: Retinal is a light-sensitive molecule that is found in the rod cells of the eye. When light enters the eye through the retina, the 11-**cis** diastereomer of retinal is converted to the all-**trans** diastereomer, changing the shape of the molecule and the way that it binds to the vision protein rhodopsin. This initiates a chain of events that leads to a signal being sent to the vision center of the brain.

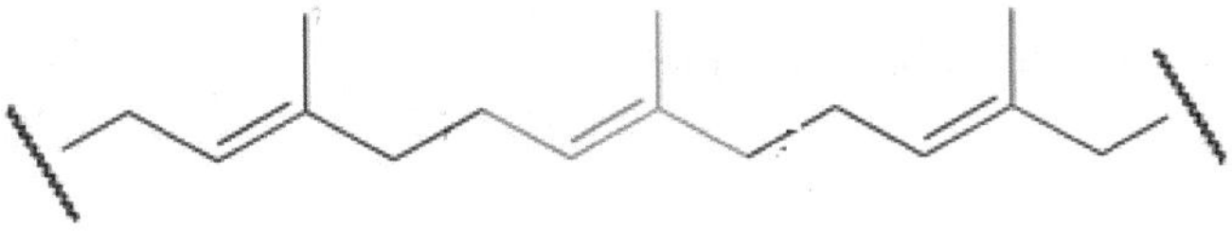

Trans -isoprenoids

(serve as cholesterol precursor)

- higher melting point

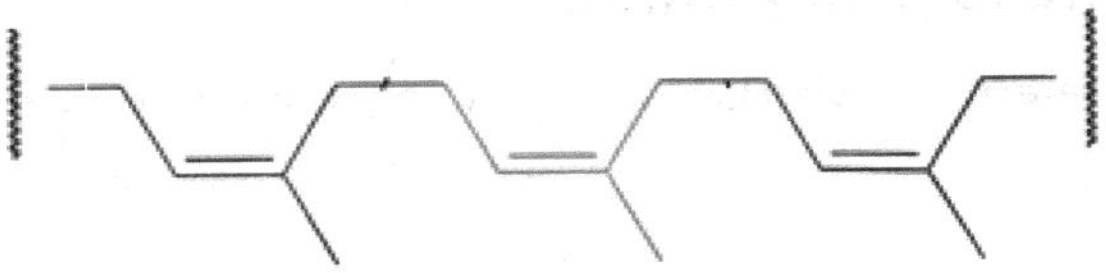

Cis -isoprenoids

(found in rubber)

- higher boiling point

Isomer Properties

Isomer	Physical Properties	Chemical Properties
Constitutional	Different	Different
Conformational	Same	Same
Cis/Trans	Different	Same
Diastereomer	Different	Same
Enantiomer	same	Same*

*except for how they rotate plain polarized light

11. R-ethanbutol is a drug used to treat tuberculosis while S-ethanbutol causes blindness. Scientists could use which of the following to most effectively separate purify a racemic mixture of the drug?

    A. Reaction with (+)-brucine followed by recrystallization
    B. Column chromatography with a polar solvent
    C. Reaction with acetic acid followed by fractional distillation
    D. Reaction with pyridine followed by vacuum distillation

12. Which of the following amino acids has 4 possible stereoisomers?

    A. Glycine
    B. Isoleucine
    C. Cysteine
    D. Tyrosine

Timed MCAT Practice Passage

Mastery of the MCAT sciences is a two-part process. First you must study to understand (not just memorize!) the science content, and then you must study the content actively and challenge yourself within the context of the exam

1. Complete your reading of the passage (3-4 minutes).
   - Write down what you believe to be the primary science content underlying the passage.
   - What facts or concepts do you anticipate will be tested? When you are done with the questions determine if you were correct. What passage clues were there to imply related topics that showed up in the questions?
   - Were there any key terms or important scientific relationships you missed?
   - Were you able to draw any conclusions from the data, if presented?

2. Complete the practice questions on your own (4-5 minutes)
   - Rephrase each question in your own mind after reading it to clarify the task.
   - Research the relevant area(s) of the passage or your own knowledge for information related to the task.
   - Respond to the question by choosing the answer that fits your research/calculations *and* satisfies the task.
   - If no answer seems obvious, eliminate answers that fail to have support in the passage or in the relevant science.

3. Analyze your wrong answer choices to the questions you missed.
   - Did you understand the task in the question?
   - What skill type was the question?
   - Did you know the science/formula/concept needed to answer the question?
   - Did you recognize the science being hinted at?
   - Were you able to find information in the passage quickly when you needed it?
   - Were there any necessary scientific concepts you failed to apply to the question?
     - If so, why?
   - If you made a mistake in calculations, have you identified your mistake?

The structure of a polypeptide was determined beginning with the identification of its constituent amino acids. A purified sample of the polypeptide was denatured and then hydrolyzed by a strong acid at 110°C for 24 hours. The individual amino acids released by the treatment were then separated by cation-exchange chromatography. In this technique, amino acids bind to, with differing affinities, negatively charged groups attached to resins applied along the column.

Following treatment with a series of eluting solutions, the separated amino acids contained in the eluate from the column were heated with ninhydrin—a reagent that forms the blue-purple compound Ruhemann's Purple with most amino acids, amines and ammonia.

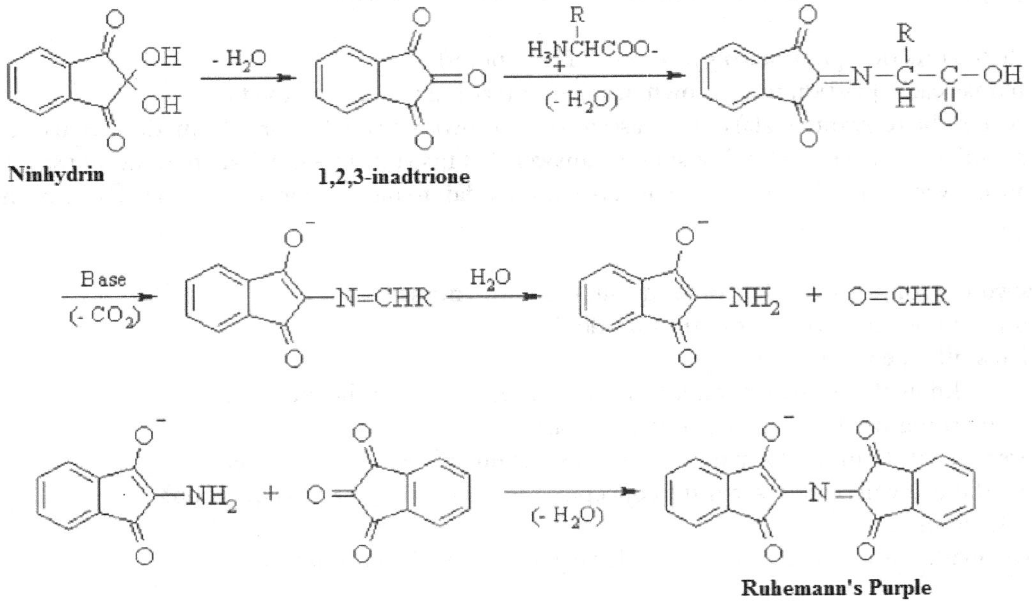

Ninhydrin $\xrightarrow{-H_2O}$ 1,2,3-inadtrione $\xrightarrow[(-H_2O)]{H_3\overset{+}{N}CH(R)COO^-}$ =N–CH(R)–C(=O)–OH

$\xrightarrow[(-CO_2)]{Base}$ –N=CHR $\xrightarrow{H_2O}$ –NH_2 + O=CHR

–NH_2 + O= $\xrightarrow{(-H_2O)}$ –N=

Ruhemann's Purple

Figure 1 The ninhydrin reaction between ninhydrin and a free amino acid.

The amount of each amino acid present was then determined spectrophotometrically by measuring the amount of blue-purple light absorbed.

The specific position of each amino acid in the polypeptide chain was also found. Edman reagent (phenylisothiocyanate) was used to label a terminal residue under mildly alkaline conditions, resulting in the formation of a phenylthiocarbamoyl. Under acidic conditions, the terminal amino acid of the polypeptide was cleaved, releasing free polypeptide and phenylthiohydantoin (PTH), an amino acid derivative that can be identified. Edman reagent was applied repeatedly, shortening the peptide bond obtained following each cycle. The steps of the Edman degradation are shown in Figure 2.

Passage taken from the Next Step Biochemistry review book, Chapter 5

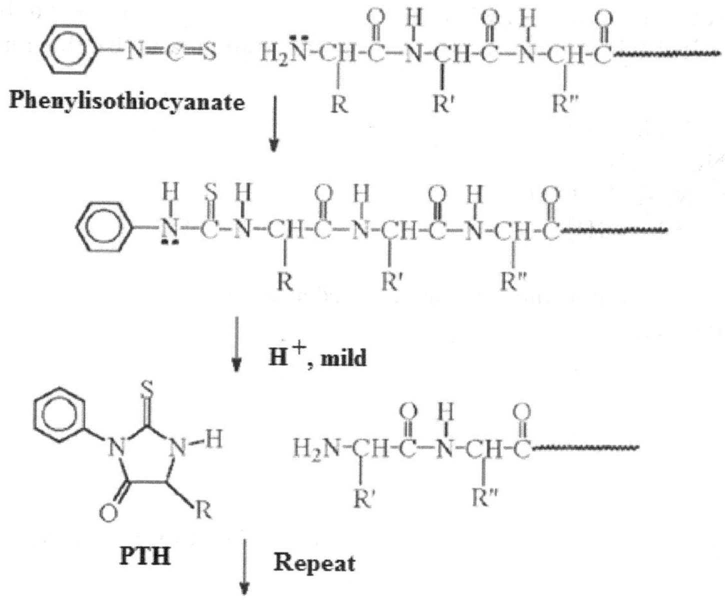

Phenylisothiocyanate

H^+, mild

PTH

Repeat

Figure 2 Edman degradation of a polypeptide

There are limits on the length of polypeptides that can be sequenced by this method. Over time, the yield of PTH-amino acid products decreases relative to the background level of PTH-amino acids. Repetitive yield is a measure of the percent of detectable material remaining after each turn of the cycle. Longer polypeptides can be sequenced from greater initial sample sizes and larger repetitive yields. They may also be cleaved by peptidase enzymes to create shorter polypeptides for sequencing.

more purple light absorbed = more amino acid in eluate

Cation

- + amino acids stick to negative groups attached to column, - amino acids slip through (separating them by charge)

Cation exchange Chromatography
↳ exchange matrix has (-) charged groups to target cationic molecules
↳ raise ph of solution to deprotonate AA Residues

Passage taken from the Next Step Chemistry and Physics Strategy and Practice book, Chapter 3, Timed Section 1, Passage 1

13. It was discovered that the rate of the ninhydrin reaction is first order with respect to both 1,2,3-indantrione and α-amino acid. Which of the following forms of the reactants would maximize the initial reaction rate? (Note: R = $C_8H_4O_2$)

    A. [RC=O^+H] and [H_2NCHRCOO$^-$]
    B. [RC=O] and [H_3^+NCHRCOO$^-$]
    C. [RC=O^+H] and [H_3^+NCHRCOOH]
    D. [RC=O] and [H_2NCHRCOOH]

14. Which of the following molecules is the product obtained at the end of the Edman degradation of the polypeptide Ala-Gly-Phe-Asp?

    A. PTH-Ala
    B. PTH-Gly
    C. PTH-Phe
    D. PTH-Asp

15. What is most likely true of the eluant solutions used to recover free amino acids from the ion-exchange column employed?

    A. They are hydrophobic.
    B. They possess a characteristic salt concentration.
    C. They must be capable of denaturing disulfide linkages.
    D. They must contain digestive enzymes.

16. At the conclusion of the process, which of the following would most efficiently allow for the elution of the target polypeptides from the chromatography column discussed in the passage?

    A. Increase the temperature of the solution in the column
    B. Decrease the temperature of the solution in the column
    C. Add 300 mL of 0.25 M HI to the column
    D. Add 150 mL of 0.50 M CsOH to the column

17. Which of the following best describes the formation of the bond between Edman reagent and a polypeptide in step 1 of Figure 2?

    A. Addition reaction
    B. Dehydration reaction
    C. Neutralization reaction
    D. Elimination reaction

Loss of a π Bond

Figure 2

Build Your Science Foundation—Isomer Worksheet Exercise

Isomers

Isomers: molecules with the same molecular formula but a different arrangement of atoms.
Divided into: Constitutional isomers vs. Stereoisomers

Different connections between the atoms:
Constitutional isomers e.g. cyclobutane, butene are both C_4H_8

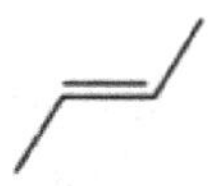

Same connections between the atoms:
Stereoisomers – divided into: configurational and conformational

Freely interconvert w/o breaking bonds:
Conformational isomers e.g. chair, boat cyclohexane

Requires bond breaking to interconvert:
Configurational isomers – divided into: enantiomers and diastereomers

Non-superimposable mirror images:
Enantiomers e.g. R and S 2-hydroxypropanoic acid

Not mirror images:
Diastereomers – comes in several different types:

Only one stereo center has been flipped:

Geometric Isomers
Vary around double bond (E/Z, cis/trans):

Epimers
Sugars that only vary at one stereocenter
e.g. Glucose and Galactose

Anomers
An epimer based on a cyclic sugar

Mutarotation: conversion between α and β anomers

α-D-glucopyranose

β-D-glucopyranose

Isomer Worksheet Exercise Level 1

Isomers

Isomers: molecules with the same molecular formula but a different arrangement of atoms.

Divided into: Constitutional isomers vs. Sterioisomers

Different connections between the atoms:

Constitutional isomers e.g. cyclobutane, butene are both C_4H_8

Same connections between the atoms:

Sterioisomers – divided into: configurational and conformational

Freely interconvert w/o breaking bonds:

Conformational isomers e.g. chair, boat cyclohexane

Requires bond breaking to interconvert:

Configurational isomers – divided into enantiomers and diastereomers

Non-superimposable mirror images:

Enantiomers e.g. R and S 2-hydroxypropanoic acid

Not mirror images:

Diastereomers – comes in several different types:

Only one stereo center has been flipped:

Geometric Isomers

Very around doublebond (E/Z, cis/trans)

Epimers

Sugars that only vary at one stereocenter

e.g. Glucose and Galactose

Anomers

An epimer based on a cyclic sugar

Mutarotation – conversion between α and β isomers

α-D-glucopyranose

β-D-glucopyranose

Isomer Worksheet Exercise Level 2

Isomers

Isomers: molecules with the same molecular formula but a different arrangement of atoms.

Divided into: Constitutional isomers vs. Steriosisomers

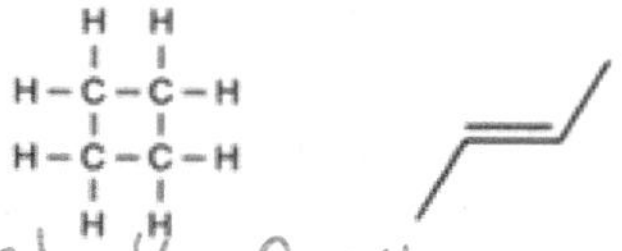

Different connections between the atoms:

Constitutional e.g. Cyclobutane, butene are both C_4H_8

Same connections between the atoms:

Steriosomers – divided into: configurational and Conformational

Freely interconvert w/o breaking bonds:

Conformational isomers e.g. chair, boat cyclohexane

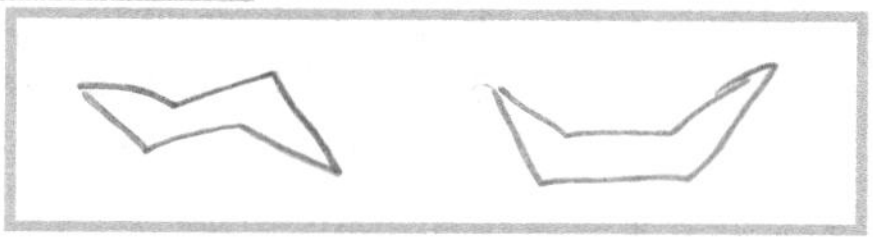

Requires bond breaking to interconvert:

Configurational isomers – divided into enantiomers and diastereomers

Non-superimposable mirror images:

Enantiomers e.g. R and S 2-hydroxypropanoic acid

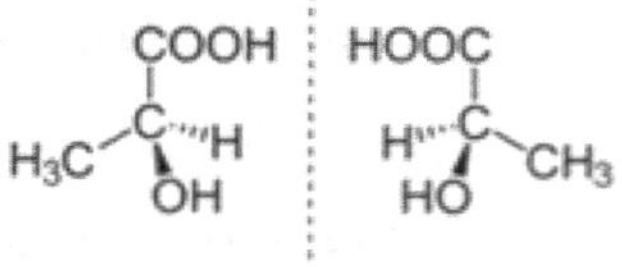

Not mirror images:

Diastereomers – comes in several different types:

Only 1 steriocenter has been flipped

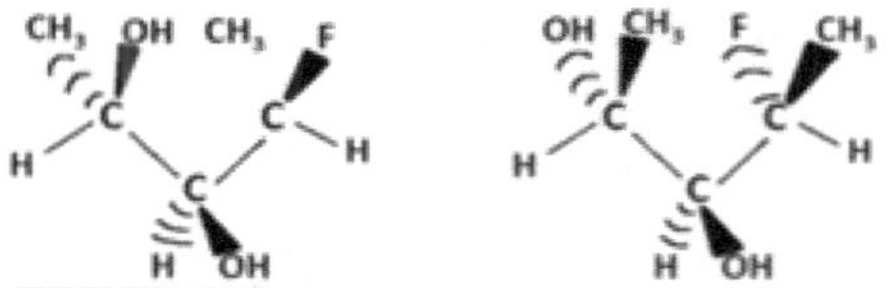

Geometric Isomers

Vary around double Bond (E/Z, cis/trans)

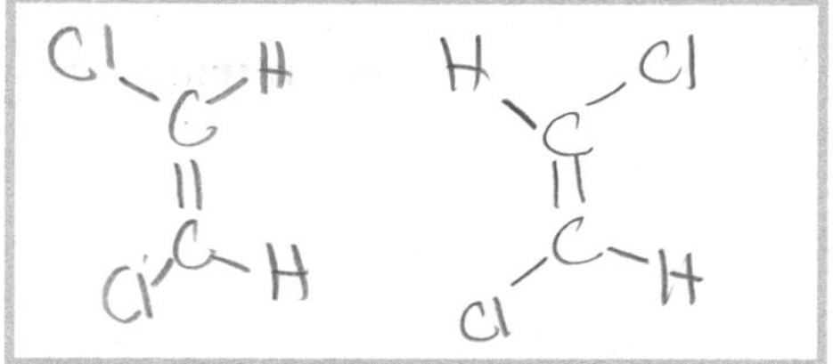

Epimers

Sugars that only vary at one stereocenter

e.g. Glucose and Galactose

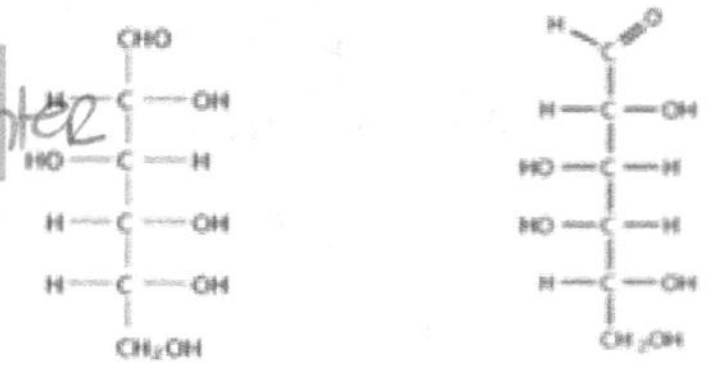

Anomers

An epimer based on a cyclic sugar. Mutarotation: Conversion between α and β anomers

α-D-glucopyranose

β-D-glucopyranose

Isomer Worksheet Exercise Level 3

Isomers

Isomers: molecules with the same molecular formula but a different arrangement of atoms.

Divided into: Constitutional isomers vs. ______

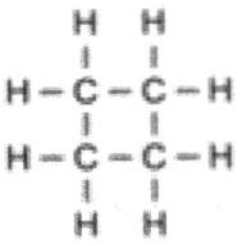

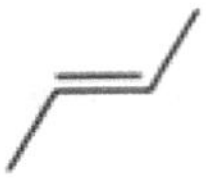

Different connections between the atoms:

______ e.g. ______

Same connections between the atoms:

______ – divided into: configurational and ______

Freely interconvert w/o breaking bonds:

______ e.g. chair, boat cyclohexane

Requires bond breaking to interconvert:

Configurational isomers – divided into ______ and diastereomers

Non-superimposable mirror images:

______ e.g. R and S 2-hydroxypropanoic acid

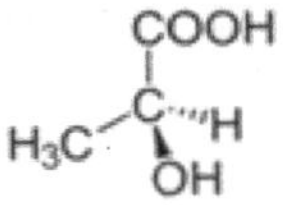

Not mirror images:

Diastereomers – comes in several different types:

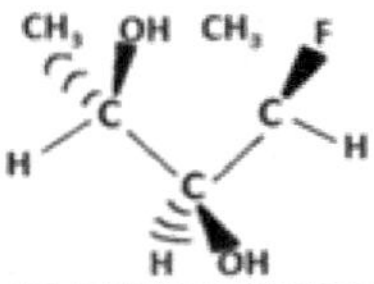

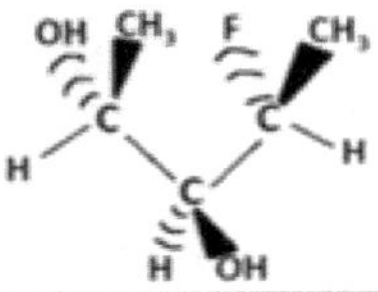

Geometric Isomers

Epimers

Sugars that ______

e.g. ______

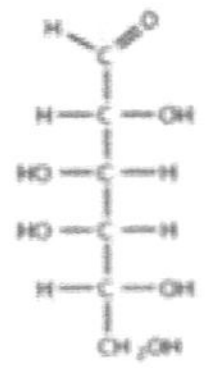

Anomers

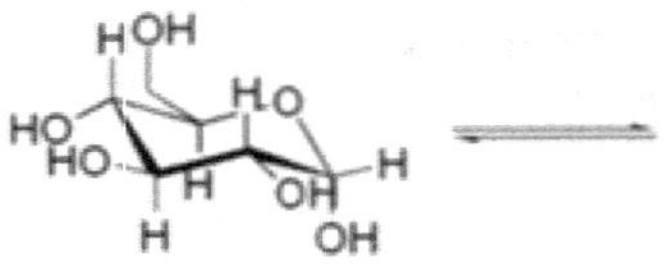

α-D-glucopyranose

β-D-glucopyranose

Diagnosing Reactions

Nucleophiles

Electrophiles

Leaving groups

SN1 Mechanism

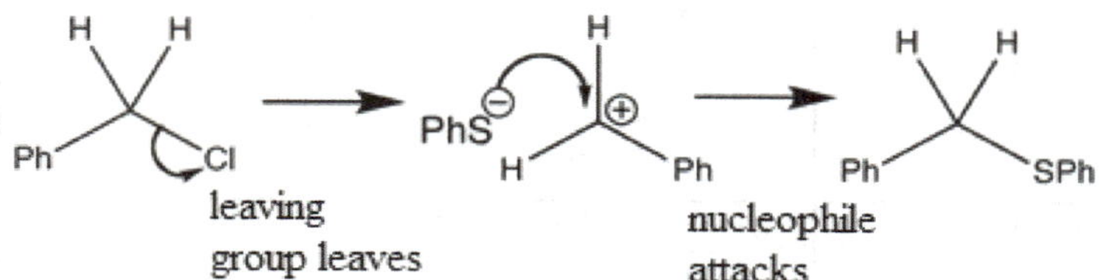

SN2 Mechanism

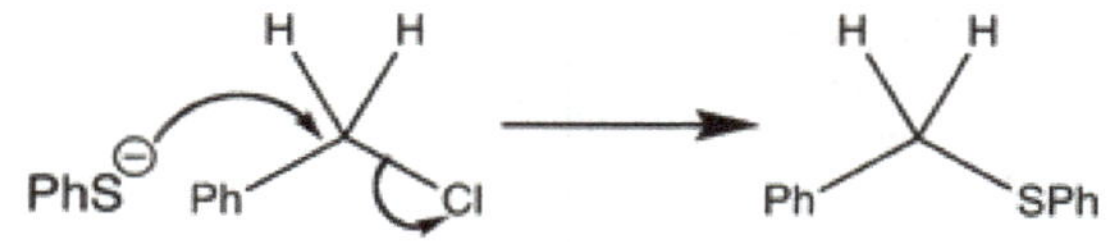

SN1 Reaction Conditions

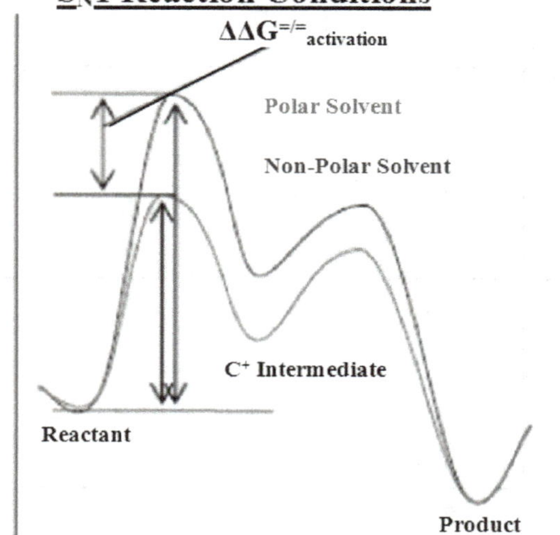

SN2 Reaction Conditions

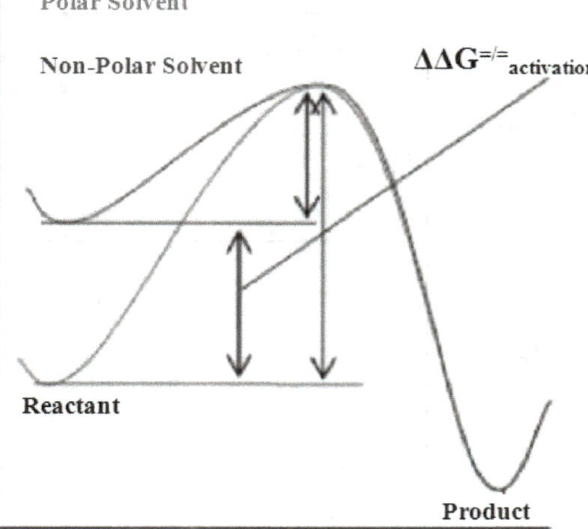

	S_N1	S_N2
Mechanism	2 step, Cation intermediate	1 Step backside attack
Kinetics	1st order rate = [R-L]	2nd order rate = [Nuc][R-L]
Leaving Group Effect	Best are weak bases	Best are weak bases
Nucleophile Effect	No strong Nucleophile needed	Strong nucleophile preferred
Carbon Structure Effect	3>2>1>methyl	methyl >1 >2 >3
Stereochemistry	elimination of Chirality / racemization	Inversion of stereo configuration
Solvent Effect	Favored By polar protic	Polar aprotic

strength generally correlates with basicity

Rank the following in order of a) increasing acidity and b) increasing nucleophilic ability

NH_3 < > R-NH_2 > < R_2-NH > < R_3-N

electron donating groups will make nitrogen atoms more basic

Ignore elimination reactions!

Unimolecular vs. Bimolecular Substitution Differential

Nuc/Base Strength	methyl	1°	2°	3°
strong/strong	*SN2*	*SN2*	neither	neither
strong/weak	*SN2*	*SN2*	*SN2*	no reaction
weak/strong	no reaction	neither	neither	neither
weak/weak	no reaction	no reaction	*SN1*	*SN1*

Steps to identifying your substitution reaction

1) Determine if you have a strong nucleophile, if not rule out Sn2
2) Determine if you have a potential carbocation, if not rule out Sn1
3) ID your solvent. Polar protic favors Sn1, aprotic favors Sn2

polar protic = water, alcohol, carboxylic acids
polar aprotic - acetone, DMSO, DMF

18. Excess 3-bromohexane is reacted with $NaOCH_3$ in N,N-dimethylformamide (polar aprotic solvent). Which of the following will be expected from this situation?

A. A partially racemic mixture of products (Sn1)
B. Capture of an intermediate molecule (Sn1)
C. Addition of $NaOCH_3$ raises the reaction rate
D. No reaction will occur

- good leaving group
- strong nucleophile
- polar aprotic
⇒ Sn2

2° alkyl halide; Br - leaving group

Na-O- ionize in solution = strong nucleophile

Biologically Important Reactions

Hemiacetals, hemiketals, and sugars

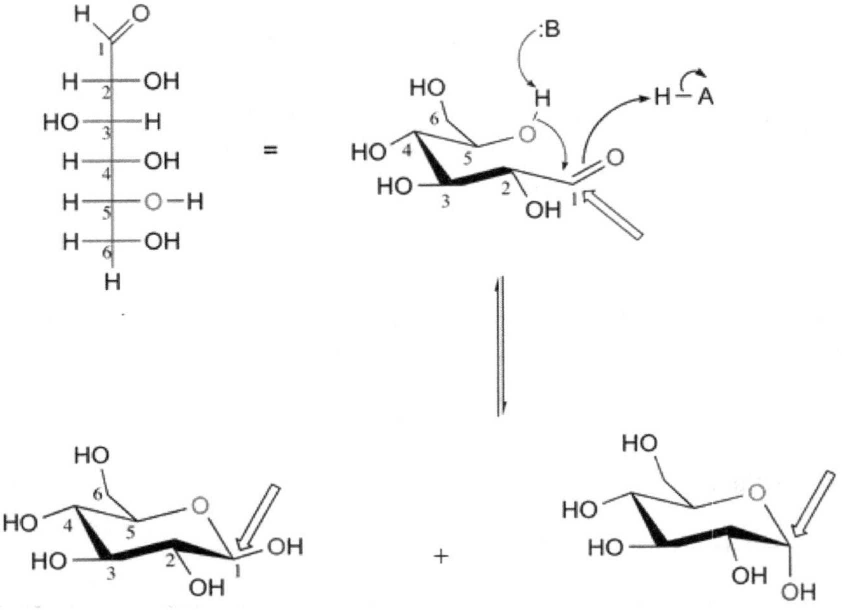

___ - glucopyranose

___ - glucopyranose

Nucleophilic attack in polysaccharide formation

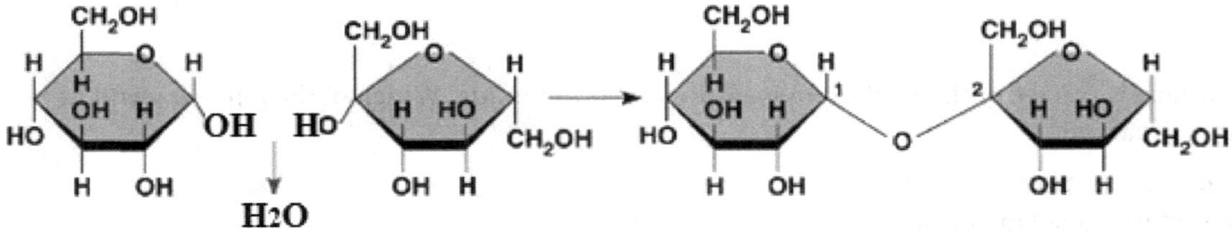

Glucose

Fructose

Sucrose (1-2 glycoside link)

Sucrose synthesis (dehydration reaction)

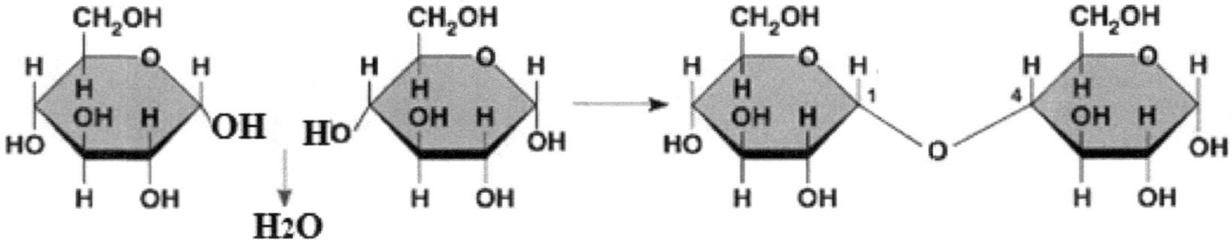

Glucose

Glucose

Maltose (1-4 glycoside link)

Maltose synthesis (dehydration reaction)

Alpha-glycosidic links vs. beta-glycosidic links and digestion

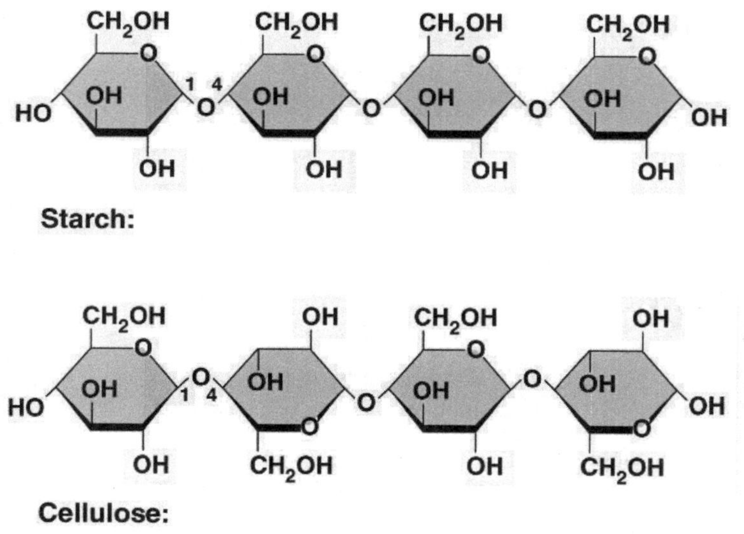
CH2OH
OH
HO
1
4
O
Starch:
Cellulose:

What monomer is included in both starch and cellulose?

Nucleophiles and peptide formation

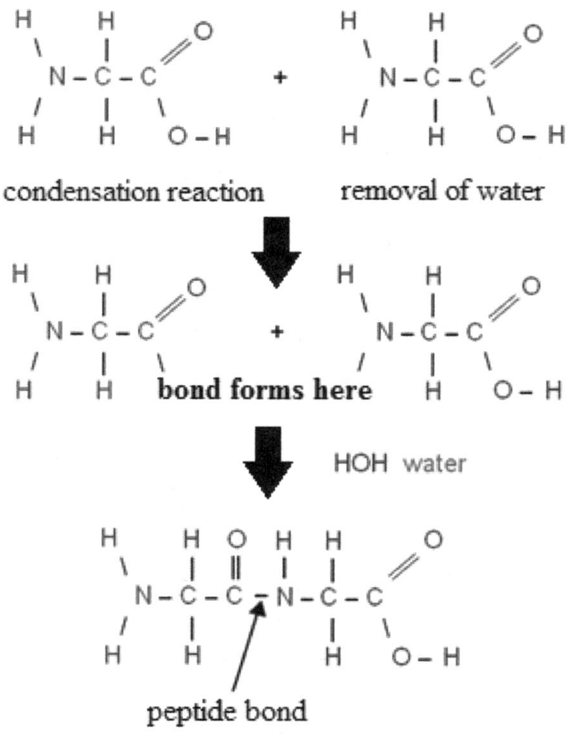
condensation reaction
removal of water
bond forms here
HOH water
peptide bond

Nucleophiles and triacylglycerol synthesis

$$\begin{array}{l} CH_2-OH \\ | \\ CH-OH \\ | \\ CH_2-OH \end{array} \quad + \quad \begin{array}{l} HO-C(=O)-C_{17}H_{35} \\ HO-C(=O)-C_{17}H_{35} \\ HO-C(=O)-C_{17}H_{35} \end{array} \quad \rightarrow \quad \begin{array}{l} CH_2-O-C(=O)-C_{17}H_{35} \\ | \\ CH-O-C(=O)-C_{17}H_{35} \\ | \\ CH_2-O-C(=O)-C_{17}H_{35} \end{array}$$

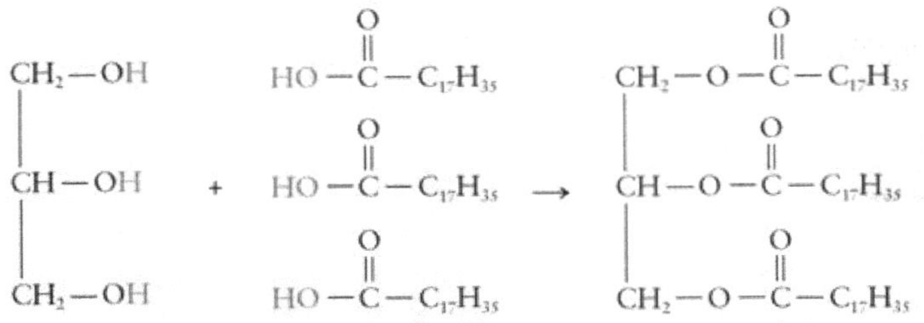

$3H_2O$

Glycerol + Fatty acids → Triacyl glycerol

What kind of reaction is triacylglycerol synthesis?

Is ester hydrolysis reversible in acidic conditions? How about basic conditions?

Saturated fats vs. Unsaturated fats

Saturated fatty acid

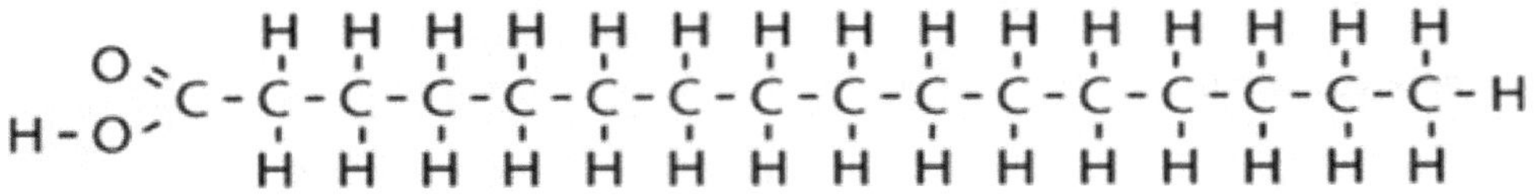

Unsaturated fatty acid

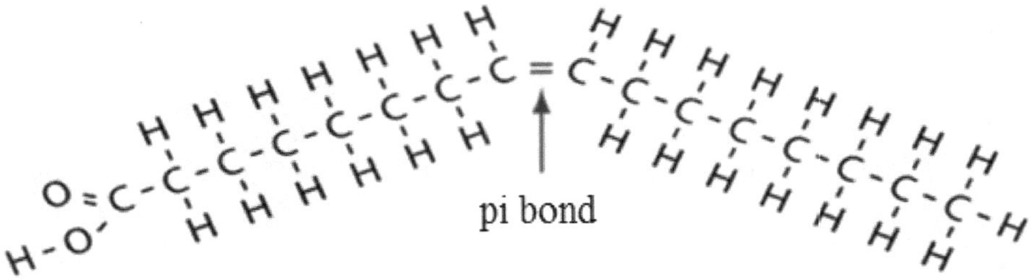

pi bond

Oils tend to be ______________________ while solid fats tend to be ______________________.

What would be the expected bond angles at a point of unsaturation?

Phospholipids:

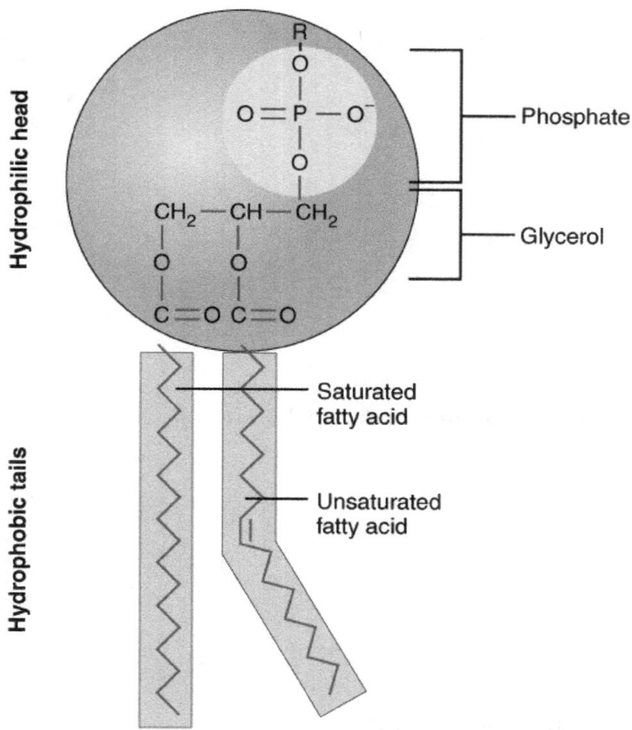

Fatty acid unit

Sugar unit

glucose or galactose

Cerebroside
(a glycolipid)

What forces allow the phospholipids to form a bilayer in the cell membrane?

What shape would a single layer of phospholipids form in the human body?

Glycolipids:

What are some functions of glycolipids in the body?

Lipopolysaccharide composition is a major distinction between what classes of prokaryotes?

Which part of the cell membrane is most likely to be altered in autoimmune disease?

A. Carbohydrate chains of glycoproteins
B. Sequence of amino acids in the channel proteins
C. Types of fatty acids in the phospholipids
D. Phosphate groups of the phospholipids

This page left intentionally blank.

MCAT Practice Passage

Clivorine is a potent toxic compound extracted from the plant *Ligularia hodgsonii Hook.* Studies suggest that clivorine induces mitogen-activated protein kinase phosphorylation, leading to renal failure. An adverse event associated with short term ingestion of clivorine is the formation of calcified kidney stones comprised of calcium phosphate $Ca_3(PO_4)_2$.

Researchers wished to study clivorine-treated human kidney K-5 cell growth. K-5 cells were seeded in 96-well microplates at a density of 10^3/well and were treated with clivorine (100 μM) for 12, 24 and 48 h. Then 0.75 mg/mL MTT was added and was incubated with cells for 5 h in a CO_2 incubator. When reduced in a cell, either enzymatically or through direct reaction with biomolecules. MTT turns blue to purple and may form an insoluble precipitate. Formazan dyes are useful for cell proliferation and toxicity assays since they only stain living, metabolically active cells.

At last the cells were dissolved in 10% SDS-0.01 M HCl in a CO_2 incubator for 12 h. The intensity was measured using a reader for ELISA under an absorption wavelength of 570/630 nm (Figure 2).

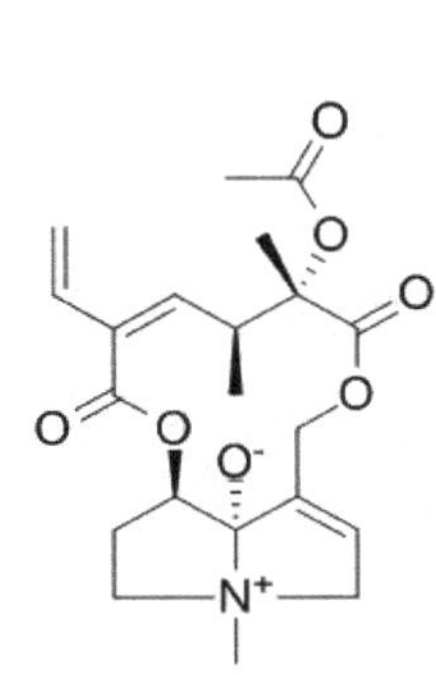

Figure 1 Clivorine

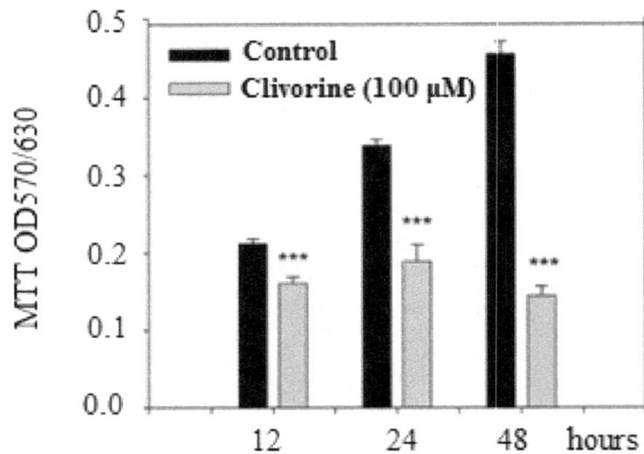

Figure 2 Time course of clivorine on K-5 cells growth. ***P ⩽ 0.001 compared with absence of clivorine. Data are means ± SE of three independent experiments

Next, researchers sought to identify the mechanism of the anti-proliferative function of clivorine in K-5 cells. After 48 h of clivorine (100 μM) treatment, fluorescence-activated cell sorting analysis of cell distribution in K-5 cells was performed as seen in Figure 2. Clivorine treatment had no effect on p53 protein levels.

Cell cycle	Percentage of the cell number	
	Control	Clivorine (100 μM)
G_0–G_1	50.14 ± 8.37	46.40 ± 4.00
G_2–M	20.11 ± 4.90	20.90 ± 1.32
S	19.80 ± 12.25	22.20 ± 6.36
G_2/G_1	12.00 ± 0.09	11.98 ± 0.01

Table 1 Analysis of cell distribution in K-5 cells after 48 h treatment

19. The research findings best support which of the following conclusions?

    A. Clivorine inhibits human normal kidney K-5 cell mitosis.
    B. Clivorine induces human normal kidney K-5 cell apoptosis.
    C. Clivorine reduces p53 protein expression leading to K-5 cell death.
    D. Clivorine decreases human normal kidney nuclear replication.

20. Which of the following molecules is most likely to cause MTT to turn purple in kidney cells?

    A. ATP
    B. Cytochrome p450 oxidase
    C. NADH kinase
    D. NADPH

21. MTT belongs to a class of compounds known as tetrazoles. Which of the following structures would be found in MTT?

A.

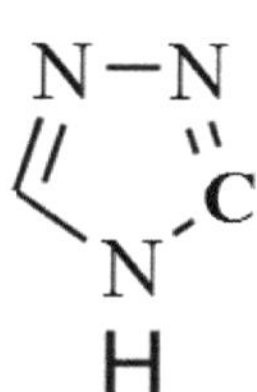

C.

C–C
C
N
H

B.

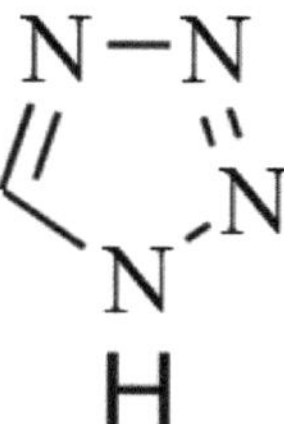

D.

C–C
C
C
H

22. Which functional groups are found on clivorine?

    A. Ether, ketone, amide
    B. Ether, ester, alkyne
    C. Ester, amine, alkene
    D. Aldehyde, ester, ether

Problem-solving Cooldown:

23. All of the following statements correctly describe an S_N1 reaction EXCEPT:
    A. Aprotic solvents stabilize the carbocation via hydrogen bonding.
    B. S_N1 reactions follow first-order kinetics.
    C. The trend of S_N1 substrate favorability is 3° > 2° > 1°.
    D. If the substrate is chiral, a partially or fully racemic mixture results.

24. How will the reaction profile for an S_N2 reaction differ when going from using a 1° substrate to a 2° substrate?
    A. The reaction with a 2° substrate would follow second order kinetics, while the reaction with the 1° substrate would follow first order kinetics
    B. The reaction with a 2° substrate would have a lower activation energy
    C. The reaction with a 2° substrate would have a higher activation energy
    D. The reaction with a 2° substrate would have a lower energy of reactants

25. The rate law for an S_N1 reaction is provided by:
    A. rate = k[substrate].
    B. rate = k[substrate][nucleophile].
    C. rate = k[nucleophile].
    D. rate = $k[\text{substrate}]^2[\text{nucleophile}]$.

26. The following molecules are what kind of isomer?

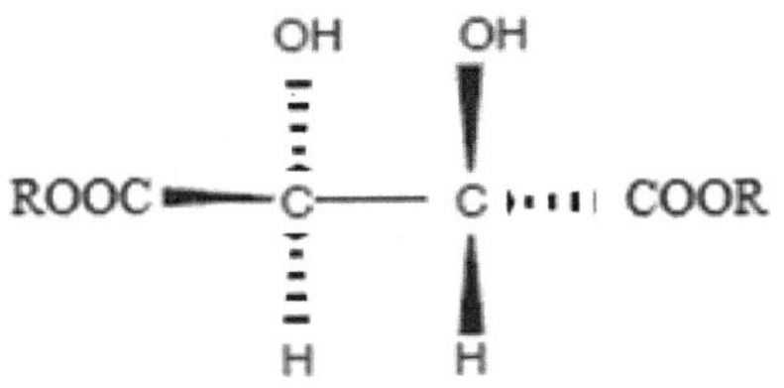

OH OH
ROOC—C—C COOR
H H

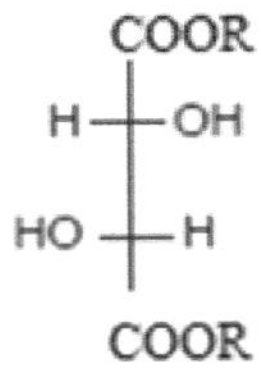

COOR
H—OH
HO—H
COOR

    A. Constitutional isomers
    B. Enantiomers
    C. Cis/trans isomers
    D. Conformational isomers

To Do After Lesson 6

- [ ] Read General Chemistry and Organic Chemistry Chapters 9 and 10
- [ ] Read Biology Chapters 5 and 6
- [ ] Read Biochemistry Chapters 3 and 4
- [ ] Complete Organic Chemistry QBank 1: Stereochemistry, Alkanes, and Alcohols

This page left intentionally blank.

LESSON

7

Biochemistry 1

To Do Before Lesson 7

- ☐ Read General Chemistry and Organic Chemistry Chapters 9 and 10
- ☐ Read Biology Chapters 5 and 6
- ☐ Read Biochemistry Chapters 3 and 4
- ☐ Complete Organic Chemistry QBank 1: Stereochemistry, Alkanes, and Alcohols

In Lesson 7

Problem-solving Warm-up
Effective Reading in the Sciences
Amino Acids
Protein Structure
MCAT Practice Passage
Non-enzymatic Protein Function
Nucleic Acids
Problem-solving Cooldown
Test-like Thinking: CARS Practice Passage

To Do After Lesson 7

- ☐ Read Biochemistry Chapters 5 and 6
- ☐ Read Psychology and Sociology Chapters 1, 2, and 3
- ☐ Complete Biochemistry QBank 3: Amino Acids and Bioenergetics

Problem-solving Warm-up

1. Which of the following amino acids has a hydrophobic side chain?

   A. Thr
   B. Cys
   C. Pro
   D. His

2. Which of the following amino acids has a net negative charge at pH = 7.1?

   A. Ser
   B. Cys
   C. Glu
   D. His

3. Which of the following amino acids will exist primarily with a net positive charge at pH = 7.1?

   A. Thr
   B. Trp
   C. Lys
   D. His

4. All amino acids in human serum albumin will have which of the following configurations?

   A. L
   B. D
   C. R
   D. S

5. Which ribonucleotide will have the lowest molecular weight?

   A. deoxyadenine
   B. adenine
   C. deoxyguanine
   D. guanine

This page left intentionally blank.

Effective Reading in the Sciences

Cyclic adenosine monophosphate (cAMP), also known as (4aR,6R,7R,7aS)-6-(6-aminopurin-9-yl)-2-hydroxy-2-oxo-4a,6,7,7a-tetrahydro-4H-furo[3,2-d][1,3,2]dioxaphosphinin-7-ol , is a well-characterized second messenger derived from ATP and commonly found in the human body. cAMP is a member of a class of molecules which form the building blocks of nucleic acids, but also serve as the metabolic precursors for ribose, deoxyribose and the various nitrogenous bases.

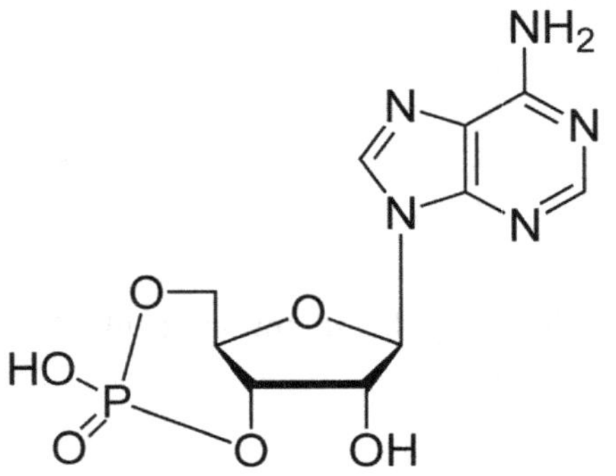

Figure 1 cAMP

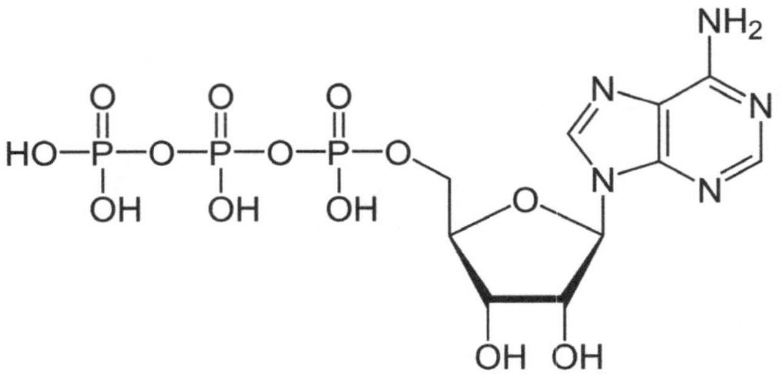

Figure 2 ATP

cAMP related changes can promote both pro-apoptotic responses and anti-apoptotic responses. The enzyme adenylate cyclase converts ATP to cyclic AMP, which activates protein kinase (PK). PK phosphorylates ion channels, allowing Na^+ ions to rush into the cell. Aberrant activities in cAMP-mediated cellular pathways are linked to abnormal cell growth and proliferation, particularly in some cancers.

A defect recognizable in diabetes is faulty insulin release in response to glucose infusion. There is evidence that the cyclic AMP mechanism may be defective. Insulin deficiency leaves unopposed the actions of hormones which stimulate the production of cyclic AMP, thereby contributing to the excess serum glucose and ketosis seen in the later stages of the disease.

Passage taken from the online Next Step QBank

6. According to passage information, which of the following facts related to cyclic adenosine monophosphate is NOT true?

   A. The sugar ring is formed by the nucleophilic attack on the primary phosphate's oxygen by the penultimate ring carbon on the pentose sugar.
   B. Reversal of cAMP's effect on sodium channels may require either a kinase or a phosphatase enzyme.
   C. cAMP binding to protein kinase A indirectly stimulates glycogenolysis.
   D. Epinephrine does not need to cross the cell membrane to initiate a cAMP cascade.

7. Which of the following is NOT an evolutionary advantage humans gain from intracellular signal transduction cascades?

   A. The ability to "amplify" the signaling effect of one molecule
   B. The ability to have a variety of biochemical triggers precipitate a single downstream action within the cell
   C. The ability to have a single biochemical trigger precipitate a variety of downstream actions within the cell
   D. The ability to regulate signal transduction at multiple points of biochemical interaction

8. According to the passage, which of the following compounds, *in vivo*, would the researcher observe structures most similar to cAMP?

   A. Polysaccharides
   B. Nucleosides
   C. Glycoproteins
   D. Nucleotides

9. The versatility lent by the sugar-phosphate backbone to the structure of nucleic acids permits which of the following?

   A. The formation of grooves adjacent to bound base pairs, providing histone binding sites.
   B. The exceptional structural stability of dsDNA
   C. The ability to induce either positive or negative supercoiling
   D. The looped conformation of the DNA backbone in G-quadraplexes found in telomeres.

Amino Acids

Aliphatic—

Aromatic—

Acidic—

Basic—

Hydroxylic—

Sulfur-containing—

Amidic (containing amide group)—

Peptide bond

EXAMPLE

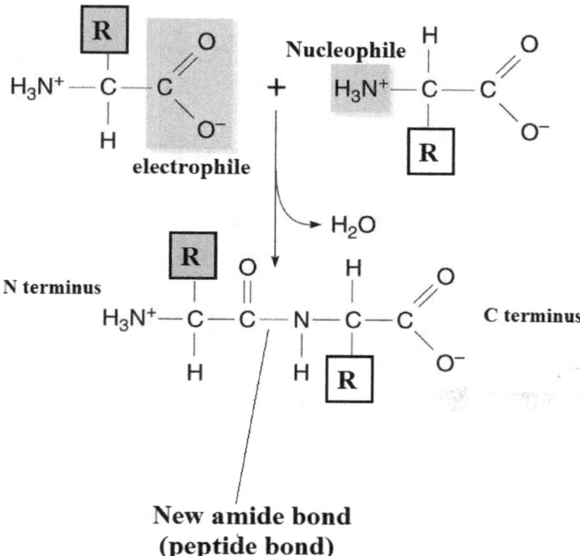

Separation of Proteins

Size exclusion chromatography

Ion exchange chromatography

Anion exchange

Cation exchange

Affinity chromatography

Purification of Proteins

SDS-PAGE

2-D Gel Electrophoresis

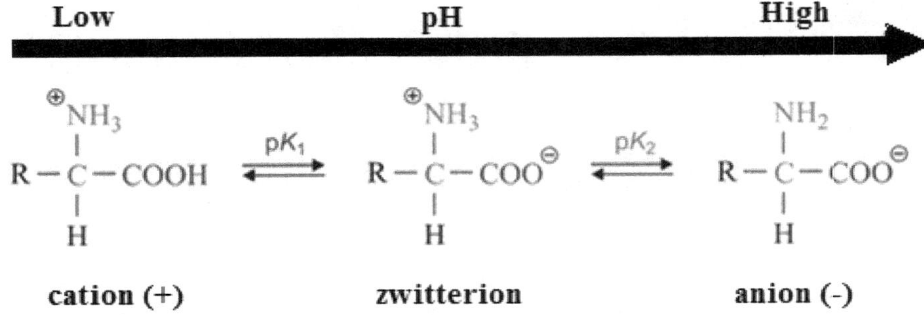

When pH > pK_a the ______________________ form predominates.

When pH < pK_a the ______________________ form predominates.

When pH = pK_a the ______________________ form predominates.

pK_a of acidic AA

pK_a of basic AA

EXAMPLE

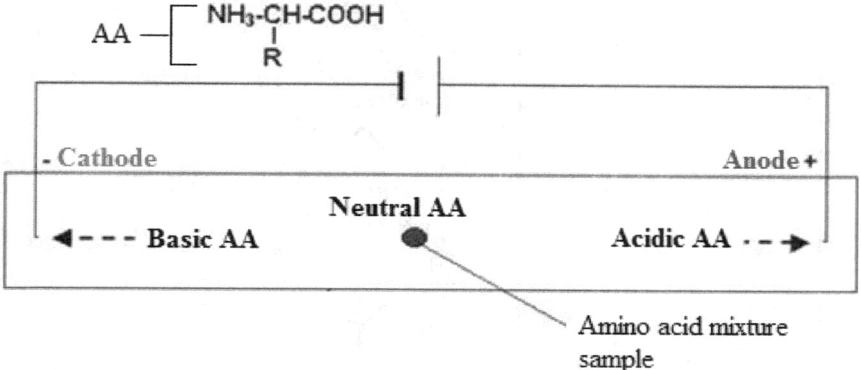

When placed into an electrophoretic gel at a pH = 8, to which node will the following amino acids migrate?

(i) Ala (ii) Pro (iii) Glu (iv) Arg

pK_a and pI

Acidic AA

Basic AA

Polypeptide hydrolysis

Mass spec proteomics

Protein Structure

Level	Description	Stabilizing F	Example (Hb)
Primary			Gly-Ser-Asp-Cys
Secondary			Pleated sheet; Alpha helix
Tertiary			Pleated sheet; Alpha helix
Quaternary			

One of the problems in certain forms of schizophrenia is a loss-of-function mutation to peptidyl transferase. What process is most likely to be halted in these patients?

A. Binding of the mRNA template to the ribosome
B. Construction of the cellular ribosome
C. Construction of the primary structure of neuroproteins
D. tRNA recognition of mRNA codons.

A polar-substrate binding enzyme is most likely to have threonine residues richly populating which region?

OH O
H_3C OH
NH_2

A. The interior of the enzyme
B. The exterior of the enzyme
C. The active site of the enzyme
D. Within an alpha-helical structure

Amino Acid Structure

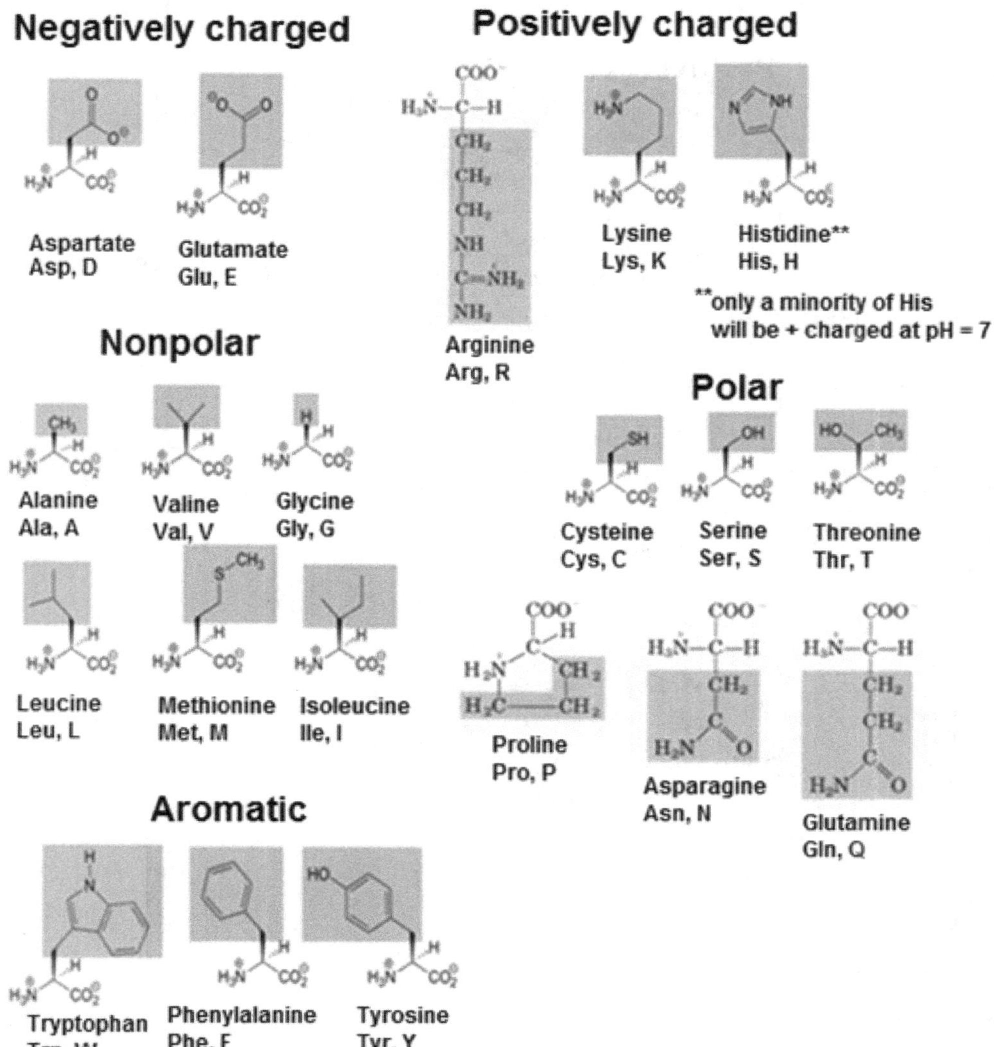

Strategy

You should prioritize your AA studying as follows in order to maximize efficiency and points: 1. full name and side group chemical behavior; 2. three-letter abbreviation; 3. one-letter abbreviation; 4. exact structure; 5. pKa of side chain

Amino Acid Structure Worksheet Exercise—Level 1

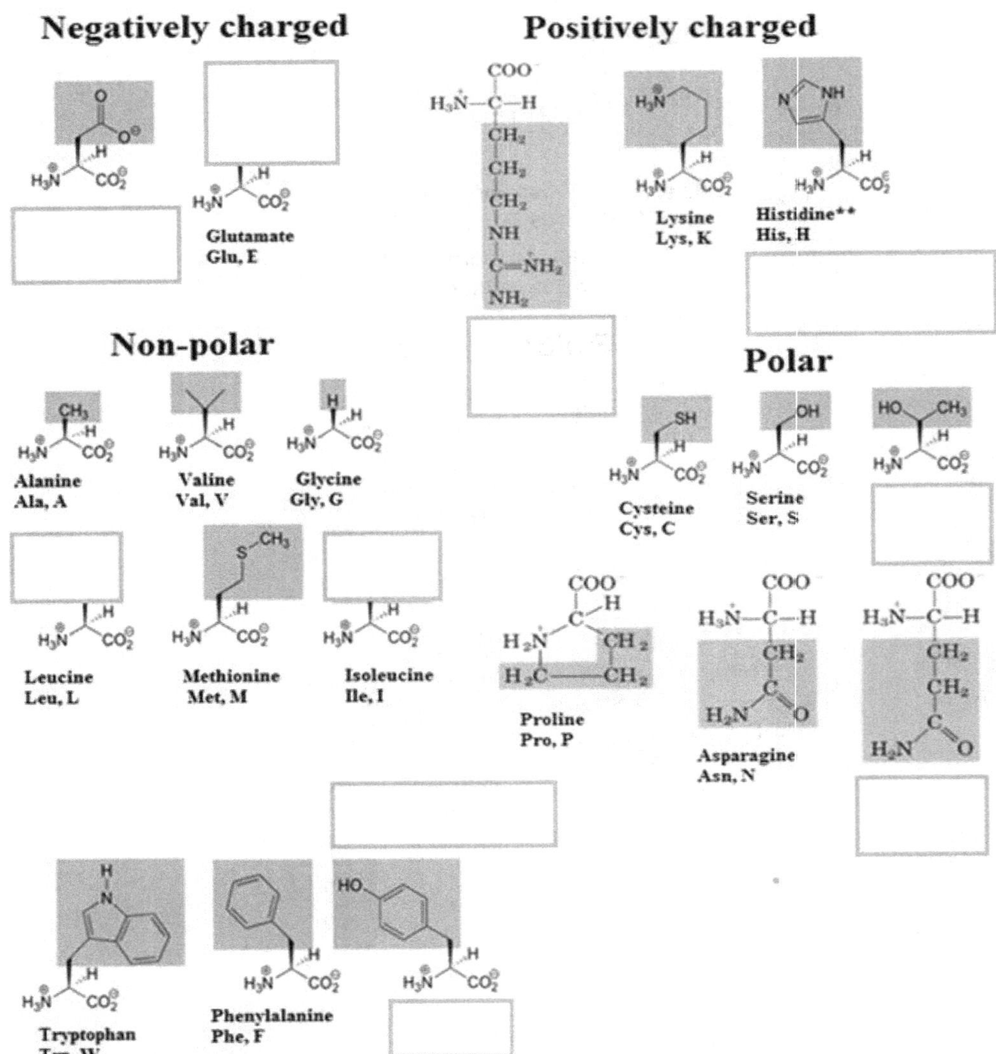

Amino Acid Structure Worksheet Exercise—Level 2

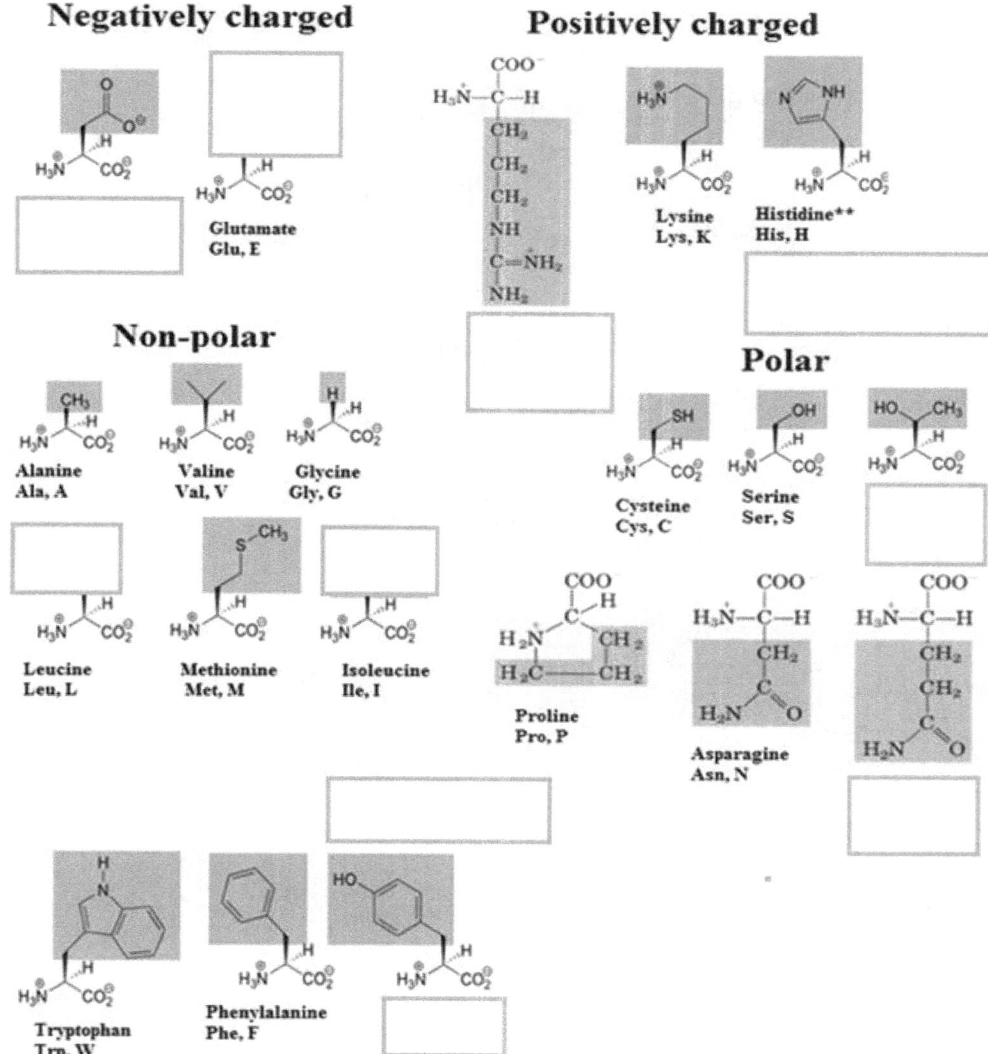

Amino Acid Structure Worksheet Exercise—Level 3

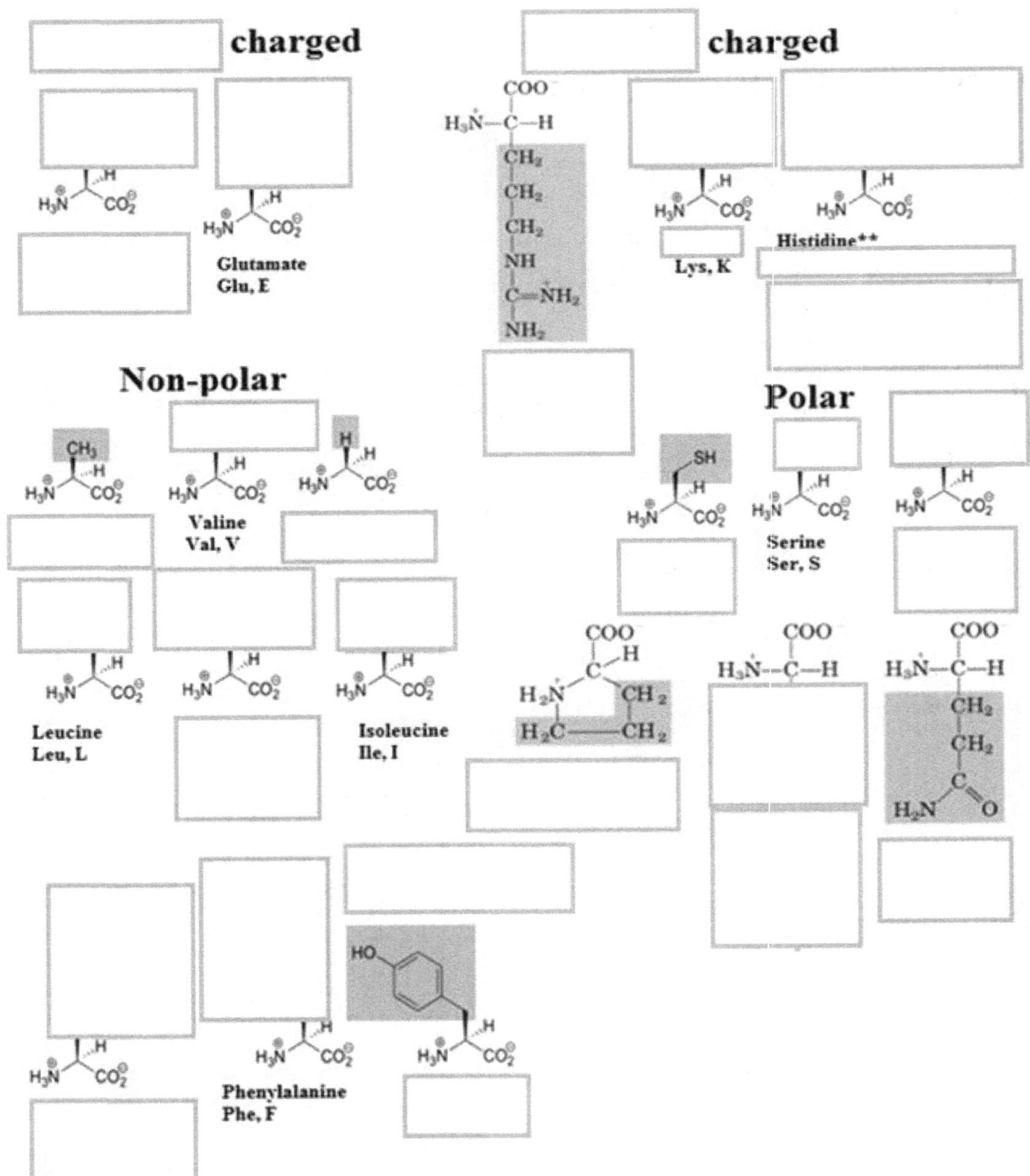

Amino Acid Recall Exercise

Amino Acid	3 Letter Abbrev.	1 Letter Abbrev.	Side Chain Property	Side Chain Structure

Timed MCAT Practice Passage

Mastery of the MCAT sciences is a two-part process. First you must study to understand (not just memorize!) the science content, and then you must study the content actively and challenge yourself within the context of the exam.

1. Complete your reading of the passage (3-4 minutes).
   - Write down what you believe to be the primary science content underlying the passage.
   - What facts or concepts do you anticipate to be tested? When you are done with the questions determine if you were correct. What passage clues were there to imply related topics that showed up in the questions?
   - Were there any key terms or important scientific relationships you missed?
   - Were you able to draw any conclusions from the data, if presented?

2. Complete the practice questions on your own (4-5 minutes)
   - Rephrase each question in your own mind after reading it to clarify the task.
   - Research the relevant area(s) of the passage or your own knowledge for information related to the task.
   - Respond to the question by choosing the answer that fits your research/calculations *and* satisfies the task.
   - If no answer seems obvious, eliminate answers that fail to have support in the passage or in the relevant science.

3. Analyze your wrong answer choices to the questions you missed.
   - Did you understand the task in the question?
   - What skill type was the question?
   - Did you know the science/formula/concept needed to answer the question?
   - Did you recognize the science being hinted at?
   - Were you able to find information in the passage quickly when you needed it?
   - Were there any necessary scientific concepts you failed to apply to the question?
     - If so, why?
   - If you made a mistake in calculations, have you identified your mistake?

This page left intentionally blank.

Keratin is a family of fibrous structural proteins which make up the human fingernail among other structures. Keratin is formed from a series of monomers that assemble into bundles to form intermediate filaments. The intermediate filaments are tough and insoluble and form strong "un-mineralized" tissues found in many mammalian and non-mammalian species. The reactions below summarize the in vitro lysing of disulfide bridges (induced either by hydrogen peroxide, acetic acid, or thioglycolic acid) formed in keratin.

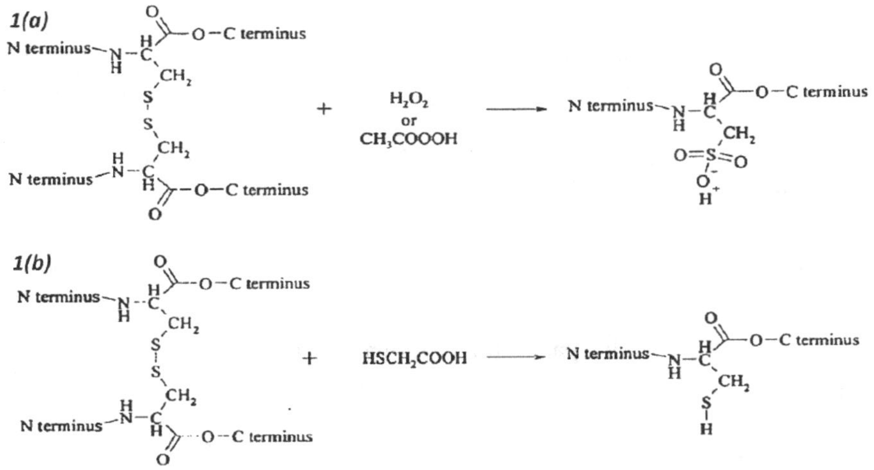

1(a)

N terminus–NH–CH(–C(=O)–O–C terminus)–CH₂–S–S–CH₂–CH(–C(=O)–O–C terminus)–NH–N terminus + H_2O_2 or CH_3COOOH ⟶ N terminus–NH–CH(–C(=O)–O–C terminus)–CH_2–$S(=O)_2$–O^- H^+

1(b)

N terminus–NH–CH(–C(=O)–O–C terminus)–CH₂–S–S–CH₂–CH(–C(=O)–O–C terminus)–NH–N terminus + $HSCH_2COOH$ ⟶ N terminus–NH–CH(–C(=O)–O–C terminus)–CH_2–S–H

Reactions 1(a) and 1(b): Lysing of disulfide bridges formed in keratin

Disulfide bridges occur between charged functional groups in abnormal pH environments, due largely to keratins' relatively high concentration of sulfur-containing amino acids. Disulfide bridges are part of a larger family of covalent or ionic polymer bonds that link one polymer chain to another. In addition to the inter/intra-molecular hydrogen bonds and interactions occurring in a protein, these crosslinks contribute to the insolubility of keratins, unless exposed to sufficiently strong dissociating or reducing agents. These crosslinks are needed for mechanically stable structures in the human body.

The more flexible and elastic keratins of hair have fewer disulfide bridges than the keratins in fingernails. Hair and other "α-keratins" consist of α-helically coiled single protein strands (with regular intra-chain H-bonding), which are then further twisted into so-called "superhelical" strands that may comprise a macro "coiled-coil" structure.

The β-keratins of reptiles and birds, on the other hand, are typically found in the scales, shells, and claws of reptiles. Figure 1 below illustrates the typical structure of a β-keratin.

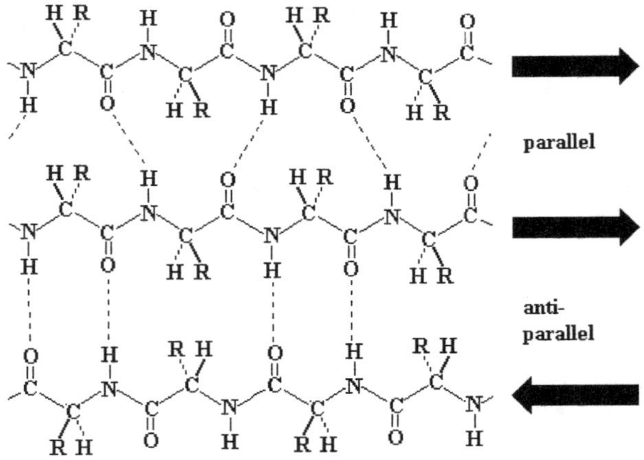

Figure 1 Structure of β-keratin

Passage taken from the online Next Step QBank

11. All of the following protein structures are likely to be found as surface proteins in the eukaryotic membrane EXCEPT:

A. DAT, a protein used to recycle dopamine from the synapse.
B. spectrin, a cytoskeletal protein which maintains plasma membrane integrity.
C. CD4-R, a glycoprotein that assists in immune cell function.
D. glycophorin A, which bears the antigenic determinants for blood type.

12. Which of the following best explains why disulfide links are rarely found intracellularly in the human body?

A. Disulfide bonds are only formed in an oxidizing environment.
B. Disulfide bridges stabilize conformations that would otherwise break down in the cytosol.
C. Methionine and cysteine are the only amino acids which can form disulfide links.
D. Cysteine which is not involved in disulfide bridge formation can stabilize alpha helices.

13. Carbon-14 is frequently used by researchers in isotopic labeling of enzymes; however, under certain conditions, it can be subject to both β^- and β^+ decay. Which of the following isotopes might be observed if a sample of C-14 in use by a researcher were subjected to β^+ decay?

A. Boron-14
B. Nitrogen-15
C. Nitrogen-14
D. Boron-15

14. Disulfide bridges that form under natural conditions generally:

A. stabilize proteins, because the energy absorbed by the formation of the intramolecular bond increases the overall energy of the protein.
B. destabilize proteins, because the energy absorbed by the formation of the intramolecular bond reduces the overall energy of the protein.
C. stabilize proteins, because the energy released by the formation of the intramolecular bond reduces the overall energy of the protein.
D. destabilize proteins, because the energy released by the formation of the intramolecular bond reduces the overall energy of the protein.

15. Real-time enzyme-catalyzed crosslink formations can be observed with specialized spectroscopy. This method uses enzymes that contain radioactive isotopes of biologically-common elements in *in vitro* reaction media. Which of the following physical properties could these spectroscopic methods use to differentiate between radioactive isotopes and other elements in the reaction?

I. Mass True
II. Vibrational Mode – elasticity and link of covalent bonds, False
III. Nuclear stability True

A. I only
B. I and III only
C. II and III only
D. I, II, and III

Non-enzymatic Protein Function

EXAMPLE

Ion channels

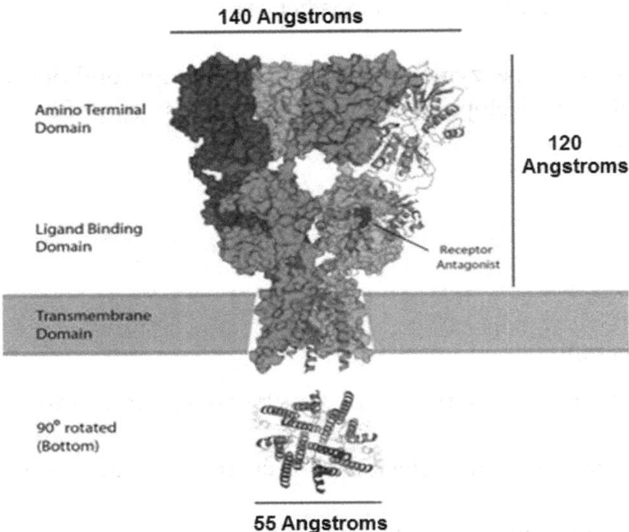

Transport protein

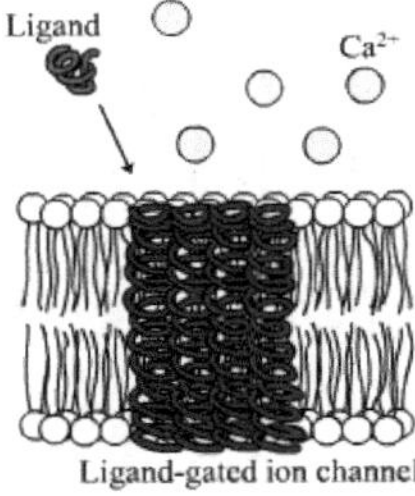

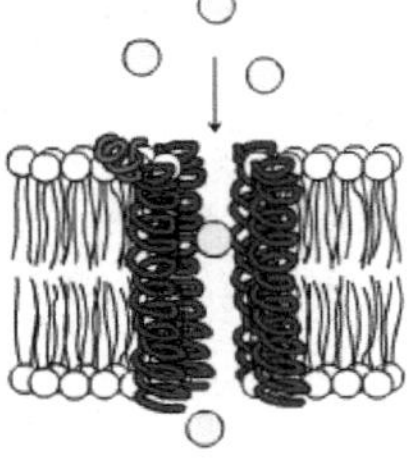

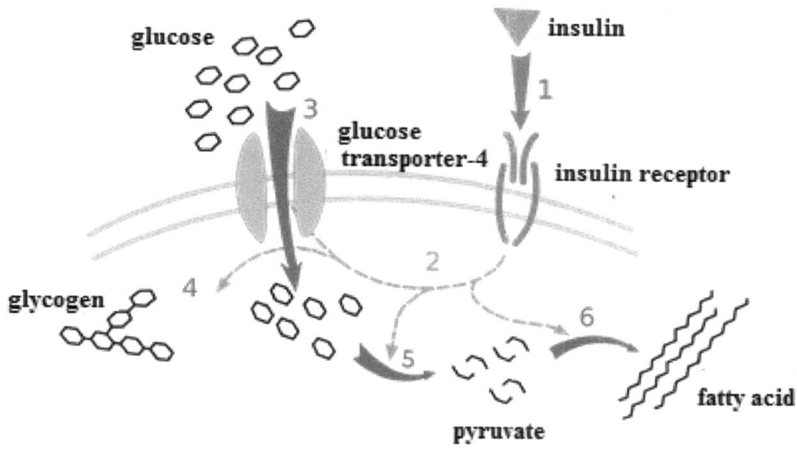

Immune System

EXAMPLE

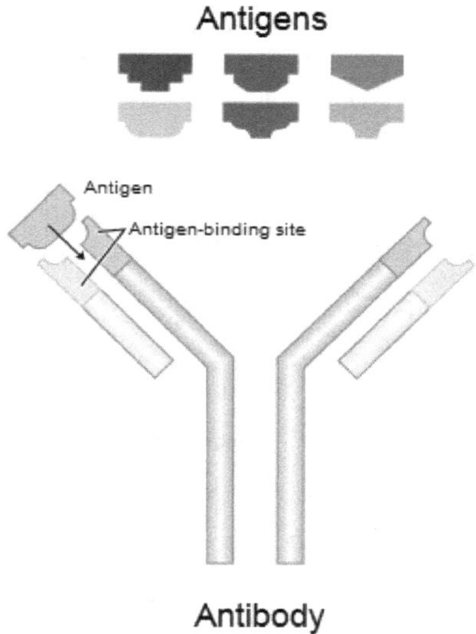

Antigens

Antibodies

Heavy chain

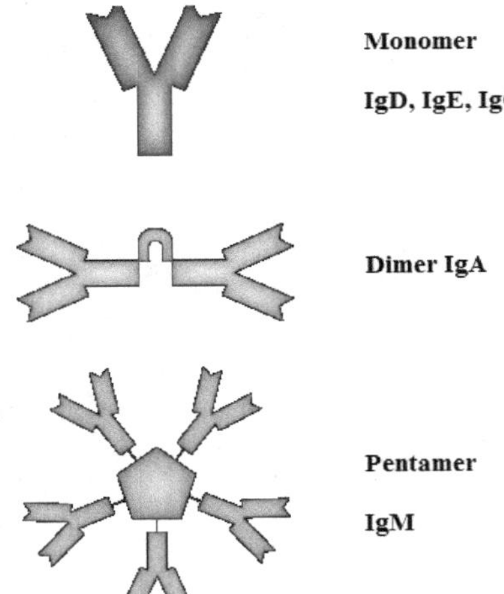

Light chain

Variable domain

Constant domain

Motor Proteins

EXAMPLE

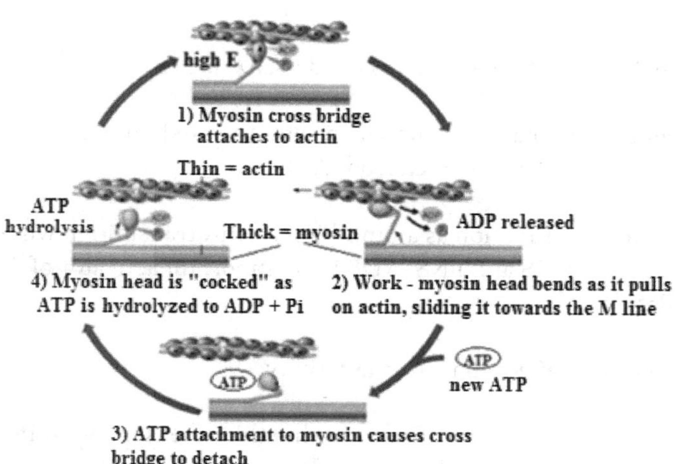

Sarcomere

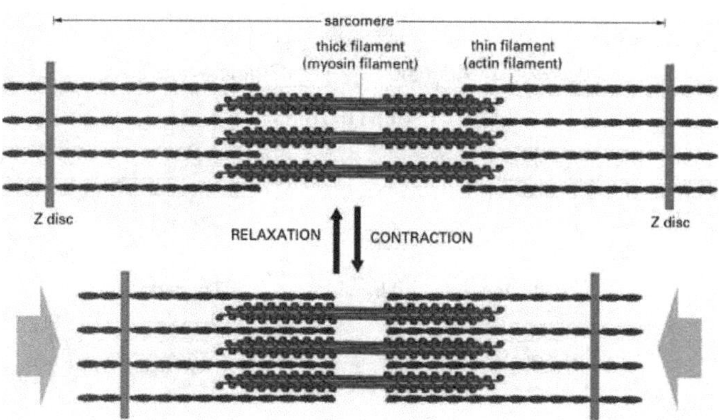

A band

I band

Z line

H zone

Nucleic Acids

Nucleotide Functions:

1. Energy stores for future use in phosphate transfer reactions. These reactions are predominantly carried out by ATP.

2. Forming a portion of several important coenzymes such as NAD^+, $NADP^+$, FAD and coenzyme A.

3. Mediators of cellular processes such as second messengers in signal transduction events. The predominant second messenger is cyclic-AMP (cAMP), a cyclic derivative of AMP formed from ATP.

4. Neurotransmitters and signal receptor ligands. Adenosine can function as an inhibitory neurotransmitter, while ATP also affects synaptic neurotransmission throughout the CNS and PNS. ADP is an important activator of platelet functions resulting in control of blood coagulation.

5. Controlling numerous enzymatic reactions through allosteric effects on enzyme activity.

6. Activated intermediates in numerous biosynthetic reactions. For example S-adenosylmethionine is involved in CH_3 transfer reactions as well as sugar coupled nucleotides involved in glycogen and glycoprotein synthesis.

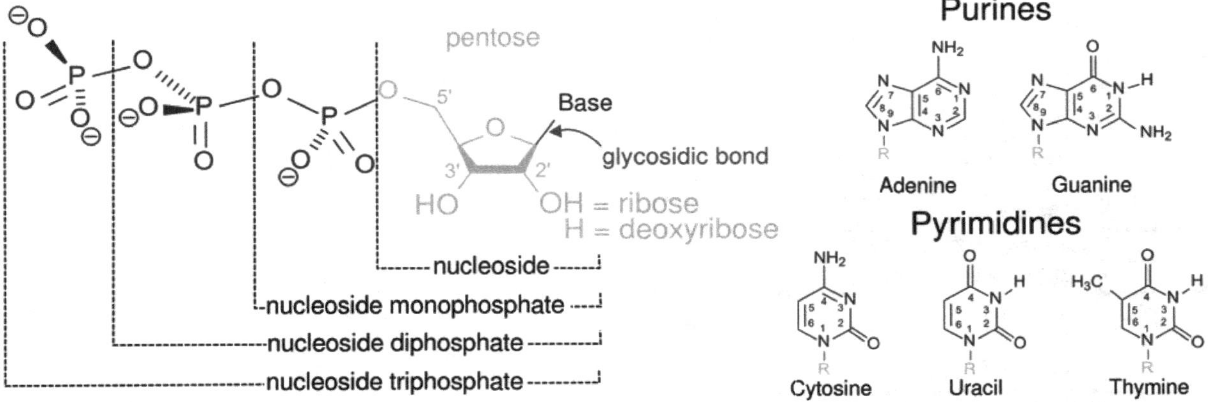

Base Stacking

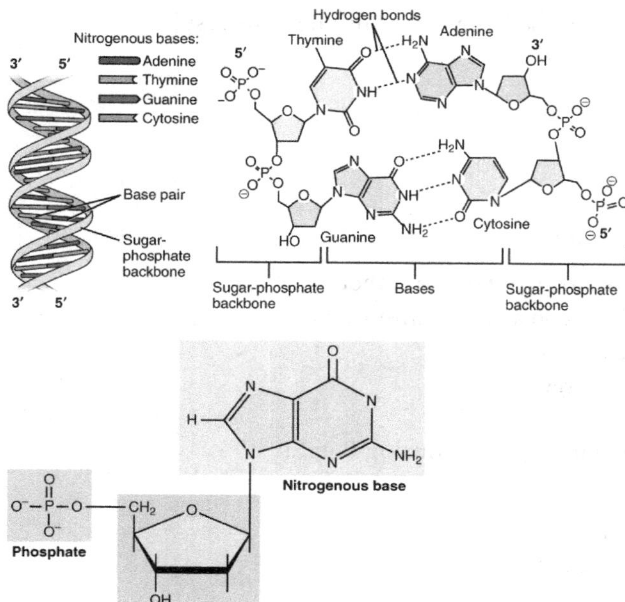

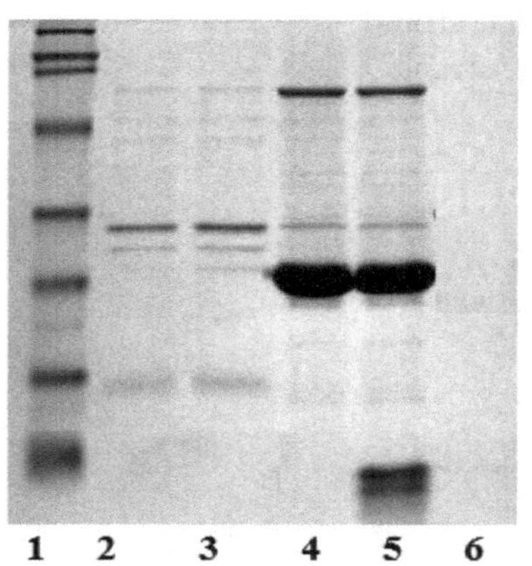

13. The PCR process involves heating the DNA prior to the addition of RNA primers. A point is reached at which the DNA molecules exist as single strands. Which of the following DNA sequences will require the highest temperature to achieve this?

    A. 5'-ATTCTGCTATTA-3
    B. 5'-ATGCUUUTATTA-3'
    C. 5'-GTTCTGCTATTA-3'
    D. 5'-ACGCCTGCTAGC-3'

Lane 1 is a ladder of DNA fragments from 50 to 400 bp in length.

1 2 3 4 5 6

14. Agarose gel electrophoresis is performed on DNA obtained after an experiment run on portions of gene A. If lanes 4 and 5 used the same protocol, which of the following best explains the additional band in lane 5?

    A. The sample in lane 5 was contaminated with DNases.
    B. DNA primers hybridized to each other and were amplified, generating larger fragments along with the desired fragment.
    C. The sample in lane 5 was contaminated with genomic DNA.
    D. Preparation of the sample for lane 4 mistakenly forgot to remove an intron.

Problem-solving Cooldown

15. If the voltage of the power supply in gel electrophoresis is increased, how will this affect the results?

    A. The pH will increase and destroy the sample molecules
    B. The sample molecules will move faster
    C. The sample molecules will move slower
    D. There is no effect of voltage on gel electrophoresis

16. Must SDS be used to separate rotavirus proteins during PAGE?

    A. Yes, because it allows negatively charged peptides to be attracted to the cathode.
    B. Yes, because it facilitates a common charge across all the constituent amino acids.
    C. No, because amino acids all have a common negative charge.
    D. No, because amino acids all have a common positive charge.

17. Must SDS be used to separate the various genes in the rotavirus genome during PAGE?

    A. Yes, because it allows the nucleic acids to be unwound.
    B. Yes, because it acts to segregate the sequences based on size.
    C. No, because nucleic acids all have a common negative charge.
    D. No, because nucleic acids all have a common positive charge.

18. Most of the readily available energy stored in ATP is stored during the:

    A. manufacture of guanosine.
    B. phosphorylation of AMP to ADP.
    C. phosphorylation of ADP to form ATP.
    D. decomposition of ATP to ADP.

19. Which of the following sequences would be ideal for use as a forward primer in the PCR amplification of the following gene sequence?

5'-CTGCGA...GCTTAA-3'	Nontemplate strand
3'-GACGCT...CGAATT-5'	Template strand

    A. 5'- GACGCT... -3'
    B. 5'- CTGCGA... -3'
    C. 5'- GCTTAA... -3'
    D. 5'- CGAATT... -3'

This page left intentionally blank.

Test-like Thinking: CARS Practice Passage

The North American Free Trade Agreement (NAFTA) was one of the most significant international treaties liberalizing trade. It became effective on January 1st, 1994 and eliminated most tariffs on trade between the US, Canada and Mexico. Over the course of the subsequent decade, it phased in further elimination of tariffs until, by 2004, all goods could be traded freely between the three nations. In conjunction with strengthened protections for intellectual property and environmental concerns, this tariff elimination has produced economic impacts that, on balance, have been modestly positive.

In Canada, the largest impact has been an increase in trade in agricultural goods, although interestingly the increase has been accompanied by a reduction—both in absolute and relative terms—in the US/Canada trade imbalance in the agricultural sector. Despite a general trend towards a loss in manufacturing jobs in developed nations, since the passage of NAFTA the number of manufacturing jobs in Canada has remained relatively constant. Mexico has arguably been the biggest beneficiary of NAFTA, with thousands of maquiladoras (manufacturing plants that focus on assembling final products from manufactured components) springing up on the US/Mexico border, providing tens of thousands of relatively high-paying jobs for low skill workers. In the U.S. the net economic impact has been more neutral, with the most pronounced impacts on the U.S. meat industry. Elimination of agricultural tariffs combined with a rising middle class in Mexico has seen Mexico transition from an insignificant part of U.S. meat exports to its second-largest international consumer.

NAFTA is not without its critics, however. Special interest groups, nonprofit watchdog groups, and legal scholars have all expressed grave concerns over NAFTA's Chapter 11 and Chapter 19 provisions, which relate to dispute resolution. Chapter 11 contains provisions which allow individual investors or corporations to sue the U.S., Mexico, or Canada. Concerns largely hinge on the fact that NAFTA allows suits against governments even when those governments are acting in ways that would be seen as the normal exercise of governmental power to protect the health and welfare of citizens. For example, the American corporation Metalclad won a $15.6 million award in a suit against the Mexican government when the Mexican state of San Luis Potosi blocked Metalclad from building a hazardous waste landfill over environmental concerns. Another corporation, Lone Pine Resources, has filed a $250 million claim against the Canadian government because the Canadian province Quebec blocked fracking (a form of oil exploration and extraction), again on environmental concerns.

Even more worrying are the provisions under Chapter 19 that circumvent normal judicial review. Chapter 19 covers actions relating to antidumping and countervailing duty impositions. That is, if a company is accused of dumping products (selling across country lines at an artificially low price to drive out competition), or if a country is subsidizing a particular industry then that country's trade partner can impose a countervailing duty. For example, if the Canadian government were subsidizing a particular product, allowing Canadian sellers to offer the product cheaply in Mexico at below-market price, then the Mexican government would be permitted to impose an import duty on that product to offset the subsidy. The concern arises from the fact that Chapter 19 includes a dispute resolution procedure in which a panel of five individuals (typically lawyers who specialize in trade issues) are empowered to review any determination made by a country's judicial system. Thus, the panel could theoretically overturn a decision of the United States Supreme Court if the panel felt that the decision was incorrect under NAFTA.

20. Which of the following is most in agreement with the views of nonprofit watchdog groups, as those views are described in the third paragraph?

A. Since the shareholders of any given corporation might all be citizens of a country not party to NAFTA, a corporation should never have the right to sue a government that is party to NAFTA.

B. Governments should have sovereign immunity from lawsuits filed by corporations when those governments are acting to protect the health and welfare of their citizens.

C. Environmental concerns are paramount when evaluating business decisions.

D. Multi-million dollar judgments against government agencies are a necessary recourse for companies to compensate them for losses when governments take actions that damage their interests.

21. The author would most likely agree with each of the following EXCEPT:

I. Free trade agreements typically end up having a net negative effect on the economies of the participating countries.

II. Rising incomes and an expanding middle class can be associated with increased meat consumption.

III. The specialized nature of trade disputes requires legal mechanisms that side-step the normal judicial systems of the countries involved.

A. II only

B. I and II only

C. I and III only

D. II and III only

22. A Mexican company seeks to open a recycled material processing plant outside a given city and is able to get approval from Canada's environmental and business management agencies. But, the construction is stopped by the municipal government, which refuses to permit zoning for the construction of the plant, citing concerns about noise and pollution. Under NAFTA, the company:

A. could file suit against the municipal government and could potentially win tens or hundreds of millions of dollars in compensation.

B. would be entitled to push for a countervailing duty imposed on imports of recycled materials.

C. has no recourse and must simply accept the losses associated with the planning stages of plant building.

D. would relocate its plant to Mexico.

23. Which of the following trade treaty provisions would the author be LEAST likely to endorse?

A. An update to NAFTA that further strengthens the environmental protections for trade goods created by various extractive industries

B. A provision that, instead of eliminating all tariffs and duties, reduces them to a very low level in order to generate a fund providing temporary financial assistance to workers whose jobs are displaced after the treaty is signed

C. A mechanism that provides for corrective action in order to reduce trade imbalances in each major economic sector

D. A provision strengthening intellectual property protection for patents and providing for an appeals board consisting of scientists and specialized patent attorneys to review dispute resolution decisions made by member nations' court systems

24. Which of the following import taxes would be permissible under NAFTA?

A. A 15% duty imposed by the US government on Mexican clothing imports to offset the subsidies received by the textile industry under a Mexican economic stimulus package

B. A $100 tariff on each bushel of organic produce grown in hothouses near the US-Mexican border that is then sold across the border

C. An import duty that automatically doubles the wholesale price of a certain computer component manufactured in the US and which was being sold at a loss in Canada

D. A tariff imposed as a result of a lawsuit filed under NAFTA's Chapter 11 provisions

To Do After Lesson 7

- ☐ Read Biochemistry Chapters 5 and 6
- ☐ Read Psychology and Sociology Chapters 1, 2, and 3
- ☐ Complete Biochemistry QBank 3: Amino Acids and Bioenergetics

LESSON 8

Psychology 1

To Do Before Lesson 8

- ☐ Read Biochemistry Chapters 5 and 6
- ☐ Read Psychology and Sociology Chapters 1, 2, and 3
- ☐ Complete Biochemistry QBank 3: Amino Acids and Bioenergetics

In Lesson 8

Problem-solving Warm-up
Sensation and Perception
Effective Reading
Cognition and Language
Turning Abstract into Concrete
MCAT Practice Passage
Emotion and Stress
Learning and Memory
Problem-solving Cooldown
Test-like Thinking: Practice CARS Passage

To Do After Lesson 8

- ☐ Read Psychology and Sociology Chapters 4, 5, and 6
- ☐ Read Biology Chapters 7 and 8
- ☐ Complete Psychology and Sociology QBank 1: Sensation and Consciousness

Problem-solving Warm-up

1. The pain-killing effect of acupuncture is most likely due to:

   A. sensory adaptation.
   B. stabilization of nystagmus.
   C. the triggering of afferent protective systems.
   D. endorphin release.

2. Amplification-based hearing aids will NOT be effective treatment for patients with which kind of deafness?

   A. Ossicle fusion
   B. Nerve loss
   C. Conduction
   D. Auditory aphasia

3. The visual deficiency known as astigmatism is the result of:

   A. an iris that is too short.
   B. a pupil that is too long.
   C. uneven distribution of light receptors in the retina.
   D. a misshapen cornea or lens.

4. New mothers with post-partum depression take longer than non-depressed women to recognize briefly-flashed pictures related to pregnancy, birth, and babies. This is an example of which phenomena?

   A. Aversive stimulation
   B. Perceptual defense
   C. Absolute threshold
   D. Denial

5. A researcher finds a correlation of 0.35 between the number of years of post-secondary education and annual income. The most likely conclusion to reach is:

   A. the annual income data is positively skewed.
   B. more years of post-secondary education are associated with lower annual income.
   C. one who attended three years of college will have an income of $35,000.
   D. higher personal income is associated with greater time spent in education.

Sensation and Perception

Sensation

Perception

Prosopagnosia

Absolute threshold vs. difference threshold

Absolute threshold

Vision

Hearing

Smell

Taste

Touch

Difference threshold

Weber's Law ($\Delta I/I = K$)

Signal detection theory

Sensory adaptation

Physiological nystagmus

Pre- vs. post-attentive processing

Pre-attentive

Post-attentive

Senses Worksheet Exercise: Answer Key

SENSE	STIMULUS	ORGAN	RECEPTOR	SENSATION
Sight				
Hearing				
Skin sensations				
Smell				
Taste				
Vestibular Sense				
Kinesthesis				

Senses Worksheet Exercise: Level 1

SENSE	STIMULUS	ORGAN	RECEPTOR	SENSATION
Sight				
Hearing				
Skin sensations				
Smell				
Taste				
Vestibular Sense				
Kinesthesis				

Senses Worksheet Exercise: Level 2

SENSE	STIMULUS	ORGAN	RECEPTOR	SENSATION
Sight				
Hearing				
Skin sensations				
Smell				
Taste				
Vestibular Sense				
Kinesthesis				

Perception

Gestalt principles

Similarity	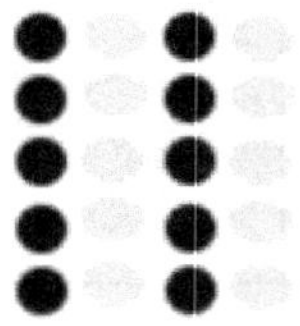
Proximity	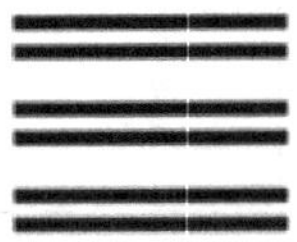
Continuity	
Closure	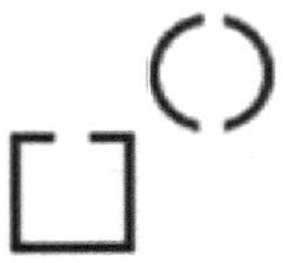

Distance perception

Perception

Perceptual constancy

Shape

Size

Brightness

Factors that affect perception

Feelings

Expectations

Motivations

Effective Reading in the Sciences

Sensory integration refers to the way in which information is inputted and organized within an individual. When sensory integration is functioning well in a sensory system, the body is able to integrate information from various sources, including proprioceptive, visual, auditory, or vestibular sources, in a process called multimodal sensory integration (MSI). However, this system can become dysregulated, leading to problems perceiving sensory information. Some professionals have termed this problem "sensory processing disorder (SPD)." However, there is controversy about whether this disorder represents a distinct disorder or is a symptom of another disorder.

Those who contend that SPD doesn't represent a distinct disorder state that symptoms associated with SPD, including heightened sensitivity to light or loud sounds or feeling highly bothered by the scratchiness of clothing, are often observed in other disorders, such as autism or ADHD. In addition, research into treatments to address SPD, primarily intended to integrate sensory processing, has been inconclusive.

Those who believe that SPD is a distinct disorder point out that SPD, while co-morbid with other disorders, exists in isolation of other disorders. They contend that there are characteristic behaviors observed in those with the disorder and that there are even sub-classifications within the disorder. The recognition of SPD is important because it contributes to the development of long-term social and intellectual difficulties. To further define SPD, researchers have studied neurological patterns among those individuals with SPD and those without it. Because MSI involves a number of activities, a number of brain areas are implicated in processing sensory information.

White matter areas of the brain have been suspected of having a role in disordered sensory processing. To investigate the relationship, researchers assessed the axonal diameter (axonal diameter) of children who had been diagnosed with SPD (SPD) and those who hadn't (non-SPD). Furthermore, to investigate the relationship between SPD severity and white matter properties, researchers correlated the axonal diameter of each participant with his multisensory processing score, a representation of multisensory processing difficulties (higher scores meant greater sensory processing difficulties). The results are presented in the following graph. The R^2 p-value for the SPD group was 0.56 and for the non-SPD group was 0.02. Assume a 0.05 level of significance.

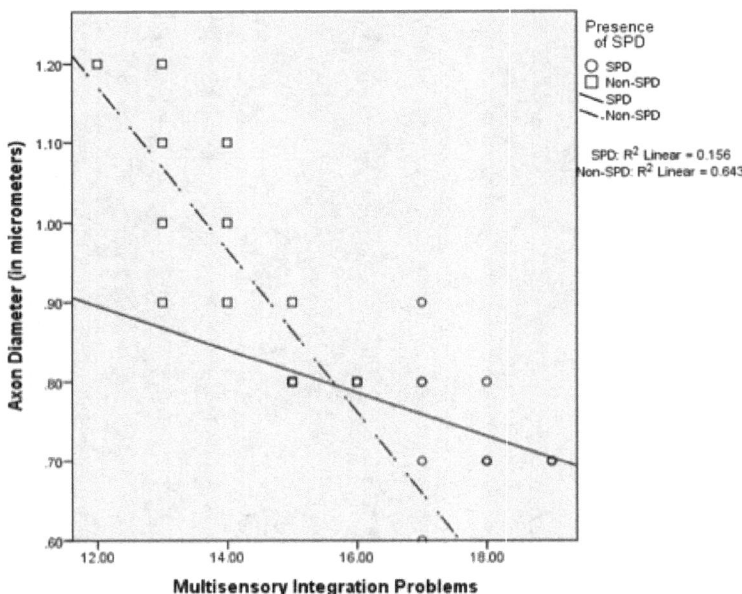

Figure 1 Correlation between axon diameter and MSI problems by presence or absence of SPD

6. Which of the following results from the study support the assertion that SPD is not a unique disorder?

    I. Increased MSI problems were associated with increased axonal diameter.
    II. Average axon diameter was different between the SPD and non-SPD group.
    III. The correlation between MSI problems and axon diameter within the SPD group was non-significant.

    A. I only
    B. II only
    C. III only
    D. II and III only

7. Which of the following strategies would NOT be helpful to determine whether or not SPD is a distinct disorder?

    A. Incorporating children with autism and ADHD into the study
    B. Using a longitudinal study design to compare white matter characteristics of children before they develop SPD and after they develop SPD
    C. Examining the overall correlation between MSI Problems and axon diameter
    D. Testing the predictive validity of criteria to diagnose SPD within children

8. Which of the following findings, if true, would support the assertion that SPD is a distinct disorder?

    A. Different average axonal diameters between SPD and non-SPD groups
    B. A 2 sample t-test comparing the average number of MSI problems between SPD and non-SPD groups returning a p-value of 0.16
    C. Similar constellations of MSI problems in those with SPD compared with those without
    D. Equal axonal diameters in both SPD and non-SPD groups

9. Which of the following is NOT a sensory process that an SPD patient may have difficulty with?

    A. Balance
    B. Feeling changes in temperature
    C. Understanding social cues
    D. Visually perceiving objects

Cognition and language

Influences on development

Genetic influence (motor milestones)

Environmental influence (social milestones)

Piaget's theory of cognitive development

	Age Range	Developmental Milestone
Stage 1		
Stage 2		
Stage 3		
Stage 4		

Intelligence

1. Learn
2. Recognize problems
3. Solve problems

Heredity vs. environment

School attendance and IQ

Breastfeeding and IQ

Adopted vs. biological children and IQ

Fraternal vs. identical twin IQ

Galton's evolutionary theory

Simon-Binet test

Mental age vs. chronological age

Prejudices and bias

MCAT thinking exercise

Is intelligence a single ability, or does it involve an assortment of multiple skills and abilities?

Are intelligence tests biased? If so, what are common sources of this bias?

Types of Intelligence

Gardner theory

Logical-mathematical

Interpersonal

Linguistic

Spatial

Existential

Kinesthetic

Intrapersonal

Triarchic theory

Analytical

Creative

Practical

Strategy

Turning Abstract into Concrete

Vocabulary

Concepts

Significance of concept

Move back and forth between the above while studying

Content vs. practice

Test-maker logic on the exam

Objective vs. subjective questions

Study strategy

Active study

Reading/notes

Videos/notes

Specific or personal examples of a concept in action

Test yourself!

Repetition of ALL OF THE ABOVE

Timed MCAT Practice Passage

Mastery of the MCAT sciences is a two-part process. First you must study to understand (not just memorize!) the science content, and then you must study the content actively and challenge yourself within the context of the exam.

1. Complete your reading of the passage (3-4 minutes).
   - Write down what you believe to be the primary science content underlying the passage.
   - What facts or concepts do you anticipate to be tested? When you are done with the questions determine if you were correct. What passage clues were there to imply related topics that showed up in the questions?
   - Were there any key terms or important scientific relationships you missed?
   - Were you able to draw any conclusions from the data, if presented?

2. Complete the practice questions on your own (4-5 minutes)
   - Rephrase each question in your own mind after reading it to clarify the task.
   - Research the relevant area(s) of the passage or your own knowledge for information related to the task.
   - Respond to the question by choosing the answer that fits your research/calculations *and* satisfies the task.
   - If no answer seems obvious, eliminate answers that fail to have support in the passage or in the relevant science.

3. Analyze your wrong answer choices to the questions you missed.
   - Did you understand the task in the question?
   - What skill type was the question?
   - Did you know the science/formula/concept needed to answer the question?
   - Did you recognize the science being hinted at?
   - Were you able to find information in the passage quickly when you needed it?
   - Were there any necessary scientific concepts you failed to apply to the question?
     - If so, why?
   - If you made a mistake in calculations, have you identified your mistake?

This page left intentionally blank.

Multitasking is often seen to be an efficient way of managing time, but what is involved in multitasking? First of all, multitasking could involve simultaneous attention towards more than two tasks or it could involve switching, or successive attention, between two tasks. There is a cost involved with multitasking that leads to slower or worse performance on a task than if focused on that task alone. It is of interest to know at what level multitasking impacts performance. For example, the act of memorizing information requires several steps including encoding and retrieval of information, among other steps.

Researchers sought to evaluate the impact divided attention had on these processes. Participants were shown information they were to memorize and then recall. Participants were first placed in the encoding multitasking condition. In this condition, half of the participants were shown two pieces of information simultaneously which they were asked to memorize (simultaneous encoding). The other half were shown one piece of information first and then the other information second (control encoding). Participants were then tested on their recall of this information. Then participants participated in the retrieval multitasking condition. In this condition, participants were all shown the information in the same way. Then half of the participants were asked to recall half of the information simultaneously with the other half (simultaneous recall). The other participants were asked to recall half of the information and then recall the other half (control recall). The average number of pieces of information that were recalled are presented in the following graph.

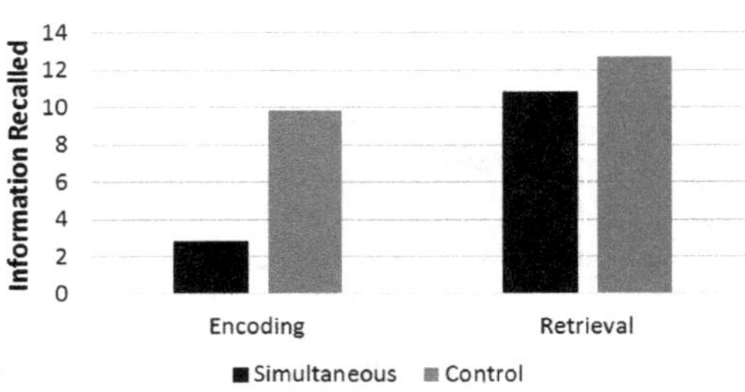

Figure 1 Amount of information recalled by participants in simultaneous and control conditions when encoding and recalling

¶1

¶2

Figure 1

10. In what process does multitasking most negatively impact information recall?

    A. Encoding
    B. Retrieval
    C. Both encoding and retrieval equally
    D. Multitasking does not impact recall

11. What other stage of memory could be impacted by multitasking?

    A. Storage
    B. Consolidation
    C. Mentalization
    D. Discrimination

12. Which of the following would likely get a person's attention?

    I. Hearing one's name in another conversation
    II. Hearing the loudness of the television after it has slowly been turned up over time
    III. A threatening face in a crowd

    A. I only
    B. III only
    C. I and III only
    D. I, II, and III

13. The results of the study suggest what about driving while talking on a phone?

    A. It does not impact attention as long as it is a hands-free phone
    B. It will impact a person who is traveling along an unfamiliar route
    C. It will impact a person who is traveling along a familiar route
    D. It will impact a person's ability to drive

Emotion and stress

Emotion

Thought

Physiology

Behavior

James-Lange theory

Cannon-Bard theory

Schachter-Singer theory

Biology of emotion

Lazarus theory

Facial feedback theory

Limbic system

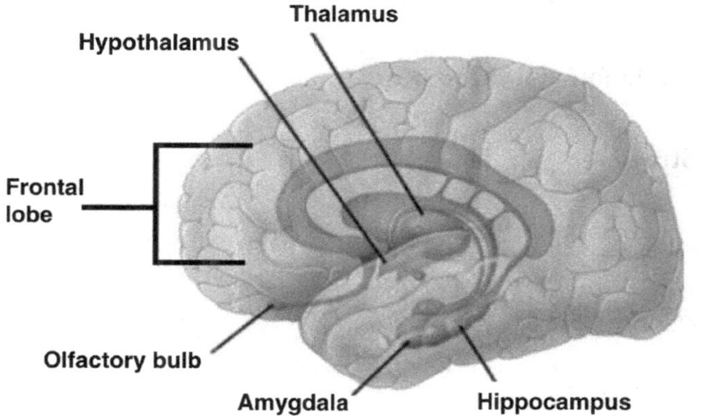

Hypothalamus

Hippocampus—what's "on your mind"

Amygdala (emotional value)

Cingulate gyrus (olfaction)

Basal ganglia (reward)

Prefrontal cortex

Autonomic nervous system (hormonal regulation of mood, emotion)

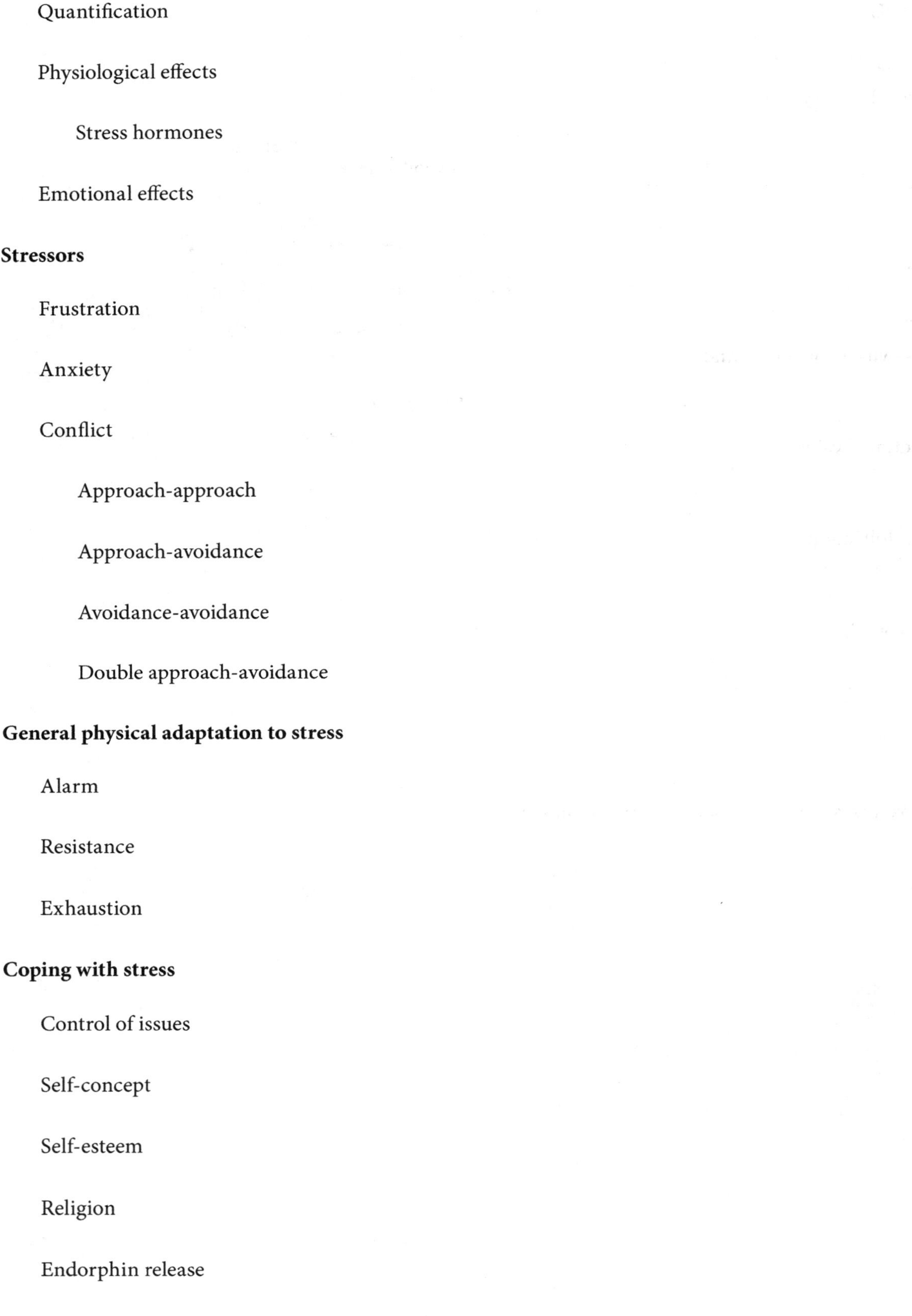

Stress

Quantification

Physiological effects

Stress hormones

Emotional effects

Stressors

Frustration

Anxiety

Conflict

Approach-approach

Approach-avoidance

Avoidance-avoidance

Double approach-avoidance

General physical adaptation to stress

Alarm

Resistance

Exhaustion

Coping with stress

Control of issues

Self-concept

Self-esteem

Religion

Endorphin release

Learning and Memory

Sensory memory

Short-term memory

Phase 1—transfer to consciousness

Phase 2—working memory

What happens when short term memory is full and another bit of information enters?

Long-term memory

Declarative

Semantic

Episodic

Non-declarative

When the MCAT arrives, your test strategies and passage skills should be in your ___________________.

How we remember short-term

Primacy effect

Recency effect

Distinctiveness

Frequency effect

Associations

Reconstruction

How we remember long-term

Significance and strength

Vision

Hearing

Repetition

Dynamic or static?

What are some possible mechanisms by which we forget?

Problem-solving Cooldown

14. When a physician arrives at home to do some notes, she realizes she left her patient list at the office. According to the recency effect, the patients she will most likely recall are:

    A. the patients she has met most frequently.
    B. in the final 1/3 of the list.
    C. the patients she has treated the longest.
    D. in the first 1/3 of the list.

15. Which of the following should be measured by researchers in order to evaluate long-term memory retrieval?

    I. Memory recall
    II. Memory recognition
    III. Memory relearning

    A. I only
    B. II only
    C. I and II only
    D. I, II, and III

16. All of the following are considered reasons for forgetting EXCEPT:

    A. faulty encoding.
    B. information decay.
    C. motivation.
    D. retention.

17. While in the middle of a rehab session, a veteran experiences a vivid, accurate recollection of the wartime incident in which he lost his legs. This should be recorded in the chart as:

    A. reconstructive memory.
    B. a flashback.
    C. a flashbulb memory.
    D. a hallucination.

18. Neurologists studying Alzheimer's disease and its effect on memory retrieval would be best served by studying:

    A. testosterone.
    B. acetylcholine.
    C. norepinephrine.
    D. glutamate.

Test-like Thinking: CARS Practice Passage

The aesthetic conceptions of Chinese artists have inarguably been deeply influenced by a special philosophy of nature in which the relation of the two principles, female and male, yin and yang, is the source of the universe. When they become detached from this primordial unity, these principles create the forms of the world by every varying degree of combination. Earth corresponds to the female and heaven corresponds to the male. Everything that is formed by the mingling of earth and heaven, of yin and yang, of female and male. While the mountain, enveloped in mists, illustrates the union of these principles, the legacy of such forces revealed in physical objects by no means stops there: whether fantastical or realistic, the animals and plants of Chinese paintings express the same conception.

The dragon, ancestor to all animals bearing feathers or scales, represents the element of water. Expressed as the waters of the earth and the mists of the air, water corresponds to the heavenly principle. The dragon is often seen breaking through the clouds, unveiling for an instant the immensity of the heavenly mystery. The tiger symbolizes the earthly principle, representing fur and hair-laden quadrupeds as distinct from birds and reptiles. The tiger's ferocious form often lurks in the midst of a storm, defying the winds that bend bamboo and uproot trees, challenging the furies of nature that often seem to be hostile to the expression of the universal soul. Bamboo symbolizes wisdom and the pine tree symbolizes will-power and life itself. The flowering plum tree symbolizes a harmonization between the two principles, representing virginal purity.

In this way, Chinese art has developed a system of allusions quite similar to the allegories of Western classics, but also superior in that these allusions never degenerate into frozen symbols. Rather, they keep close to nature, investing paintings with vibrant life. In great Chinese works, human consciousness seems to vanish and make way for the dawning consciousness of infinitude.

Buddhism takes this a step further, not giving any credence at all to the reality of the world. In Buddhism, forms are transitory and the universe is an illusion that eternally flows into an unending future. Outside of the supreme tranquility that is enlightenment, in the six worlds of desire, all things that are susceptible to pain and death pursue their evolution. Souls travel along this closed cycle in diverse forms, from the world of hell to the world of the gods, advancing or retreating in accordance with their behavior and actions in previous existences. A stone, a plant, an insect, and even a god: these are only illusory forms, each one possessing a soul on its way to the supreme tranquility. These objects and plants and animals and gods have the same moral character as man and their goal is the same: seeking tranquility in the vast world of illusion.

In the changes of the universe, Buddhists perceive the primal substance that pervades all creation: this perception breeds an intimacy with things which no other creed possesses. In this way, all creation, from inanimate objects to the most highly evolved beings, is endowed with a sense of kinship that naturally finds tender and stirring expression in the Chinese artist's interpretation of nature.

19. Which of the following best describes why the author chose to introduce Buddhism into the text?

    A. To further contextualize Chinese art, placing it into the religious and spiritual context of Chinese history
    B. To further separate Chinese art from Western art, proving its superiority through spirituality
    C. To further illuminate how Chinese artists so effectively and rousingly depict the natural world in their work
    D. To further illustrate how much influence the six worlds of desire have over human behavior and endeavor

20. Based upon the passage, which of the following statement would the author be most likely to agree with?

    A. Chinese artists have produced the greatest paintings of all time.
    B. Buddhism is the central driving force behind great Chinese art.
    C. Western art often fails to keep close to nature.
    D. Western art is less concerned with nature and more concerned with the human experience.

21. There is a young American artist that wants to immerse himself into the style of Chinese painting explained in this passage. Based upon the passage, which of the following would the author most likely recommend as a place to begin this immersion?

    A. Studying the philosophy of yin and yang
    B. Studying the tenets of Buddhism
    C. Studying the anatomy and physiology of tigers
    D. Studying the tension between Western and Eastern art

22. Based upon the passage, which of the following most closely reflects a balance between yin and yang?

    A. The human mind
    B. The Chinese artist
    C. The plum tree in bloom
    D. Bamboo amidst a storm

23. Suppose a journalist sits down with the author of this passage to discuss Buddhism. The journalist asks, "Why is it that Buddhism is so helpful to Chinese artists?" Which of the following statements might the author answer with?

    A. Buddhism's notion of all souls eventually achieving supreme tranquility informs the harmony of great Chinese paintings.
    B. Buddhism's notion of illusory forms informs the ability of painters to express principles through stock animals and plants.
    C. Buddhism's notion of the six worlds of desire informs the artist's understanding of physical limitations in terms of making art.
    D. Buddhism explains a purpose to life, it explains apparent injustice and inequality around the world, and it provides a code of practice or way of life that leads to true happiness.

To Do After Lesson 8

- ☐ Read Psychology and Sociology Chapters 4, 5, and 6
- ☐ Read Biology Chapters 7 and 8
- ☐ Complete Psychology and Sociology QBank 1: Sensation and Consciousness

LESSON 9

Biology 2

To Do Before Lesson 9

- ☐ Read Psychology and Sociology Chapters 4, 5, and 6
- ☐ Read Biology Chapters 7 and 8
- ☐ Complete Psychology and Sociology QBank 1: Sensation and Consciousness

In Lesson 9

Problem-solving Warm-up
Effective Reading in the Sciences
Nervous System
Deciphering Biological Data
MCAT Practice Passage
Circulatory System
Classical Genetics
Problem-solving Cooldown
Test-like Thinking: CARS Practice Passage

To Do After Lesson 9

- ☐ Read Biochemistry Chapters 7 and 8
- ☐ Read Chemistry and Organic Chemistry Chapters 11 and 12
- ☐ Complete Biology QBank 2: Gene Expression and Classical Genetics

Problem-solving Warm-up

1. A man touches a hot stove. Which of the following accurately describes the direction of the nerve impulse and type of neuron that carries pain information from hand to brain?

   A. Moving distally, in an efferent neuron
   B. Moving proximally, in an efferent neuron
   C. Moving distally, in an afferent neuron
   D. Moving proximally, in an afferent neuron

2. Which of the following is NOT a higher function of the nervous system?

   A. Ventilation
   B. Fear
   C. Memory
   D. Language

3. Which of the following digestive enzymes is secreted by the small intestine?

   A. Lipase
   B. Amylase
   C. Carboxypeptidase
   D. Aminopeptidase

4. Fetal circulation is able to shunt oxygenated blood away from the developing liver to the brain by the function of the:

   A. ductus arteriosus.
   B. ductus venosus.
   C. foramen ovale.
   D. pulmonary shunt.

5. The victim of a car accident is brought into the emergency room with kidney trauma. An ultrasound shows extensive damage to the renal capsule and organ damage. This patient will most likely be able to maintain:

   A. normal blood pH.
   B. normal urine solute concentrations.
   C. normal blood pressure.
   D. normal blood temperature.

This page left intentionally blank.

Effective Reading in the Sciences

Reading science passages on the MCAT means being able to keep track of important (i.e. likely to be tested) information in the passage. You must be able to anticipate, recognize, and understand scientific concepts presented in many different forms.

Heart rate is highly susceptible to changes in hormone levels. Epinephrine, when secreted in response to certain stimuli, dramatically increases heart rate. Myocardium also secretes the hormone atrial natriuretic peptide (ANP). ANP is secreted by atrial myocytes in response to elevated blood pressure, causing compensatory smooth muscle response and corrective sodium changes in the blood. These lead to a reduction in blood volume and thus reduction in systemic blood pressure.

In fetal circulation, there is an opening between the left and right atria known as the foramen ovale that allows a portion of the blood to go directly from the right atrium to the left atrium. The blood that does not enter the left atrium is pumped into the right ventricle before entering the pulmonary artery. Fetal hearts also have a connection between the pulmonary artery and aorta, which allows the blood that does not pass through the foramen ovale to be shunted into systemic circulation. After birth, changes in pulmonary pressure cause these pathways to close. In rare cases, the foramen ovale remains into adulthood and is known as atrial septal defect.

In a physiology lab at a local hospital, a student discovers two action potential recordings collected the prior week that have been lost from a patient file. Attached notes indicate the electrode recordings were taken in two separate muscle tissues in a single healthy patient. In an effort to avoid any errors in treating the patient, the student attempts to match the recordings to the appropriate muscle tissue.

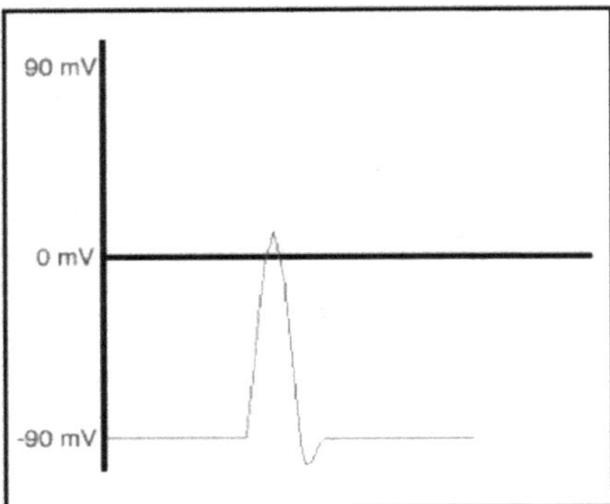

Action Potential Recording A

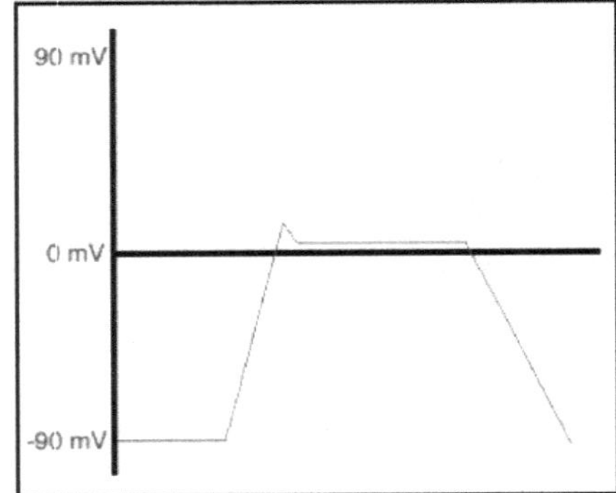

Action Potential Recording B

Figure 1 Recording of unknown muscle tissue

Passage taken from the Next Step online QBank

6. Which of the following represents the path that blood travels from the time it enters the adult heart to the time it enters systemic circulation?

   A. Right Atrium → Mitral Valve → Pulmonary Vein → Left Ventricle → Aorta
   B. Left Atrium → Tricuspid Valve → Pulmonary Artery → Right Atrium → Aorta
   C. Right Atrium → Tricuspid Valve → Pulmonary Artery → Pulmonary Vein → Left Ventricle
   D. Right Ventricle → Mitral Valve → Aorta → Tricuspid Valve → Pulmonary Vein

7. The student concludes Recording A is from cardiac muscle and Recording B is from skeletal muscle. Is he correct?

   A. Yes, cardiac muscle action potentials have no refractory period whereas skeletal muscle action potentials have both an absolute and a relative refractory period.
   B. No, skeletal muscle action potentials have a larger depolarization than cardiac muscle action potentials, so Recording A is actually skeletal muscle and Recording B is cardiac muscle.
   C. Yes, Recording B is likely from a skeletal muscle that is being flexed, which is why there is a depolarized plateau seen in the recording.
   D. No, cardiac muscle has an influx of Ca^{2+} ions that balances out the outflux of K^+ ions leading to a plateau in the action potential, so Recording A is actually skeletal muscle and Record B is cardiac muscle.

8. Which of the following hormone levels would produce effects that would counteract high levels of ANP?

   I. High levels of angiotensin I
   II. Low levels of angiotensinogen
   III. High levels of aldosterone

   A. III only
   B. I and II only
   C. I and III only
   D. I, II, and III

9. An individual born with an atrial septal defect might have which of the following symptoms?

   A. Difficulties regulating body temperature
   B. ANP deficiency
   C. Hyperactivity
   D. Shortness of breath when exercising

10. The mean arterial pressure (MAP) is used to describe the average blood pressure during a single cardiac cycle in a part of the circulatory system. Where in the body is the MAP the highest?

    A. Inferior vena cava
    B. Right ventricle
    C. Aorta
    D. Arterioles

Nervous System

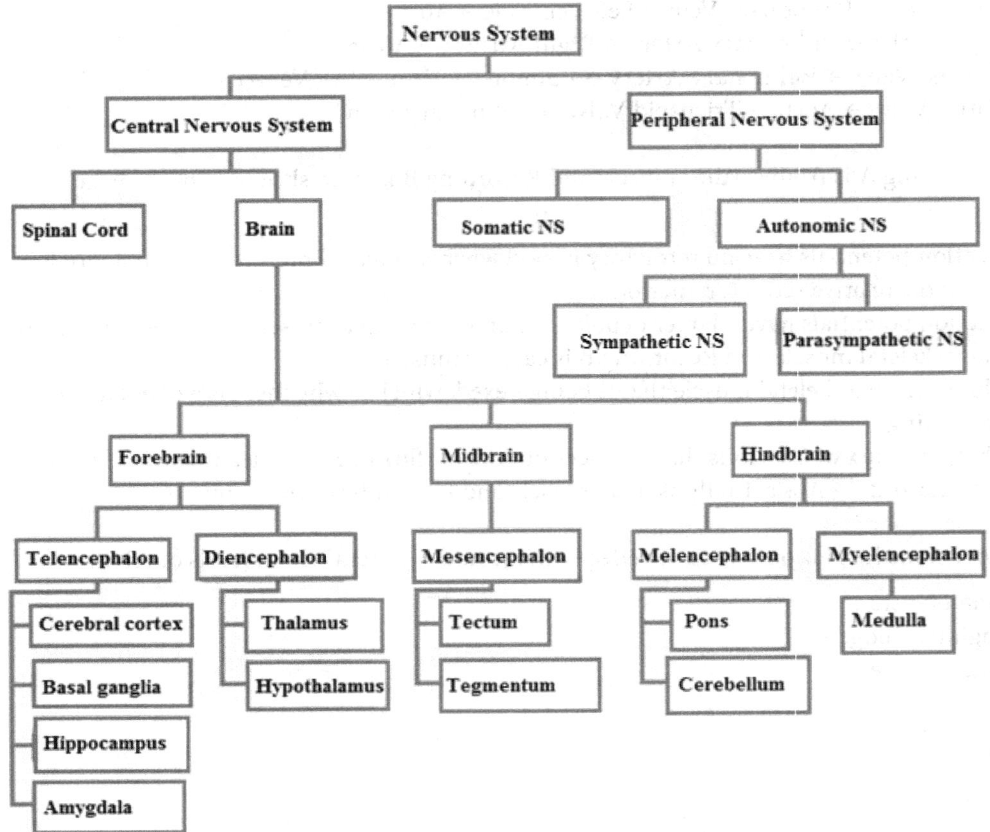

Where on the spine do afferent and efferent nerves synapse?

What are physiological responses that indicate parasympathetic activation? Sympathetic activation?

What is the difference between grey matter and white matter?

How might gyrencephalization assist the cerebral cortex with its primary functions?

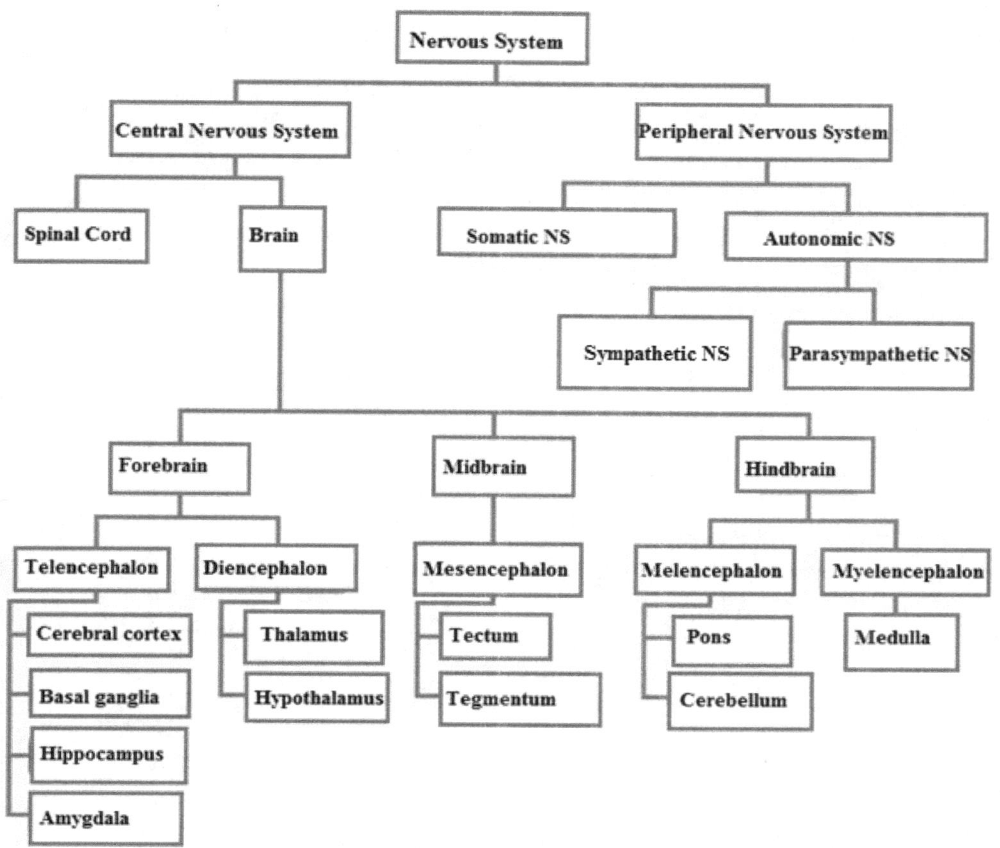

Bridge to Psychology

Which of the regions above are thought to play a role in:

Emotion

Working Memory

Coordinated Body Movement

Hormonal Regulation

Anatomy of a Neuron

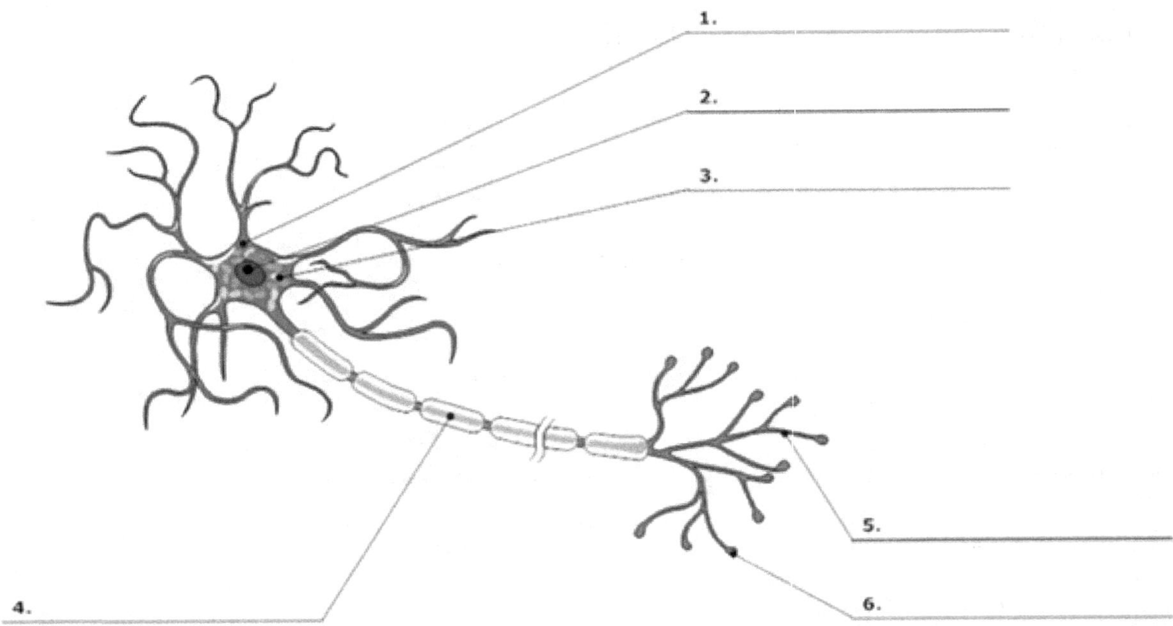

Common Neurotransmitters

Saltatory Conduction

Myelinated vs. Unmyelinated Conduction Velocities

Synaptic Cleft

Action Potential Transmission

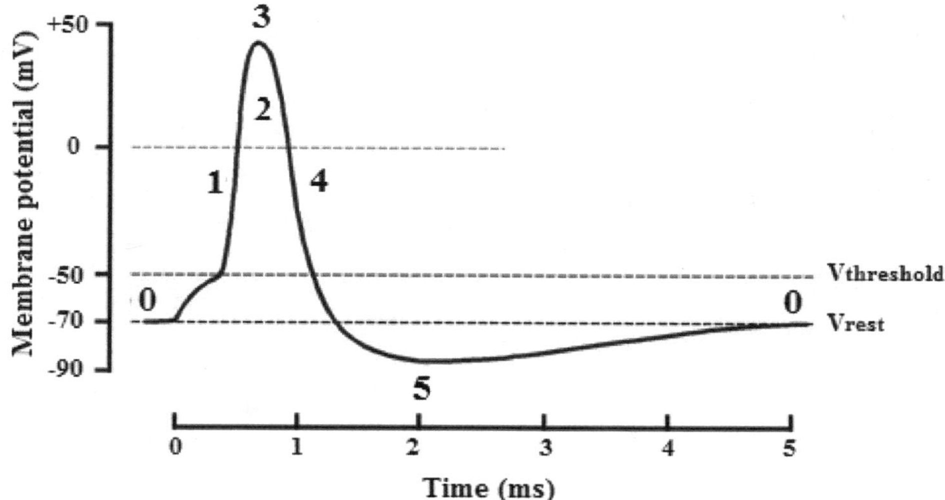

Na/K ATPase Pump and Resting Potential

Threshold

Depolarization (skeletal muscle duration vs. cardiac muscle duration)

Overshoot

Repolarization

Hyperpolarization

Leak Currents

Feedback Loops

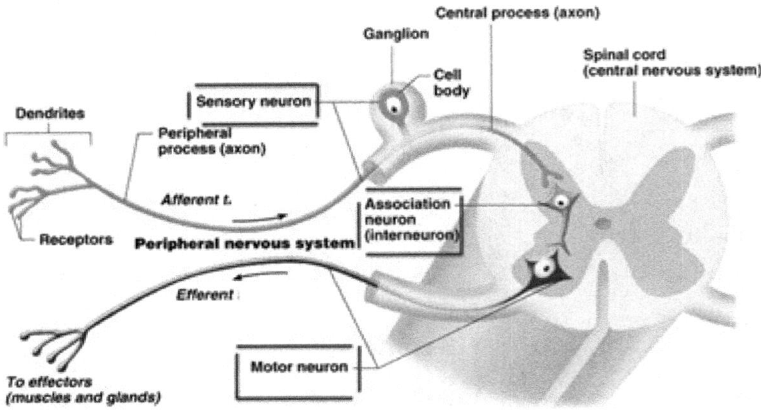

Reflex Arcs

1.

2.

3.

4.

5.

6.

Deciphering Biological Data

Reading science passages on the exam means being able to understand familiar and unfamiliar lab techniques and methods of presenting biological findings.

No matter how unusual or new the data seems, remember this test is first and foremost a standardized exam, so you *will* be able to relate it to science which you already know.

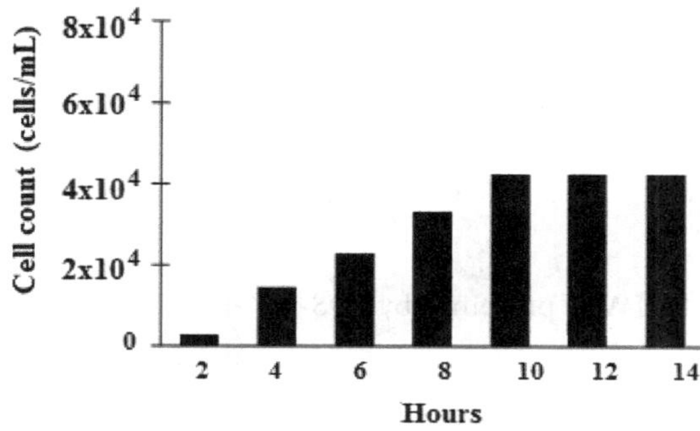

Figure 1 Levels of cellular mitosis in controlled medium

Trends:

Outliers:

Statistics:

Conclusions:

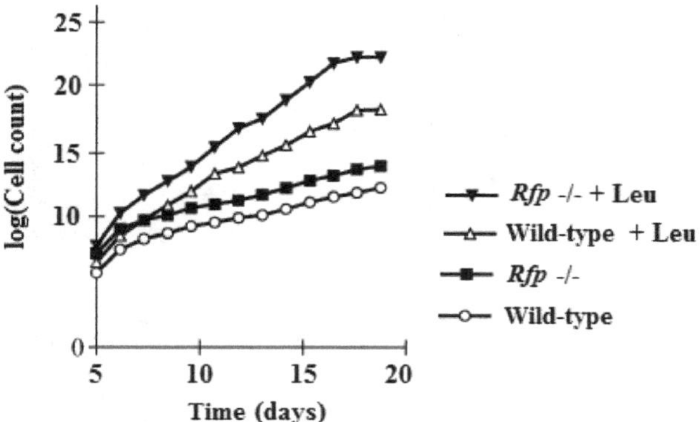

Figure 1 Cell count of wild-type and *Rfp* knockout *Listeria* strains with and without Leu

Trends:

Outliers:

Statistics:

Conclusions:

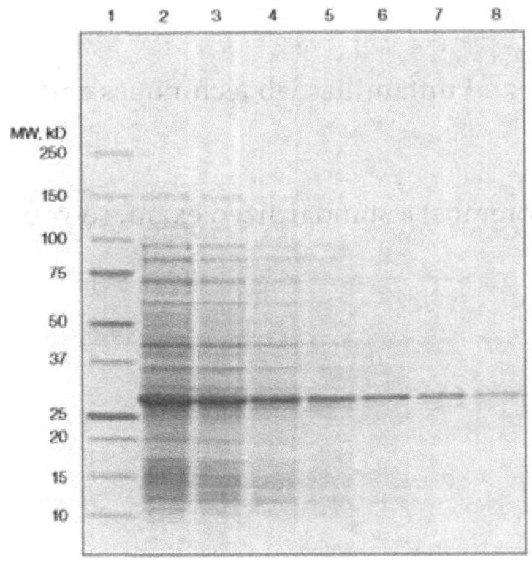

Figure 1 MW determination of protein X

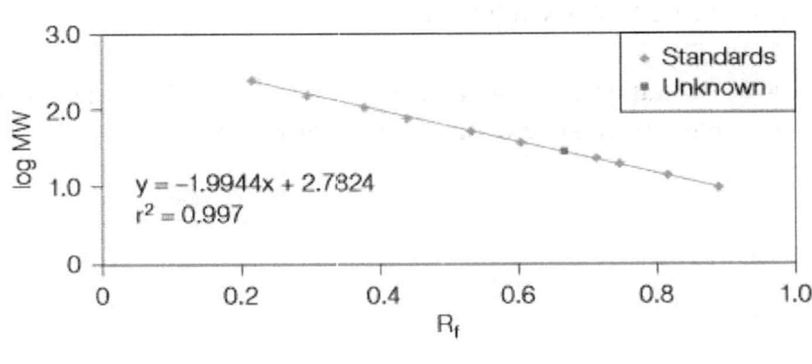

Figure 2 MW of protein X by SDS-PAGE

Trends:

Outliers:

Statistics:

Conclusions:

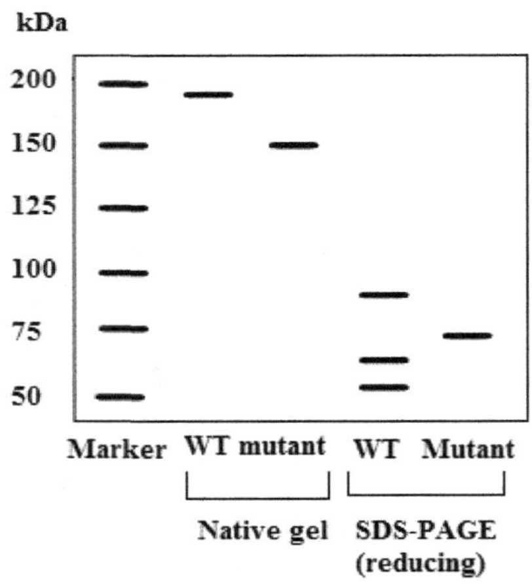

Figure 1 Native gel and SDS gel electrophoresis of protein A

What is the difference between reducing and non-reducing SDS-PAGE?

What can be concluded about the structure of the wild-type/mutant protein?

What can be concluded about the AA composition of the wild-type/mutant protein?

What can be concluded about the oligomeric bonding of the wild-type/mutant protein?

Error Bar Types

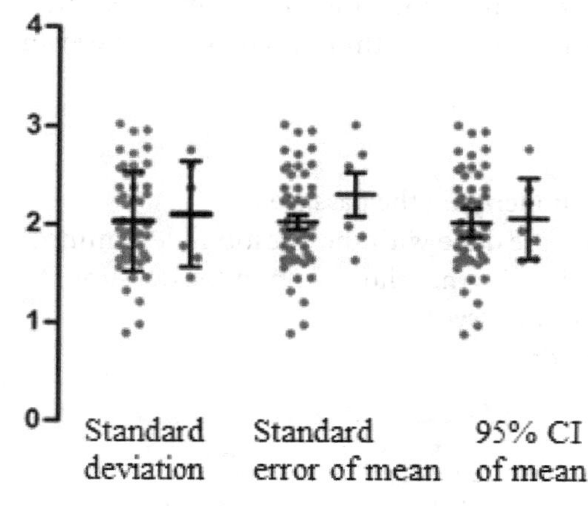

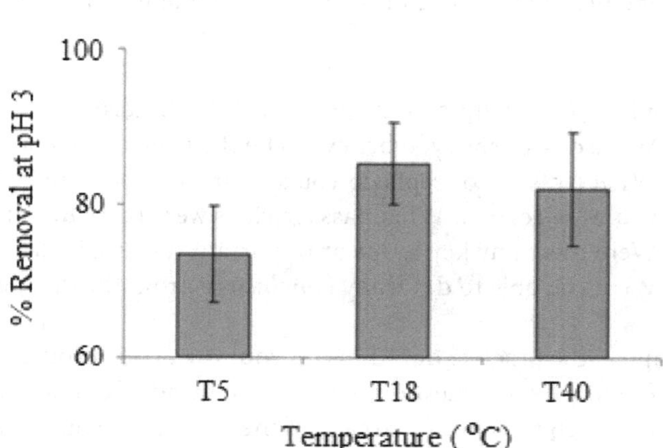

Std. Dev.

SEM

95% Confidence Interval

Error bar type	Overlapping error bars Conclusion	Non-overlapping error bars Conclusions
SD		
SEM		
CI		

Timed MCAT Practice Passage

Mastery of the MCAT sciences is a two-part process. First you must study to understand (not just memorize!) the science content, and then you must study the content actively and challenge yourself within the context of the exam.

1. Complete your reading of the passage (3-4 minutes).
   - Write down what you believe to be the primary science content underlying the passage.
   - What facts or concepts do you anticipate to be tested? When you are done with the questions determine if you were correct. What passage clues were there to imply related topics that showed up in the questions?
   - Were there any key terms or important scientific relationships you missed?
   - Were you able to draw any conclusions from the data, if presented?

2. Complete the practice questions on your own (4-5 minutes)
   - Rephrase each question in your own mind after reading it to clarify the task.
   - Research the relevant area(s) of the passage or your own knowledge for information related to the task.
   - Respond to the question by choosing the answer that fits your research/calculations *and* satisfies the task.
   - If no answer seems obvious, eliminate answers that fail to have support in the passage or in the relevant science.

3. Analyze your wrong answer choices to the questions you missed.
   - Did you understand the task in the question?
   - What skill type was the question?
   - Did you know the science/formula/concept needed to answer the question?
   - Did you recognize the science being hinted at?
   - Were you able to find information in the passage quickly when you needed it?
   - Were there any necessary scientific concepts you failed to apply to the question?
     - If so, why?
   - If you made a mistake in calculations, have you identified your mistake?

This page left intentionally blank.

The human autonomic nervous system (ANS) is comprised of the sympathetic and the parasympathetic nervous system. Transmission in the ANS is mediated by two types of neurons, pre-ganglionic and post-ganglionic. Pre-ganglionic neurons (solid lines in Figure 1) originate from the thoracolumbar region of the vertebrae (T1-L2). These neurons connect with ganglia before they synapse with post-ganglionic neurons (dashed lines Figure 1) whose axons extend to many different target organs in the body. Parasympathetic nerves typically have long pre-ganglionic and short post-ganglionic axons, while sympathetic nerves have short pre-ganglionic and long post-ganglionic axons.

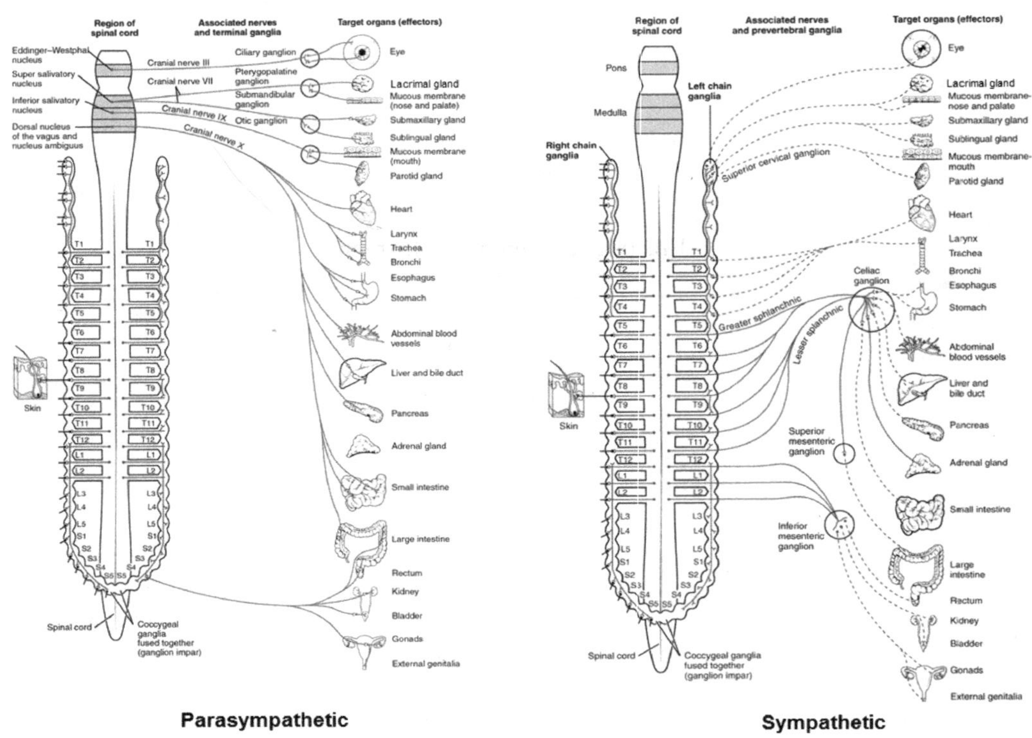

Figure 1 Organization of the Autonomic Nervous System

Two patients participated in a study on the ANS. Baseline measurements are taken on two patients. Patient 1 is then brought into a room and is asked to sit down at a table with a bowl of 5 °C soup placed on it. Patient 1 is told to begin eating the soup. At the same time in a separate room, Patient 2 is provided the same setup with identical instructions, but 3 minutes into eating, a wire is pulled to cause a flap of the table to collapse. This causes the bowl of soup to abruptly drop into the lap of Patient 2, who was observed to jump out of his chair in response. Thirty seconds after the table collapses, both patients are brought into a third room for observation.

Passage taken from the Next Step online QBank

11. If there are equal levels of myelination across types, compared to a parasympathetic nerve, the conduction time in the pre-ganglionic axon of a sympathetic nerve will be:

    A. longer than that of the parasympathetic nerve.
    B. shorter than that of the parasympathetic nerve.
    C. equal to that of the parasympathetic nerve.
    D. There is not enough information to answer this question.

12. The levels of insulin and glucagon are measured in Patient 1 and Patient 2 at the same time point in their meals, shortly after the table collapses on Patient 2. Which of the following statements regarding the hormone levels of the two patients, relative to baseline measurements, is correct?

    A. Patient 1 will have high levels of insulin; Patient 2 will have high levels of glucagon.
    B. Patient 1 will have low levels of insulin; Patient 2 will have low levels of glucagon.
    C. Patient 1 will have high levels of insulin; Patient 2 will have low levels of glucagon.
    D. Patient 1 will have low levels of insulin; Patient 2 will have high levels of glucagon.

13. Parasympathetic nervous system post-ganglionic neurons activate muscarinic receptors on target tissue through which neurotransmitter?

    A. Muscarine
    B. Serotonin
    C. Epinephrine
    D. Acetylcholine

14. It is observed that the pupillary radius in one of the patients is increased compared to baseline when brought into the third room. This was most likely:

    A. Patient 1 because pre-ganglionic cholinergic neurons are activated.
    B. Patient 1 because his sympathetic nervous system is activated.
    C. Patient 2 because pre-ganglionic cholinergic neurons are activated.
    D. Patient 2 because his parasympathetic nervous system is activated.

Circulatory System

The heart serves as a mechanical pump to circulate blood to the tissues and back.

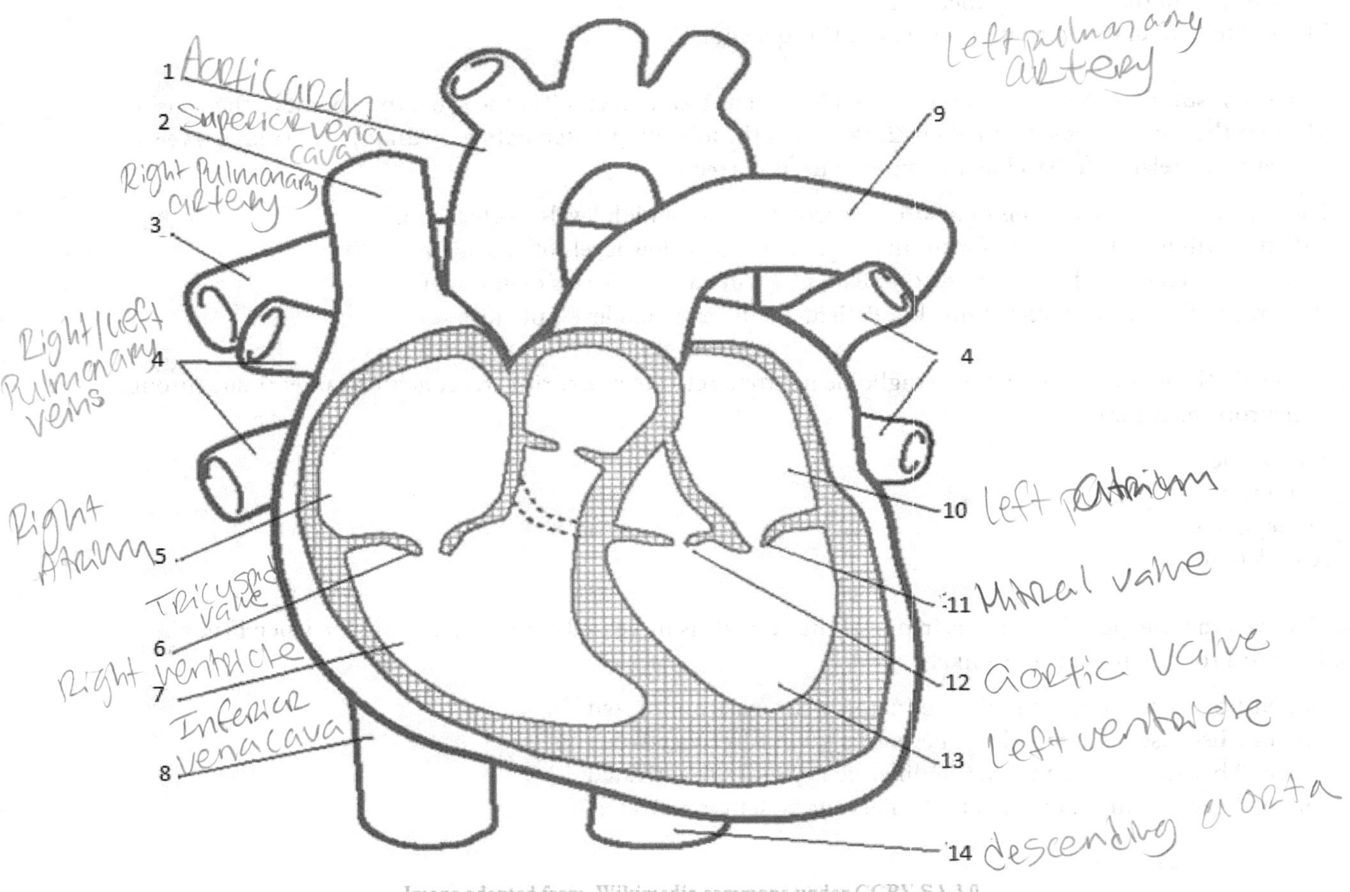

Image adapted from Wikimedia commons under CCBY SA 3.0

What is the path blood takes through the body?

What are the 3 main structural differences in fetal circulation compared with adult circulation?

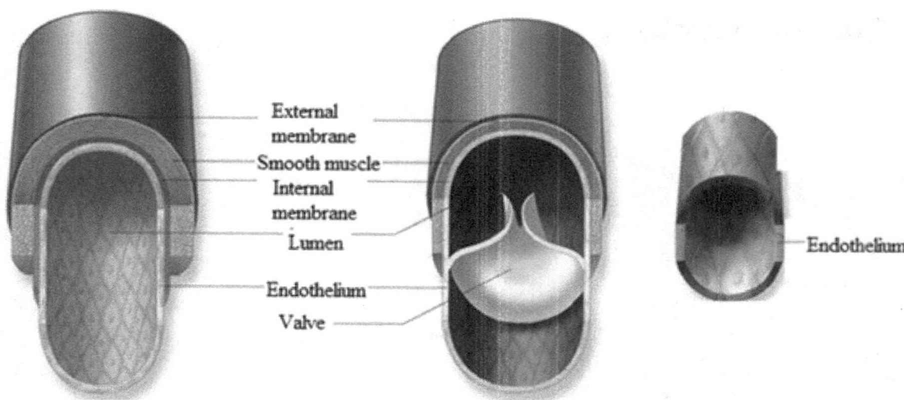

Vessel:	**Vessel:**	**Vessel:**
Purpose:	**Purpose:**	**Purpose:**
Direction:	**Direction:**	**Direction:**
Pressure:	**Pressure:**	**Pressure:**
Velocity:	**Velocity:**	**Velocity:**

Blood Type	Antigens expressed	Antibodies produced	Can donate to	Can receive from
A+				
B-				
AB+				
O-				

Electrical Signal of the Cardiac Cycle

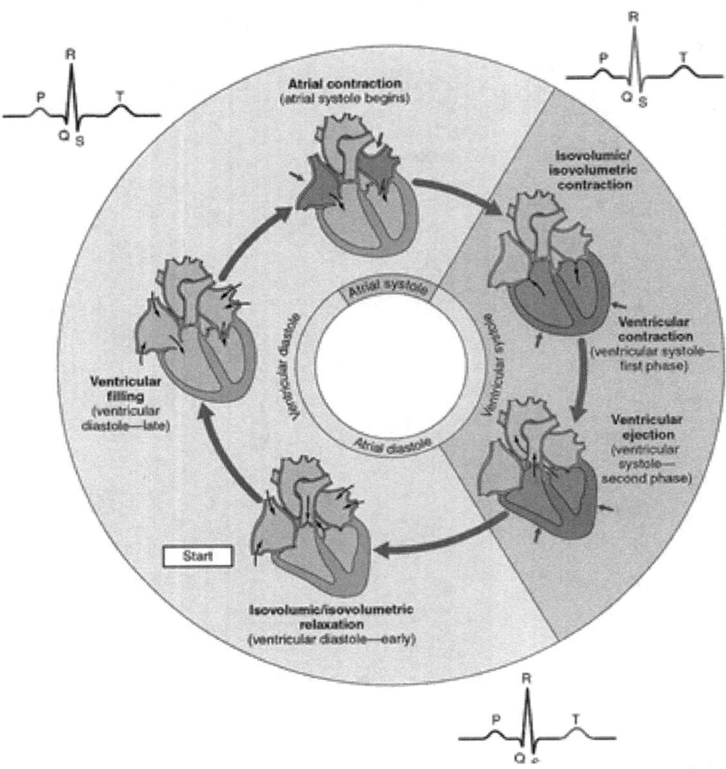

What is the path for the electrical signal of the heart?

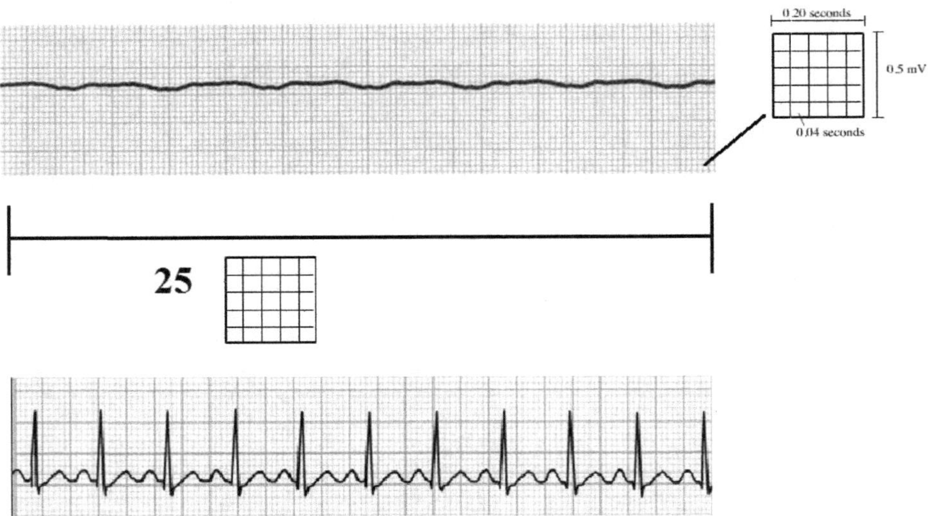

If normal adult heart rate is 60-100 bpm, what heart rates do these ECG strips show?

Hemoglobin and Oxygen Delivery

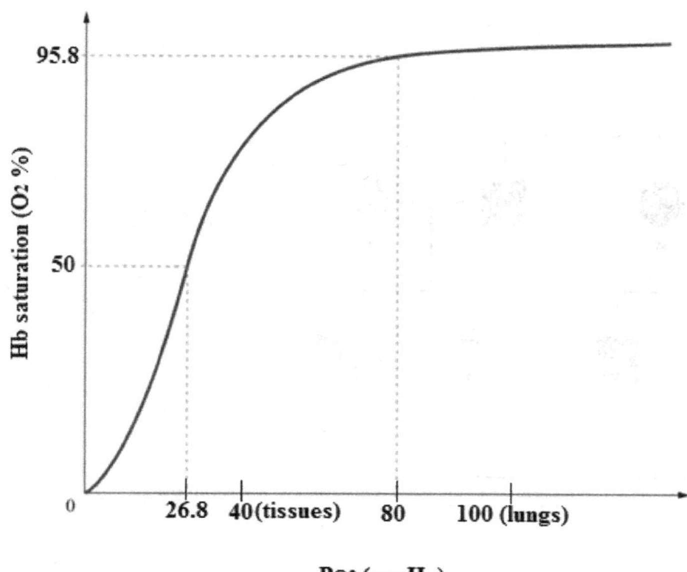

What protein phenomenon explains the shape of the Hb dissociation curve?

Bohr Effect (pH changes)

$$H_2O + CO_2 \longleftrightarrow H_2CO_3 \longleftrightarrow H^+ + HCO_3^-$$

DPG changes

T changes

How would the curve for myoglobin compare to the plot for Hb? Fetal Hb?

Classical Genetics

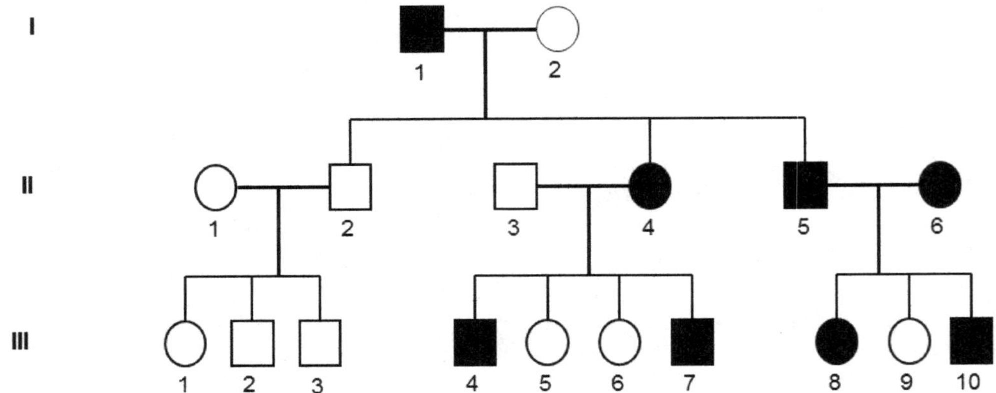

Inheritance Pattern ___________________________________

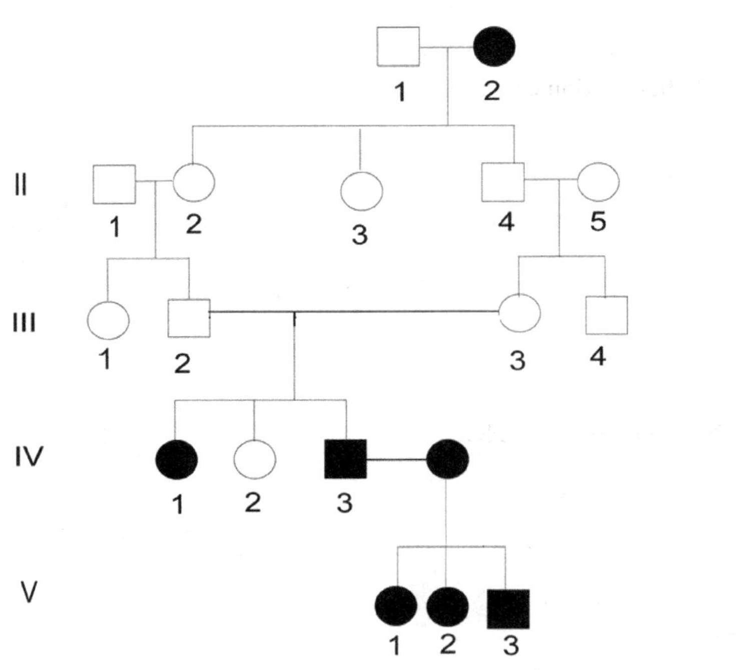

Inheritance Pattern ___________________________________

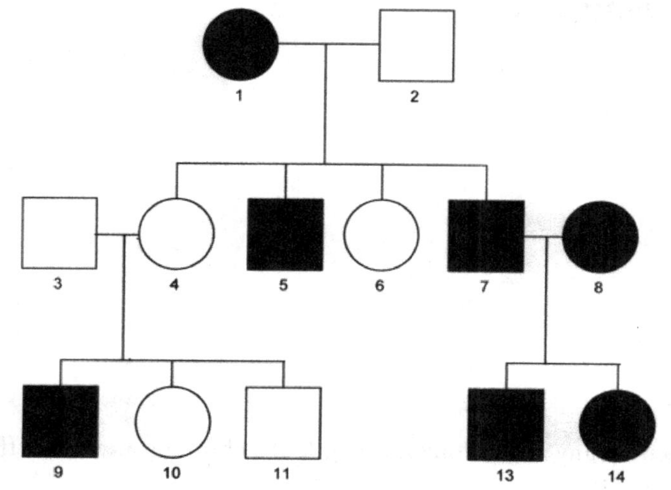

Inheritance Pattern ______________________________

Test cross

Dihybrid cross

Monohybrid cross

Prevalence vs. dominance

Crossover Frequency and Genetic Mapping

Crossover

Genetic mapping

To an approximation, crossovers are *equally* likely to occur at any point along the length of a chromosome. Thus, the probability of a crossover between two genes is proportional to:

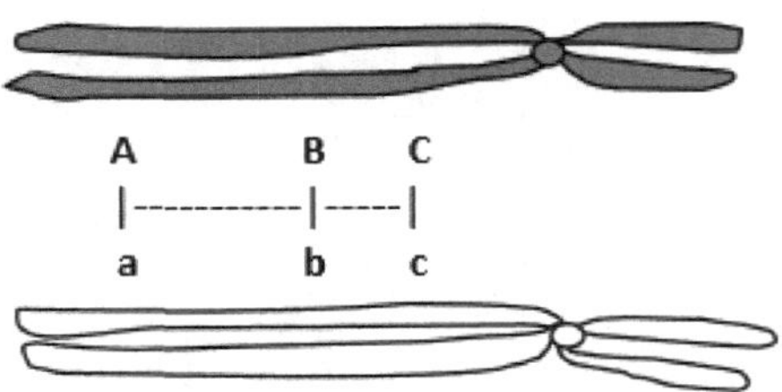

If AB is twice as long as BC, and the probability of a BC crossover = 0.40, what is the probability of a crossover occurring between A and B?

A. 0.20
B. 0.40
C. 0.50
D. 0.80

A wild-type fruit fly (heterozygous for gray body color and normal wings) was mated with a black fly with vestigial wings. The offspring had the following phenotypic distribution:

wild-type, 350
black-normal, 150
black-vestigial, 350
gray-vestigial, 150

What is the recombination frequency between these genes for body color and wing type?

A. 30%
B. 50%
C. 70%
D. 90%

Problem-solving Cooldown

15. The cells that tear down and remodel bone are known as:

    A. osteoblasts.
    B. osteoclasts.
    C. osteocytes.
    D. macrophages.

16. Which bone would contain significant amounts of red bone marrow in an adult?

    A. Humerus
    B. Sternum
    C. Radius
    D. Tibia

17. Which of the following is NOT true about reflexes?

    A. Reflexes involve at least three neurons and all arc through the spinal cord
    B. The knee-jerk reflex is an example of a monosynaptic reflex
    C. Reflexes are automatic, subconscious responses
    D. Some reflexes rely on stretch receptors to sense external stimuli

18. The portion of the brain involved in understanding speech and using words is located in the:

    A. frontal lobe.
    B. occipital lobe.
    C. temporal lobe.
    D. parietal lobe.

19. Which of the following is NOT a chemical class of hormones?

    A. Steroid
    B. Carbohydrate
    C. Glycoprotein
    D. Peptide

Test-like Thinking: CARS Practice Passage

Flint, Michigan has become the unfortunate poster child for unsafe drinking water, but public health advocates have been pointing out for years that heavy metals and other contaminants have been present at unsafe levels in our tap water in many municipalities the US. Despite this, others counter that tap water is generally very safe and is almost always safer than bottled water, collected rainwater, or other alternatives.

Those who fear for the safety of tap water point to the failure of state and federal regulatory agencies to properly assess the contaminant levels in Flint's water. However, critics of bottled water remind us of the fact that the same federal government (albeit in the form of the Food and Drug Administration (FDA) rather than the Environmental Protection Agency (EPA)) is in charge of regulating the safety of bottled water. Furthermore, unlike tap water (which is regulated in every single state at the state and federal levels, and in many municipalities at the municipal level as well), bottled water has no state or local oversight in over 20% of states.

Health concerns over bottled water have been steadily growing since a report in 1999 by the Natural Resources Defense Council (NRDC) which revealed several startling findings. First, over 25% of the samples taken from all major brands were simply tap water in a bottle, with no additional processing or treating. An additional 2.2% of the brands were found to be contaminated with either one or more microorganism species or with one or more chemical above the safe limits established by the EPA for tap water. Based on its findings, the NRDC recommended that individuals should generally use tap instead of bottled water unless testing specific to their home has revealed an issue with their tap water.

Bottled beverage trade groups have offered several strong rebuttals to the NRDC's study, alleging that both the testing methodology and the samples used made for nearly-useless results. The key issue they point out is that the NRDC's analysis of bottled water didn't actually include any simultaneous testing of tap water. The bottled water samples were simply compared against a set of federal guidelines. The trade groups contend that had the NRDC done a simultaneous study including a representative set of tap water samples, they would have noted that tap water was often adulterated at levels similar to or higher than those found in bottled water. Despite these vociferous objections, bottled water advocates have only ever been able to produce a single study of their own—a small analysis carried out in just a matter of days in the late 1980s, done by a private lab working on contract for a bottled water manufacturer.

Both tap water advocates and bottled water trade groups tend to ignore two major issues. First, the environmental concerns associated with making and distributing bottled water are enormous. When one accounts for the energy needed to create the plastic bottle, fill and process it, and ship it to its final point of sale, each liter of bottled water produced consumes over three liters of water. Each liter of such water also creates carbon emissions equivalent to running a diesel generator for nearly a day and a half.

Second and more importantly, the plastic bottle itself is a source of health concern. Research is only just now beginning to reveal the harmful effects of phthalates and other chemicals that leach out of the bottle into the water. These chemicals appear to have a negative effect on the development of boys, both in utero and during puberty.

20. The passage implies that the bottled water critics mentioned in the second paragraph believe which of the following?

    A. The federal government is largely ineffectual when attempting to ensure the safety of its citizens.
    B. In the states in which bottled water is subject to state and local oversight, bottled water is at least as safe as tap water.
    C. Tap water is regulated at the state and municipal levels in every county.
    D. Even in Flint, Michigan the tap water is safer than bottled water.

21. Suppose a customer at a restaurant had a choice of purchasing a soda from the fountain dispenser (using a disposable paper cup) or a bottled soda in a plastic bottle. Which would the author likely recommend?

    A. The fountain dispensed soda
    B. The bottled soda
    C. Neither, as tap water is a better beverage choice
    D. We cannot infer the author's preference.

22. The arguments put forth by bottled water advocates would be most strengthened if each of the following were found true EXCEPT:

    A. An independent investigation of federal agencies found that, among agencies studies, workers at the FDA demonstrated a much higher level of competence and adherence to federal guidelines than those at the EPA.
    B. The private lab that carried out the study discussed was run by and employed a number of very prestigious chemists and public health scientists.
    C. Tap water contamination occurs much more frequently than previously suspected and often goes unnoticed for months or even years due to lax testing schedules at the municipal level.
    D. The federal guidelines used in the NRDC study were only proposed model guidelines that were never implemented because they were deemed much too strict.

23. The author would most likely advocate for which of the following?

    A. Federal subsidies for bottled water for Americans living near or below the poverty line.
    B. Further study of the effects of polymer additive leaching on human health.
    C. Legislation opposing the distribution of products with disastrous environmental impact.
    D. Regulations banning the sale of bottled water.

24. The fourth paragraph implies which of the following?

    A. The research conducted by the NRDC was marked by methodological flaws that make its results useless.
    B. Tests done of tap water at the local, state, and federal levels involve comparing tap water samples to other locally-available bottled water samples.
    C. The author believes that the research done by the NRDC is more credible than the research put forth by bottled water trade groups.
    D. Less than 2.2% of samples taken of tap water sources are infected with microorganisms.

To Do After Lesson 9

- ☐ Read Biochemistry Chapters 7 and 8
- ☐ Read Chemistry and Organic Chemistry Chapters 11 and 12
- ☐ Complete Biology QBank 2: Gene Expression and Classical Genetics

LESSON 10

Chemistry 2

To Do Before Lesson 10

- ☐ Read Biochemistry Chapters 7 and 8
- ☐ Read Chemistry and Organic Chemistry Chapters 11 and 12
- ☐ Complete Biology QBank 2: Gene Expression and Classical Genetics

In Lesson 10

Problem-solving Warm-up
Kinetics and Equilibrium
Effective Reading in the Sciences
Solubility
MCAT Practice Passage
Thermochemistry
MCAT Practice Passage
Problem-solving Cooldown
Test-like Thinking: CARS Practice Passage

To Do After Lesson 10

- ☐ Read General Chemistry and Organic Chemistry Chapter 8
- ☐ Read Psychology and Sociology Chapters 7 and 8
- ☐ Read Biology Chapters 9 and 10
- ☐ Complete Chemistry QBank 1: Atoms and Reactions

Problem-solving Warm-up

1. Assuming total dissociation, which of the following will have the lowest pH?

   A. 2 M HCl
   B. 2 N H_2CO_3
   C. 2 M H_2SO_4
   D. 3 N H_3PO_4

2. If the K_{sp} of CaO is equal to 4.9×10^{-13}, at what [Ca^{2+}] would we expect precipitate to form?

   A. 7×10^{-7} M
   B. 4.9×10^{-6} M
   C. 7×10^{-5} M
   D. 4.9×10^{-4} M

3. In the presence of a common ion which of the following must happen?

   A. K_{sp} will increase
   B. K_{sp} will decrease
   C. Molar solubility will increase
   D. Molar solubility will decrease

4. Which of the following is NOT expected to be soluble in water?

   A. $CaSO_4$
   B. K_2SO_4
   C. Na_2SO_4
   D. $MgSO_4$

5. Based upon the values given in the table below, which of the following species is the strongest base?

Formula	pK_a
NH_3	8.34
CH_3NH_2	9.65
$(CH_3)_2NH$	11.54
$(CH_3)_3N$	11.17

A. NH_3
B. CH_3NH_2
C. $(CH_3)_2NH$
D. $(CH_3)_3N$

Kinetics and Equilibrium

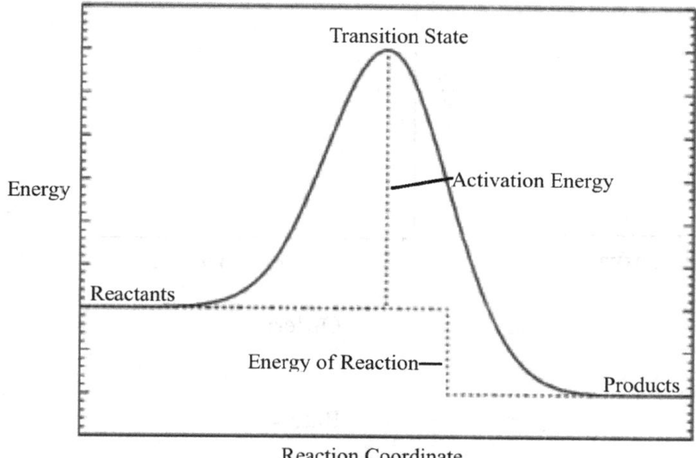

Activation Energy—

Energy of Reaction—

Kinetics vs. Thermodynamics

Rate =

Rate Law—

$$\text{Rate} = k[X]^n$$

Rate-Determining Step—

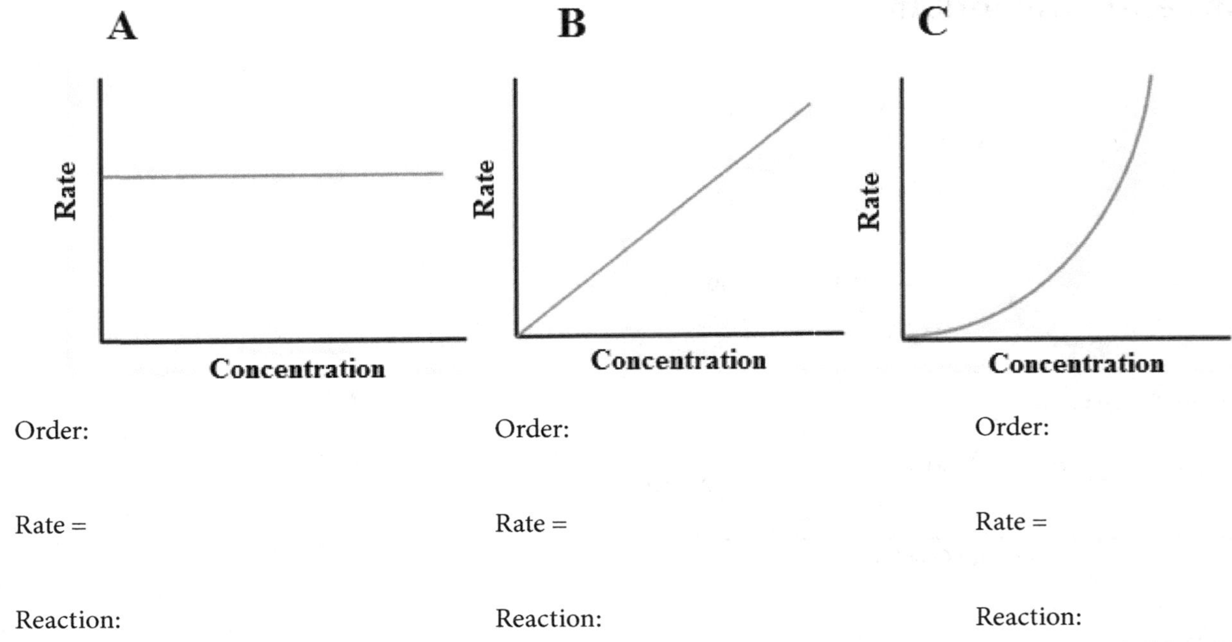

Order:	Order:	Order:
Rate =	Rate =	Rate =
Reaction:	Reaction:	Reaction:

What are the units of the y-axis in order to obtain a linear graph of [concentration] vs time?

Trial	[A]	[B]	[C]	Rate (M/s)
1	0.35	0.35	0.6	1.72×10^{-6}
2	1.05	0.7	0.6	3.01×10^{-5}
3	0.71	0.7	1.2	1.36×10^{-5}
4	1.05	0.35	0.6	1.54×10^{-5}

This reaction, if elementary would be designated ________________________________.

Factors that Affect Reaction Rates

Catalyst—

Concentration—

Temperature—

Pressure—

Light—

Fill in the figure below:

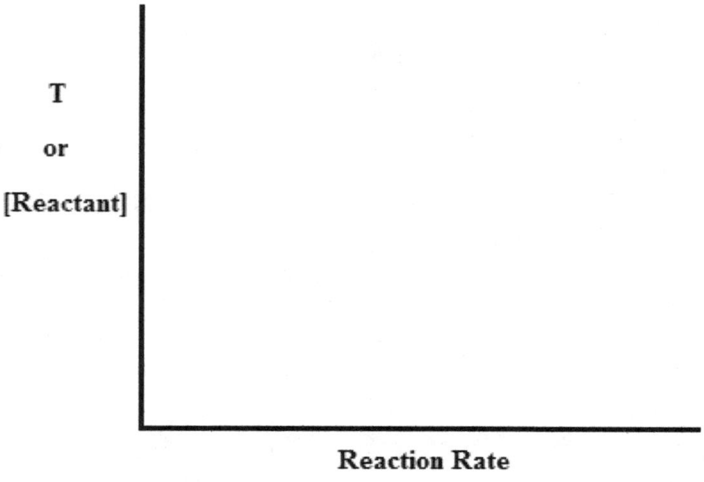

T

or

[Reactant]

Reaction Rate

Mechanism 1

$NO + NO \longleftrightarrow N_2O_2$

(fast)

$N_2O_2 + O_2 \rightarrow NO_2$

(slow)

6. What is the rate law for mechanism 1 above?

   A. $k[NO]^2[N_2O_2]$
   B. $k[O_2][NO_2]$
   C. $k[NO]^2[O_2]$
   D. $k[N_2O_2][O_2]$

Equilibrium

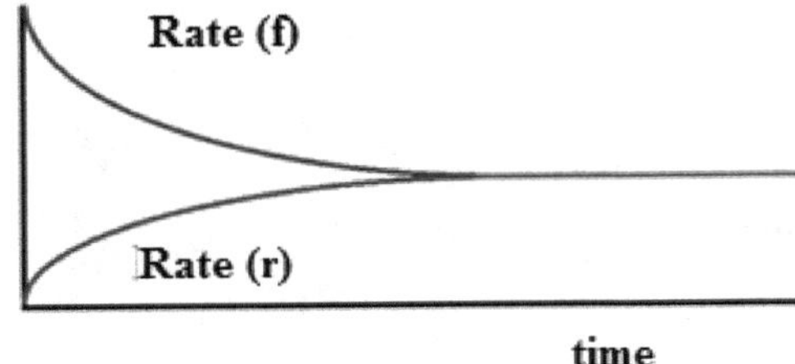

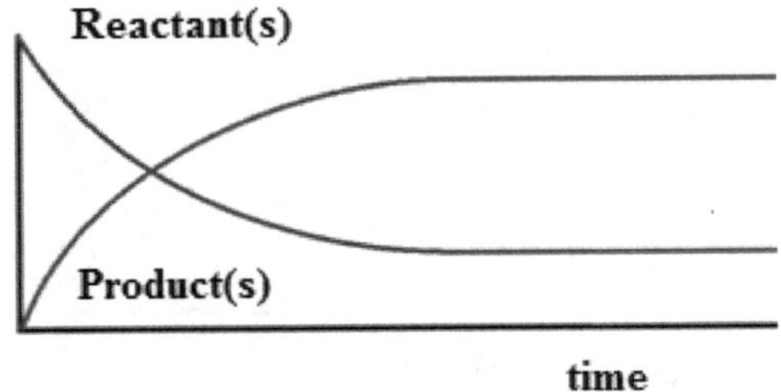

A reaction will be at equilibrium if:

____

is equal to

____

At equilibrium:

Concentrations of products and reactants

The net change of products and reactants

Equilibrium is a ________________________ state.

The Equilibrium Constant (K_{eq})

$$aA + bB \longleftrightarrow cC + dD$$

K_{eq} =

$$CO_2\,(g) + H_20\,(l) \longleftrightarrow H_2CO_3\,(aq)$$

K_{eq} =

________________________ and ________________________ are NOT included in K_{eq} expressions.

Why must this be the case?

Stress Applied to Equilibrium

Le Chatelier's Principle states that if a stress is applied to a system at equilibrium, the position of the equilibrium will shift to minimize the stress.

In the human body, this is known as ______________________________.

Example

$2\ N_2\ (g) + 6\ H_2O\ (l) \longleftrightarrow 4\ NH_3\ (aq) + 3\ O_2\ (g)$ $\Delta H = +\ 41$ kJ/mol

	Equilibrium will:
Increasing $[H_2O(l)]$	
Increasing $[NH_3]$	
Increasing Pressure	
Increasing Temperature	
Addition of a Catalyst	
Decreasing $[O_2]$	

Effective Reading in the Sciences

Hydrofluoric acid (HF) burns are a unique clinical entity. Dilute solutions deeply penetrate before dissociating, thus causing delayed injury and symptoms. Burns may leave the overlying skin intact, and pain may be severe with little surface abnormality. Severe burns occur after exposure of concentrated hydrofluoric acid to 1% or more body surface area (BSA), exposure to hydrofluoric acid of any concentration to 5% or more BSA, or inhalation of hydrofluoric acid fumes from a 60% or stronger solution.

The two mechanisms that cause tissue damage are corrosive burn from the free hydrogen ions and chemical burn from tissue penetration of the fluoride ions. Fluoride ions penetrate and form insoluble salts with calcium and magnesium. Soluble salts also are formed with other cations but dissociate rapidly, and further tissue destruction occurs.

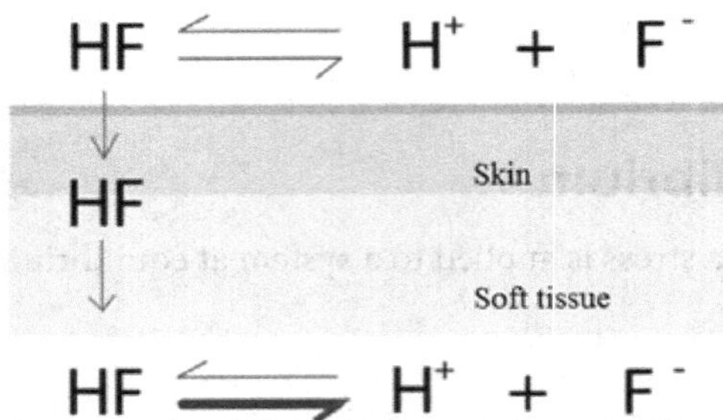

Figure 1 Mechanism of skin penetration and underlying soft tissue destruction by HF

Systemic toxicity occurs secondary to depletion of total body stores of calcium and magnesium, resulting in enzymatic and cellular dysfunction, and ultimately in cell death. The systemic effects are related to electrolyte disturbances such as acidosis, fluorosis and hyperkalemia, which can lead to disturbances of renal, hepatic and fatal cessation of cardiac function. Patient populations at risk for systemic toxicity are any burns with >50% HF concentration, exposure of >5% total BSA with any HF concentration, and inhalation or ingestion of HF.

¶1

¶2

Figure 1

¶3

Adapted from Whitaker, Eckert et al., "Occupational Hydrofluoric Acid Injury—Washington State 2001–2013", CDC 2015

7. According to the passage, which of the following steps best explains the systemic toxicity due to HF exposure?

A. $H_3O^+ + F^- \rightarrow H_3O^+F^-$
B. $MgF_2 \rightarrow Mg^{2+} + 2F^-$
C. $Ca^{2+} + 2F^- \rightarrow CaF_2$
D. $HF + H_2O \rightarrow H_3O^+ + F^-$

8. The figure below shows the approximate surface area proportions of specific body regions.

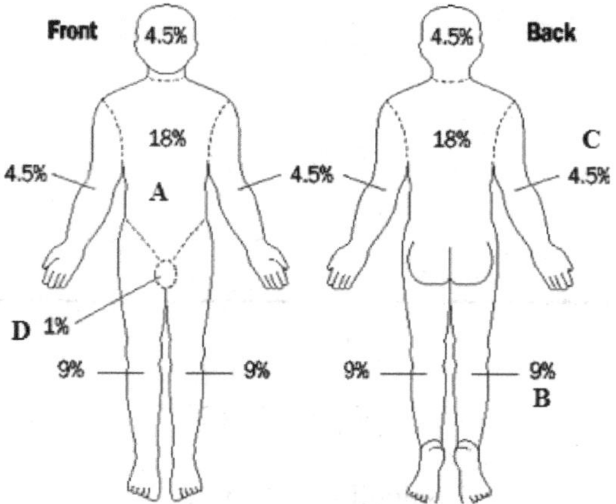

Which HF accident would cause a physician to consider systemic toxicity?

I. Exposure of 5% HF solution to region A
II. Exposure of 15% HF solution to region B
III. Exposure of 25% HF solution to region C
IV. Exposure of 45% HF solution to region D

A. I only
B. I and II only
C. I, II, and III only
D. III and IV only

9. Compared to other hydrogen halide burns, the liquefaction necrosis of deeper tissues with little skin surface destruction is unique to HF burns because the molecule is:

A. highly polar compared to HCl.
B. highly acidic compared to HCl.
C. highly lipophilic compared to HCl.
D. highly protic compared to HCl.

10. Pain out of proportion to physical examination findings is a hallmark finding in HF burns. All of the following could explain this increased pain perception EXCEPT:

A. local hyperkalemia effect secondary to ion binding by fluorine.
B. cell membrane permeability to potassium is increased by local calcium depletion.
C. fluoride ions inhibit adenylate cyclase in myocardial cells.
D. fluoride ions are believed to directly inhibit Na^+/K^+ pumps.

11. The uniquely low acidity of HF among hydrogen halides is often attributed to the high strength of the H-F bond. Yet, spectroscopic analysis shows that HF ionizes almost completely in water. Which of the following best resolves this discrepancy?

A. The hydration enthalpy for the fluoride ion is equal to the strength of the H-F bond.
B. The hydration enthalpy for the fluoride ion is less than the strength of the H-F bond.
C. The endothermic dissociation of HF yields free hydronium ions in solution.
D. Upon dissociation, fluoride ions form weak bonds with hydronium ions in solution.

Solubility

Solute: Solvent:

Molar solubility

$$A_XB_Y\ (s) + H_2O\ (l) \longleftrightarrow xA^{Y+}\ (aq) + yB^{X-}\ (aq)$$
$$K_{sp} = [A^{Y+}]^X[B^{X-}]^Y$$

Solubility Product Constant

$Mg_3\ (PO_4)_2\ (s) + H2O\ (l) \longleftrightarrow 3Mg^{2+}\ (aq) + 2PO_4^{3-}\ (aq)$ $K_{sp} = 1.08 \times 10^{-28}$

$CaF_2\ (s) + H_2O\ (l) \longleftrightarrow Ca^{2+}\ (aq) + 2F^{-}\ (aq)$ Mol. Solubility = 2.1×10^{-4} M

Solving for molar solubility using K_{sp}

Solving for K_{sp} using molar solubility

Strategy

Math Shortcut: Solubility problems on the exam may provide volumes in mL, but most equations require that volume be converted to L. The following relationships can save you valuable time.

grams → moles	concentration → moles
divide mass by molec. weight	*multiply M by volume*

Solution	**K_{sp} vs. Ion Product**
Unsaturated Solution	
Saturated Solution	
Supersaturated Solution	

What is the concentration of magnesium in a saturated solution of $Mg_3(PO_4)_2$? ($K_{sp} = 1.08 \times 10^{-28}$).

Which of the following compound will have the greatest solubility?

KCl ($K_{sp} = 1.8x10^{-12}$)   NaI K_{sp} = ($9.0x10^{-18}$)   CuBr ($K_{sp} = 4.9x10^{-13}$) Ag_2CrO_4 ($K_{sp} = 3.2x10^{-14}$)

Common Ion Effect

Factors Affecting Solubility

Solid in Liquid

Liquid in Liquid

Gas in Gas or Aqueous Solvent

Henry's Law $P_{gas} = C/k$

P_{gas} Partial pressure of the gas
k A constant for a particular gas in a given solvent
C Concentration of the gas dissolved in the solution

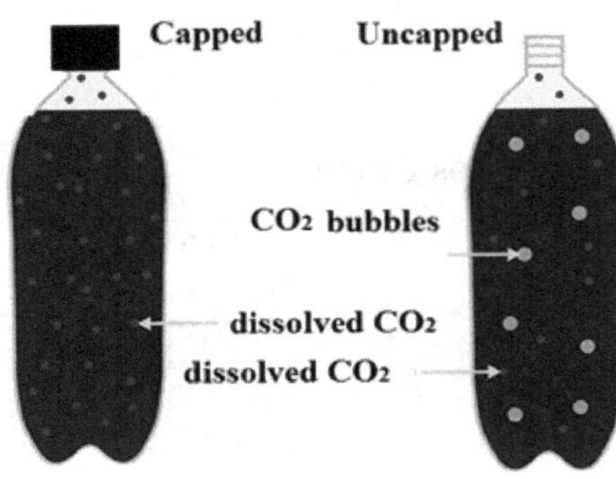

Calculate the $[CO_2]$ in a can of soda with a partial pressure of CO_2 of 10 atm over the liquid at 298 K. (note k CO_2 in water at 298 K = 3.15×10^{-2} mol/L•atm)

Timed MCAT Practice Passage

Mastery of the MCAT sciences is a two-part process. First you must study to understand (not just memorize!) the science content, and then you must study the content actively and challenge yourself within the context of the exam.

1. Complete your reading of the passage (3-4 minutes).
    - Write down what you believe to be the primary science content underlying the passage.
    - What facts or concepts do you anticipate to be tested? When you are done with the questions determine if you were correct. What passage clues were there to imply related topics that showed up in the questions?
    - Were there any key terms or important scientific relationships you missed?
    - Were you able to draw any conclusions from the data, if presented?

2. Complete the practice questions on your own (4-5 minutes)
    - Rephrase each question in your own mind after reading it to clarify the task.
    - Research the relevant area(s) of the passage or your own knowledge for information related to the task.
    - Respond to the question by choosing the answer that fits your research/calculations *and* satisfies the task.
    - If no answer seems obvious, eliminate answers that fail to have support in the passage or in the relevant science.

3. Analyze the questions.
    - Did you understand the task in the question?
    - What skill type was the question?
    - Did you know the science/formula/concept needed to answer the question?
    - Did you recognize the science being hinted at?
    - Were you able to find information in the passage quickly when you needed it?
    - Were there any necessary scientific concepts you failed to apply to the question?
        - If so, why?
    - If you made a mistake in calculations, have you identified your mistake?

Natural gas production is possible though hydraulic fracturing techniques that release trapped natural gas from rock layers that were previously inaccessible. This process involves drilling and subsequent pumping of aqueous fluids into a sedimentary rock layer under high pressure. The gas that is produced is 90% methane, but also contains small amounts of other short-chain hydrocarbons. Natural gas produces much more energy and less carbon dioxide per carbon atom than other fuels. Natural gas also does not contain significant amounts of impurities, like the sulfur in coal that can contribute to air pollution and acid rain.

Production of natural gas releases excess methane into the atmosphere. Methane is a potent biofuel which can also be produced under anaerobic conditions by certain bacteria. Engineered strains of *Ralstonia eutropha* take in carbon dioxide and hydrogen and produce branched alcohols, which can serve as an energy source. Plants can be cultivated to produce cellulose, though the potency of the polymer as fuel is far less than that of those currently used. Table 1 compares the heats of reaction for methane to several other potential organic fuels.

Formula	ΔH (kJ/mol)	Density (25°C, kg/m³)
CH_4 (*g*)	-890	0.71
C_3H_8 (*l*)	-2402	493
C_8H_{18} (*l*)	-5470	703
C_2H_5OH (*l*)	-1370	789
$C_6H_{12}O_6$ (*l*)	-2800	1540
C (*s*) amorphous	-390	1994

Table 1 Standard heats of combustion for carbon fuels

Propane is often used for cooking. It is stored under pressure inside 1 kg tanks tank as a colorless, odorless liquid. As pressure is released, the propane vaporizes and turns into gas that is used in combustion. An odorant, ethyl mercaptan, is added for leak detection.

Figure 1 Ethyl mercapthan

Passage taken from the Next Step online QBank

12. At standard conditions, approximately what mass of propane would be required to raise the temperature of 4 kg of water to just below the boiling point of water?

A. 10 g
B. 23 g
C. 56 g
D. 75 g

13. Which of the fuels given below releases the LEAST amount of energy per CO_2 produced when used as a fuel?

A. CH_4 (*g*)
B. C_2H_5OH (*l*)
C. $C_6H_{12}O_6$ (*s*)
D. C_8H_{18} (*l*)

14. One problem using coal as a fuel is the production of gases that can contribute to acid rain. Which of the following elements found in coal would NOT generate rain-acidifying oxides?

A. Sulfur
B. Calcium
C. Phosphorus
D. Nitrogen

15. Which of the following regions of the infrared spectrum would be most useful in detecting ethyl mercaptan?

A. 1600-1750 cm^{-1}
B. 2500-2600 cm^{-1}
C. 3500-3700 cm^{-1}
D. 3000-3300 cm^{-1}

16. Biofuel research aims for renewable sources that would be carbon neutral, meaning the carbon used to make the fuel comes directly from the atmosphere. Which of the following are potentially C-neutral?

I. Methane produced by human GI flora
II. Alcohols derived from *Ralstonia eutropha*
III. Cellulose derived from plant matter

A. I only
B. I and II only
C. II and III only
D. I, II, and III

Thermochemistry

System A (30 K) ⟺ System B (50 K)

Heat exchange

0th Law

Final T: Final T:

Open:

Closed:

Isolated:

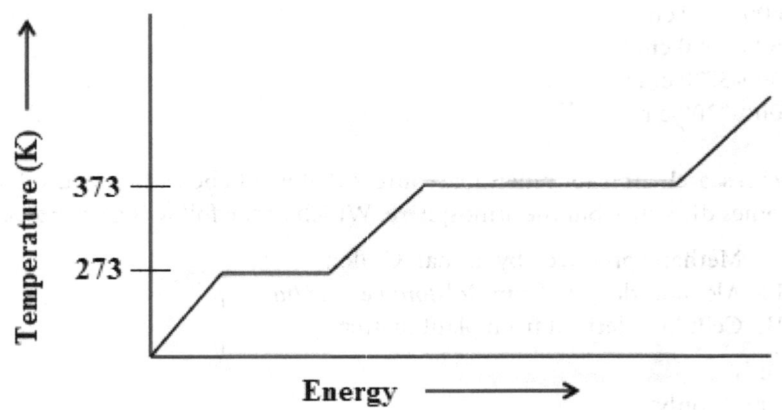

Heat Added to System (Q)

Heat capacity

What is this substance?

Specific heat

$c_{H20} =$

1st Law

$\Delta U = Q - W_{by}$

ΔU is the change in internal energy of a system

Q is the heat exchanged between the system and its surroundings

W_{by} is the work done *by* the system. This equation assumes the convention $W_{by} > 0$.

$W_{by} = -W_{on}$ AND $W_{on} = -W_{by}$

A gas in a system has constant pressure. The surroundings around the system lose 75 J of heat and do 450 J of work on the system. What is the internal energy of the system?

Work Done By a Gas

Expansion

Compression

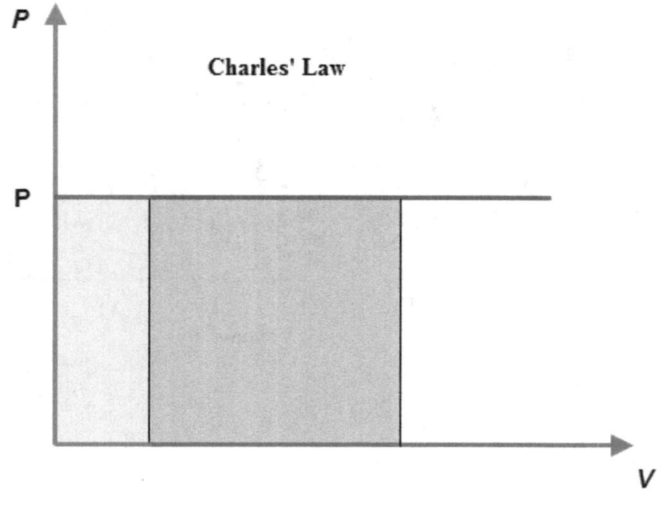

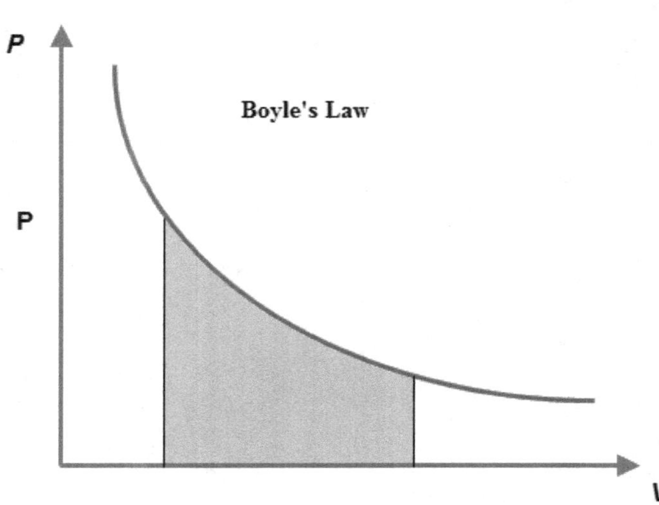

Ideal Gas Processes

<table>
<tr><th colspan="2">Process</th><th>Heat Transfer (Q)</th><th>W_{by} (W= PΔV)</th><th>Revised Equation</th><th>ΔU</th></tr>
<tr><td rowspan="2">Adiabatic</td><td>Compression</td><td></td><td></td><td></td><td></td></tr>
<tr><td>Expansion</td><td></td><td></td><td></td><td></td></tr>
<tr><td>Isovolumetric</td><td></td><td></td><td></td><td></td><td></td></tr>
<tr><td rowspan="2">Isobaric
(V ≈ T)</td><td>Compression</td><td></td><td></td><td></td><td></td></tr>
<tr><td>Expansion</td><td></td><td></td><td></td><td></td></tr>
<tr><td rowspan="2">Isothermal</td><td>Compression</td><td></td><td></td><td></td><td></td></tr>
<tr><td>Expansion</td><td></td><td></td><td></td><td></td></tr>
</table>

1

2

3

4

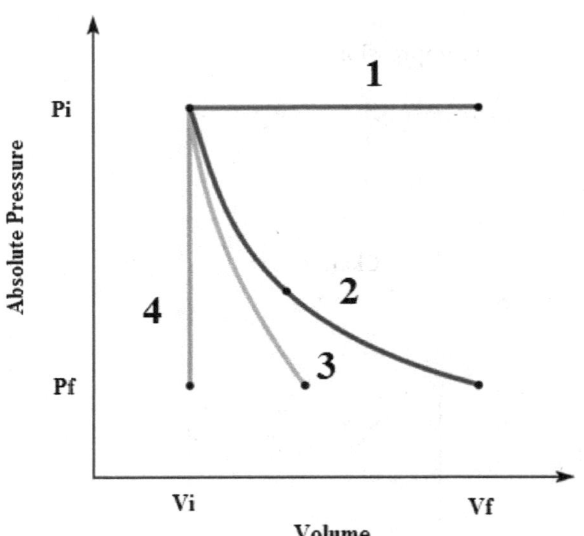

Entropy ΔS (J/K)

Enthalpy ΔH (kJ/mol)

$\Delta H > 0$

$\Delta H = 0$

$\Delta H < 0$

Hess's Law

Gibbs Energy $\Delta G = \Delta H - T\Delta S$ $\Delta G = \Delta G° + RT \ln(K_{eq})$

$\Delta G > 0$

$\Delta G = 0$

$\Delta G < 0$

MCAT Practice Passage

The Carnot cycle can be represented using a pressure-volume graph (see Figure 1). Progressing from point A through point D, a Carnot engine uses a working gas to operate in a Carnot cycle, which operates between temperatures T_h and T_l where $T_h > T_l$.

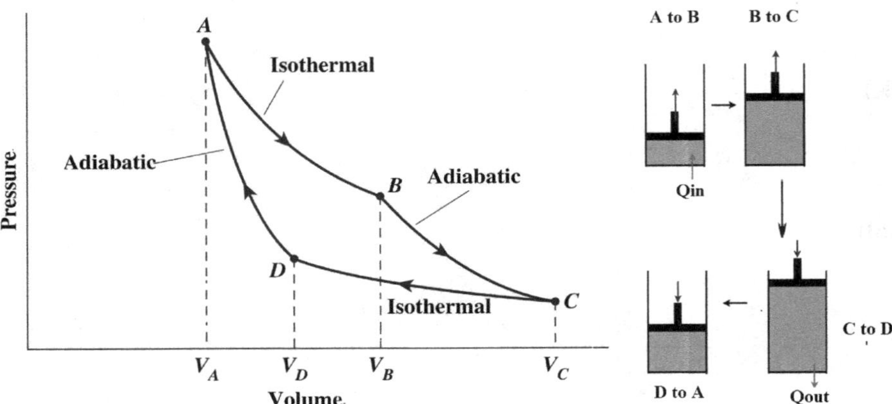

Figure 1 Schematic of Carnot engine cycle

Carnot's theorem states that for a heat engine operating between T_h and T_l to be as efficient as a Carnot engine operating between the same two temperatures, it must operate reversibly. A reversal of the Carnot cycle allows work to be converted to heat exhaust, as observed in the operation of a commercial freezer. In a freezer heat is absorbed from the interior when a specialized liquid coolant passes though and is turned into gas. A compressor in the rear of the freezer returns the gas to the liquid state, and the cycle begins anew.

Engine efficiency (Ɇ) can be expressed as the ratio of the output work to the input heat of a system. Work (ρ) can be found using equation 2, where $T_c = T_l$ is the temperature of the cold sink and T_h is the temperature of the heat source (in Kelvin).

Ɇ $= (T_h - T_c)/T_h \times 100$

Equation 1

$$\rho \leq 1 - T_c/T_h$$

Equation 2

17. What does the efficiency of a Carnot engine describe?

    A. The maximum mechanical work that can be converted to heat.
    B. The maximum heat that can be converted to mechanical work.
    C. The minimum mechanical work that can be converted to heat.
    D. The minimum heat that can be converted to mechanical work.

18. Which of the following would make a heat engine more efficient?

    A. Increase the heat expelled as exhaust.
    B. Increase the friction inside the engine.
    C. Increase the temperature of the cold sink.
    D. Increase the temperature of the heat sink.

19. Which of the following is true of the system when going from Point C to Point D in the cycle?

    A. No heat is exchanged with between the engine and the surroundings.
    B. The volume of the system increases.
    C. The surroundings perform work on the system.
    D. The internal energy of the system increases.

20. Which molecule would make the most effective coolant in a freezer used to store biological materials?

    A. Ammonia, $T_{boil} = 242$ K
    B. Propane, $T_{boil} = 230$ K
    C. n-Butane, $T_{boil} = 273$ K
    D. Water, $T_{boil} = 373$ K

Problem-solving Cooldown

21. Which of the following is NOT a state function?

    A. Displacement
    B. Enthalpy
    C. Work
    D. Entropy

22. A researcher investigating the relationship between air temperature and the growth of thermophilic bacteria will most likely find that growth rates:

    A. on cloudy nights are higher than those on clear nights.
    B. recorded on clear days will be lower than those on cloudy days.
    C. will be random.
    D. will be the same regardless of cloud cover.

23. A research team wishes to investigate the nighttime temperatures on both cloudy nights and clear nights. The data are expected to show:

    A. temperatures recorded on cloudy nights will be higher.
    B. temperatures recorded on clear nights will be higher.
    C. temperatures recorded will be random.
    D. the temperatures recorded will be the same.

24. Match the process to its shortcut in the equation $\Delta U = Q - W_{\text{by system}}$

1. Isothermal	A. $Q = 0$
2. Adiabatic	B. $W_{\text{by system}} = 0$
3. Isobaric	C. $\Delta U = 0$
4. Isochoric	D. $W_{\text{by system}} = P\Delta V$

25. Given the following heat engine, $Q_H = 50$ J, $Q_C = 40$ J. What must be the value of W and the efficiency of the engine?

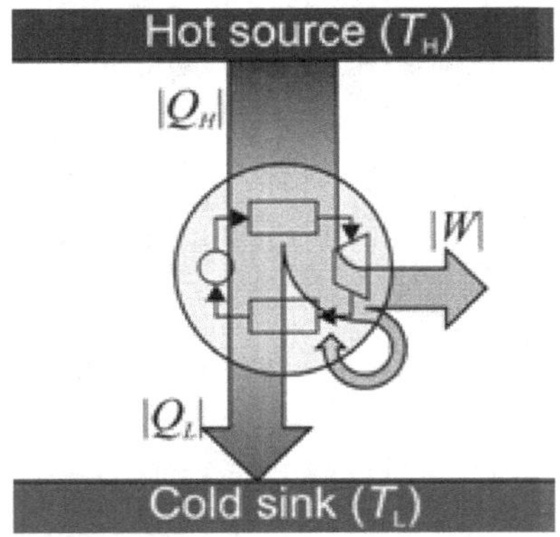

    A. 10 J, 20%
    B. 20 J, 40%
    C. 90 J, 20%
    D. 90 J, 40%

This page left intentionally blank.

Test-Like Thinking: CARS Practice Passage

The "dreamtime" serves not so much as a representation of Australian Aboriginal mythology as it does an example of how the combination of Western academic frameworks and subsequent commercial ambitions can serve less as a lens to see through and more as a screen on which Western notions are projected. The term was coined in the early 1970s as a mistranslation of the Arrernte term *altjira* that was meant to reference the timeless void that precedes creation. It is to this place that great Aboriginal heroes return after their deaths, where the ancestors live, along with other supernatural entities.

Creation itself is thought of as an act, not of an individual omnipotent and omnipresent deity, but rather as a project carried out by a multitude of heroic figures traveling across the formless chaos that preceded creation. These heroes laid down songlines across the land, spanning all of Australia with the songlines giving shape and definition to existence as well as binding it together and preventing existence from flying apart into the void. This Dreaming place where the creators live is also synonymous with several other aspects of aboriginal culture. Individuals believe that before they are born and after they die, their lives are the Dreaming. When a child is born, he or she becomes the caretaker responsible for the part of the Dreaming that is instantiated in his or her life.

The appropriation of the dreamtime as an idea in the popular culture began slowly through the 1960s and 70s, and by the late 1980s became one of the common myths used in some forms of New Age and feminist spirituality. While these movements tended to lean much more heavily on distorted and superficial elements of Hindu religious culture, symbols, and systems (most notably components of the Ayurveda), notions about Native American and Aboriginal purity in the mold of Rousseau's Noble Savage eventually became standard elements in them. In this mold, Western civilization, Christianity, and post-Enlightenment rationality are seen as corrupting influences that degrade humanity's essential goodness. By the early 2000s, references to the dreamtime were showing up not just in obscure academic journals or New Age literature, but in movies, comic books, and even video games.

This incorporation of dreamtime ideas and symbols into Western academic and creative efforts inevitably carried with it a crass commercialization that crept back into Aboriginal culture itself. As early as the late 1970s, Aboriginals began using the term Dreaming to refer not just to their creation myth, but to a system of totemistic design, artwork, and stories representing and connected to the dreamtime, over which an individual can have ownership. One would be hard-pressed to imagine a greater irony than Aboriginal groups adopting Western notions of property—especially intellectual property—as a part of their millennia-old religious views.

Such ownership ideas have carried with them two pernicious elements of Western cultural views towards property: exclusion and legalistic dispute resolution. One of the core Western ideas about property is exclusion; that is, to own a thing is to be able to exclude others from it. A person has a legitimate claim to the use of force when ejecting others from owned land or in the reclaiming of chattels. At the end of the 20th century, Aboriginal tribes began treating it as a crime for one person to tell the Dreaming story that "belongs" to another. Violations of these rules as well as other disputes started being funneled into the formal Australian court system, with its focus on strict rules and abstract forms rather than more traditional content-based processes.

26. A certain Yupik tribe that has legal permission to hunt a species of seal which is otherwise protected by endangered species laws begins altering its hunting style to gather more seal meat to sell to specialized bush meat wholesalers. The author would characterize this behavior as:

    A. analogous to the reaction Australian Aboriginals had towards the Dreaming and dreamtime.
    B. an example of a culture that was able to resist Western influences.
    C. an excellent demonstration of a society's ability to adapt to survive changing times.
    D. an insult to the Dreaming of Seals that would be owned by one or another Yupik tribe.

27. The author refers to the "Noble Savage" in the third paragraph in order to:

    A. prove that Rosseau's ideas about anthropology were incorrect.
    B. provide an example of an idea presented in the first paragraph.
    C. support recent changes to Aboriginal attitudes towards their own religion.
    D. qualify his overall thesis with an exception.

28. The passage implies that, prior to the 1970s, which of the following was most likely true?

    A. Aboriginal children, when born, were not seen as expressions of the Dreaming.
    B. The concept of exclusion had no place in Aboriginal culture or dispute resolution.
    C. The concept of property was not applied to the material culture of Aboriginals.
    D. Aboriginal totemistic art was considered part of the physical, rather than metaphysical world.

29. The author's attitude towards the Australian court system can best be described as:

    A. respectful of its worth in providing formal dispute resolution that avoids violence.
    B. concerned about its ability to properly address claims related to intellectual property.
    C. dismissive of its value in resolving any cases.
    D. disappointment about its overtaking traditional Aboriginal dispute resolution.

30. Each of the following facts are provided as support for the author's main thesis EXCEPT:

    I. Aboriginals adopted Western notions of property, most notably intellectual property, and applied these notions to their own content-based dispute resolution processes.
    II. Aboriginal culture began to be used and referenced in Western frameworks such as feminist spirituality and video games.
    III. Western New Age philosophies use the Melanesian concept of *masalai* to describe the detrimental effect of capitalist greed on the human soul.

    A. II only
    B. III only
    C. I and III only
    D. II and III only

To Do After Lesson 10

- ☐ Read General Chemistry and Organic Chemistry Chapter 8
- ☐ Read Psychology and Sociology Chapters 7 and 8
- ☐ Read Biology Chapters 9 and 10
- ☐ Complete Chemistry QBank 1: Atoms and Reactions

Sociology and Full Length 1 Review

LESSON 11

To Do Before Lesson 11

- [ ] Read General Chemistry and Organic Chemistry Chapter 8
- [ ] Read Psychology and Sociology Chapters 7 and 8
- [ ] Read Biology Chapters 9 and 10
- [ ] Complete Chemistry QBank 1: Atoms and Reactions

In Lesson 11

Full Length 1 Review
Lessons Learned Journal
What Does Your Score Tell You?
Problem-solving Warm-up
Social Interaction
Discrimination
Effective Reading in the Sciences
Social Institutions
Culture
MCAT Practice Passage
Problem-solving Cooldown

To Do After Lesson 11

- [ ] Read Psychology and Sociology Chapters 9 and 10
- [ ] Read Biochemistry Chapters 9 and 10
- [ ] Read Physics Chapter 9
- [ ] Complete Psychology and Sociology QBank 5: Sociological Approaches and Culture

FL 1 Review - Complete this portion of the lesson after taking FL#1

How did you do on Full Length 1 compared to your diagnostic?

	Chem/Phys Foundations	CARS	Bio/Biochem Foundations	Psych/Soc Foundations
Higher than my diagnostic				
Same as my diagnostic				
Lower that my diagnostic				

How did you keep track of passage information: highlighting, note-taking, both?

	Chem/Phys Foundations	CARS	Bio/Biochem Foundations	Psych/Soc Foundations
Highlighting				
Note-taking				
Both				

Did you run out of time or have to rush on any section?

	Chem/Phys Foundations	CARS	Bio/Biochem Foundations	Psych/Soc Foundations
Time ran out				

Expectations vs. reality

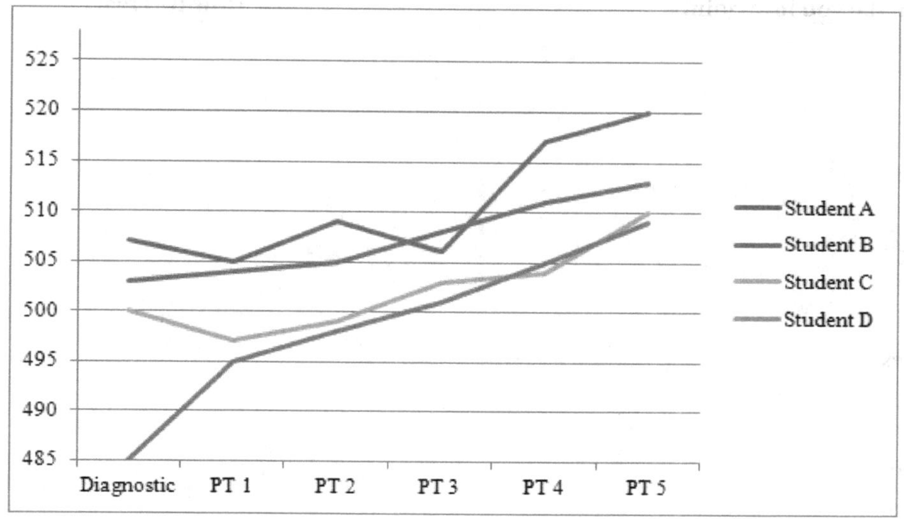

What do these trends tell you about score progression?

____

What should you focus on from FL 2 and beyond?

____

How did you use the onscreen timer?

____

Where do you spend most of your time, reading the passage or answering questions?

____

How did you keep track of passage information, highlighting, note-taking, both, neither?

____

Do you have any scratch work from the exam? What does it look like?

____

Are you caught up with the recommended course homework?

____

Pathologies that make you lose points	**How to Treat**
Attitude	
Familiarity	
Endurance/Pacing	
Content weaknesses	
Lack of recognition	
Careless mistakes	
Timing	

What is the best way to identify and then eliminate these factors?

Reviewing Science Questions

Which questions do you review?

1. Correct and confident

2. Correct but uncertain

3. Guessed and correct

4. Incorrect

The most important questions to review are ________________ and ________________. Why?

Where can you find lots of detail on the questions you missed, already collected for you?

Learning from Your Mistakes

When you review your Full Length exam, you want to prepare your notes to make a detailed list:

1. Reread and rephrase each missed question and see why you missed it.
    i. Was it a concept, interpretation of concept/data, careless mistake, miscalculation or missed passage detail?

2. Read through the correct answer and explanation so you understand why the correct answer IS the only correct answer. Put it in your own words

3. Put, in your own words, why you think you missed the question. Be specific!

4. Note whatever scientific concept or term you do not recognize or know on your study list.

5. Make note of what question types were missed (e.g. Skill 1, 2, 3 or 4)

Chemistry/Physics Foundations Full Length 1

11. Another possible method of separating 2-methylundecanal and 2-methylundecanoic acid could be based on:
    A. their differences in the rotation of plane-polarized light.
    B. a mass spectrometry analysis.
    C. an extraction based on their differing solubility.
    D. the very different scent profiles of each molecule.

1.

2.

3.

4.

5.

This page left intentionally blank.

Psychology/Sociology Foundations Full Length 1

4. African-American patients who are in the pre-encounter stage of Cross's Nigrescence Model of African-American identity development might have what attitude towards Caucasian-American healthcare providers?

    A. They would regard them as superior practitioners and not question their medical advice.
    B. They would regard them with distrust and prefer to be treated by an African-American practitioner.
    C. They would recognize historical injustices in medical care towards racial minorities and work to empower African-American patients to self-advocate.
    D. They would judge the medical advice given to them in a culture-free manner.

1.

2.

3.

4.

5.

CARS Review

Most Common CARS Mistakes

1. Failure to read efficiently
   i. Ideas are more important (i.e. testable) than details

2. Failure to understand the question
   i. NOT, EXCEPT...

3. Failure to locate relevant information in passage
   i. Read too quickly or skimmed passage

Prepare your notes to make a detailed list:

1. Reread each missed question and see why you missed it.
   i. Was it a failure to identify arguments, recognize detail, locate relevant information, draw an inference, or did you overlook a passage detail?

2. Read through the correct answer and explanation so you understand why the correct answer IS the only correct answer. Put it in your own words.

3. Put, in your own words, why your answers fails to satisfy the question. Be specific!

4. Make note of what question types were missed (e.g. Skill 1, 2 or 3).

CARS review is all about learning to bring your thinking in line with __________________________.

How can you develop your ability to identify flaws in the wrong answers in CARS?

CARS Full Length 1

40. Which of the following is an example of Representation by Regulated Interaction according to the author's definition?

    A. In videogames in general, an avatar might take a hit from an enemy and it is represented to the player as a vibration in the videogame controller.
    B. In *Batman: Arkham Asylum*, the player avatar is poisoned and begins hallucinating. While hallucinating, the avatar changes form. In this form, the avatar no longer runs in response to movement commands from the player, but shuffles slowly instead.
    C. In *Grand Theft Auto*, in order to find out how Liberty City is laid out, what the character's tasks are, and the options available to complete them, the player must direct the avatar in such a way as to gather this information about the world.
    D. In videogames, facts about the character are represented to the player visually, such as the color of the characters skin or eyes, and audibly, such as the way they talk.

1.

2.

3.

4.

What questions should you ask when looking for flaws in an answer choice?

What are the common wrong answer types the test-makers will use in CARS?

When the Review is Complete

You will have a Lessons Learned Journal full of all the valuable information you have obtained, one for each section of the exam.

The LLJ will also provide you with a list of homework assignments to complete over the next 3-5 days

Lessons Learned Journal

Passage/Q #	Question Type	Topic	Reason for Lost Points	Lesson Learned

Electronic vs. Paper LLJ

Test Strategies

Continuation

Refinement

Replacement

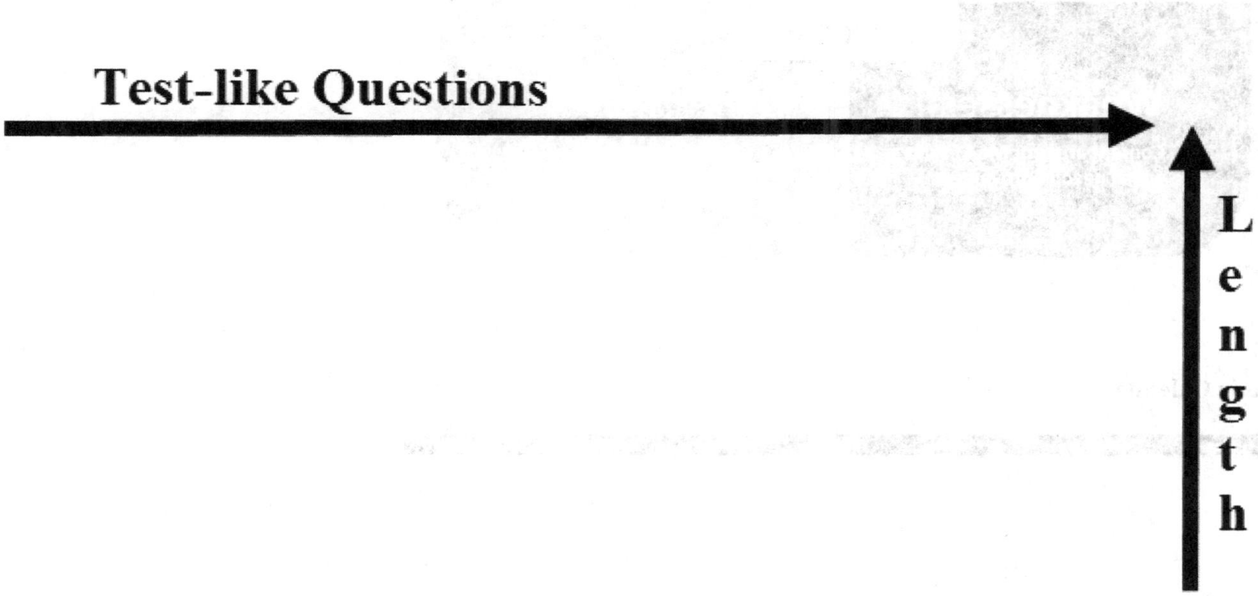

Test-like Questions

Length

Practice and Next Step Resources

What Does Your Score Tell You?

Motivation

SWOT Analysis

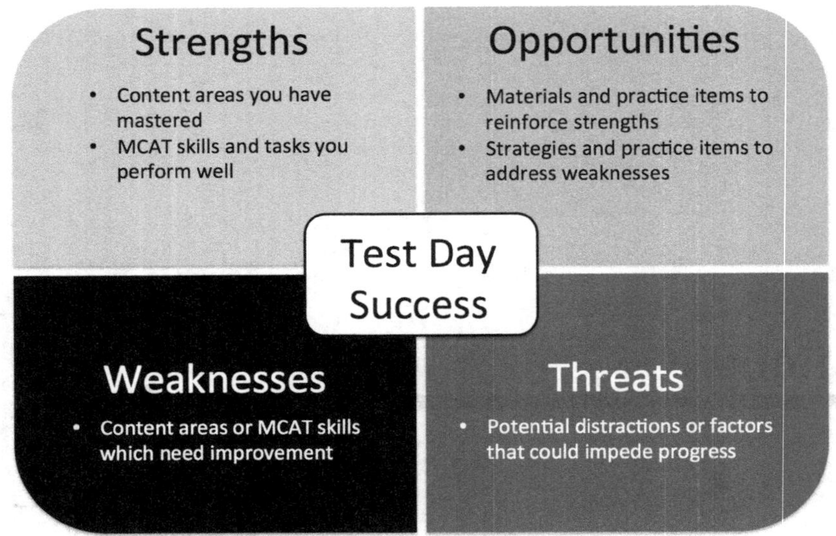

Study Calendar

Monday	Tuesday	Wednesday	Thursday	Friday	Saturday	Sunday
				1	2	3
4	5	6	7	8	9	10
11	12	13	14	15	16	17
18	19	20	21	22	23	24
25	26	27	28	29 Big day!	30	

Problem-solving Warm-up

1. A new resident is feeling ill so she decides to go to the restroom before seeing a patient. While she does, a nurse and technician welcome the patient and collect information in order for the patient visit to run smoothly. This scenario is best explained by which sociological concept?

   A. Conflict resolution
   B. Symbolic interactionism
   C. Functionalism
   D. Role exit

2. A new resident is feeling ill so she decides to go for a physical and discovers she is pregnant. The resident informs her program director that she will have to drastically adjust her work hours in preparation for duties as a mother. This scenario is best explained by which sociological concept?

   A. Conflict resolution
   B. Symbolic interactionism
   C. Functionalism
   D. Role exit

3. A medical student is annoyed that a resident is late for a patient appointment for the third time in a week. The student considers confronting the resident more strongly this time when they arrive, but decides to speak with the resident after the patient leaves, in order to avoid impacting patient care. The medical student is employing which sociological concept?

   A. Conflict resolution
   B. Symbolic interactionism
   C. Functionalism
   D. Role exit

4. Which of the following would be considered an ascribed status?

   A. Chief resident
   B. Husband
   C. Prisoner
   D. Uncle

5. Which of the following could be considered a master status?

   A. CEO
   B. Transgendered
   C. Athlete
   D. All of the above

Social Interaction

Status

1.

2.

3.

4.

5.

6.

Achieved

Ascribed

Master

Role

Role Conflict vs. Role Strain

Role Exit

Social Network

Primary Group

Secondary Groups

In-group vs. Out-group

Group Size

Formal Organization

Bureaucracy

Ideal Bureaucracy

Views on Bureaucracy

Organizational Democracy

Formal Organization

Self-presentation

Gender and Emotion

Culture and Emotion

Impression Management

Front-stage Self

Back-stage Self

Communication

Verbal

Nonverbal

Social Behavior

Attraction

Aggression

Attachment

Evolution of Social Behavior

What are some potential evolutionary reasons which explain the persistence of the following social behaviors?

Inclusive Fitness

Mating

Game Theory

Frequency and strength of "optimal" behavior

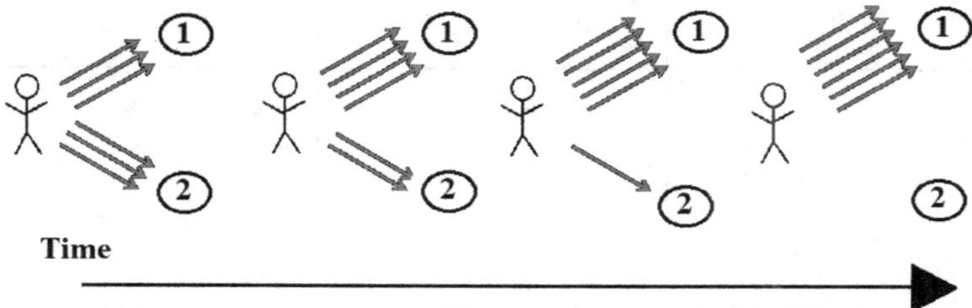

Erikson's Stages of Psychosocial Development

Success

Failure

Stage	Psychosocial Obstacle	Virtue Developed	Age (expected)	Example Behavior
1				
2				
3				
4				
5				
6				
7				
8				

What is an important aspect of development that Erikson fails to adequately explain?

Erikson's Stages of Development—Worksheet Exercise—LEVEL 1

Stage	Psychosocial Obstacle	Virtue Developed	Age (expected)	Example behavior
1	Trust vs. mistrust		0-18 months	If care has been harsh or inconsistent, the infant will develop a sense of mistrust and will not have confidence in the world around them or in their abilities to influence events.
2	Autonomy vs. shame			
3		Purpose	3 to 5 years	Children will plan activities, make up games, and initiate activities with others.
4		Competency	5-12 years	The child's peers will gain significance and will become a major source of their self-esteem. The child feels the need to win approval by demonstrating skills that are valued by others.
5	Ego identity vs. Role confusion			
6	Intimacy vs. isolation	Love	18 to 40 years	Person will share themselves more intimately with others. They will explore relationships leading to long term commitments with someone other than a family member.
7		Care	40 to 65 years	Person will establish a career, settle down within a relationship, begin a family and develop a sense of being a part of the bigger picture.
8	Ego integrity vs. despair	Wisdom	65+ years	Productivity will slow, and the person will enter life as a retired person. During this time they contemplate accomplishments and are able to develop integrity if they perceive themselves as successful in life.

Erikson's Stages of Development—Worksheet Exercise—LEVEL 2

Stage	Psychosocial Obstacle	Virtue Developed	Age (expected)	Example behavior
1	Trust vs. mistrust		0-18 months	.
2	Autonomy vs. shame			
3		Purpose	3 to 5 years	Children will plan activities, make up games, and initiate activities with others.
4		Competency		The child's peers will gain significance and will become a major source of their self-esteem. The child feels the need to win approval by demonstrating skills that are valued by others.
5	Ego identity vs. Role confusion			
6	Intimacy vs. isolation	Love	18 to 40 years	Person will share themselves more intimately with others. They will explore relationships leading to long term commitments with someone other than a family member.
7		Care		
8	Ego integrity vs. despair			Productivity will slow, and the person will enter life as a retired person. During this time they contemplate accomplishments and are able to develop integrity if they perceive themselves as successful in life.

Erikson's Stages of Development—Worksheet Exercise—LEVEL 3

Stage	Psychosocial Obstacle	Virtue Developed	Age (expected)	Example behavior
1				
2				
3				
4		Competency		
5				
6		Love		
7	Generativity vs. stagnation			
8				

Discrimination

Direct

Indirect

Positive

Negative

Individual Discrimination

Institutional Discrimination

LEVEL	EXAMPLE	DAMAGE LEVEL
National		
Cultural		
State		
Local		
Group/Organization		
Individual		

Role of Prejudice

Agents of Discrimination

Power

Prestige

Class

This page left intentionally blank.

Effective Reading in the Sciences

Reading science passages on the MCAT means being able to keep track of important (i.e. likely to be tested) information in the passage. You must be able to anticipate, recognize, and understand scientific concepts presented in many different forms.

Attachment theory is based on the idea that there is a relationship between the early patterns of interactions of parents and children and later child development. Diana Baumrind initially classified three patterns of child behavior. The first was termed Pattern I and is characterized by children being secure, self-reliant, and explorative. In the second, Pattern II, children tend to withdraw, are distrustful, and are discontent. The third, Pattern III, describes children who have little self-control, retreat from novel experiences, and lack self-reliance.

Baumrind postulated that parenting styles lead to children developing one of these patterns. Experiments allowed researchers to classify preschool children as belonging to one of the patterns based on five criteria: self-control, approach-avoidance tendency, self-reliance, subjective mood, and peer affiliation. Children who exhibit Pattern I behavior are viewed as having the healthiest development, so efforts have been made to foster this behavior in children. A study was conducted to determine if parenting style training would translate to desirable child behavior. Results of parental training are shown in Figure 1.

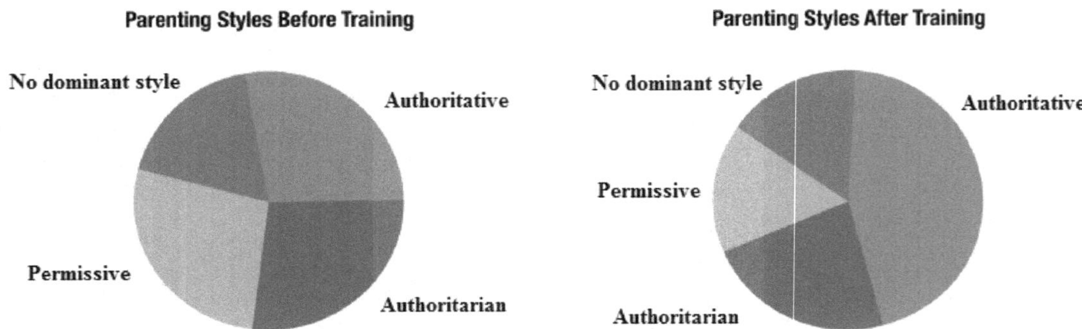

Figure 1 Parenting style pre and post training (n = 30)

Parenting behavior was observed and coded. Associations emerged: Parents of Pattern I children (i.e. Pattern I parents) were designated authoritative. These parents respected the child independence but held the children to a position once decided. They demonstrated control of the children, were supportive, and communicated clearly. Pattern II parents were designated authoritarian. These parents exhibited highly controlling behavior. They provided little nurturance, avoided reasoning with the children, and failed to encourage communication. Pattern III parents were called permissive parents. These couples were not controlling of the children. They were less organized, less secure about their parenting, and tended to use withdrawal of love as a consequence for child behavior.

Passage taken from the Next Step online QBank

6. It can be expected that after incorporating the same training from the study into community outreach programs, which pattern of behavior will decrease in the child population to the greatest extent?

   A. Pattern I
   B. Pattern II
   C. Pattern III
   D. Patterns I and III

7. An infant who demonstrates Pattern I behavior whose parents used an authoritative style most probably has what attachment type with his parent?

   A. Anxious-ambivalent
   B. Avoidant
   C. Disorganized
   D. Secure

8. Which of the following is LEAST likely be observed when studying behavior in children of authoritarian parents?

   A. These children associate obedience and success with love.
   B. These children display low self-esteem and mistrust of others.
   C. These children act conceited and unashamed around others.
   D. These children have a profound lack of social competence.

9. Authoritative parents are most likely to help their child resolve which Erikson developmental stage first?

   A. Intimacy vs. isolation
   B. Trust vs. mistrust
   C. Formal operations vs. concrete operations
   D. Oedipal vs. latency

10. If a child does not have a secure bond with his caregivers and later is unable to form secure relationships, he may have missed what period of time for learning?

    A. Attachment period
    B. Authoritative period
    C. Imprinting period
    D. Authoritarian period

Social Institutions

Education

Hidden curriculum

Teacher expectancy

Segregation/stratification

Family

Kinship

Diversity of structure

Marriage and divorce

Domestic violence

Religion

Religiosity

Organized religion

Government

Power

Economic systems

Political systems

Division of labor

Healthcare

Medicalization

Delivery of health care

Illness experience

Epidemiological impact

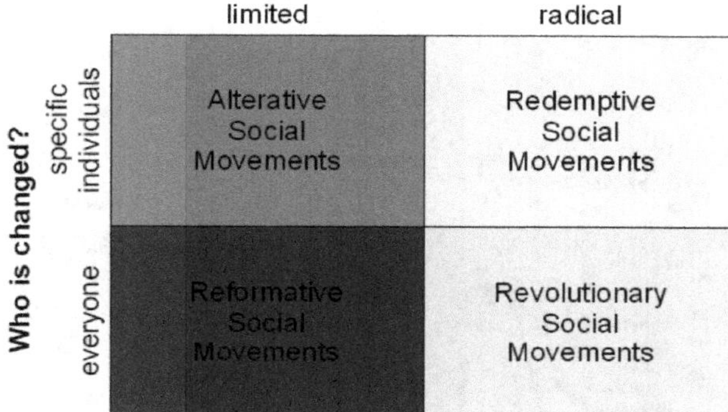

Social Change

Religious

Political

Economical

Culture

Beliefs vs. Values

Language

Rituals vs. Symbols

Material Culture

Symbolic Culture

Culture Shock

Honeymoon

Negotiation

Adjustment

Mastery

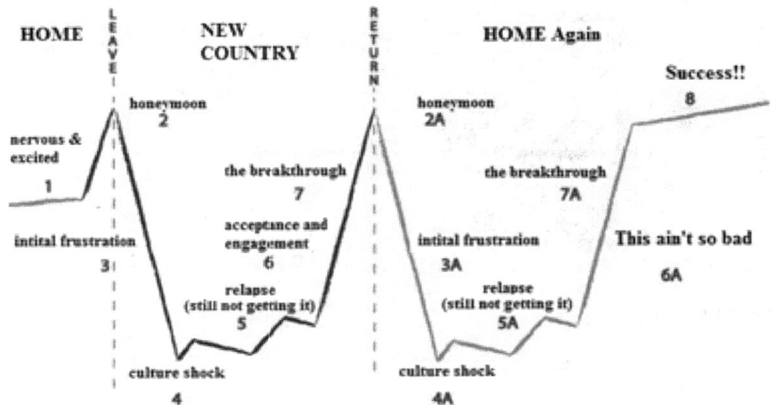

Culture Lag and Medical Technology

Assimilation

Multiculturalism

Subcultures

Counterculture

Popular Culture

Transmission of Culture

Meme

Diffusion of Culture

Timed MCAT Practice Passage

Mastery of the MCAT sciences is a two-part process. First you must study to understand (not just memorize!) the science content, and then you must study the content actively and challenge yourself within the context of the exam.

1. Complete your reading of the passage (3-4 minutes).
    - Write down what you believe to be the primary science content underlying the passage.
    - What facts or concepts do you anticipate to be tested? When you are done with the questions determine if you were correct. What passage clues were there to imply related topics that showed up in the questions?
    - Were there any key terms or important scientific relationships you missed?
    - Were you able to draw any conclusions from the data, if presented?

2. Complete the practice questions on your own (4-5 minutes)
    - Rephrase each question in your own mind after reading it to clarify the task.
    - Research the relevant area(s) of the passage or your own knowledge for information related to the task.
    - Respond to the question by choosing the answer that fits your research/calculations *and* satisfies the task.
    - If no answer seems obvious, eliminate answers that fail to have support in the passage or in the relevant science.

3. Analyze your wrong answer choices to the questions you missed.
    - Did you understand the task in the question?
    - What skill type was the question?
    - Did you know the science/formula/concept needed to answer the question?
    - Did you recognize the science being hinted at?
    - Were you able to find information in the passage quickly when you needed it?
    - Were there any necessary scientific concepts you failed to apply to the question?
        - If so, why?
    - If you made a mistake in calculations, have you identified your mistake?

This page left intentionally blank.

There are factors which uniquely impact the mental health of women of retirement age in Japan. Japanese women typically decrease their volunteer work in their community as they arrive at retirement age. Reasons for this include that women most frequently volunteer through their children's schools and as their children graduate there are fewer opportunities for this. Lessening volunteer work is correlated with higher levels of depression. In addition, due to cultural norms many Japanese women of retirement age are also supporting an elder family member in their homes, which may require a great deal of time. The relationship between women caretakers and their elderly family members may be stressful, and can result in a number of conflicts.

To address these unique needs Japan has adopted programs to assist them. The Long-Term Care Initiative of 2000 strives to coordinate care resources for the elderly and provide psychosocial support for their caregivers. In Japan, seeking mental health services outside of the home is still taboo, especially among older individuals. To meet the need of women of retirement age, case managers first identify those in highest need. Those caregivers who are providing care for family members with high levels of health needs typically have the highest stress levels. Case managers target these caregivers as a priority, providing services such as social talk and educating about approaching and avoiding styles of care.

Social talk consists of interactions between caregivers and case managers that provide an opportunity for caregivers to express themselves and their frustrations, much as might occur in a therapy session. Avoidance strategies consist of the caregiver taking space and time for herself in order to address her own needs. Approaching strategies consist of formulating ways for the caregiver to enlist the elderly in their own care. These interventions have been shown to reduce caregiver stress.

Passage taken from the Next Step online QBank

11. Which of the following is NOT a cultural factor described in the passage that might account for increased levels of stress among Japanese women of retirement age?
    A. Need to support elderly relatives
    B. Emphasis on education
    C. Reduced volunteerism
    D. Reluctance to access public mental health resources

12. Asking an elderly mother-in-law to assist in preparing breakfast is an example of which kind of support strategy?
    A. Approaching strategy
    B. Social talk
    C. Care initiative
    D. Avoidance strategy

13. Which of the following is an example of an effective strategy to reduce stress associated with generational inequity discussed in the passage?
    A. Providing extra resources for elderly individuals living with younger family members
    B. Increasing attachment among family members living with each other
    C. Encouraging women caregivers to take time to do activities they enjoy
    D. Helping women caregivers understand the developmental needs of elderly family members

14. What is a possible reason for taking care of elderly family members and avoiding mental health services outside of the home in Japan?
    A. Socialization
    B. Psychoanalytic drive
    C. Cognitive dissonance
    D. Altruism

15. A recent visit by a healthcare worker to Japan left her shocked at the inhumane treatment of those with mental illness. While normal in the villages she visited, such behavior would be illegal in her home country. If her guide advised her not to judge the workers because the behavior is "the way it has always been done here" and is how they understand mental illness, this guide is illustrating the concept of:
    A. cultural transmission.
    B. cultural sensitivity.
    C. cultural relativism.
    D. cultural diffusion.

Problem-solving Cooldown

16. In which of the following scenarios is the subject most clearly exhibiting cognitive dissonance?

    A. A wealthy businessman who never got a college degree pushes his daughter to attend an expensive private university.
    B. An oncologist who knows the dangers of smoking continues to experience pleasure when smoking.
    C. A successful attorney is proud her daughter is admitted to a top law school.
    D. A grief counselor feels guilt after the death of a loved one because he chooses not to seek help for the significant negative effects of his grief.

17. The social phenomenon of groupthink is characterized by all of the following EXCEPT:

    A. a significant over-rating of the decision-making abilities of members of the in-group.
    B. a decrease in the creativity of individual group members in contributing to solutions the in-group wants to achieve.
    C. high group loyalty, allowing members to feel safe raising controversial issues and proposing alternative solutions.
    D. an effort to minimize conflict and ensure consensus.

18. According to attachment theory, which of the following children is most likely to attach to a male psychologist, previously unknown to the child, in the course of a psychological study?

    A. A two month old female infant raised in a safe, stable environment
    B. A five month old male infant raised in a safe, stable environment
    C. An eight month old male infant raised by a single caregiver who frequently neglects the child
    D. A thirteen month old female infant raised by two caregivers who occasionally neglect the child

19. Each of the following are aspects of the McDonaldization of Society EXCEPT:

    A. rationalization of decisions into cost/benefit analysis structures and away from traditional modes of thinking.
    B. bureaucratic organization that formalizes well-establish division of labor and impersonal structures.
    C. dissolution of hierarchical modes of authority into collaborative team-based decision protocols.
    D. an intense effort on achieving sameness across diverse markets.

20. A parent wishes to encourage her daughter to complete her homework every night without resorting to extrinsic motivation. Which of the following strategies would be best?

    A. Allow her daughter to set her own homework study schedule, and praise her effectiveness when she sticks to that schedule.
    B. Create an internal sense of competitiveness by fostering a competition between the daughter and the daughter's best friend who is in all of the same classes.
    C. Remind the daughter that getting good grades are their own reward, good grades are the result of hard work, and that good grades should generate a sense of accomplishment.
    D. Offer to increase the daughter's allowance if she completes her homework each week.

To Do After Lesson 11

- ☐ Read Psychology and Sociology Chapters 9 and 10
- ☐ Read Biochemistry Chapters 9 and 10
- ☐ Read Physics Chapter 9
- ☐ Complete Psychology and Sociology QBank 5: Sociological Approaches and Culture

This page left intentionally blank.

LESSON 12

Physics 2

To Do Before Lesson 12

- ☐ Read Psychology and Sociology Chapters 9 and 10
- ☐ Read Biochemistry Chapters 9 and 10
- ☐ Read Physics Chapter 9
- ☐ Complete Psychology and Sociology QBank 5: Sociological Approaches and Culture

In Lesson 12

Problem-solving Warm-up
Fluid Dynamics
Effective Reading in the Sciences
Electrostatics and Magnetism
Circuits
MCAT Practice Passage
Problem-solving cool down

To Do After Lesson 12

- ☐ Read Physics Chapter 10
- ☐ Read Biology Chapters 11 and 12
- ☐ Complete Physics QBank 2: Waves, Fluids, and Electrostatics

Problem-solving Warm-up

1. A small, electrically neutral rubber ball contacts a glass window. The two objects do not stick to each other. However, when the ball is positively charged it sticks to the window. The window is most likely:

    A. an ideal conductor.
    B. electrically positive.
    C. electrically negative.
    D. electrically neutral.

2. What is the magnitude of work required to move a charge of +2 C from infinity to a distance X from a second charge +Q through a potential difference of 50 V?

    A. 25 J
    B. 50 J
    C. 100 J
    D. 200 J

3. A -1 C point charge with a mass of 1 kg is placed at 3R. What is its speed at 2R?

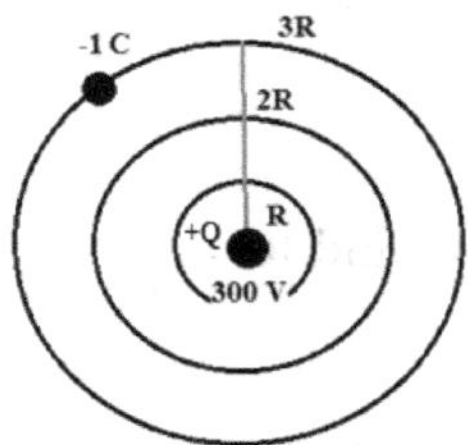

    A. 1 m/s
    B. 10 m/s
    C. 15 m/s
    D. 20 m/s

4. A nucleus of U-238 splits into two fragments that have different masses but the same charges. Which of the following must be true after the split? The fragments are moving:

    A. apart and exert the same force on each other.
    B. closer together and exert unequal force on each other.
    C. apart and have the same acceleration.
    D. closer together and have the same velocity.

5. How should a magnetic field be oriented for a negative test charge to pass through the space below in a linear path?

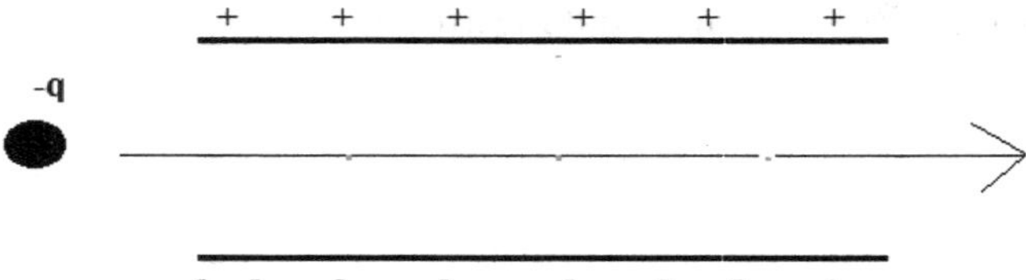

    A. Out of the page
    B. Into the page
    C. Up
    D. Down

Fluid Dynamics

Density:

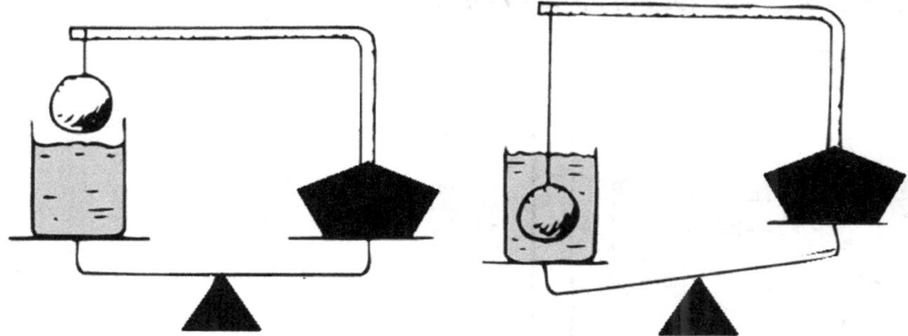

Draw the free body diagram for both scenarios above and determine what property of the sphere has changed to allow the tipping shown.

Buoyant Force

Specific Gravity

The buoyant force will be equal in weight to ________________________________.

Conservation of Mass: $A_1v_1 = A_2v_2$

Conservation of Energy: $P_1 + ½ \rho(v_1)^2 + \rho gh_1 = P_2 + ½ \rho(v_2)^2 + \rho gh_2$

What are the three types of energy described in the Bernoulli equation?

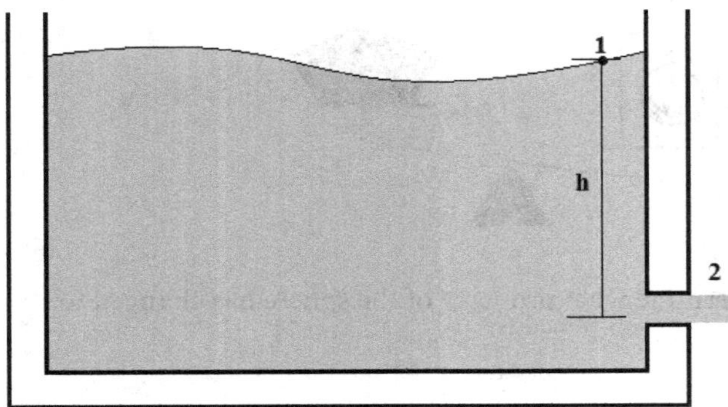

If points 1 and 2 are exposed to the atmosphere and the hole in the tank is very tiny, what is the fluid velocity at point 2?

A. $2gh_2$
B. h_2/h_1
C. $\sqrt{(2gh)}$
D. h_1/h_2

There are now three holes in the side of the tank, covered to start with. One hole is 1/4 of the way down from the top, while the other two are 1/2 and 3/4 of the way down. Which hole shoots the water furthest horizontally?

Poiseuille's Law and the Autonomic Nervous System

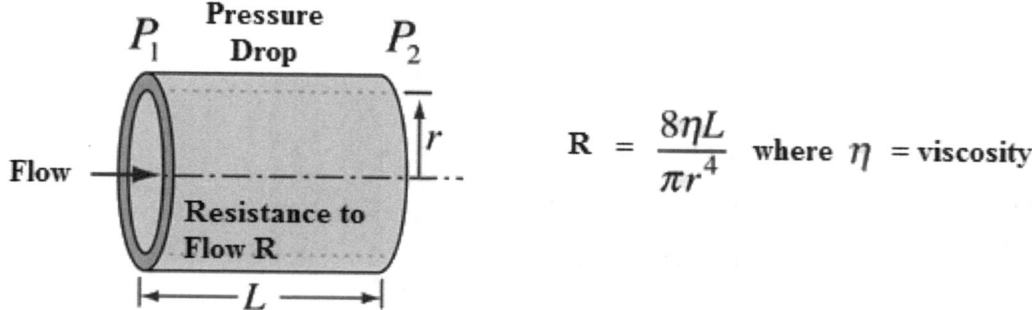

If the original blood flow rate is 200 mL/s, which of the following will cause the greatest increase in blood flow rate?

A. Quadrupling the length of the vessel
B. Halving the viscosity of the blood
C. Doubling the radius of the vessel
D. Doubling the pressure at P_1

What would be the expected new flow rate and pressure required to restore normal blood flow if the radius of the aorta is reduced to 50% of its original value? (Flow = $\Delta P/R$, Normal ΔP = 120 mmHg and normal flow = 100 mL/min)

A. 6 mL/min, 75 mm Hg
B. 6 mL/min, 1920 mm Hg
C. 60 mL/min, 240 mm Hg
D. 60 mL/min, 120 mm Hg

Which of the following structures is MOST likely to experience turbulent flow?

A. Larger straight vessels like the abdominal aorta
B. Long curved vessels without branches like the arch of the aorta
C. Short curved branch points like the mesenteric arteries
D. The arterioles

The vessels that are the dominant contributors to flow resistance are the ________________________.

Strategy

Test Day Short-cuts

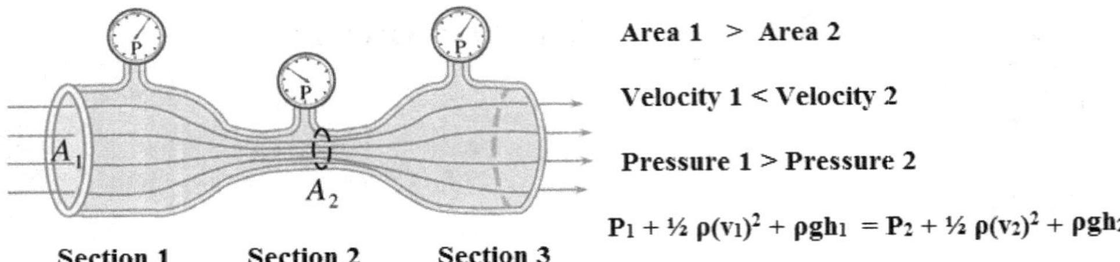

Area 1 > Area 2

Velocity 1 < Velocity 2

Pressure 1 > Pressure 2

$$P_1 + \frac{1}{2}\rho(v_1)^2 + \rho g h_1 = P_2 + \frac{1}{2}\rho(v_2)^2 + \rho g h_2$$

Simple Pitot Tubes

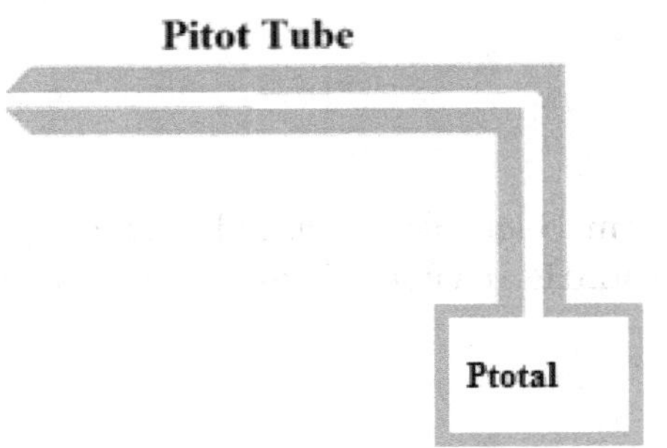

Pitot-Static Tube

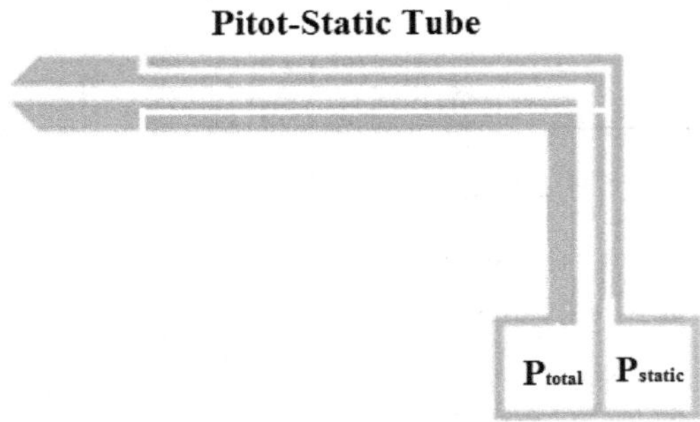

Where would a pressure sensor need to be placed in order to detect the dynamic pressure?

At what fluid velocities might a pitot-static tube fail to give accurate measurements? Why?

Surface Tension and Respiration

During inhalation, where would you expect the pressure to be greater, P_1 or P_2? During exhalation?

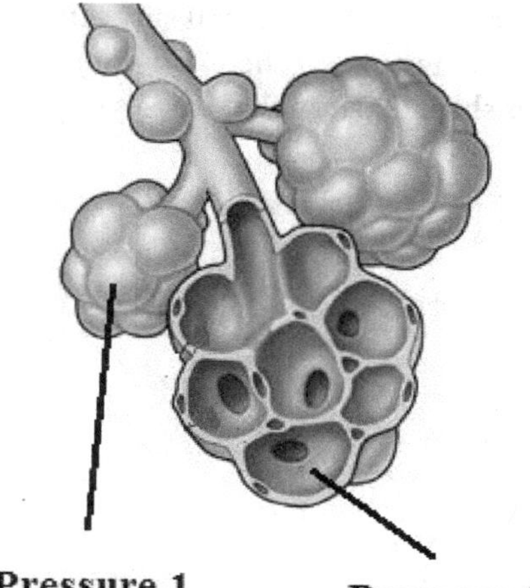

The amount of net pressure required for inflation of the ________________ is dictated by the

________________ on the outside of these balloon-like structures.

________________ is the molecule responsible for coating these structures and reduces

________________ by a factor of 15 in order to ensure efficient inflation.

At what volume of the structure does this molecule have its greatest effect?

Why is this important to efficient oxygen transport?

Effective Reading in the Sciences

Like most arteries, the abdominal aorta is elastic, which allows it to be filled with blood under high pressure. An aneurysm develops when the wall of the artery becomes weakened and distended. Aneurysms usually are discovered before they produce symptoms, such as back pain, but they may rupture if they become too large. An adult man is admitted to the ER complaining about pain just below their ribs on their left side. The intern on call suspects there is occlusion in one of the major branches of the abdominal aorta and sets out to determine if there is a problem with the patient's splenic artery. The splenic artery (SA) is a short and wide cylinder shaped artery that carries oxygenated blood from the aorta to the spleen as shown in figure 1.

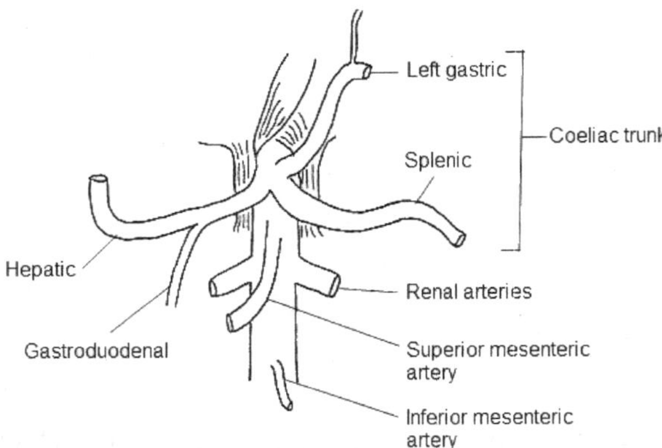

Figure 1 Structure and main branches of the abdominal aorta

Ultrasound diagnostics are completed to determine the dimensions of the patient's SA as well as the speed with which blood flows through the vessel. The results of the diagnostics along with reference values are shown in table 1

Vessel Parameter	Diag. Results	Reference Values
Length	30 mm	25 mm
Radius	10 mm	15 mm
Blood speed	200 mm/s	500 mm/s

Table 1 Results of SA diagnostics compared to reference values

After reading the results, the intern decides to perform a stent with balloon angioplasty in order to improve blood flow to the spleen. They consult a manual before performing the procedure, a portion of which is shown in figure 2.

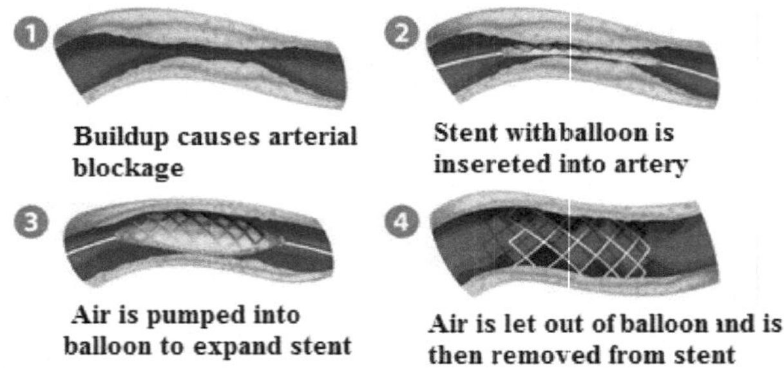

Figure 2 Procedure for stent with balloon angioplasty

6. If stent placement doubles the diameter of an artery, what effect would be expected in the blood speed in this section of the artery?

   A. The velocity will decrease by 75%
   B. The velocity will decrease by 50%
   C. The velocity will increase by 50%
   D. The velocity will increase by 100%

7. An occlusion of the superior mesenteric artery will most likely lead to increase in blood pressure in all of the following vessels EXCEPT:

   A. hepatic artery.
   B. gastroduodenal artery.
   C. left renal artery.
   D. inferior mesenteric artery.

8. If the blood of the patient was replaced with a liquid of lower density but the same viscosity, what would be observed?

   A. The lower density fluid would flow with the same speed since it has both a lower weight and a lower inertia
   B. The lower density fluid would flow with smaller speed since it has a greater inertia
   C. The lower density fluid would flow with greater speed since the pressure in the vessels would be greater
   D. The lower density fluid would flow with lower speed since it has a lower weight

9. According to the diagnostic results, compared to a normal adult, how much longer will it take for an erythrocyte to pass through the complete length of the patient's splenic artery?

   A. 0.05 s
   B. 0.10 s
   C. 0.15 s
   D. 0.20 s

10. The viscosity of blood is related to the protein composition and temperature of the plasma. Which of the following correctly describes the relationship between temperature, protein composition and blood viscosity?

    A. Viscosity is directly proportional to both protein concentration and temperature.
    B. Viscosity is inversely proportional to both protein concentration and temperature.
    C. Viscosity is directly proportional to protein concentration and inversely proportional to temperature.
    D. Viscosity is inversely proportional to protein concentration and directly proportional to temperature.

Electrostatics and Magnetism

The MCAT emphasizes integration and testing of relationships. Many times the successful use of a formula or equation will depend on the relationships of the equation, not raw calculation.

When learning equations, focus on the relationship between the variables and how they influence each other. Knowing units will also allow you to derive a needed equation in a pinch.

	Equation	Units	Relationships
Coulomb's Law			
Electrical Potential Energy			
Electric Potential			
Electric Field			
Magnetic Field			
Magnetic Force			

Electric Field

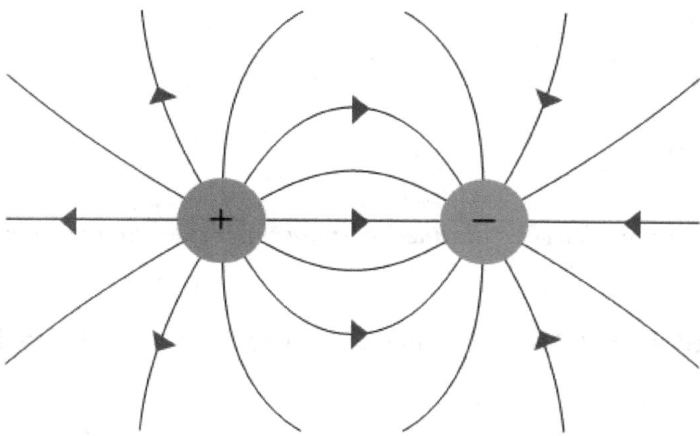

Electric field lines will always point in the direction a ________________ charge would be accelerated in the field.

Draw a plot showing the relationship between electrical potential energy on charge Q_1 and the distance between Q_1 and Q_2 if:

(a) Q_1 is positive and Q_2 is positive
(b) Q_1 is negative and Q_2 is positive

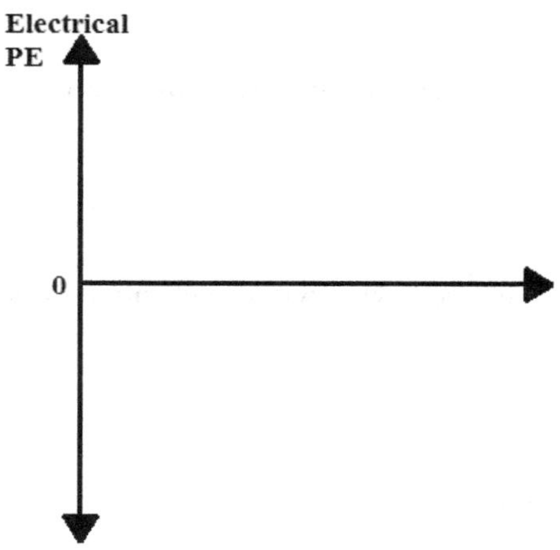

Voltage is the ratio of ________________ to ________________.

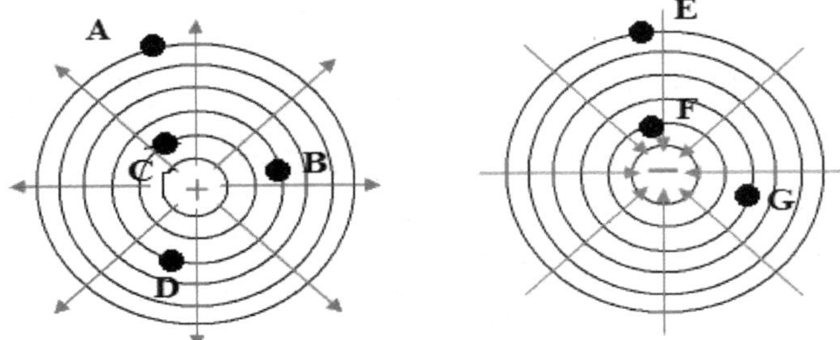

In the above figure each line is twice the distance from the center charge as the line 1 position closer (For example, Point G is twice as far from the center charge as Point F).

What can be said about the voltage of a 1 C charge placed at point B compared to the voltage on a 3 C charge placed at point D?

How do their electrical potential energies compare?

What will happen to the potential energy of a -2 C charge if it is moved from G to E?

If the voltage at point C is 30 V, what is the work required to move a 10 C charge from an infinite distance away from the positive charge to point B?

If a +5 C charge has a mass of 2 kg and is placed at point E (V = 64 volts) and released, what will its velocity be when it reaches point F?

A transcranial magnetic stimulation (TMS) coil uses a figure-8 configuration (shown below) to use capacitors to generate a 2-3 T magnetic field over electrically active tissue.

In order to ensure a uniform, focused magnetic field, what should be the direction of current in each portion of the coil?

Clockwise, clockwise
Counterclockwise, counterclockwise
Clockwise, counterclockwise
Alternating the direction in each coil continuously

To maximize the depolarization effect on the tissue, how should the operator hold the coil over the target tissue?

With the coil oriented parallel to the target tissue
With the coil oriented 45° to the target tissue
With the coil oriented 90° to the target tissue
It does not matter how the coil is oriented

Which of the following would NOT increase the strength of the TMS stimuli?

Decrease the coil resistance
Increase the current in the coil
Add a capacitor in series with the coil
Add a capacitor in parallel with the coil

Circuits

Resistors

Simplify the following circuit:

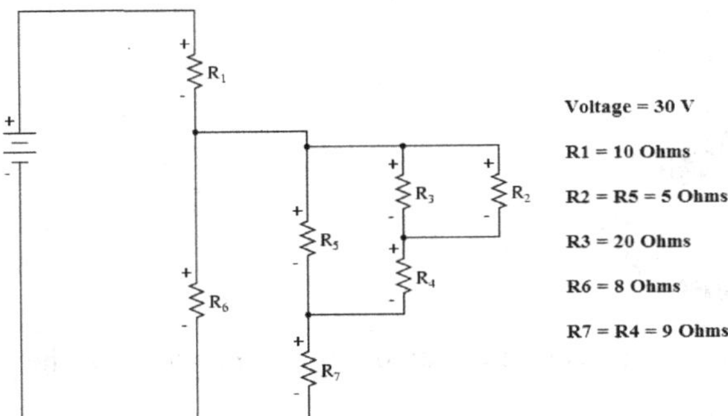

Will the current be higher in R_7 or R_3?

R_{tot} =

I_{tot} =

If the diameter of the circular resistor R_6 is doubled, what is the value of its new resistance?

How does the voltage in R_5 compare to the voltage in R_4?

Capacitance

Simplify the following circuit:

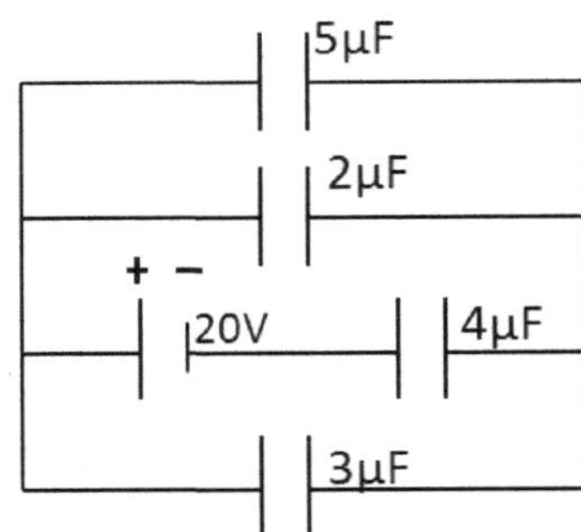

What is C_{tot}?

Removing the 3 μF capacitor will:

________________ the total capacitance of the circuit and ________________ the charge drawn from the battery.

________________ the charge stored on the 2 μF capacitor and ________________ the voltage on the 4 μF capacitor.

$C_{new} = k\varepsilon_o A/d$ and $Q_{tot} = V_{batt}C_{tot}$

Why does area (A) affect capacitance?

Timed MCAT Practice Passage

Mastery of the MCAT sciences is a two-part process. First you must study to understand (not just memorize!) the science content, and then you must study the content actively and challenge yourself within the context of the exam.

1. Complete your reading of the passage (3-4 minutes).
    - Write down what you believe to be the primary science content underlying the passage.
    - What facts or concepts do you anticipate to be tested? When you are done with the questions determine if you were correct. What passage clues were there to imply related topics that showed up in the questions?
    - Were there any key terms or important scientific relationships you missed?
    - Were you able to draw any conclusions from the data, if presented?

2. Complete the practice questions on your own (4-5 minutes)
    - Rephrase each question in your own mind after reading it to clarify the task.
    - Research the relevant area(s) of the passage or your own knowledge for information related to the task.
    - Respond to the question by choosing the answer that fits your research/calculations *and* satisfies the task.
    - If no answer seems obvious, eliminate answers that fail to have support in the passage or in the relevant science.

3. Analyze your wrong answer choices to the questions you missed.
    - Did you understand the task in the question?
    - What skill type was the question?
    - Did you know the science/formula/concept needed to answer the question?
    - Did you recognize the science being hinted at?
    - Were you able to find information in the passage quickly when you needed it?
    - Were there any necessary scientific concepts you failed to apply to the question?
        - If so, why?
    - If you made a mistake in calculations, have you identified your mistake?

Magnetic levitation trains operate using what is known as a linear motor, which allows the trains to move at high speed in a straight line. Linear motors are electric induction motors that produce motion in a straight line rather than rotational motion. In a traditional electric motor, the rotor spins inside the circular, static part known as a stator. In a linear motor, the stator is unwrapped and laid out flat and the rotor moves over it in a straight line.

Linear induction motors are powered by alternating current (AC). Two pairs of electromagnetic coils (Figure 1) are energized by an AC supply. Each pair of coils is energized together. The current in each coil oscillates according to the equation

$$I_t = I_{max} \sin(\omega t)$$

where ω is the angular frequency. When the current in one pair is at a maximum, the current is the other pair is 0 A and vice-versa.

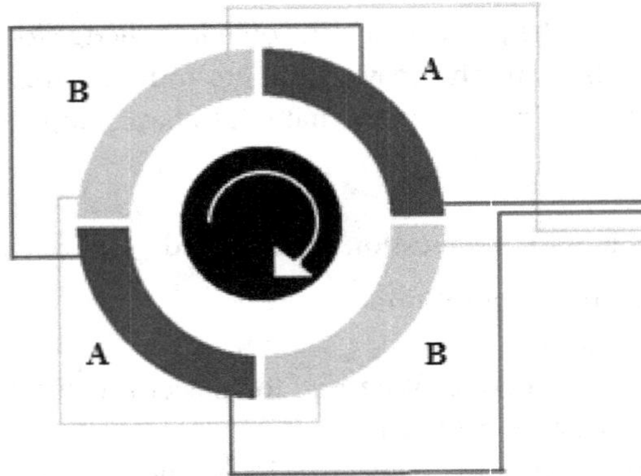

Figure 1 AC induction motor

As the coils are powered, the magnetic field they produce between them induces an electric current in the rotor. This current produces its own magnetic field that tries to oppose the magnetic field from the outer coils. The interaction between the two fields causes the rotor to turn. As the magnetic field alternates between the coil pairs, it rotates around the motor, which forces the rotor to spin in the same direction and at the same speed. A direct current (DC) motor uses a similar principle but generates mechanical work using a DC circuit.

11. To what degree are the two pairs of electromagnetic coils in the induction motor out of phase with each other?

    A. 0°
    B. 45°
    C. 90°
    D. 180°

12. How are the coils in each pair in the motor wired together?

    A. Pair A is wired in series, Pair B is wired in parallel
    B. Pair A is wired in series, Pair B is wired in series
    C. Pair A is wired in parallel, Pair B is wired in series
    D. Pair A is wired in parallel, Pair B is wired in parallel

13. If the AC power frequency of a motor is 150 Hz, what is the angular frequency?

    A. 25 rad/sec
    B. 75 rad/sec
    C. 450 rad/sec
    D. 950 rad/sec

14. Which of the following changes to an electromagnetic coil in a DC motor would NOT decrease the strength of its magnetic field generated?

    A. Decrease the diameter of the wire in the coil
    B. Decrease the current through the coil
    C. Decrease the resistivity of the coil
    D. Increase the diameter of the coil

15. A proton is moving at 10 m/s when it enters a region with a uniform electric field (E) and uniform magnetic field (B), which is oriented perpendicular to the proton's velocity. If the velocity remains unchanged, which of the following must be true?

    A. The magnitude of B is 10 times the magnitude of E.
    B. The electric field is oriented in the opposite direction to the magnetic field.
    C. The electric field is oriented in the same direction to the magnetic field.
    D. The magnitude of E is 10 times the magnitude of B.

Problem-solving Cooldown

Questions 16-18 use the following circuit. The switch is continuously thrown from position 1 to position 2 and back.

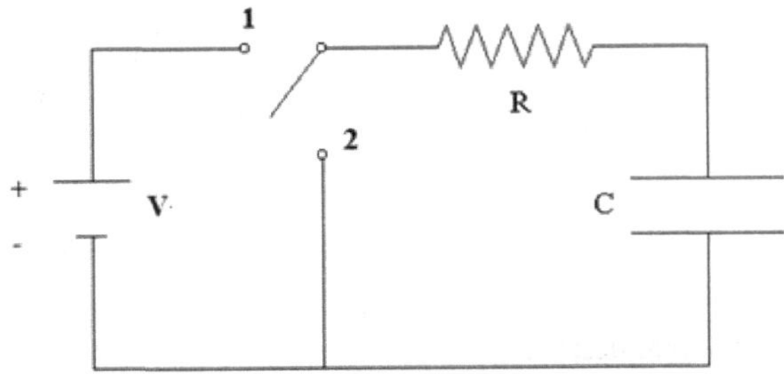

16. Which of the following correctly plots the voltage on a capacitor versus time for the following circuit?

A.

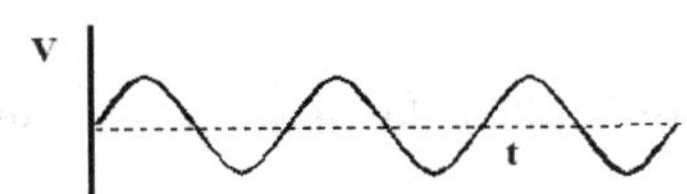

B.

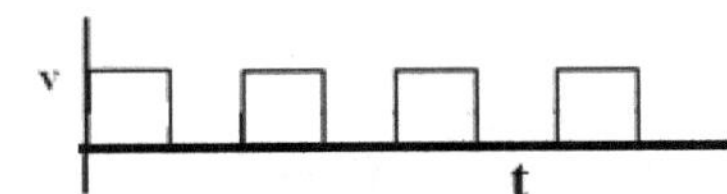

C.

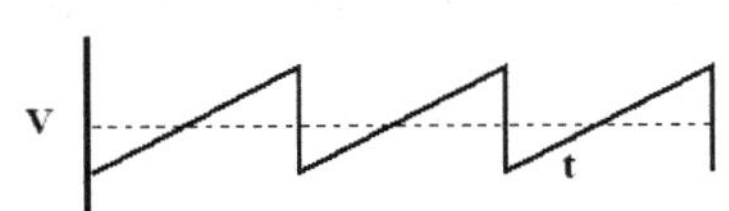

D.

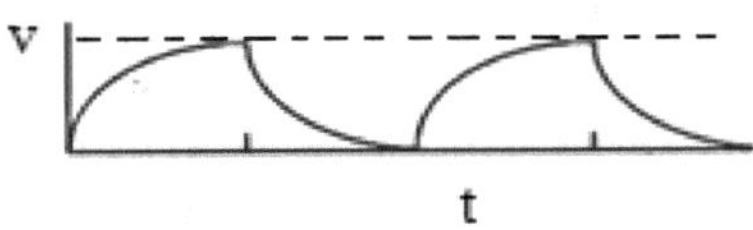

17. Which of the following correctly plots the total voltage across the circuit?

A.

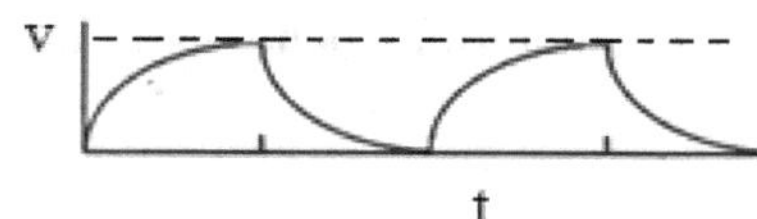

B.

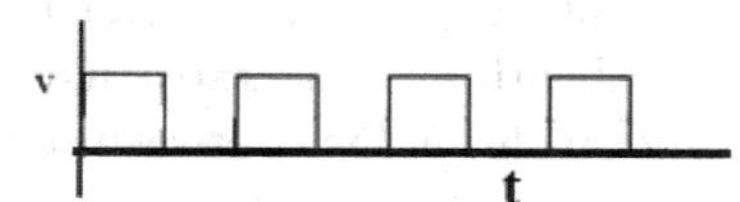

C.

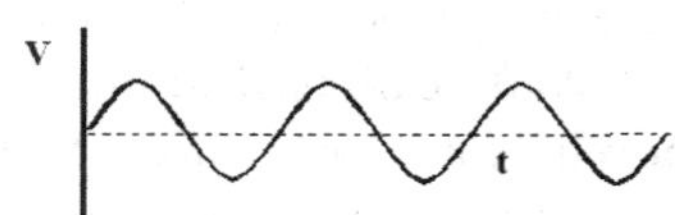

D.

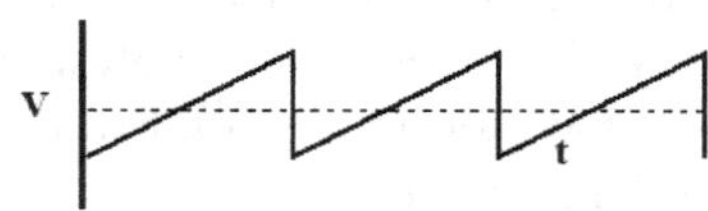

18. If the switch were left in position 1 and a new resistor is added in series to R, how would the voltage across the capacitor change?

A. V_{max} would increase
B. V_{max} would decrease
C. V_{max} would be reached quicker
D. V_{max} would be reached slower

19. What will be the magnetic force exerted on a neutron moving with a velocity of 30 m/s up though a magnetic field (B = 3 T) oriented downwards?

A. 0 N
B. 45 N
C. 90 N
D. 180 N

20. Which of the following components CANNOT store potential energy?

A. Capacitors
B. Resistors
C. Inductors
D. Batteries

Test-like thinking: CARS Practice passage

About his own *magnum opus*, *Infinite Jest* (pub. 1996), David Foster Wallace is reputed to have said that Wood's criticism—calling *Infinite Jest* "another example of hysterical realism"—was the highest praise he ever read about the work. One can well imagine why. British literary critic James Wood had a long history of directing vitriol at postmodern literature, including such widely lauded figures as Thomas Pynchon and Don DeLillo. His essay in the July 24, 2000 edition of the New Republic first coined the term in response to Zadie Smith's *White Teeth*. Although he devoted no small portion of his analysis to showing trends that began with Pynchon reached their zenith with Wallace, Smith's *White Teeth* came in for the harshest criticism. One cannot help but suspect this was because Wood just didn't enjoy the book, but that as a professional literary critic, he felt obliged to express that dislike in a bloviating long form essay.

Wood's criticism aside, *Infinite Jest* was an enormous success both commercially and artistically. In the decade following its publication, the book sold over a million copies—an unheard of feat for a thousand-page work that is unapologetically literary. The novel seemed to secure its place on everyone's end-of-year and end-of-decade "best of" lists from the very day it was first published. Interestingly, even critics (including the aforementioned James Wood) who initially expressed a strong distaste for the work later came to revise their views. The cynic might assert that this revision is simply eulogizing in response to Wallace's tragic suicide in 2008. Nonetheless, the impact *Infinite Jest* had on other promising young writers is undeniable. After holding that it felt "rather willed and secondhand . . . [and] ultimately irritating," in 2000 in a New York Times review, A. O. Scott later said of Wallace that he was "the best mind of his generation" and that *Infinite Jest* "set his generation's benchmark for literary ambition."

Much of the negative response to the work both among normal readers and professional critics stems from its enormous scope and intentionally fractured nature. The latter is illustrated within the narrative itself, as the plot skips around in chronology between several tangentially related (or wholly unrelated) plot threads and ultimately ends with no clear resolution for any characters, but for the ones we know are dead before the main plot begins. Wallace himself admitted to friend and fellow novelist Jonathan Franzen that even he himself thinks it's a "story [that] can't fully be made sense of." The fracturing of the story also works in the structure of the book. Wallace peppers the main narrative with nearly 400 end notes, many of which themselves have footnotes. Following each of these notes in turn forces the reader's attention to the physical act of reading itself. Given how several of the footnotes break across pages, one can easily understand Harold Bloom's complaint about the book having "[the] arrogance to expect every reader to keep four bookmarks . . . on hand [for] a single tome."

. . . Yet it is the surprisingly tender heart of the work that shows Wallace's true gifts. For all of its encyclopedic bravado the story is frequently very, very funny while also serving as a deeply thoughtful meditation on melancholy. It's no wonder that Wallace's own struggles with clinical depression should show through in his work.

1. The passage suggests that *Infinite Jest* would have been better received by its critics if:
   A. its story had be more coherent and focused.
   B. the critics had been better educated.
   C. it had expanded the main narrative to subsume the foot- and end-notes and provide more resolution.
   D. the critics were fans of *White Teeth*.

2. Which of the following authors would most likely be impacted by reading *Infinite Jest*, according to the passage?
   A. A young man who was still dreaming of work as a novelist, who later went on to write a series of very highly successful genre novels in both the mystery and fantasy genres
   B. A journalism student who sought to work on issues related to local politics in and around the town where she grew up
   C. An aspiring novelist, 23 years old when *Infinite Jest* was published, who then delved deeper into postmodern literature
   D. A poet interested in the impact of fractured storytelling on the reader's psyche

3. The author's attitude towards James Woods's literary critique of *Infinite Jest* can best be described as:
   A. unqualified approval.
   B. concerned that it demonstrates Woods's lack of qualification as a literary critic.
   C. objectively evaluative.
   D. disagreement and faint disdain.

4. The author's main thesis is that:
   A. critics who spoke poorly about *Infinite Jest* later came revise their opinions and this reveals the true genius of Wallace's *magnum opus*.
   B. the novel *Infinite Jest*, although a difficult read, is both a literary and commercial success that has at its heart an emotional expressiveness that belies its surface complexity.
   C. David Foster Wallace was able to mix literary genius and emotional expressiveness in part due to his own struggles with clinical depression.
   D. postmodern literature begin in the early 20th century with the work of Pynchon and DeLillo but reached its highest form in the works of late 20th century geniuses like David Foster Wallace.

5. The passage implies that which of the following is true?
   A. Mental illnesses such as depression are the hallmark of great novelists.
   B. Being a commercial success in an essential component of critical success for literary fiction.
   C. *Infinite Jest* is a highly overrated example of literary fiction.
   D. David Foster Wallace thought highly of the work of Thomas Pynchon.

To Do After Lesson 12

- [ ] Read Physics Chapter 10
- [ ] Read Biology Chapters 11 and 12
- [ ] Complete Physics QBank 2: Waves, Fluids, and Electrostatics

LESSON 13

Biochemistry 2

To Do Before Lesson 13

- [ ] Read Physics Chapter 10
- [ ] Read Biology Chapters 11 and 12
- [ ] Complete Physics QBank 2: Waves, Fluids, and Electrostatics

In Lesson 3

Problem-solving Warm-up
Effective Reading in the Sciences
Regulation of Carbohydrate Metabolism
Pentose Phosphate Pathway
MCAT Practice Passage
Hormonal Regulation of Metabolism
Metabolism of Fatty Acids
Metabolism of Proteins
MCAT Practice Passage
Problem-solving Cooldown

To Do After Lesson 13

- [ ] Read Psychology and Sociology Chapters 11 and 12
- [ ] Read Biochemistry Chapters 11 and 12
- [ ] Complete Timed Section 1 from the Verbal Practice: 108 Passages book
- [ ] Complete the Chemical and Physical Foundations section from the AAMC Online Official Guide at e-mcat.com

Problem-solving Warm-up

1. If the conversion of monosaccharide A to polysaccharide B leads to an equilibrium with a majority of polysaccharide B, which of the following must be true?

   A. $\Delta G° = 0$
   B. $\Delta G° > 0$
   C. $\Delta G° < 0$
   D. $\Delta G° = K_{eq}$

2. An isomerase:

   A. transfers part of one molecule to another molecule.
   B. rearranges groups within a molecule.
   C. removes a group from a molecule forming a double bond, or adds a group to a double bond.
   D. joins two molecules together using energy from ATP.

3. The synthesis of proteins from amino acids is an example of a(n):

   A. anabolic reaction.
   B. catabolic reaction.
   C. exergonic reaction.
   D. spontaneous reaction.

4. Which of the following has the highest ratio of energy released per gram of material?

   A. Alcohols
   B. Proteins
   C. Fats
   D. Carbohydrates

5. Allosteric enzymes are commonly found in what metabolic regulatory system?

   A. Competitive inhibition
   B. Enzyme induction
   C. Feedback inhibition
   D. Enzyme repression

This page left intentionally blank.

Effective Reading in the Sciences

Reading science passages on the MCAT means being able to keep track of important (i.e. likely to be tested) information in the passage. You must be able to anticipate, recognize, and understand scientific concepts presented in many different forms.

There are at least 10 different types of glycogen storage disease (GSDs). The types are put into groups based on the enzyme that is missing. The most common forms of GSD are types I, III and IV. About one in 20,000 people can have a type of GSD.

GSD I, also known as von Gierke disease, results from the loss of a phosphorylation-state modifying enzyme and causes a characteristic enlarged liver in those who are afflicted. GSD III, also known as Cori disease, results from a lack of a glycogen debranching enzyme. This causes the body to form glycogen molecules that have an abnormal structure. This abnormal structure prevents the glycogen from being broken down into free glucose. In GSD IV there is no significant increased amount of glycogen in the tissues. In this type of GSD, there is lack of glycogen branching enzyme, which leads to the formation of glycogen with fewer branch points and longer outer chains. This abnormal glycogen is thought to stimulate the immune system and produce glycogen deposits that cause a scarring of the liver, muscle and heart tissues.

A major complication for these patients is hypoglycemia with severe drops in blood glucose even after eating. A research study was conducted to quantify the difference in blood glucose levels in patients with GSD type I. The blood glucose levels of 100 subjects diagnosed with GSD I and 100 healthy volunteers were monitored for 24 hours. Meals were provided to both groups at hours 0 and 12. Group post-meal average blood glucose levels as a function of time are shown in figure 1.

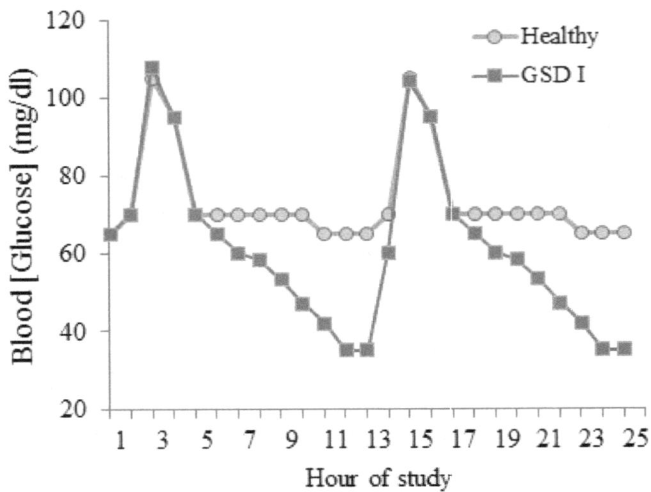

Figure 1 Blood glucose levels post-meal for both healthy and GSD I groups.

6. If experiments are performed on the blood solubility of the glycogen produced by GSD I, III and IV patients, which of the following results is expected?

    A. I > IV > III
    B. IV > III > I
    C. III > IV > I
    D. III > I > IV

7. Based on the results of the group study, the enzyme defective in GSD I is LEAST likely to:

    A. add phosphate groups to its target.
    B. catalyze gluconeogenesis.
    C. catalyze glycogenolysis.
    D. remove phosphate groups from its target.

8. Study physicians took fasting blood samples of all participants prior to the onset of the experiment. Which of the following is expected in the GSD I samples?

    I. Hyperlipidemia
    II. Lactic acidemia
    III. Hyperuricemia

    A. I only
    B. I and II only
    C. II and III only
    D. I, II and III

9. According to the results shown in Figure 1, if a healthy person eats a meal at 12pm, when will their body begin to release glucagon?

    A. 2pm
    B. 3pm
    C. 5pm
    D. 7pm

10. Which of the following best explains the characteristic liver of GSD I patients?

    A. Decreased glycogen in the liver leads to inflammation and swelling
    B. Increased blood flow to the liver as a result of increased demand for glucose
    C. Increased glycogen in hepatocytes causes the cells to absorb water and swell
    D. Increased branching of the glycogen molecules prevents efficient packing

Carbohydrate Metabolism

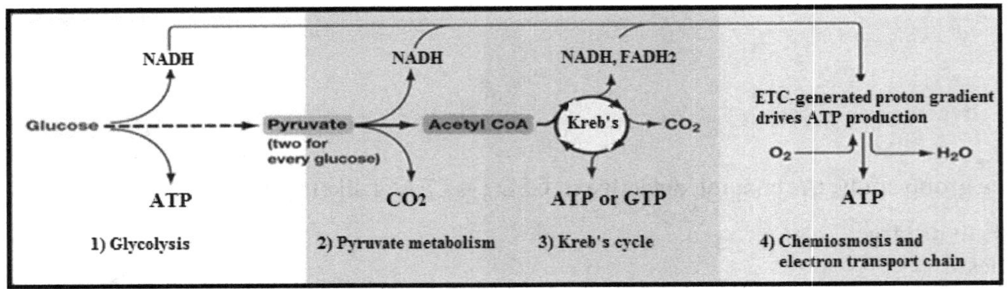

Phase I, glucose splitting (-2 ATP)

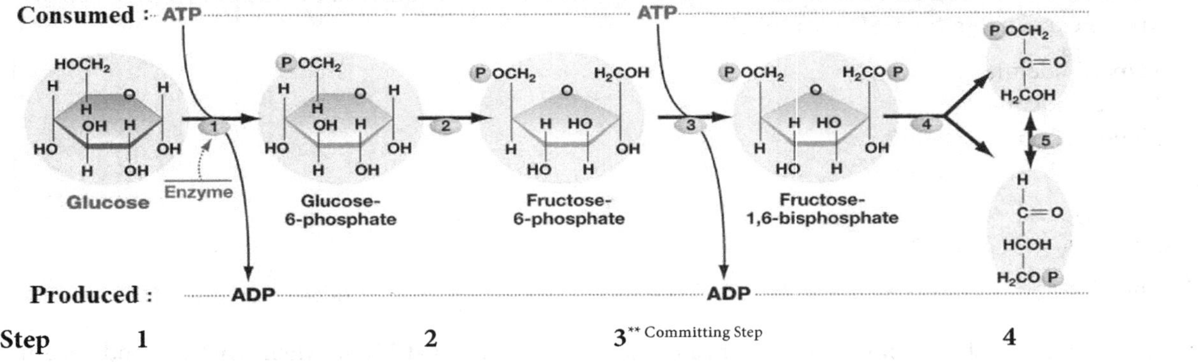

Step 1 2 3** Committing Step 4 5

Enzyme

Reversible

A) phosphoglucose isomerase *B) hexokinase* *C) triose phosphate isomerase*
D) phosphofructokinase *E) aldolase* *F) G-3-P dehydrogenase*
G) phosphoglycerate kinase *H) pyruvate kinase* *I) phosphoglycerate mutase* *J) enolase*

Besides glucose, what other molecules can enter the glycolytic pathway?

Phase II, Energy is produced (+4 ATP)

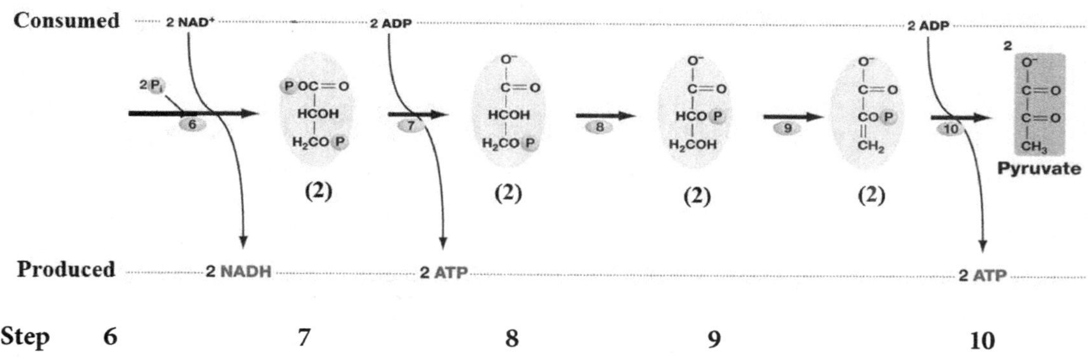

Step 6 7 8 9 10

Enzyme

Reversible

A) phosphoglucose isomerase *B) hexokinase* *C) triose phosphate isomerase*
D) phosphofructokinase *E) aldolase* *F) G-3-P dehydrogenase*
G) phosphoglycerate kinase *H) pyruvate kinase* *I) phosphoglycerate mutase* *J) enolase*

During periods of low energy needs, what alternative process can the pyruvate produced be used for?

Regulation

In step 3, high levels of ________________________ bind to the allosteric site of ________________________,

causing a conformational change and shutting down the enzyme.

In step 3, low to mid levels of ______________________ bind to the active site of ______________________.

________________, ________________or ________________ (an indicator of low ATP) can speed up the conversion

of pyruvate to ________________.

Gluconeogenesis

Similarities

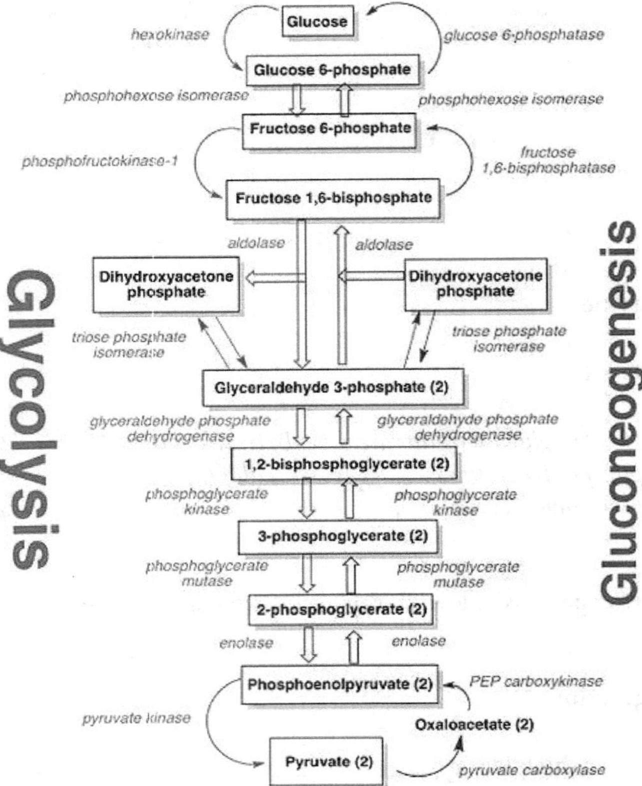

Differences

Regulation

Glycogen Synthesis and Breakdown

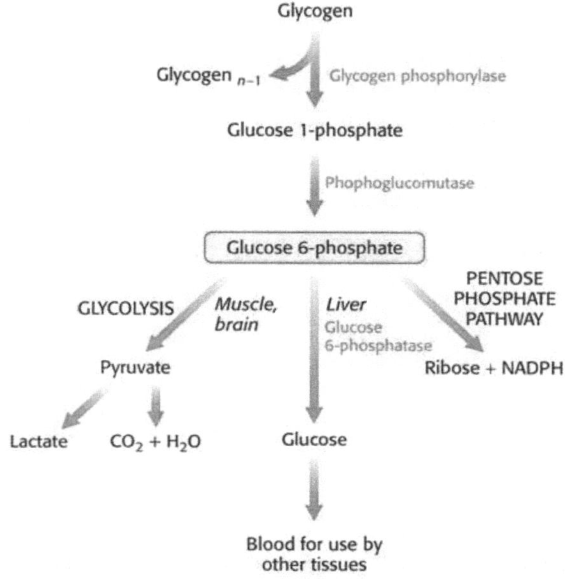

Location

Function

Dominant Linkage

Energetics

The liver has glucose-6-phosphatase, yet muscle does not. Why?

Effect of Epinephrine and Glucagon

Fermentation

When there is an absence of ________________________, glycolysis will be the primary source of ATP.

________________________ must be regenerated in order to allow glycolysis to continue.

During fermentation in human cells, pyruvate accepts electrons from ________________________.

11. The only goal of fermentation is:
    A. reduction to allow glycolysis to continue.
    B. oxidation to allow glycolysis to continue.
    C. phosphorylation to allow glycolysis to continue.
    D. ATP production to allow glycolysis to continue.

12. The ratio of ATP generated in aerobic conditions to the ATP generated in anaerobic conditions is approximately:
    A. 10:1.
    B. 20:1.
    C. 30:1.
    D. 40:1.

13. Which stage of aerobic respiration produces ATP and NADH while releasing CO_2?
    A. Glycolysis
    B. Krebs cycle
    C. Electron transport chain
    D. Fermentation

14. The fermentation products produced by human and yeast cells, respectively, are:
    A. ethanol and lactic acid.
    B. lactic acid and ethanol.
    C. ethanol and methanol.
    D. lactic acid and ethanoic acid.

Pentose Phosphate Pathway

This path oxidizes glucose to make NADPH and other carbohydrates for biosynthesis.

While glycolysis is a ____________________ process, the PPP can act as a ____________________ process, building several compounds from glycolytic intermediates.

The major route for reduction of ____________________. to ____________________ is the reaction of glucose-6-phosphate through two successive reactions.

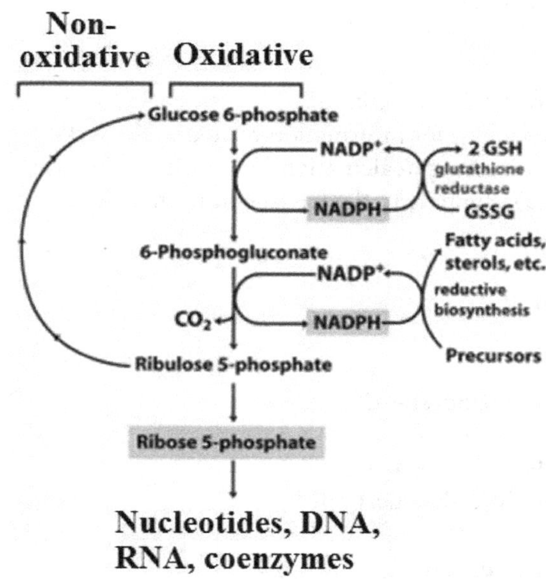

Oxidative

Non-oxidative

Carbon tracking for the entire PPP:

Oxidative Phase 6C + 6C + 6C → (3x1C) + 5C + 5C + 5C

Sugar Interconversion Phase: 5C + 5C + 5C → 6C + 6C + 3C

Timed MCAT Practice Passage

Mastery of the MCAT sciences is a two-part process. First you must study to understand (not just memorize!) the science content, and then you must study the content actively and challenge yourself within the context of the exam.

1. Complete your reading of the passage (3-4 minutes).
   - Write down what you believe to be the primary science content underlying the passage.
   - What facts or concepts do you anticipate to be tested? When you are done with the questions determine if you were correct. What passage clues were there to imply related topics that showed up in the questions?
   - Were there any key terms or important scientific relationships you missed?
   - Were you able to draw any conclusions from the data, if presented?

2. Complete the practice questions on your own (4-5 minutes)
   - Rephrase each question in your own mind after reading it to clarify the task.
   - Research the relevant area(s) of the passage or your own knowledge for information related to the task.
   - Respond to the question by choosing the answer that fits your research/calculations *and* satisfies the task.
   - If no answer seems obvious, eliminate answers that fail to have support in the passage or in the relevant science.

3. Analyze your wrong answer choices to the questions you missed.
   - Did you understand the task in the question?
   - What skill type was the question?
   - Did you know the science/formula/concept needed to answer the question?
   - Did you recognize the science being hinted at?
   - Were you able to find information in the passage quickly when you needed it?
   - Were there any necessary scientific concepts you failed to apply to the question?
     - If so, why?
   - If you made a mistake in calculations, have you identified your mistake?

This page left intentionally blank.

The mechanism by which polypeptide chains fold into unique three-dimensional structures is still a focus of much research today. It has been determined that proteins prefer to adopt conformations that are the most thermodynamically stable, which at times necessitates bonds to be formed between amino acids that are significantly far apart from each other in the native chain. The folding of a protein is largely attributed to the chemical structure of the individual amino acids that comprise it. In order for a protein to find the most stable structure, sometimes it must undergo a number of trials and errors, and proteins can adopt many different conformations depending upon the solutions they are in.

Scientists were interested in looking at the denaturation capabilities of a number of different organic solvents. They dissolved soybean proteins into a number of highly hydrophobic solvents, immiscible with water, and heated them to three temperatures: 20 °C (i.e., room temperature), 60 °C, and 100 °C. The scientists then tested the absorbance of the solutions, and used this as a proxy to quantify the amount of native protein contents that remained in the solution following the treatment. They repeated the experiment with solvents that had fairly high hydrophobicity but were able to dissolve slightly into water. The results of these experiments can be found in Tables 1 and 2 below.

Table 1 Denaturation (60 minutes) of defatted soybean flour proteins with completely water-immiscible organic solvents

Solvents	**Absorbance at 20 °C**	**Absorbance at 60 °C**	**Absorbance at 100 °C**
Benzene	0.275	0.241	0.242
sec-Amyl acetate	0.283	0.270	0.241
Trichloroethylene	0.283	0.242	0.219
Water	0.250	0.202	0.192

Table 2 Denaturation (60 minutes) of defatted soybean flour proteins with partially water-miscible organic solvents

Solvents	**Absorbance at 20 °C**	**Absorbance at 60 °C**	**Absorbance at 100 °C**
Methyl ethyl ketone	0.304	0.268	0.263
n-Butanol	0.266	0.210	0.184
Isopropanol	0.240	0.194	0.176
Water	0.250	0.202	0.192

15. Which of the following amino acids would most likely be in the inner core of a protein immersed in water?

    A. Asparagine
    B. Tryptophan
    C. Glutamate
    D. Lysine

16. Based on the results of the experiments, which of the following organic molecules is most likely to denature soybean proteins at high temperatures?

    A.

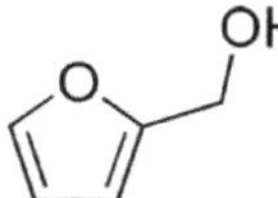

    C.

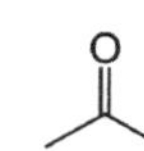

    B.

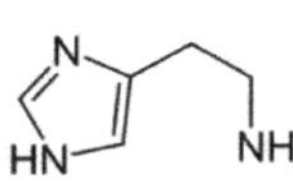

    D.

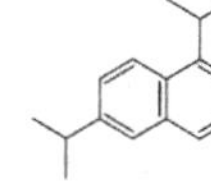

17. All of the following bonds could contribute to a protein's tertiary structure except:

    A. S-S.
    B. O-H.
    C. C-O.
    D. N-H.

18. Which of the following solvents would be most effective at denaturing soybean proteins at room temperature?

    A. Trichloroethylene
    B. Isopropanol
    C. Water
    D. Methyl ethyl ketone

19. Why did the scientists specifically include the denaturation results for water as a solvent?

    A. To demonstrate that water denatures proteins more effectively at higher temperatures than lower temperatures
    B. To demonstrate that water is the most effective denaturing solvent tested
    C. To demonstrate that some partially-miscible solvents denature proteins more effectively than water itself
    D. To demonstrate that soybean proteins do not contain hydrophobic residues

20. Heat most likely denatures proteins by:

    A. improving the thermodynamic stability of the bonds in the protein.
    B. disrupting hydrogen bonds and nonpolar hydrophobic interactions.
    C. disrupting covalent bonds and nonpolar hydrophobic interactions.
    D. disrupting ionic bonds and improving nonpolar hydrophobic interactions.

Pyruvate Decarboxylation and the Citric Acid Cycle

In order to continue with aerobic respiration, pyruvate must be converted to Acetyl CoA.

Pyruvate → (CO_2) Decarboxylation → Oxidation ($2e^-$) → Transfer to CoA (CoA) → Acetyl CoA

Net Reaction: Pyruvate + CoA + NAD^+ → Acetyl CoA + CO_2 + NADH + H^+

______ NADH total ______ $FADH_2$ total ______ ATP total ______ CO_2 total

ΔG Glucose: -686 kcal/mol ATP: 7.5 kcal/mol

The total energy produced by all ATPs is ____________ kcal/mol.

The % of energy recovered from aerobic respiration is ____________.

EXAMPLE

______ NADH from glycolysis

______ NADH from pyruvate decarboxylation (PD)

______ NADH from Krebs cycle

______ $FADH_2$ from Krebs cycle

______ total ATP from glycolysis

______ total ATP from Krebs cycle

______ net ATP/NADH from glycolysis

______ net ATP/NADH from PD and Krebs

______ net ATP/$FADH_2$

______ Total ATP from glucose

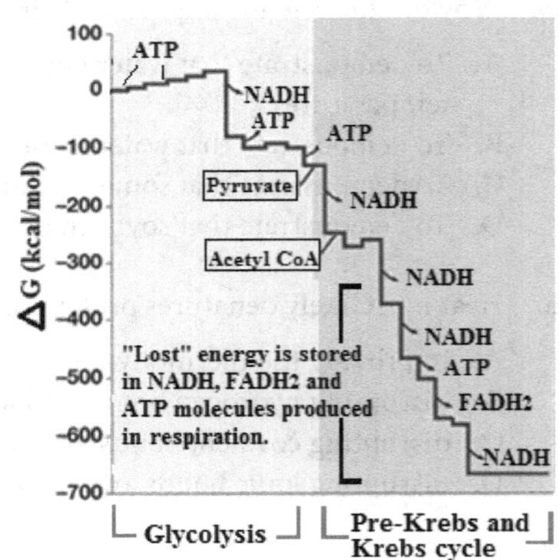

21. Membrane traffic diseases can impede the Krebs cycle due to damage to which cell membrane component?

    A. Cholesterol
    B. Integral proteins
    C. Glycoproteins
    D. Lipoproteins

22. Citrate is produced by the:

    A. ribosome.
    B. peroxisome.
    C. mitochondrion.
    D. smooth endoplasmic reticulum.

23. Acetyl CoA can also be used by the cell in fatty acid creation. Which of the following is true of this path?

    A. Fatty acid creation is reductive, while the Krebs cycle is oxidative.
    B. Both fatty acid creation and the Krebs cycle take place in the cytoplasm.
    C. Fatty acid creation is oxidative, while the Krebs cycle is reductive.
    D. Both fatty acid creation and the Krebs cycle take place in the mitochondrial matrix.

Build Your Science Foundation

For biochemistry on the MCAT, there is no shortage of information to learn. The MCAT can expect you to know multi-step metabolic pathways but the best way to do this is to start with the most important steps and understand the overall flow of the reaction. Placing your emphasis on understanding will maximize recall and your test score.

Rule #1:

Rule #2:

Rule #3:

Rule #4:

Rule #5:

Rule #6:

Rule #7:

Rule #8:

Biochemistry Mnemonics

Glycolysis Steps

Glycolysis Enzymes

Citric Acid Cycle Compounds

Citric Acid Cycle Enzymes

Pyruvate Products of Complete Oxidation

Have you made your own mnemonics for learning biochemistry? If so, what are they?

Hormonal Regulation of Metabolism

Insulin

Glucagon

Epinephrine

Hypothalamus

Adipose Tissue

Fasting State

Fed State

Hormonal Regulation of Blood [glucose]

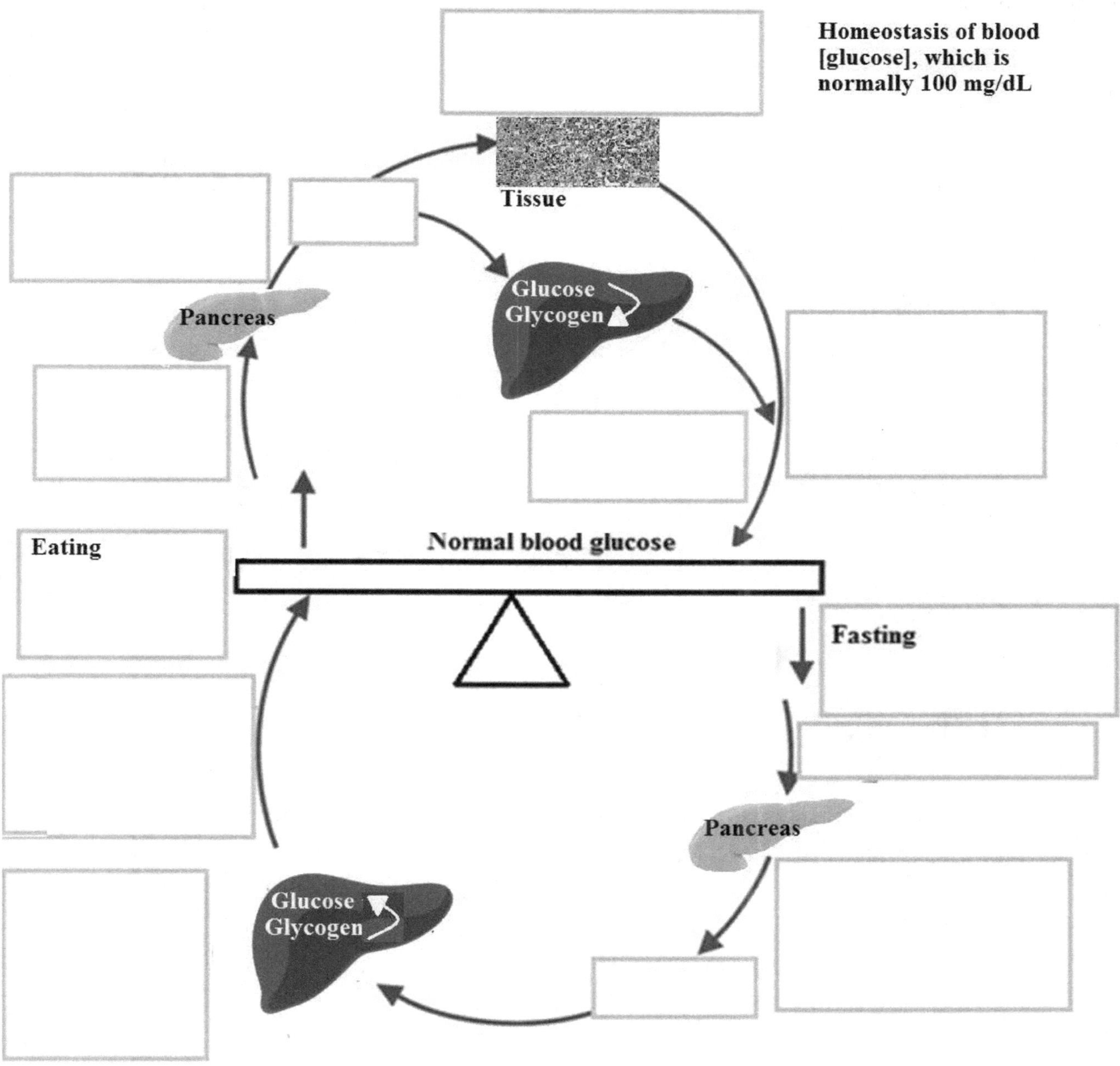

Metabolism of Alternative Fuels

Metabolism of Fatty Acids

Metabolism of Alternative Fuels

Metabolism of Proteins

Problem-solving Cooldown

24. Predominantly, what type of energy facilitates cell activity?

    A. Thermal
    B. Electrical
    C. Atomic
    D. Chemical

25. What is the most common electron carrier among biological systems?

    A. FAD
    B. NAD
    C. Coenzyme A
    D. Cytochrome C

26. During the process of translocation, glucose is brought into the cell and is chemically modified into what compound to prevent it from leaving the cell?

    A. Acetyl-CoA
    B. ATP
    C. Pyruvate
    D. Glucose 6-phosphate

27. Fatty acids can also be utilized by the body for fuel. The metabolism of an 8-carbon fatty acid will produce how many ATP molecules?

    A. 36
    B. 48
    C. 64
    D. 96

28. For each molecule of glucose that undergoes aerobic respiration, how many carbon dioxide molecules are released?

    A. 2
    B. 4
    C. 5
    D. 6

This page left intentionally blank.

Test-like Thinking: CARS Practice Passage

While there is no such thing as "elder poetry", at the end of the 20th century a number of publishers started to release small collections of poems by both young and old writers that specifically addressed themselves to the experiences of elderly people. While these poems struggled with the experiences of older citizens, it is essential to distinguish them from the over-simplified label "elder poetry", which would suggest that American culture is split into "young" and "old". While the day-to-day experiences of both such groups diverge from each other (especially at the ends of the spectrum), the salient fact is less their divergence than their overlap. The renowned expert on aging, Donald Leigh, correctly put it thus:

Elderly poets ought not be analyzed as a wholly separate group on the grounds of the false notion that they are all alike, or that they even follow similar lyrical or stylistic patterns that somehow reflect their senescence. But, in our increasingly youth-obsessed culture, the elderly do have a special literary place that can be described. Such description must, perforce, include the ever increasing marginalization of elderly voices in our society, the isolation felt as a consequence of that marginalization, the gradual diminishment of both personal, that is to say mental, and political, that is economic, power.

A decade into the 21st century, there is by now a sizable body of poetic works that focus on these personal and public experiences of the elderly. That the public experiences of a youth oriented culture inform the private sphere is axiomatic. The youth orientation fundamentally means any society whose dominant mode is a capitalist marketplace is one in which the marketplace focuses nearly all of its energy in appealing to younger consumers (in the understandable paradigm that it is better to capture the brand loyalty of the young, thereby creating a lifetime of purchasing habits).

One example of an elder poet reflecting on these experiences is found in Michelle Rood's collection *December Speaks*. In the first poem, Rood reflects on young lovers who are kept apart only by the intransigence of the nearly-senile elder patriarch of the young woman's family. To fulfill their romance, the patriarch serves only as an obstacle that must be circumvented or destroyed. The lovers here represent the dynamism of the public sphere of life, and the patriarch is, perhaps, a stand-in for Rood herself.

In societies in which the elderly are still accorded respect, the poetry produced reflects the potent spark produced when experience is melded with the calming that comes with age, and with the horror of impending death. The 95 year old Lebanese poet Farid Rafiq writes in *The Olive Grove* of a farmer approaching his one hundredth birthday (demonstrating that no matter how old we become, "old" is always someone older than us). The farmer's children are powerful elder statesmen who still come to him for advice, his grandchildren are family leaders who come to pay their respects and his great-grandchildren are filled with the mindless energy of their youth, and ignore him entirely. Rafiq presents a series of poignant images reflecting the man's gradual surrender of all that mattered to him. When his birthday arrives, the man has retreated into total dementia, not as an unwilling victim of a disease, but as a voluntary choice of one seeking a final shelter from the crushing losses that have built up in his mind.

[Adapted from, "Old Writers, Young Voices" by B. Leigh, 2011.]

Passage taken from the Next Step online QBank

29. The passage discussion of the experience of young and old writers assumes that:
    A. the experience of younger poets is wholly distinct from that of older poets.
    B. there is a degree of similarity between the experience of young and old poets.
    C. the experience of rambunctious youth is inferior to the experience of literary emeriti.
    D. elder poets influence younger poets through their choice of imagery.

30. According to the passage, many elder poets write poetry that:
    A. focuses on their isolation in a culture that is obsessed with youth.
    B. shows distinctly lyrical patterns that mark them as elder poets.
    C. presents the voices of the elderly through the lens of youth.
    D. portrays the elderly as an impediment to the dynamism of youth.

31. In the final paragraph, the author asserts that:
    A. Rafiq treats dementia less seriously than he should.
    B. poems by those who feel a strong connection to their grandchildren are more respectful of the elderly than works by other poets.
    C. senility and dementia serve different literary functions based on the position of the poet in society.
    D. poetry of higher quality is produced when society accords respect to its older citizens.

32. The author implies that the relationship between elderly family members with ailing mental faculties and younger people:
    I. serves primarily as a barrier to happiness for younger people in Rafiq's poetry.
    II. reflects the experiences of the elder poet in the larger society.
    III. is fundamentally detrimental to the elderly.

    A. I only
    B. II only
    C. II and III only
    D. I, II, and III

33. Which of the following is most strongly supported by the passage?
    A. Capitalist societies are youth oriented because of their economic structure.
    B. Capitalist societies marginalize the voices of the elderly because their lyrical and stylistic patterns are unique to them.
    C. Capitalist societies have, in the 21st century, shifted into a youth orientation.
    D. Capitalist societies encourage day-to-day experiences that are widely divergent between the young and old.

To Do After Lesson 13

- ☐ Read Psychology and Sociology Chapters 11 and 12
- ☐ Read Biochemistry Chapters 11 and 12
- ☐ Complete Timed Section 1 from the Verbal Practice: 108 Passages book
- ☐ Complete the Chemical and Physical Foundations section from the AAMC Online Official Guide at e-mcat.com

LESSON 14

Psychology 2

To Do Before Lesson 14

- ☐ Read Psychology and Sociology Chapters 11 and 12
- ☐ Read Biochemistry Chapters 11 and 12
- ☐ Complete Timed Section 1 from the Verbal Practice: 108 Passages book
- ☐ Complete the Chemical and Physical Foundations section from the AAMC Online Official Guide at e-mcat.com

In Lesson 14

Problem-solving Warm-up
Personality
Effective Reading in the Sciences
Psychological Disorders
MCAT Practice Passage
Social Effects on Behavior
MCAT Practice Passage
Problem-solving Cooldown

To Do After Lesson 14

- ☐ Complete Full Timed Section 2 from the Verbal Practice: 108 Passages book
- ☐ Complete the Biological and Biochemical Foundations section from the AAMC Online Official Guide at e-mcat.com
- ☐ Complete Psychology and Sociology QBank 4: Identity, Disorders, and Groups

Problem-solving Warm-up

1. If social stratification is a potential confounder in a study to investigate the effect of education on IQ, which of the following subject selections would be most appropriate?

   A. A small sample of people from each socioeconomic status
   B. A large sample of people from each socioeconomic status
   C. A small sample of people from a single socioeconomic status
   D. A large sample of people from a single socioeconomic status

2. Five study participants are asked to wear a set of headphones and listen to classical music presented to one ear while ignoring country music presented to the opposite ear. After 5 minutes of listening, all channels were turned off and the participants were asked to write out what details they recall about the country music. This is an example of:

   A. shadowing the unattended ear.
   B. dichotic listening.
   C. trichotic listening.
   D. subjective listening.

3. Saturation is a primary danger when training animals using which conditioning technique?

   A. Instinctual drift
   B. Continuous reinforcement
   C. Variable ratio reinforcement
   D. Fixed ratio reinforcement

4. Nancy's social security number is 666871293, but she can only ever remember it as 666 87 1293. What memory device is Nancy relying on?

   A. Decay
   B. Chunking
   C. Mnemonics
   D. Hindsight bias

5. Which of the following most strongly challenges the theory that pain is an entirely physical phenomena?

   A. Referred pain
   B. Delayed pain
   C. Phantom limb pain
   D. Neuropathic pain

Personality

Humanist Perspective

Characteristics for Fully Functioning

Maslow's Hierarchy

EXAMPLE

Evolutionary Perspective

Besides survival, what is a driving force behind personality?

How might the MCAT connect the following evolutionary tasks to personality traits using evolutionary psychology?

Foes

Food

Friends

Offspring

Kin

Selection

Social Cognitive Perspective

Bobo Doll Experiment

Behavioral Model of Abnormal Psychology

5 Primary Determinants of Personality

1.

2.

3.

4.

5.

Biological Perspective

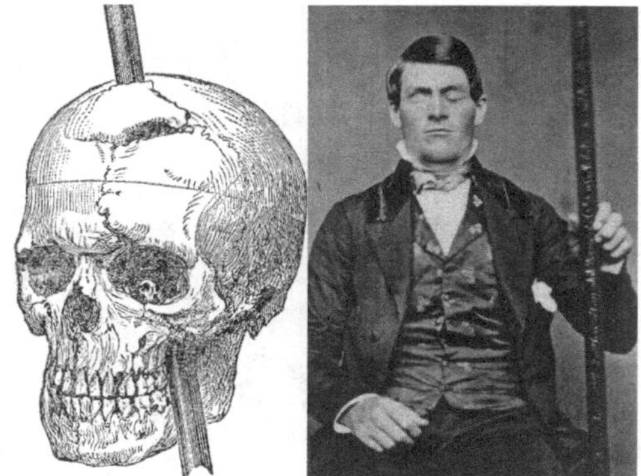

Phineas Gage

Genes and Personality

Neuroanatomy and Personality

Testosterone

Estrogen

Vasopressin

Oxytocin

Behaviorist Perspective

Watson

Habits

Thorndike

Law of Effect

Law of Exercise

How would a behaviorist explain an extremely shy child?

___

___

___

Pavlov

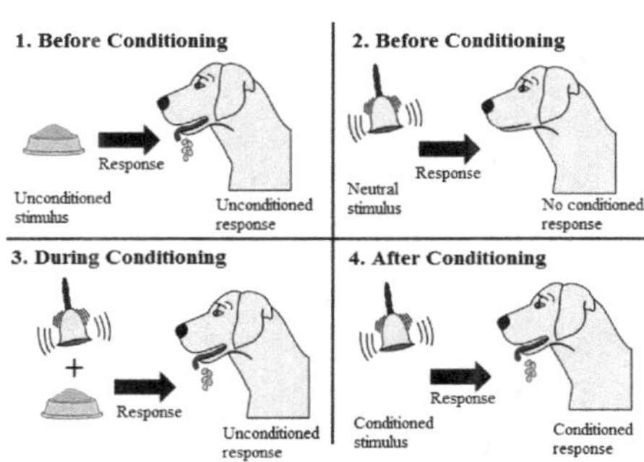

Skinner

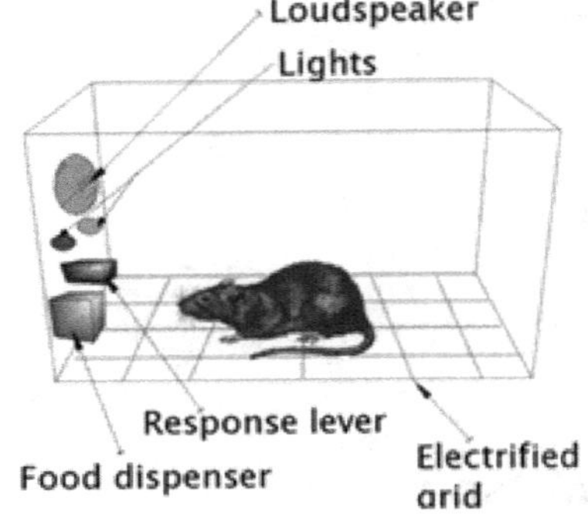
Loudspeaker
Lights
Response lever
Food dispenser
Electrified grid

Operant Conditioning

Positive vs. Negative

Reinforcement vs. Punishment

	Something is ________	Something is ________
Behavior occurs ______ often		
Behavior occurs ______ often		

Conditioning Quiz

Responding decreases with the elimination of reinforcing consequences during the extinction process of:

In ___________________ conditioning, the conditioned responses are active behaviors that operate on the environment.

Which approach can be used to condition physiological and emotional responses?

In classical conditioning, ___________________ occurs when the conditioned response decreases when the conditioned stimulus is presented alone repeatedly.

If a tone predicts an electric shock which causes the subject to startle, what does the electric shock serve as?

Is it possible for an intended punishment to function as a reinforcement?

How could a trainer convert escape learning into avoidance learning in a rat experiment involving painful air puffs?

Trait Perspective

Allport

Cattel

Extraversion vs. Introversion

Sensing vs. Intuition

Thinking vs. Feeling

Judging vs. Perceiving

Eysenck

Extraversion

Neuroticism

Psychoticism

From Acts to Personality

The "Big 5"

What is a major advantage of trait theory?

If certain behaviors are situational, how does that affect trait theory?

Effective Reading in the Sciences

Working memory is transient and allows people to consider information temporarily. The prefrontal cortex is primarily involved in working memory and is influenced by the release of dopamine or glutamate. Information in working memory has the potential to become long-term memory. The medial temporal lobe and the hippocampus, in that order, are theorized to mediate converting short-term memory into long-term memory.

Evidence for has come from the case-study of H.M., an individual who had his medial temporal lobe removed to address severe epilepsy. As a result, H.M. was unable to remember recent events. H.M. was unable to remember speaking with people with whom he had recently spoken. However, H.M. was able to recall information from far in his past, suggesting long-term memory involves a long-term change in the connections of neurons. It has been found that biochemical processes that occur proximal and distal to an event lead to long-term potentiation. The neurons share connections, whose strength and number are modified, along with an increase in NMDA activity, leading to long-term, stable relationships between the neurons.

A study was conducted in which participants with trauma-induced amnesia were exposed to new tasks and then assessed for the time necessary to master the task. The two tasks were a vocabulary /definition recall task and how to enter data into a database. Participants were "trained" by exposure to and practice with the target skill 25 times. Researchers recorded the number of words (out of 10) participants were able to recall and the number of seconds (out of 10) required to complete the data entry task at 5, 10 and 15 minutes post training. The results are shown below.

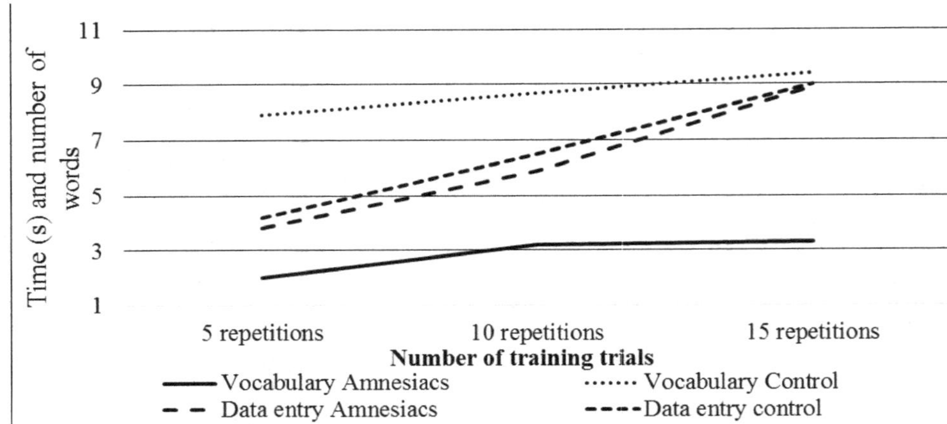

Figure 1 The words learned or time to learn a task after a number of training repetitions

6. The results of the study strongly support which of the following?

   I. Amnesiacs are able to learn declarative information as well as controls
   II. Amnesiacs are able to learn procedural information as well as controls
   III. Amnesiacs are able to learn emotional information as well as controls

   A. I only
   B. II only
   C. III only
   D. I and III only

7. H.M. would likely have the most difficulty with which memory task?

   A. Remembering the names of childhood friends
   B. Remembering how to drive to his long-time home
   C. Remembering a phone number that he just heard
   D. Remembering what he ate for lunch yesterday

8. According to the passage, what is the typical sequence of brain regions involved with memory as it passes from short to long term?

   A. Prefrontal cortex, medial temporal lobe, hippocampus
   B. Medial temporal lobe, prefrontal cortex, hippocampus
   C. Amygdala, hippocampus, medial temporal lobe
   D. Amygdala, prefrontal cortex, medial temporal lobe

9. A follow up diffusion tensor imaging study revealed that individuals highly skilled in a given task had slightly higher synaptic density compared to those with lower skills, but with additional practice over 4 weeks, were able to increase their synaptic density far more than low skilled performers after the same training. According to the passage, which of the following will also be found?

   A. Long-term potentiation among high-skill subjects took place exclusively in the hippocampus
   B. Greater levels of long-term potentiation occurred in low-skill rather than high-skilled subjects from week 1 to 4
   C. High-skill subjects have increased NMDA receptors in areas involved with the task compared with low-skill subjects
   D. The density of NMDA receptors in high-skill subjects became significantly reduced

10. Which of the following procedures would be most effective in ascertaining the brain areas involved in declarative versus procedural tasks?

    A. Observe the neural connections of a human recalling a list of family birthdays followed by a test on state capitals
    B. Use an experimental where the hippocampus is surgically ablated while a human subject is asked to tie their shoes
    C. PET scan of humans subjects describing their high school graduation and then riding a bike.
    D. Comparing the time taken for amnesiacs to complete a task recalling important historical dates or recalling events from one hour previous

Psychological Disorders

Biomedical Approach

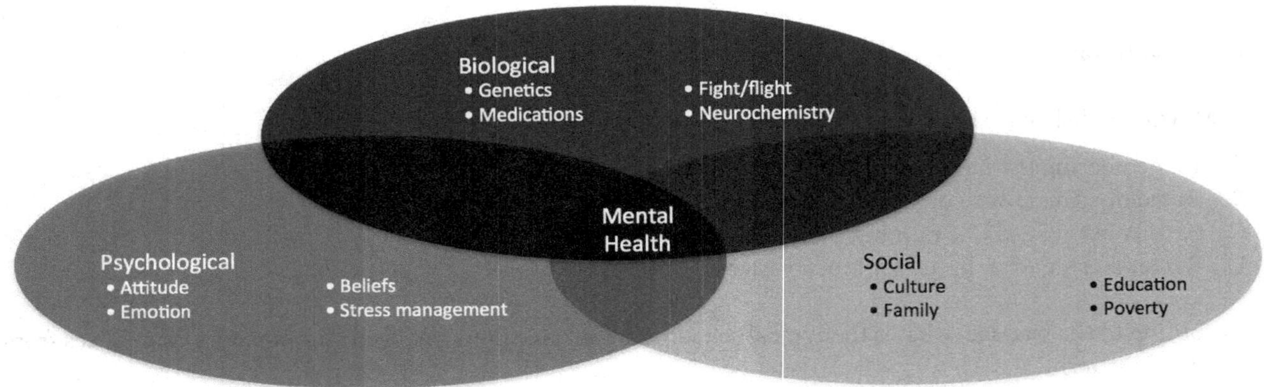

Biopsychosocial Approach

Classifying Psychological Disorders

Definition?

Neurosis

Psychosis

Types of Disorders

Anxiety

Somatic

Bipolar

Depressive

Dissociative

Anxiety Disorders

Phobia

Panic Disorder

Post-traumatic Stress Disorder

Obsessive-Compulsive Disorder

Generalized Anxiety Disorder

Somatic Disorders

Hypochondriasis

Conversion Disorder

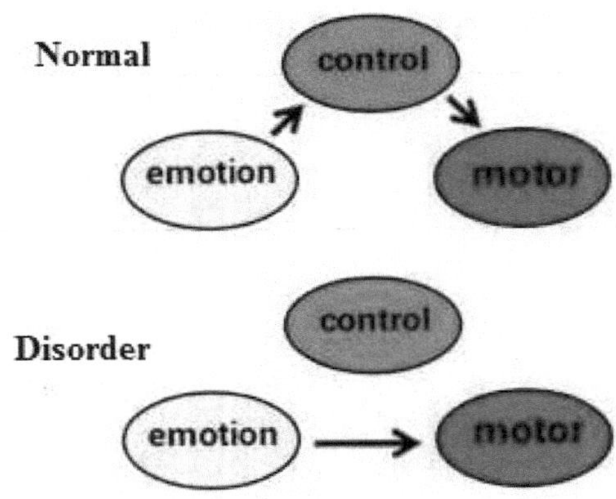

Bipolar Disorder

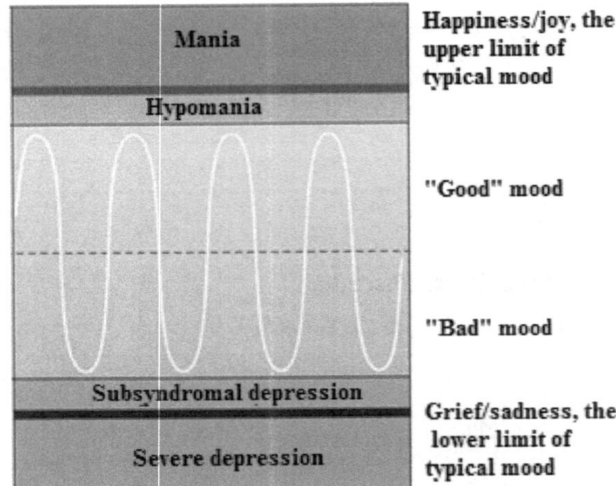

Type I

Type I Mixed

Type II

Depressive Disorders

Major Depression

Persistent Depressive Disorder

Psychotic Depression

Postpartum Depression

Seasonal Affective Disorder

Bipolar Disorder

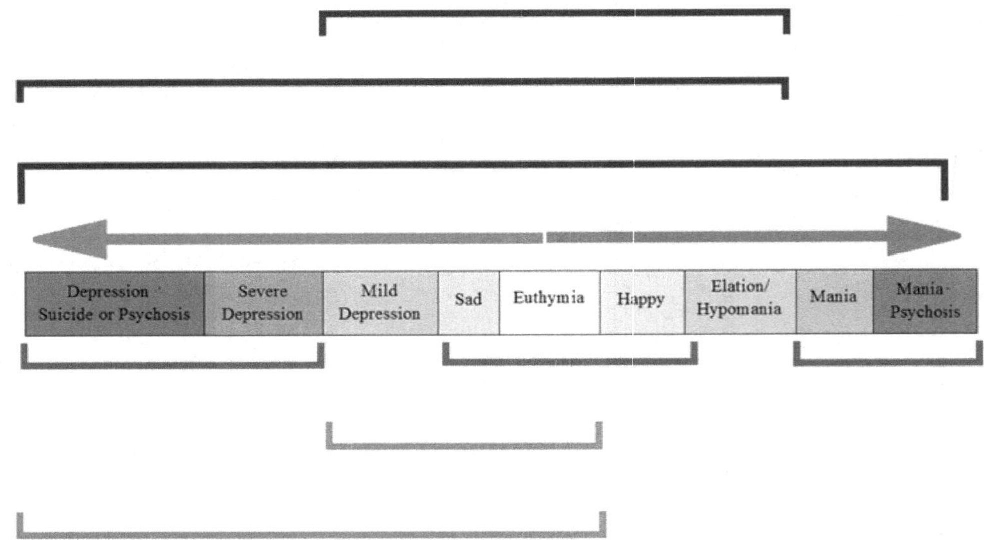

Schizophrenia

Positive Symptoms

Negative Symptoms

Paranoid

Disorganized

Catatonic

Residual

Schizoaffective

Dissociative Disorders

Amnesia

Localized

Selective

Generalized

Continuous

Dissociative Identity Disorder

Fugue State

Depersonalization Disorder

Other Dissociative Disorder

7 Major Personality Disorders

Personality Disorders Worksheet Exercise

	Disorder	Behaviors
"Odd" Behavior	Paranoid	Irrational suspicions and mistrust of others
	Schizoid	Lack of interest in social relationships
	Schizotypal	Odd behavior and/or thinking
Overly Dramatic	Antisocial	Disregard for the law and rights of others (may make up a significant portion of the prison population in some countries)
	Borderline	Instability in relationships, self-image, identity, and behavior
	Histrionic	Pervasive attention-seeking behavior, shallow or exaggerated emotions
	Narcissistic	Pervasive sense of own grandiosity; need for admiration and lack of empathy
Anxiety-ridden	Avoidant	Social inhibition; feelings of inadequacy
	Dependent	Pervasive psychological dependence on others
	Obsessive-compulsive	Rigid conformity to rules and moral codes; excessive orderliness

Personality Disorders Worksheet Exercise Level 1

	Disorder	Behaviors
"Odd" Behavior	Paranoid	
		Lack of interest in social relationships
	Schizotypal	Odd behavior and/or thinking
Overly Dramatic		Disregard for the law and rights of others (may make up a significant portion of the prison population in some countries)
	Borderline	Instability in relationships, self-image, identity, and behavior
	Histrionic	
		Pervasive sense of own grandiosity; need for admiration and lack of empathy
Anxiety-ridden	Avoidant	
	Dependent	Pervasive psychological dependence on others
	Obsessive-compulsive	Rigid conformity to rules and moral codes; excessive orderliness

Personality Disorders Worksheet Exercise Level 2

	Disorder	Behaviors
"Odd" Behavior	Paranoid	
		Lack of interest in social relationships
	Schizotypal	
Overly Dramatic		Disregard for the law and rights of others (may make up a significant portion of the prison population in some countries)
		Instability in relationships, self-image, identity, and behavior
	Histrionic	
		Pervasive sense of own grandiosity; need for admiration and lack of empathy
Anxiety-ridden	Avoidant	
	Dependent	
		Rigid conformity to rules and moral codes; excessive orderliness

Personality Disorders Worksheet Exercise Level 3

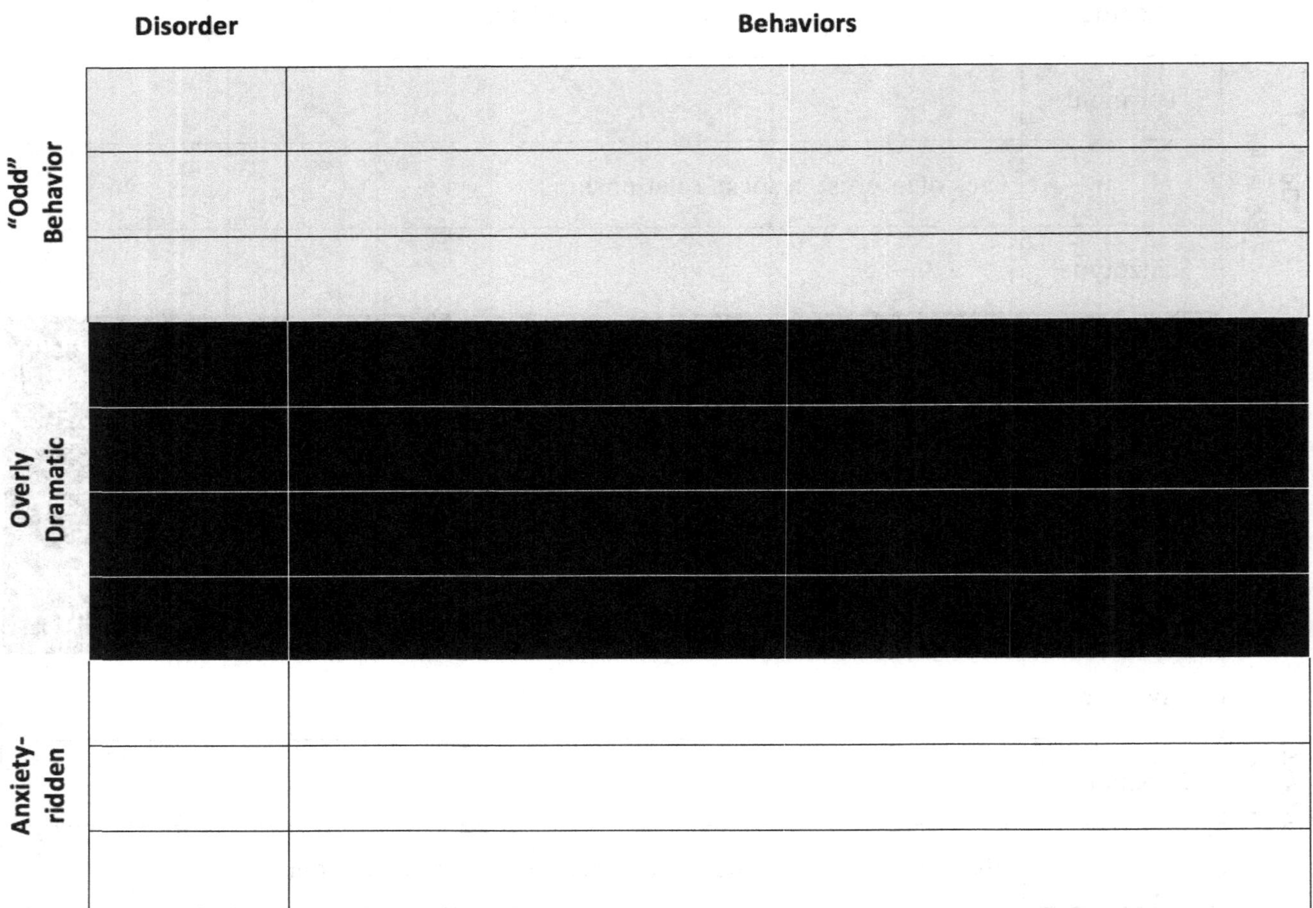

	Disorder	Behaviors
"Odd" Behavior		
Overly Dramatic		
Anxiety-ridden		

Timed MCAT Practice Passage

Mastery of the MCAT sciences is a two-part process. First you must study to understand (not just memorize!) the science content, and then you must study the content actively and challenge yourself within the context of the exam.

1. Complete your reading of the passage (3-4 minutes).
    - Write down what you believe to be the primary science content underlying the passage.
    - What facts or concepts do you anticipate to be tested? When you are done with the questions determine if you were correct. What passage clues were there to imply related topics that showed up in the questions?
    - Were there any key terms or important scientific relationships you missed?
    - Were you able to draw any conclusions from the data, if presented?

2. Complete the practice questions on your own (4-5 minutes)
    - Rephrase each question in your own mind after reading it to clarify the task.
    - Research the relevant area(s) of the passage or your own knowledge for information related to the task.
    - Respond to the question by choosing the answer that fits your research/calculations *and* satisfies the task.
    - If no answer seems obvious, eliminate answers that fail to have support in the passage or in the relevant science.

3. Analyze your wrong answer choices to the questions you missed.
    - Did you understand the task in the question?
    - What skill type was the question?
    - Did you know the science/formula/concept needed to answer the question?
    - Did you recognize the science being hinted at?
    - Were you able to find information in the passage quickly when you needed it?
    - Were there any necessary scientific concepts you failed to apply to the question?
        - If so, why?
    - If you made a mistake in calculations, have you identified your mistake?

There are three main types of aggression. The first is premeditated aggression, in which the aggression is consciously planned and executed for some expected gain. The second type is medically related aggression. This aggression is symptomatic of some medical condition. For example children with Down Syndrome may have trouble controlling their body and avoiding hitting others. The third type is impulsive aggression, which results from children having difficulty controlling their actions and reacting impulsively with aggression.

The prefrontal cortex (PFC), controls many executive functions, particularly affect. The left PFC primarily connects words to emotional experiences and encodes memories. The right PFC controls memory retrieval and visuospatial information. By age 4 the left PFC dominates nearby related areas, allowing proper interpretation of events and decision making. However, dysfunction in the PFC can result in behaviors such as inattention, impulsivity, and disorganization. This dysfunction can also result in aggression due to the difficulty of the individual to choose appropriate responses and by the deficits in executive decision making. Children with these inappropriate behaviors find themselves unable to connect with peers. This separation precludes social skill building and peer support. This leaves the child to unable to handle conflicts or frustration.

The anterior cingulate gyrus (ACG), a part of the limbic system, connects the limbic system with the PFC and serves to modulate the processing of emotional information. The ACG also helps the brain shift attention to relevant stimuli by modulating attention between affect and cognition. When the ACG is functioning properly an individual is able to encounter situations that may lead to feelings of frustration, yet reflect back on internal controls and modulate this arousal. Dysfunction may impair their ability to focus on the social expectations of a peer group, which allows them to ignore social constraints on overly aggressive behavior.

The amygdala are responsible for aversion emotions, such as fear or disgust. Low amygdala activity has been found in people with antisocial personality disorder. It is hypothesized that deficits in the amygdala lead to a lack of feeling aversive behaviors. In order to assess the relationship between aggression and brain dysfunction, researchers examined individuals with brain dysfunction in one of the areas mentioned above. Their histories of aggression were recorded and the individuals were classified according to what type of aggression they predominantly displayed.

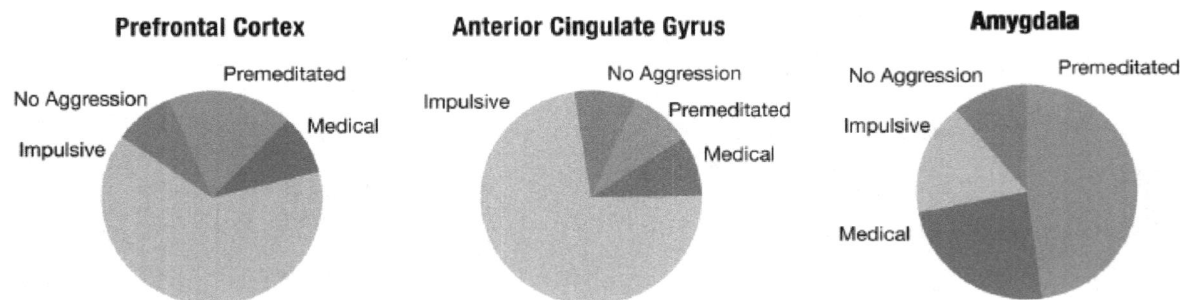

Figure 1 Comparison of aggression type with brain dysfunction location

Passage taken from the Next Step Psychology and Sociology review book, Chapter 1

11. Which of the following best explains the aggression pattern seen in those with amygdala deficits?
    A. Lack of social skills
    B. Lack of executive functioning skills
    C. Lack of fear-based learning
    D. Lack of memory

12. According to the passage, which of the following functions is most likely to deficient in a subject with dominant impulsive aggression?
    A. Emotional pain
    B. Physical development
    C. Vestibular sense
    D. Language

13. Which of the following neurological complications best explains an overly aggressive man whose dangerous behavior only lasts a short time and demonstrated elevated temporal lobe activity?
    A. Schizoid disorder
    B. Schizophrenia
    C. Epilepsy
    D. Anxiety

14. What type of intervention would be LEAST effective as treatment for an woman demonstrating aggression as a result of anterior cingulate gyrus dysfunction?
    A. Affect arousal modulation skill instruction
    B. Training on social mores
    C. Weighing the pros and cons of planning rewarding but potentially dangerous behavior
    D. Teaching empathy with other's thoughts and feelings

15. According to the passage, why would Bill, who suffers from impulsive aggression problems, also have difficulty differentiating between shapes?
    A. There is right prefrontal cortex damage.
    B. There is left prefrontal cortex damage.
    C. There is right temporal lobe damage.
    D. There is left temporal lobe damage.

Social Effects on Behavior

Social Facilitation

Co-action Effects

Audience Effects

Deindividuation

Factors in deindividuation

Bystander Effect

Social Loafing

Group Size

Expectations

Motivation

Diffusion of Responsibility

Peer Pressure

Conformity

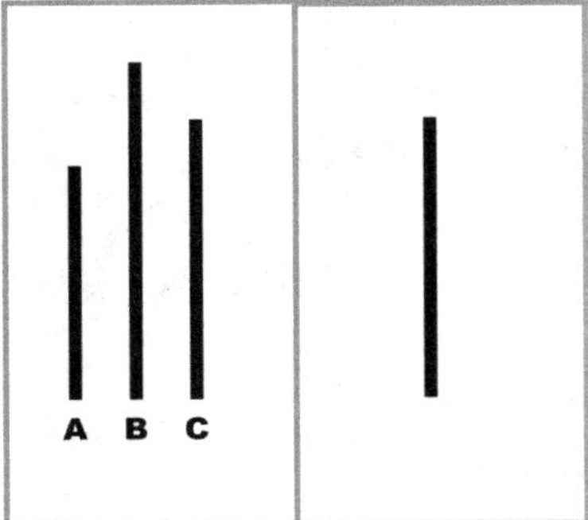

Compliance

Internalization

Conformity Types

Identification

Ingratiational

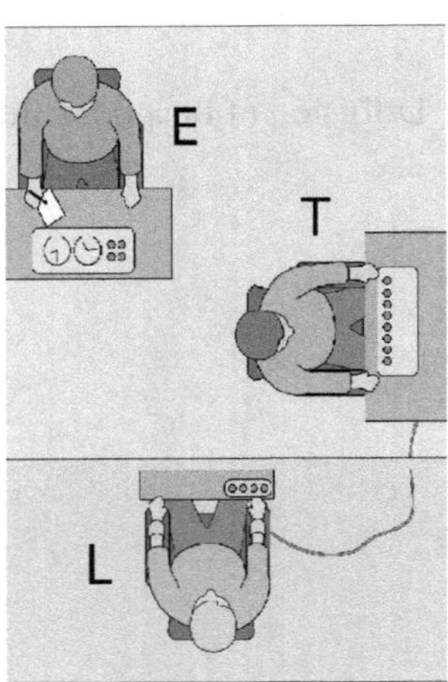

Obedience

Milgram Experiment

Stanford Prison Experiment

This page left intentionally blank.

MCAT Practice Passage

Neuroticism exists on a spectrum from primarily calm to primarily nervous. Hans Eysenck viewed personality as deriving primarily from genetic s, so he viewed neuroticism as controlled by autonomic nervous system (ANS). The ANS responds to perceived stimuli and prepares our body to emotionally respond, primarily through production of epinephrine. Eysenck theorized the ANS responded differently in different people, with some individuals being more sensitive than others.

If the ANS is chronically over responsive, the person typically displays neuroticism, which may lead to a neurotic disorder. For example, a panic attack can represented with a positive feedback loop. During a panic attack, the emotions of dread and fear, which can appear for a minor reason, or a stress trigger, or for what seems like reason at all, kick in the ANS self-preservation mechanisms, which are then perceived by the mind as real evidence that an actual threat exists. This leads to more anxiety, sweating or other somatic responses. This loop continues until the individual is incapacitated via a panic attack.

The temperament dimension of extraversion-introversion refers to the propensity for engaging with others versus spending time alone. Extraverts prefer being around others, engaging in social activities, and working in groups. Introverts enjoy solitary activities and are more reserved in group settings. Eysenck concluded the reason individuals display one factor over the other is due to their preferred arousal level, with extraverts preferring to be more aroused and introverts less aroused.

The temperament dimension of extraversion-introversion refers to the propensity for engaging with others versus spending time alone. Extraverts prefer being around others, engaging in social activities, and working in groups. Introverts enjoy solitary activities and are more reserved in group settings. Eysenck concluded the reason individuals display one factor over the other is due to their preferred arousal level, with extraverts preferring to be more aroused and introverts less aroused.

In a study based on 4-factor analysis, individuals were provided questionnaires about their preferences. Researchers looked for responses which tended to be endorsed together and formed categories of temperament from them. Participants rated the extent to which they agreed with a series of statements, ranked on a scale from 1 to 5 with 1 indicating they did not agree at all up to 5 indicating that they completely agreed. A selection of the data is reproduced in Table 1.

Table 1 Sample responses to a temperament questionnaire

	Participant Rating		
Statement	**Joe**	**Katherine**	**Sally**
I enjoy attending parties.	5	2	1
I get nervous in groups.	1	5	5
I sometimes feel as if I'm having a panic attack.	1	4	5
I enjoy doing activities alone.	2	5	4

Passage taken from the Next Step online QBank

16. Based on the data provided, which participants appear to be INFP personality types?

    A. Joe and Katherine
    B. Katherine and Sally
    C. Sally and Joe
    D. None

17. Eysenck viewed personality as primarily deriving from what?

    A. Nature
    B. Nurture
    C. Learned experience
    D. T-data

18. If the researchers concluded Joe likes all types of social gatherings due to his responses on the questionnaire, they have committed what error?

    A. Availability heuristic
    B. Self-fulfilling prophecy
    C. Mental shortcut heuristic
    D. Fundamental attribution

19. Which theoretical view of personality does NOT contrast with the view that personality is derived from temperamental dimensions?

    A. Behaviorist perspective
    B. Psychoanalytic perspective
    C. Five factor view of personality
    D. Biological perspective

Problem-solving Cooldown

21. A medical school anatomy class allows students to take quizzes as a group of 4. Why might the group quiz score be higher than any individual's quiz score?

    A. Time constraints forced upon groups foster higher quality decision-making.
    B. Group members can compensate for each other's weaknesses.
    C. Groups have the advantage of access to better decision-making resources.
    D. Individuals working alone have a better sense of error detection.

22. According to Fisher, which of the following is the proper cycle of steps a small group will progress through as they work on solving a problem?

    A. Orientation → conflict → reinforcement → emergence
    B. Emergence → orientation → conflict → reinforcement
    C. Conflict → reinforcement → emergence → orientation
    D. Orientation → conflict → emergence → reinforcement

23. A town of 4,000 residents were asked to rank a series of norms from 1-10 with 1 being the least important to observe and 10 being the most important.

	Avg. Score
Don't spoil the end of a movie.	8.8
Don't cut in line.	3.2
Don't drink straight out of the milk carton.	9.1
Don't go the wrong way down a one way street.	5.3
Don't spit into the wind.	6.2
Boys must wear blue and girls pink to bed.	5.4
Keep the newspaper sections in order when done reading.	4.9
Don't look for hidden birthday presents.	3.7

Which of the norms would be considered a more?

A. Don't go the wrong way down a one way street.
B. Keep the newspaper sections in order when done reading.
C. Don't look for hidden birthday presents.
D. Don't spit into the wind.

24. A town of 4,000 residents were asked to rank a series of norms from 1-10 with 1 being the least important to observe and 10 being the most important.

	Avg. Score
Don't spoil the end of a movie.	8.8
Don't cut in line.	3.2
Don't drink straight out of the milk carton.	9.1
Don't go the wrong way down a one way street.	5.3
Don't spit into the wind.	6.2
Boys must wear blue and girls pink to bed.	5.4
Keep the newspaper sections in order when done reading.	4.9
Don't look for hidden birthday presents.	3.7

Which of the norms would be considered a folkway?

A. Don't go the wrong way down a one way street.
B. Don't cut in line.
C. Don't drink straight out of the milk carton.
D. Don't look for hidden birthday presents.

25. Which of the following are learned through agents of socialization?

I. Attitudes
II. Values
III. Behaviors

A. I only
B. II only
C. II and III only
D. I, II and III

To Do After Lesson 14

- ☐ Complete Full Timed Section 2 from the Verbal Practice: 108 Passages book
- ☐ Complete the Biological and Biochemical Foundations section from the AAMC Online Official Guide at e-mcat.com
- ☐ Complete Psychology and Sociology QBank 4: Identity, Disorders, and Groups

LESSON 15

Biology 3

To Do Before Lesson 15

- ☐ Complete Full Timed Section 2 from the Verbal Practice: 108 Passages book
- ☐ Complete the Biological and Biochemical Foundations section from the AAMC Online Official Guide at e-mcat.com
- ☐ Complete Psychology and Sociology QBank 4: Identity, Disorders, and Groups

In Lesson 15

Problem-solving Warm-up
Effective Reading in the Sciences
Endocrine System
Mnemonic Devices
MCAT Practice Passage
Digestive System
Renal System
Build Your Science Foundation
MCAT Practice Passage
Problem-solving Cooldown

To Do After Lesson 15

- ☐ Complete Full Timed Section 3 from the Verbal Practice: 108 Passages book
- ☐ Complete the Psychological and Sociological Foundations section from the AAMC Online Official Guide at e-mcat.com
- ☐ Complete Biology QBank 5: Nervous and Endocrine Systems

Problem-solving Warm-up

1. Microvilli, which function to increase surface area, are more likely to be found in:
   A. stratified cuboidal epithelium.
   B. pseudostratified columnar epithelium.
   C. simple columnar epithelium.
   D. transitional epithelium.

2. Lactase deficiency would most likely result from damage to the:
   A. lumen of the large intestine.
   B. lumen of the pancreas.
   C. brush border of the ileum.
   D. brush border of the duodenum.

3. Which of the following is the type of cartilage found in intervertebral disks of the vertebral column?
   A. Hyaline cartilage
   B. Fibrocartilage
   C. Elastic cartilage
   D. Yellow cartilage

4. Neuroglial cells perform each of the following functions for neurons EXCEPT:
   A. carrying on phagocytosis.
   B. cell-to-cell communications.
   C. transmitting nervous impulses.
   D. supporting and binding nervous tissue.

5. Which of these is NOT a connective tissue?
   A. Blood
   B. Bone
   C. Cartilage
   D. Muscle

This page left intentionally blank.

Effective Reading in the Sciences

Reading science passages on the MCAT means being able to keep track of important (i.e. likely to be tested) information in the passage. You must be able to anticipate, recognize, and understand scientific concepts presented in many different forms.

Muscle contraction is a complicated process with many steps. It all begins with an action potential that is transmitted along a motor neuron towards muscle tissue. Efferent somatic neurons use the neurotransmitter acetylcholine.

Figure 1 Acetylcholine (left) and nicotine (right)

When the action potential reaches a muscle cell, acetylcholine is released and binds a nicotinic acetylcholine receptor on the neuromuscular junction. Nicotinic receptors are so named because they also bind nicotine. When this receptor is activated, it causes depolarization of the sarcomere and an electrochemical signal is transduced along the muscle fiber, depolarizing all the sarcomeres in the fiber. When a sarcomere is depolarized, calcium channels in the cell's membrane open, which in turn opens the calcium channels of the sarcoplasmic reticulum and calcium rushes into the cytoplasm of the muscle cells.

The actual contraction of muscle occurs as a result of calcium binding troponin C, a compound found on thin actin filaments. The binding of calcium to troponin C causes tropomyosin, which normally blocks binding sites on the thin filaments, to move. The binding sites are exposed and thick filament myosin heads can interact with thin filaments, pulling them toward the M line.

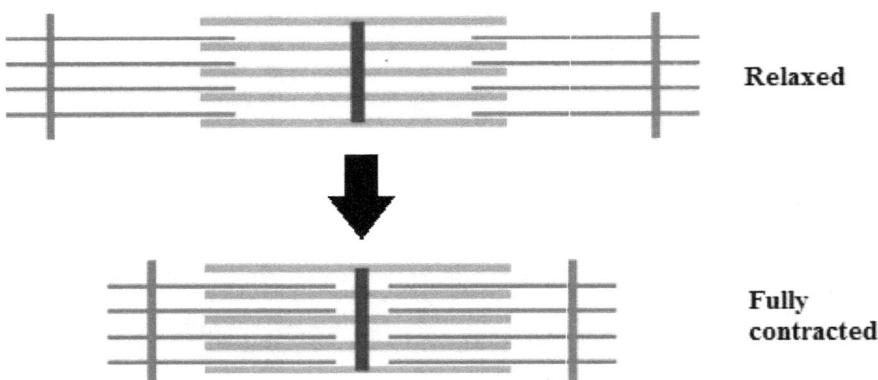

Figure 2 Sarcomere contraction

Myosin can freely bind the thin filaments. Myosin at this stage is also bound to an ADP and inorganic phosphate group, which when released, cause the stroke and pull inward toward the M line. When ATP binds myosin, myosin releases the thin filaments and the ATP is hydrolyzed, allowing the myosin to revert to its original state, ready to bind another binding site on the actin fibers. Each stroke moves the thin filaments about 10 nm closer to the M-line.

Passage taken from the Next Step online QBank

6. Which of the following shortens during the contraction of two adjacent sarcomeres?

    I. Length of H zone
    II. Distance between Z lines
    III. Length of the I band

    A. I only
    B. I and II only
    C. II and III only
    D. I, II, and III

7. Which of the following would result in paralysis of skeletal muscle?

    A. A peptide hormone that agonistically binds nicotinic acetylcholine receptors
    B. A peptide hormone that antagonistically binds muscarinic receptors
    C. A peptide hormone that antagonistically binds nicotinic acetylcholine receptors
    D. A peptide hormone that agonistically binds muscarinic receptors

8. How many sets of power strokes in myosin filaments would be required to shorten a sarcomere by 80 nm?

    A. 4
    B. 8
    C. 16
    D. It depends on the length of the sarcomere.

9. Given the need for a tertiary or quaternary nitrogen for nicotinic receptor binding, which of the following is LEAST likely to be able to bind a nicotinic receptor?

A.

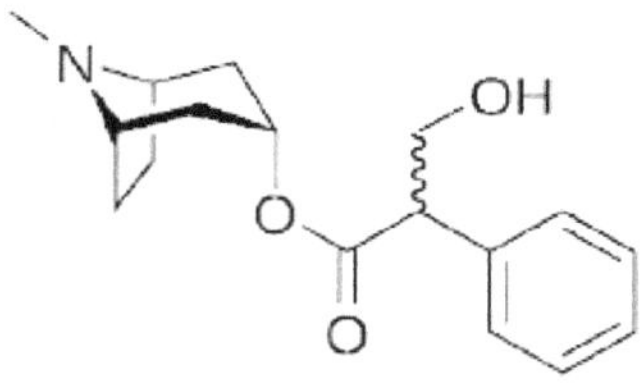

B.

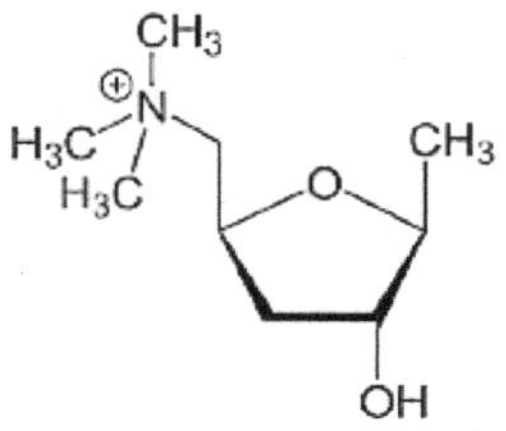

C.

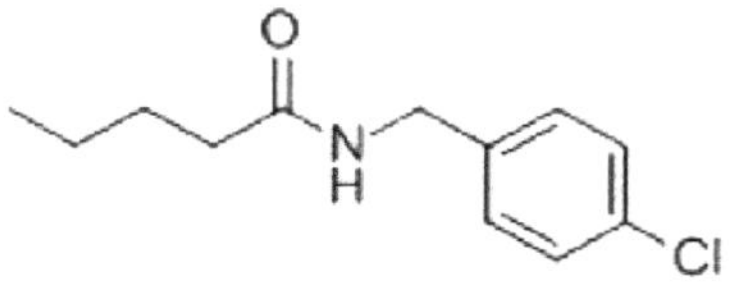

D.

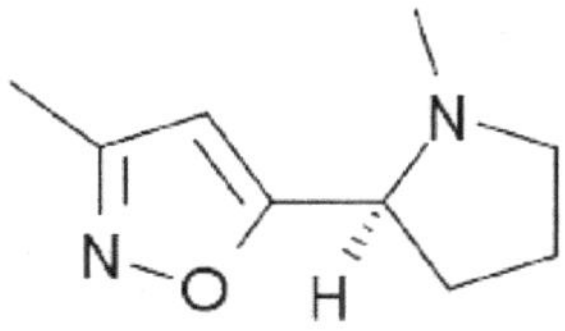

10. Which of the following must be present in abundance for skeletal muscle contraction to begin?

    I. Calcium
    II. ADP
    III. ATP

    A. III only
    B. I and II only
    C. I and III only
    D. II and III only

Endocrine System

Homeostasis

Endocrine Organs

Hypothalamus

Pituitary

Pancreas

Thyroid and Parathyroid

Adrenal Gland

Testes and Ovaries

Antagonistic Hormone Pairs

Negative and Positive Feedback Loop

The Menstrual Cycle

FSH

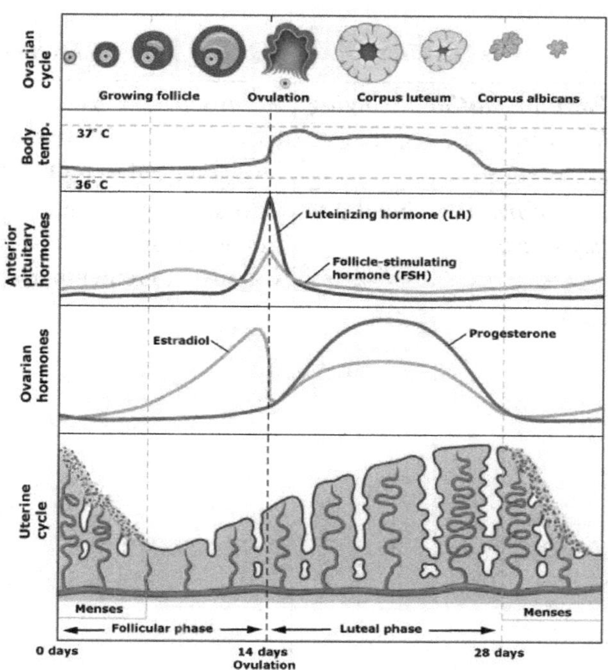

LH

Estrogen

Progesterone

hCG

Mnemonic Devices

Mnemonic devices can help you remember much of the dry facts inherent to the biological sciences. The key is to utilize mnemonics that help you most without complicating the topic. Spending a few minutes every now and then to visualize and make associations is very beneficial in the long run.

When to Use:	***Method:***	***Example:***
For information involving key words	**Acronym**—an invented combination of letters with each letter acting as a cue to an idea you need to remember.	
For information involving key words	**Acrostic**—an invented sentence where the first letter of each word is a cue to an idea you need to remember.	**FOL(d)M(a)PS**— **SEVEN UP**— **LAb RAt**— **SNoW DRoP**—
For remembering information items	**Loci Method**—Imagine placing the items you want to remember in specific locations in a room with which you are familiar.	
For ordered or unordered lists	**Chaining**—Create a story where each word or idea you have to remember will cue the next idea you need to recall.	

This page left intentionally blank.

Timed MCAT Practice Passage

Mastery of the MCAT sciences is a two-part process. First you must study to understand (not just memorize!) the science content, and then you must study the content actively and challenge yourself within the context of the exam.

1. Complete your reading of the passage (3-4 minutes).
   - Write down what you believe to be the primary science content underlying the passage.
   - What facts or concepts do you anticipate to be tested? When you are done with the questions determine if you were correct. What passage clues were there to imply related topics that showed up in the questions?
   - Were there any key terms or important scientific relationships you missed?
   - Were you able to draw any conclusions from the data, if presented?

2. Complete the practice questions on your own (4-5 minutes)
   - Rephrase each question in your own mind after reading it to clarify the task.
   - Research the relevant area(s) of the passage or your own knowledge for information related to the task.
   - Respond to the question by choosing the answer that fits your research/calculations *and* satisfies the task.
   - If no answer seems obvious, eliminate answers that fail to have support in the passage or in the relevant science.

3. Analyze your wrong answer choices to the questions you missed.
   - Did you understand the task in the question?
   - What skill type was the question?
   - Did you know the science/formula/concept needed to answer the question?
   - Did you recognize the science being hinted at?
   - Were you able to find information in the passage quickly when you needed it?
   - Were there any necessary scientific concepts you failed to apply to the question?
     - If so, why?
   - If you made a mistake in calculations, have you identified your mistake?

Secretin is secreted by the small intestine in response to lowered pH. Secretin is a linear peptide hormone.

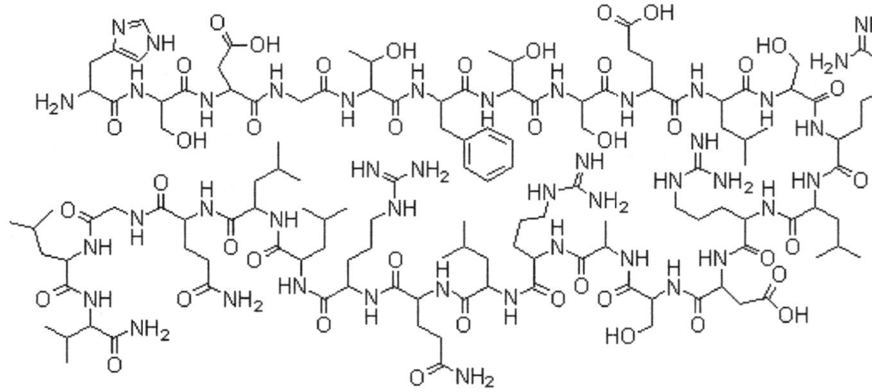

Figure 1 The structure of secretin

Cholecystokinin is an enzyme whose action is enhanced by the presence of secretin. Cholecystokinin is secreted from the duodenum when fat reaches the small intestine. Cholecystokinin stimulates contraction of the gallbladder and stimulates the pancreas to secrete enzymes to aid in digestion. The following enzymes are released by the pancreas:

Enzyme	Function
Lipase	Digest fats
Nuclease	Digest phosphodiester bonds
Trypsin	Digest proteins
Chymotrypsin	Digest proteins
Amylase	Digest starches
Carboxypeptidase	Digest peptides

Table 1 Pancreatic juice contents

Trypsinogen, chymotrypsinogen and procarboxypeptidase are zymogens, inactive forms of enzymes. They are activated by trypsin, which is itself the active form of the zymogen trypsinogen. Trypsinogen can be formed into trypsin by the enzyme enterokinase, which is released from the cells of the duodenum.

Amylase, nuclease, and lipase are able to directly catalyze the metabolism of certain molecules. Amylase functions to break down starch, a polymer of glucose molecules.

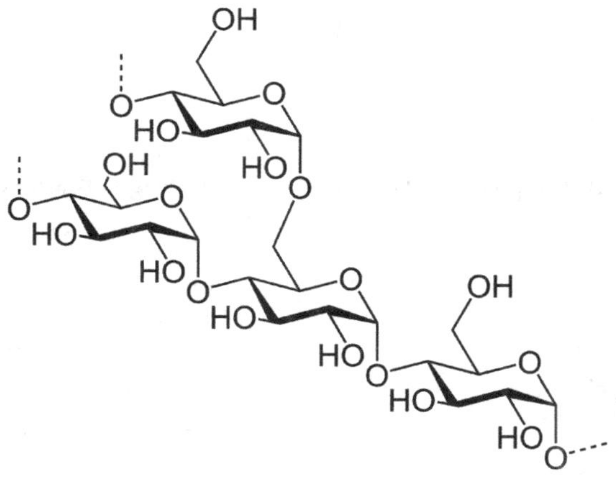

Figure 2 Starch molecule

Amylase breaks down starches into maltose subunits. Maltose is a disaccharide composed of two glucose units joined in an α(1-4) glycosidic linkage.

Passage taken from the Next Step online QBank

11. How does the small intestine know to release secretin only after a meal?

    A. The increase in hydrogen ions from the breakdown of peptides and carbohydrates lowers the pH in the small intestine.
    B. The release of hydrochloric acid from the stomach lowers the pH in the duodenum.
    C. Acetic acid, a byproduct of carbohydrate digestion, lowers the pH in the small intestine.
    D. The release of bile acids lowers the pH in the small intestine.

12. Which of the following, if absent, would lead to the biggest decrease in our ability to digest proteins?

    A. Chymotrypsinogen
    B. Chymotrypsin
    C. Carboxypeptidase
    D. Enterokinase

13. Which enzyme catalyzes the reaction below?

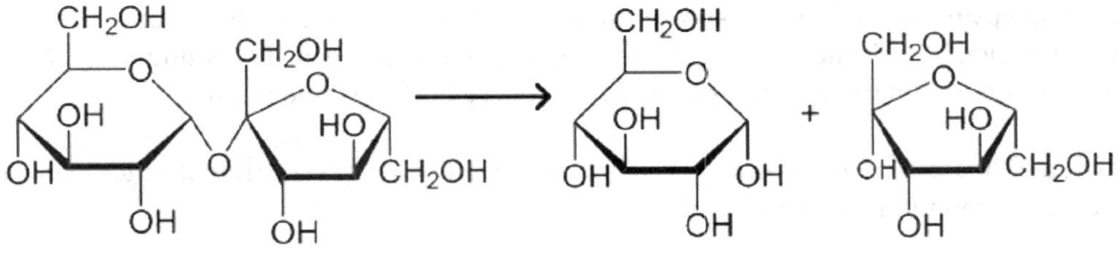

CH_2OH O OH OH OH O CH_2OH O HO CH_2OH OH → CH_2OH O OH OH OH OH + CH_2OH O HO OH CH_2OH OH

    A. Sucrase
    B. Lactase
    C. Maltase
    D. Lipase

14. According to the information in the passage, which of the following is maltose?

A.

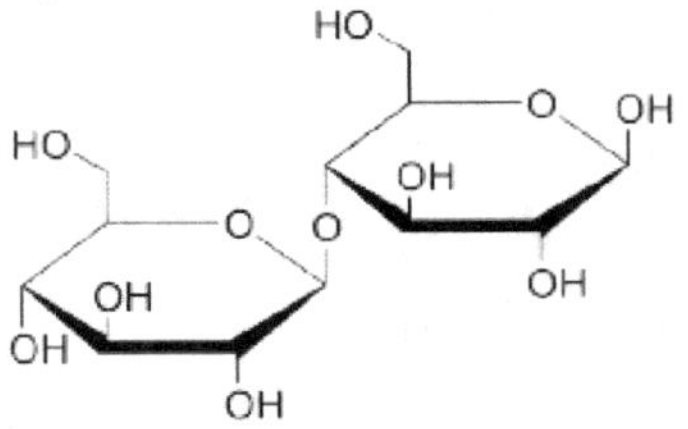

HO O OH OH O HO O OH OH OH OH

B.

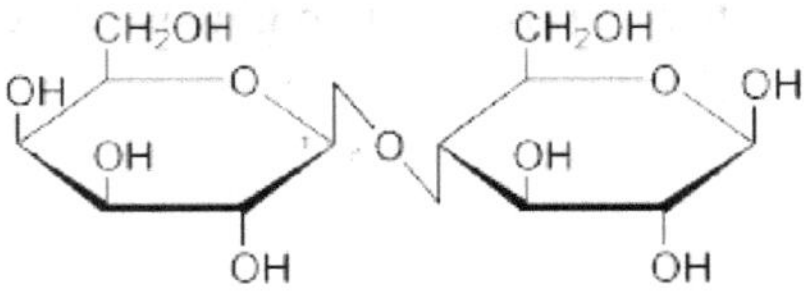

CH_2OH OH O OH OH O CH_2OH O OH OH OH

C.

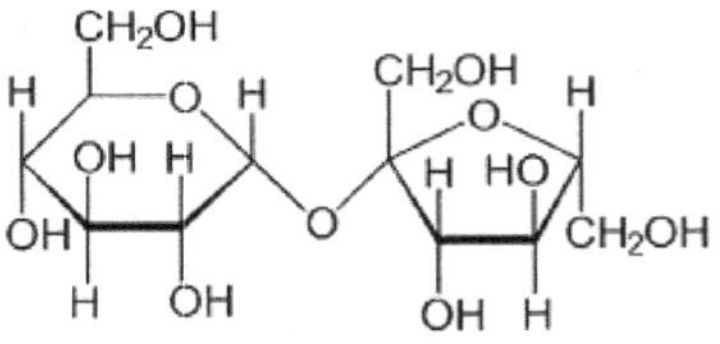

CH_2OH H O H OH H OH H OH O CH_2OH H O H HO CH_2OH OH H

D.

CH_2OH O OH OH OH O CH_2OH O OH OH OH

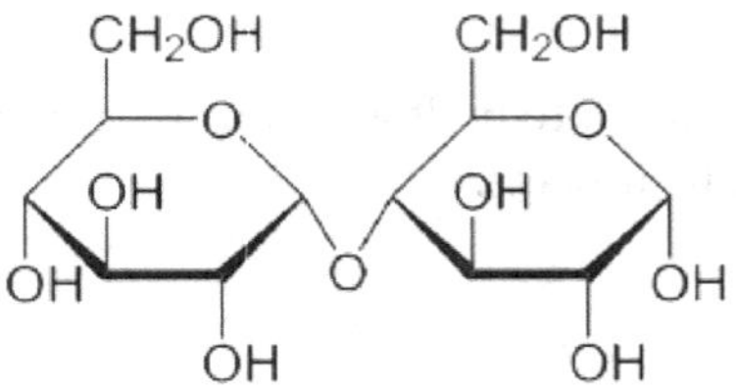

15. Which of the following is true concerning secretin?

    A. Secretin is unique because the carboxyl-terminal amino acid is an amide.
    B. Secretin is unique because it contains equal amounts of basic and acidic side groups.
    C. Secretin is unique because the amine-terminal residue contains a basic side group.
    D. Secretin is unique because the carboxyl-terminal residue is hydrophobic.

Digestive System

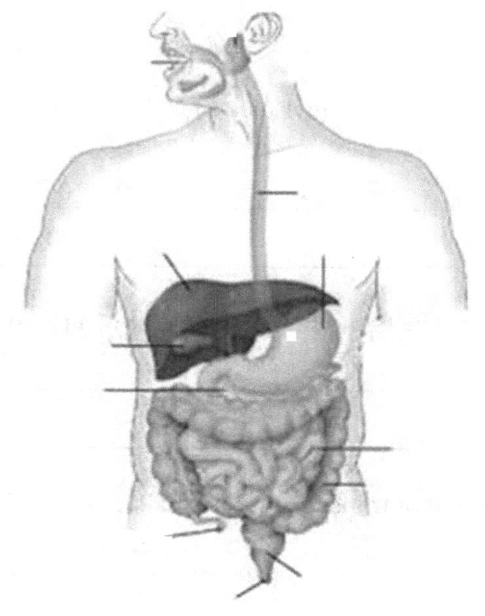

Enzyme Type	Produced in	Site of Action	Substrate

What immune-related system is required for the proper absorption and transport of fats?

If a patient reports they have had fatty, oily stools after meals for the past 3 days which digestive organ(s) are least likely to be affected?

Which digestive enzyme is most likely to be found in the esophagus of a person with a weakened cardiac sphincter?

Match the nutrient to its primary method of transport in the small intestine.

Sodium Glucose Amino Acids Nucleic Acids Fatty Acids

Cotransport Primary active transport Diffusion

Renal System

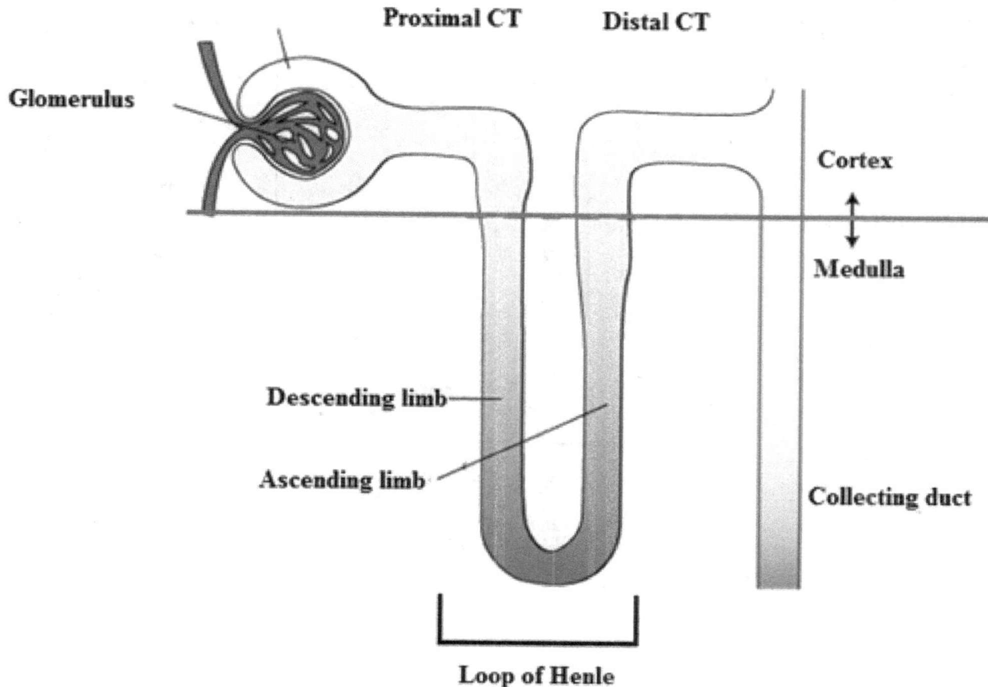

Filtration

Reabsorption

Secretion

Renin-Angiotensin (regulation of blood pressure)

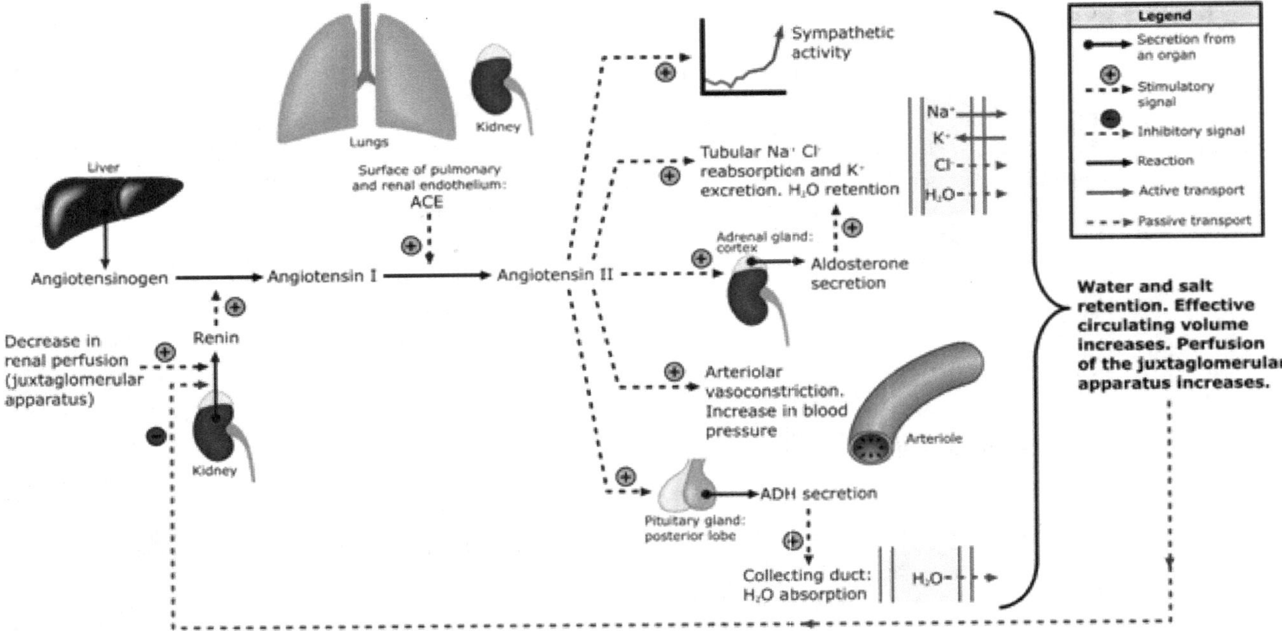

Stimulated by:

1.

2.

3.

Central diabetes insipidus is characterized by excessive excretion of dilute urine. Which renal hormone is most likely deficient in CDI?

An animal adapted to living in the desert is likely to have which portion of their nephron enlarged?

A scientist wishing to test the ability of the kidney to convey changes in blood osmolarity from the macula densa to the juxtaglomerular cells would achieve this by monitoring which class of molecule?

A. Steroid hormone
B. Peptide hormone
C. Prostaglandin
D. Neurotransmitter

All of the following are expected to be in the glomerular filtrate EXCEPT:

A. lysine.
B. glucose.
C. Na^+
D. immunoglobulin.

Which of the following statements is true about creatinine, a waste product produced by the kidney?

A. The rate of urinary excretion is equal to the rate of glomerular filtration.
B. The rate of urinary excretion is greater than the rate of glomerular filtration.
C. The rate of urinary excretion is less than the rate of glomerular filtration.
D. The rate of urinary excretion is equal to that of glucose.

Respiratory System Worksheet Exercise

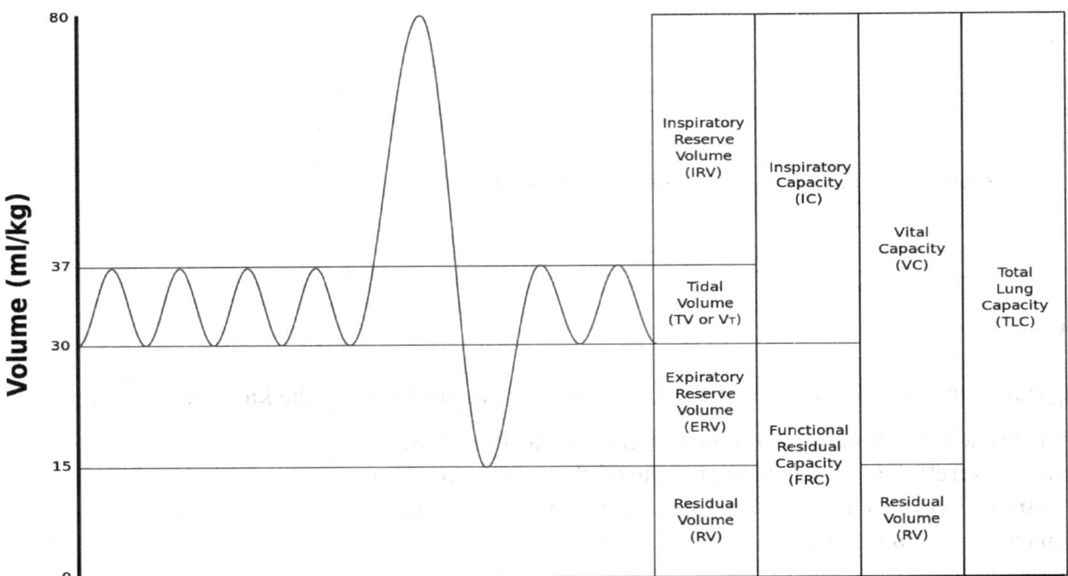

Tidal volume (TV), is the amount of air inspired during normal, relaxed breathing.

Inspiratory reserve volume (IRV), is the additional air that can be forcibly inhaled after the inspiration of a normal tidal volume.

Expiratory reserve volume (ERV), is the additional air that can be forcibly exhaled after the expiration of a normal tidal volume.

Residual volume (RV), is the volume of air still remaining in the lungs after the expiratory reserve volume is exhaled.

Total lung capacity (TLC), is the maximum amount of air that can fill the lungs.

TLC = TV + IRV + ERV + RV

Vital capacity (VC), is the total amount of air that can be expired after fully inhaling.

VC = TV + IRV + ERV

Inspiratory capacity (IC), is the maximum amount of air that can be inspired.

IC = TV + IRV

Functional residual capacity (FRC), is the amount of air remaining in the lungs after a normal expiration.

FRC = RV + ERV

Respiratory System Worksheet Exercise Level 1

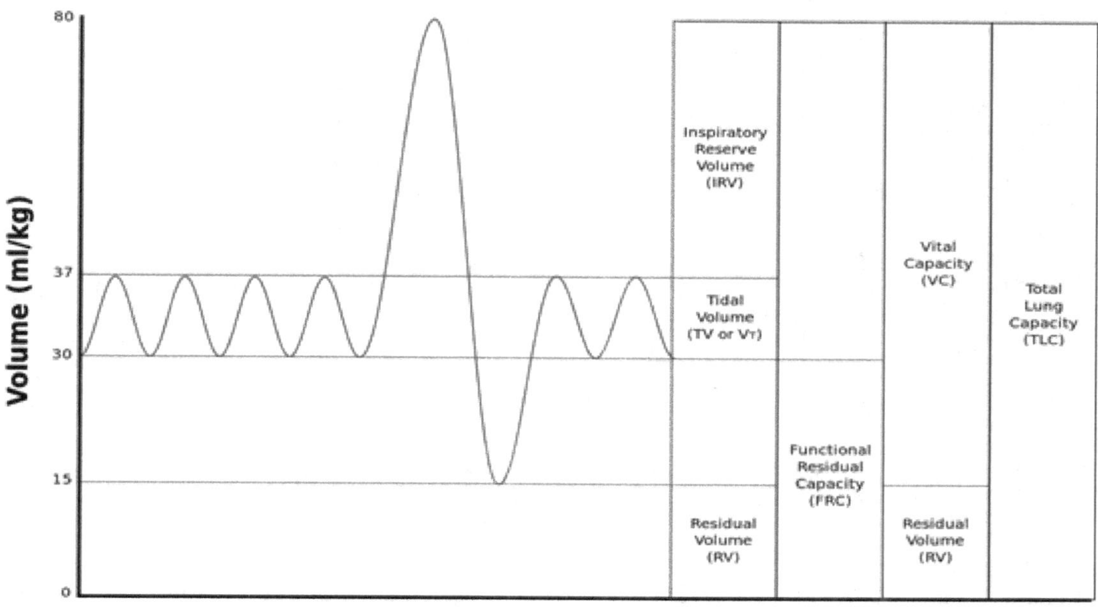

______________________________ is the amount of air inspired during normal, relaxed breathing.

Inspiratory reserve volume (IRV), is the additional air that can be forcibly inhaled after the inspiration of a normal tidal volume.

______________________________ is the additional air that can be forcibly exhaled after the expiration of a normal tidal volume.

Residual volume (RV), is the volume of air still remaining in the lungs after the expiratory reserve volume is exhaled.

______________________________ is the maximum amount of air that can fill the lungs.

______________________________ = TV + IRV + ERV + RV

Vital capacity (VC), is the total amount of air that can be expired after fully inhaling.

VC = ______________________________

Inspiratory capacity (IC), is the maximum amount of air that can be inspired.

IC = TV + IRV

Functional residual capacity (FRC), is the amount of air remaining in the lungs after a normal expiration. FRC = RV + ERV

Respiratory System Worksheet Exercise Level 2

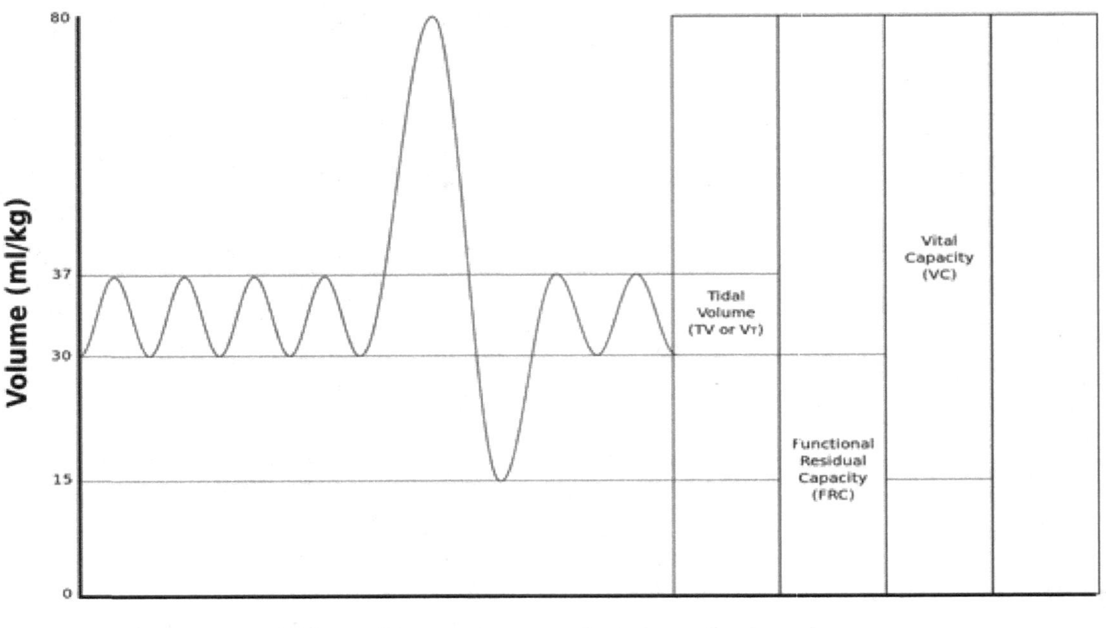

______________________ is the amount of air inspired during normal, relaxed breathing.

Inspiratory reserve volume (IRV), is the additional air that can be forcibly inhaled after the inspiration of a normal tidal volume.

______________________ is the additional air that can be forcibly exhaled after the expiration of a normal tidal volume.

______________________, is the volume of air still remaining in the lungs after the expiratory reserve volume is exhaled.

______________________ is the maximum amount of air that can fill the lungs.

______________________ = TV + IRV + ERV + RV

Vital capacity (VC), is the total amount of air that can be expired after fully inhaling.

VC = ______________________

Inspiratory capacity (IC), is the maximum amount of air that can be inspired.

IC = TV + IRV

______________________ is the amount of air remaining in the lungs after a normal expiration.

__________ = RV + ERV

Respiratory System Worksheet Exercise Level 3

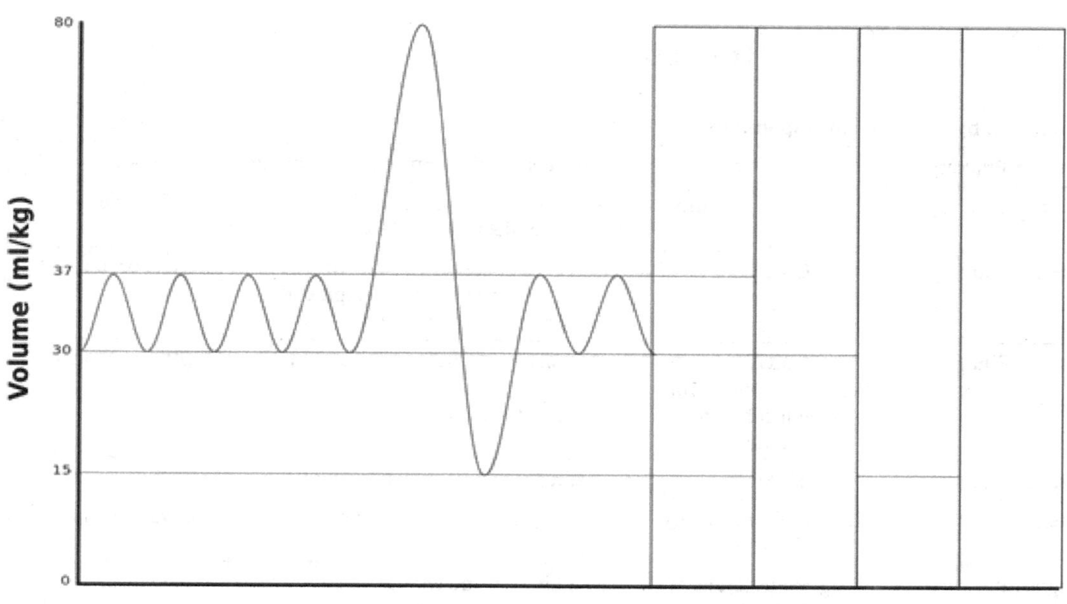

____________________ is the amount of air inspired during normal, relaxed breathing.

____________________ is the additional air that can be forcibly inhaled after the inspiration of a normal tidal volume.

____________________ is the additional air that can be forcibly exhaled after the expiration of a normal tidal volume.

____________________ is the volume of air still remaining in the lungs after the expiratory reserve volume is exhaled.

____________________ is the maximum amount of air that can fill the lungs.

____________________ = TV + IRV + ERV + RV

Vital capacity (VC), ____.

VC = ____________________

____________________ is the maximum amount of air that can be inspired.

IC = ____________________

Functional residual capacity (FRC), ____.

FRC = ____________________

Hormone Worksheet Exercise

Hormones

Hormone	Secreted by	In response to	Effect	Type
Oxytocin	Posterior Pituitary	Childbirth	Uterine contraction, Emotional Bonding	Peptide
Vasopressin (ADH)	Posterior Pituitary	High plasma osmolality	Retain water, ↑ aquaporin channels in collecting duct, DCT	Peptide
FSH	Anterior Pituitary	GnRH	♀: initiate follicle growth ♂: ↑ spermatocyte development ♀, ♂: maturation of germ cells	Glycoprotein
LH	Anterior Pituitary	GnRH ♀: estrogen spike from follicle just before ovulation	♀: ovulation, follicle becomes corpus luteum ♂: Leydig cells → ↑testosterone	Glycoprotein
ACTH	Anterior Pituitary	CRH, Stress	↑ adrenal release of corticosteroids	Peptide
TSH	Anterior Pituitary	TRH, low plasma levels of T_4 and T_3	↑ thyroid release of T_4 and T_3	Glycoprotein
Prolactin	Anterior Pituitary	Falling progesterone at end of pregnancy	Mammary gland enlargement, milk production	Peptide
Endorphin	Anterior Pituitary	Pain	Pain relief	Peptide
Growth Hormone	Anterior Pituitary	GHRH	Growth of long bones, general anabolism	Peptide
Calcitonin	Thyroid	High plasma [Ca^{2+}]	Reduce plasma [Ca^{2+}]	Peptide
T_4 & T_3	Thyroid	TSH	↑ metabolic rate	Amino Acid Tyr, but act like steroid
Parathyroid Horm.	Parathyroid	Low plasma [Ca^{2+}]	↑ plasma [Ca^{2+}]	Peptide
Glucagon	Pancreas α cells	Low blood [Glucose]	↑ blood [Glucose]	Peptide
Insulin	Pancreas β cells	High blood [Glucose]	↓ blood [Glucose]	Peptide
Somatostatin	Pancreas δ cells	Various, usually high hormone levels	Suppress: GH, TSH, CCK, insulin, glucagon	Peptide
Cortisol	Adrenal Cortex	Stress	↑ [Glucose], Immune suppression	Steroid
Aldosterone	Adrendal Cortex	ACTH, ATII, low bp	Collecting Duct, DCT: reabsorb Na^+, Secrete K^+, water retention, ↑ bp	Steroid
Epinephrine	Adrenal Medulla	Sudden stress	Sympathetic response: ↑ heart rate, breathing, etc.	Peptide / Tyr derivative
Estrogen	♀: Ovaries, ♂: Adrenal	FSH	♀: secondary sex characteristics, endometrial development during menstrual cycle, surge leads to LH surge	Steroid
Progesterone	♀: Ovary: Corpus Luteum, ♂: Adrenal	Ovulation	Thicken, maintain endometrium in preparation for implantation	Steroid
Testosterone	♂: Leydig cells of testes, ♀: Ovaries	GnRH→LH→Testos.	Development, maintenance of secondary sex characteristics	Steroid
Norepinephrine	Adrenal Medulla	Sudden stress	Sympathic responses of fight or flight	Peptide / Tyr derivative
hCG	Placenta	Implantation	Maintains corpus luteum at start of pregnancy	Glycoprotein
GnRH	Hypothalamus	Puberty, Menses	↑ LH, FSH release	Peptide

Hormone Worksheet Exercise Level 1

Hormones

Hormone	Secreted by	In response to	Effect	Type
Oxytocin		Childbirth		Peptide
Vasopressin (ADH)	Posterior Pituitary			Peptide
FSH			♀: initiate follicle growth ♂: ↑ spermatocyte development ♀, ♂: maturation of germ cells	
	Anterior Pituitary		♀: ovulation, follicle becomes corpus luteum ♂: Leydig cells → ↑testosterone	Glycoprotein
ACTH		CRH, Stress		
		TRH, low plasma levels of T_4 and T_3		Glycoprotein
Prolactin	Anterior Pituitary	Falling progesterone at end of pregnancy		
Endorphin			Pain relief	
Growth Hormone		GHRH		Peptide
Calcitonin				Peptide
T_4 & T_3	Thyroid	TSH		Amino Acid Tyr, but act like steroid
Parathyroid Horm.	Parathyroid			
	Pancreas α cells	Low blood [Glucose]		Peptide
Insulin			↓ blood [Glucose]	
	Pancreas δ cells	Various, usually high hormone levels	Suppress: GH, TSH, CCK, insulin, glucagon	Peptide
Cortisol	Adrenal Cortex			Steroid
Aldosterone	Adrendal Cortex	ACTH, ATII, low bp		
Epinephrine		Sudden stress	Sympathetic response: ↑ heart rate, breathing, etc.	Peptide / Tyr derivative
Estrogen	♀: Ovaries, ♂: Adrenal		♀: secondary sex characteristics, endometrial development during menstrual cycle, surge leads to LH surge	
Progesterone	♀: Ovary: Corpus Luteum, ♂: Adrenal	Ovulation		Steroid
	♂: Leydig cells of testes, ♀: Ovaries		Development, maintenance of secondary sex characteristics	Steroid
	Adrenal Medulla	Sudden stress	Sympathic responses of fight or flight	
hCG		Implantation		Glycoprotein
GnRH		Puberty, Menses		Peptide

Hormone Worksheet Exercise Level 2

Hormones

Hormone	Secreted by	In response to	Effect	Type
	Posterior Pituitary		Uterine contraction, Emotional Bonding	
			Retain water, ↑ aquaporin channels in collecting duct, DCT	
FSH		GnRH		
LH		GnRH ♀: estrogen spike from follicle just before ovulation		
	Anterior Pituitary	CRH, Stress	↑ adrenal release of corticosteroids	Peptide
TSH	Anterior Pituitary	TRH, low plasma levels of T_4 and T_3		
		Falling progesterone at end of pregnancy	Mammary gland enlargement, milk production	Peptide
	Anterior Pituitary	Pain		Peptide
		GHRH	Growth of long bones, general anabolism	
	Thyroid		Reduce plasma [Ca^{2+}]	
		TSH	↑ metabolic rate	
	Parathyroid		↑ plasma [Ca^{2+}]	Peptide
Glucagon			↑ blood [Glucose]	
	Pancreas β cells	High blood [Glucose]		Peptide
Somatostatin		Various, usually high hormone levels		
	Adrenal Cortex	Stress	↑ [Glucose], Immune suppression	
	Adrendal Cortex		Collecting Duct, DCT: reabsorb Na^+, Secrete K^+, water retention, ↑ bp	Steroid
Epinephrine	Adrenal Medulla	Sudden stress		
Estrogen	♀: Ovaries, ♂: Adrenal	FSH		Steroid
		Ovulation	Thicken, maintain endometrium in preparation for implantation	
Testosterone		GnRH→LH→Testos.		
Norepinephrine	Adrenal Medulla			Peptide / Tyr derivative
	Placenta	Implantation	Maintains corpus luteum at start of pregnancy	
		Puberty, Menses	↑ LH, FSH release	

Hormone Worksheet Exercise Level 3

Hormones

Hormone	Secreted by	In response to	Effect	Type
Oxytocin		Childbirth		
Vasopressin (ADH)		High plasma osmolality		
FSH				
LH			♀: ovulation, follicle becomes corpus luteum ♂: Leydig cells → ↑testosterone	
ACTH		CRH, Stress		
TSH			↑ thyroid release of T_4 and T_3	
Prolactin		Falling progesterone at end of pregnancy		
Endorphin			Pain relief	
Growth Hormone		GHRH		
Calcitonin			Reduce plasma [Ca^{2+}]	
T_4 & T_3		TSH		
Parathyroid Horm.			↑ plasma [Ca^{2+}]	
Glucagon		Low blood [Glucose]		
Insulin			↓ blood [Glucose]	
Somatostatin		Various, usually high hormone levels		
Cortisol			↑ [Glucose], Immune suppression	
Aldosterone		ACTH, ATII, low bp		
Epinephrine		Sudden stress		
Estrogen		FSH		
Progesterone			Thicken, maintain endometrium in preparation for implantation	
Testosterone			Development, maintenance of secondary sex characteristics	
Norepinephrine		Sudden stress		
hCG			Maintains corpus luteum at start of pregnancy	
GnRH		Puberty, Menses		

Hormone Worksheet Exercise Level 4

Hormones

Hormone	Secreted by	In response to	Effect	Type
		Childbirth	Uterine contraction, Emotional Bonding	
		High plasma osmolality	Retain water, ↑ aquaporin channels in collecting duct, DCT	
		GnRH	♀: initiate follicle growth ♂: ↑ spermatocyte development ♀, ♂: maturation of germ cells	
		GnRH ♀: estrogen spike from follicle just before ovulation	♀: ovulation, follicle becomes corpus luteum ♂: Leydig cells → ↑testosterone	
		CRH, Stress	↑ adrenal release of corticosteroids	
		TRH, low plasma levels of T_4 and T_3	↑ thyroid release of T_4 and T_3	
		Falling progesterone at end of pregnancy	Mammary gland enlargement, milk production	
		Pain	Pain relief	
		GHRH	Growth of long bones, general anabolism	
		High plasma [Ca^{2+}]	Reduce plasma [Ca^{2+}]	
		TSH	↑ metabolic rate	
		Low plasma [Ca^{2+}]	↑ plasma [Ca^{2+}]	
		Low blood [Glucose]	↑ blood [Glucose]	
		High blood [Glucose]	↓ blood [Glucose]	
		Various, usually high hormone levels	Suppress: GH, TSH, CCK, insulin, glucagon	
		Stress	↑ [Glucose], Immune suppression	
		ACTH, ATII, low bp	Collecting Duct, DCT: reabsorb Na^+, Secrete K^+, water retention, ↑ bp	
		Sudden stress	Sympathetic response: ↑ heart rate, breathing, etc.	
		FSH	♀: secondary sex characteristics, endometrial development during menstrual cycle, surge leads to LH surge	
		Ovulation	Thicken, maintain endometrium in preparation for implantation	
		GnRH→LH→Testos.	Development, maintenance of secondary sex characteristics	
		Sudden stress	Sympathic responses of fight or flight	
		Implantation	Maintains corpus luteum at start of pregnancy	
		Puberty, Menses	↑ LH, FSH release	

Hormone Worksheet Exercise Level 5

Hormones

Hormone	Secreted by	In response to	Effect	Type
Oxytocin				
Vasopressin (ADH)				
FSH				
LH				
ACTH				
TSH				
Prolactin				
Endorphin				
Growth Hormone				
Calcitonin				
T_4 & T_3				
Parathyroid Horm.				
Glucagon				
Insulin				
Somatostatin				
Cortisol				
Aldosterone				
Epinephrine				
Estrogen				
Progesterone				
Testosterone				
Norepinephrine				
hCG				
GnRH				

MCAT Practice Passage

Though the two conditions are characterized by similar symptoms, diabetes mellitus (DM) and diabetes insipidus (DI) have distinct and unrelated causes. In both DM and DI, patients experience polyuria (excessive urination). It is important for physicians to differentiate between DM and DI in order to properly treat their patients.

DM is caused by the impaired action of insulin in the body. People with type 1 DM produce insufficient quantities of insulin or sometimes no insulin at all. This is thought to be the result of the immune system attacking insulin-secreting cells. In type 2 DM, the body develops a gradual reduction in sensitivity to insulin, resulting in little or no response to the insulin the body produces. Type 2 DM is associated with obesity and increases the risk of many other health problems, including cardiovascular disease and nerve damage. Elevated levels of blood glucose in DM can exceed the capacity of the kidneys to reabsorb the substance.

DI is caused by the impaired action of antidiuretic hormone (ADH) on the kidneys. In central DI, the body does not produce sufficient ADH. Nephrogenic DI is characterized by normal serum ADH levels with an impaired ability of the kidney to respond to the action of ADH. Both types of DI can be hereditary in nature or caused by other factors.

A 15-year-old male with polyuria and polydipsia (excessive thirst) presents to his pediatrician. The doctor runs a series of blood and urine tests. In addition to the tests in Table 1 below, the physician performs a test to measure the patient's response to exogenous insulin, the results of which are normal.

Value	Result	Normal range
Fasting serum glucose	328 mg/dl	70-110 mg/dl
Serum ADH	3.6 pg/ml	1-5 pg/ml
Urine [glucose]	Positive	Negative
Urine osmolarity	1127 mOsm/kg	50-1200 mOsm/kg

Table 1 Results of the patient's laboratory tests. All reference ranges are for an adolescent male.

Passage taken from the Next Step online QBank

16. Nephrogenic DI is most plausibly caused by damage to ADH receptors in:

    A. the glomerulus.
    B. the pituitary gland.
    C. the collecting duct.
    D. the hypothalamus.

17. The patient's expected serum insulin levels would be:

    A. below normal.
    B. normal.
    C. above normal.
    D. The answer cannot be determined without more information.

18. Which of the following symptoms would be seen in DM but NOT in DI?

    I. Excessive hunger (polyphagia)
    II. Ketoacidosis from abnormally high fatty acid metabolism
    III. Excessive thirst (polydipsia)

    A. I only
    B. I and II only
    C. II and III only
    D. I, II, and III

19. In a healthy person, ADH is most likely to be secreted when:

    A. blood pressure is high; blood osmolality is low.
    B. blood pressure is high; blood osmolality is high.
    C. blood pressure is low; blood osmolality is low.
    D. blood pressure is low; blood osmolality is high.

Problem-solving Cooldown

20. Following apoptosis, dying cells need to be taken up into surrounding tissues via phagocytosis. Which of the following immune cells would NOT be able to carry out this function?

    A. Macrophages
    B. Eosinophils
    C. Basophils
    D. Mast cells

21. Humoral immunity depends on the production and actions of:

    A. T cells.
    B. antibodies.
    C. neutrophils.
    D. antigens.

22. A woman is brought to the ER suffering from acute narrowing of the bronchioles brought on by anaphylaxis. This will have the most direct impact on:

    A. relaxed inspiration.
    B. relaxed expiration.
    C. forced inspiration.
    D. forced expiration.

23. A man suspected of DUI is brought in for a breathalyzer analysis. At the exact moment between peak exhalation and onset of inhalation, which of the following is true?

    A. The pressure of air within the alveoli is greater than the pressure of air in the atmosphere.
    B. The pressure of air within the alveoli is less than the pressure of air in the atmosphere.
    C. The pressure of air within the alveoli is equal to the pressure of air in the atmosphere.
    D. The partial pressure of oxygen in the alveoli is less than the partial pressure of oxygen in the capillaries.

24. Which of the following chromosomal abnormalities is least likely to survive to birth in humans?

    A. Trisomy X
    B. Trisomy 21
    C. Trisomy 18
    D. Trisomy 6

To Do After Lesson 15

- ☐ Complete Full Timed Section 3 from the Verbal Practice: 108 Passages book
- ☐ Complete the Psychological and Sociological Foundations section from the AAMC Online Official Guide at e-mcat.com
- ☐ Complete Biology QBank 5: Nervous and Endocrine Systems

This page left intentionally blank.

LESSON 16

Chemistry 3

To Do Before Lesson 16

- ☐ Complete Full Timed Section 3 from the Verbal Practice: 108 Passages book
- ☐ Complete the Psychological and Sociological Foundations section from the AAMC Online Official Guide at e-mcat.com
- ☐ Complete Biology QBank 5: Nervous and Endocrine Systems

In Lesson 16

Problem-solving Warm-up
Acid-Base Chemistry
MCAT Practice Passage
Electrochemistry
Nerve Tissue
MCAT Practice Passage
Problem-solving Cooldown
Test-like Thinking: CARS Practice Passage

To Do After Lesson 16

- ☐ Complete the Critical Analysis and Reasoning Skills section from the AAMC Online Official Guide at e-mcat.com
- ☐ Complete Chemistry QBank 2: Solutions, Acids, and Electrochemistry
- ☐ Complete Chemistry QBank 3: Bonding and Phases

Problem-solving Warm-up

1. A student titrates 50 mL of unknown concentration of aqueous morpholine at 25 °C ($pK_b = 8.33$) using 0.1 M aqueous nitric acid. If the equivalence point was reached after adding 80 mL of acid solution, what was the pH of the solution when 40 mL of nitric acid had been added?

   A. 4
   B. 6
   C. 7
   D. 9

2. Which of the following compounds is expected to be the most basic?

   A. 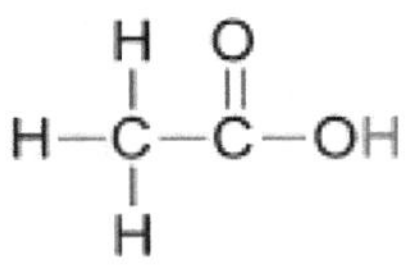
   C. 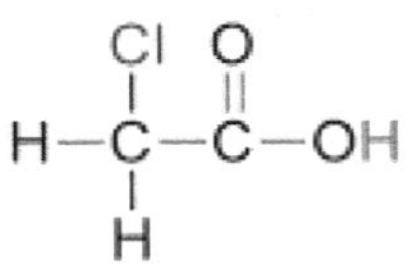
   B. 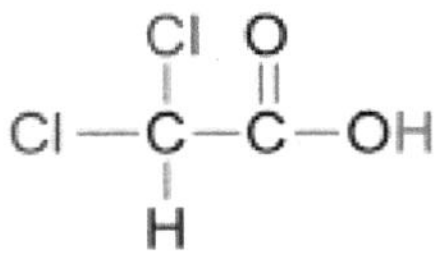
   D.

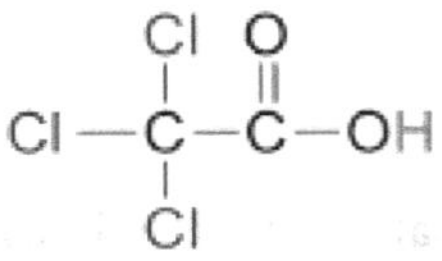

3. A patient with disrupted kidney function has a limited ability to excrete HCO_3^-. How would the accumulated ion function according to the Bronsted-Lowry model?

   A. It will function as an acid because its negative charge can attract H^+ ions.
   B. It will function as an acid in order to increase pH and buffer against increased basicity.
   C. It will function as a base in order to lower pH and buffer against increased acidity.
   D. It will function as a base by accepting an H^+ ion and maintaining near constant blood pH.

4. The reaction quotient of HCl at equilibrium with water is expected to be:

   A. >1.
   B. 1.
   C. <1.
   D. 0.

5. Which of the following amino acids is most likely to cross the cell membrane via diffusion?

   A. 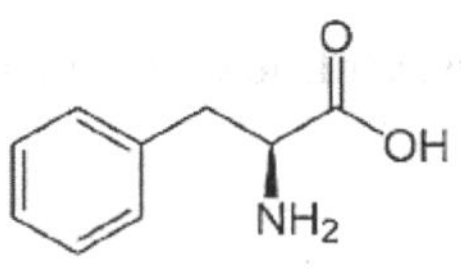
   C. 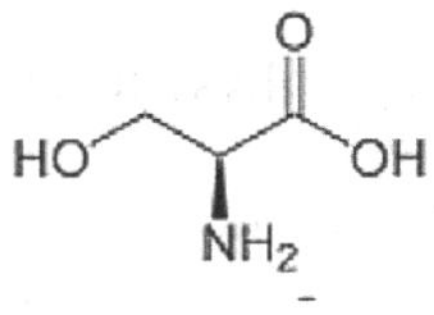
   B. 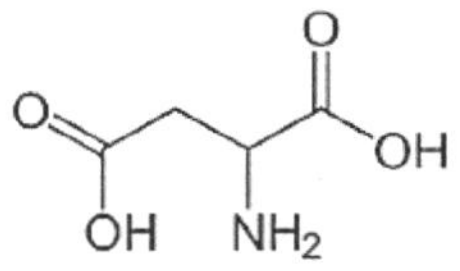
   D.

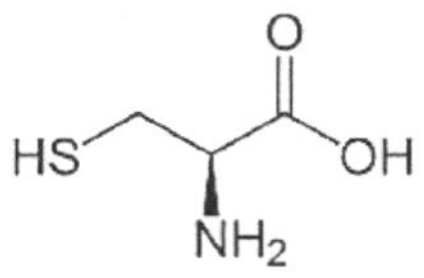

Acid-Base Chemistry

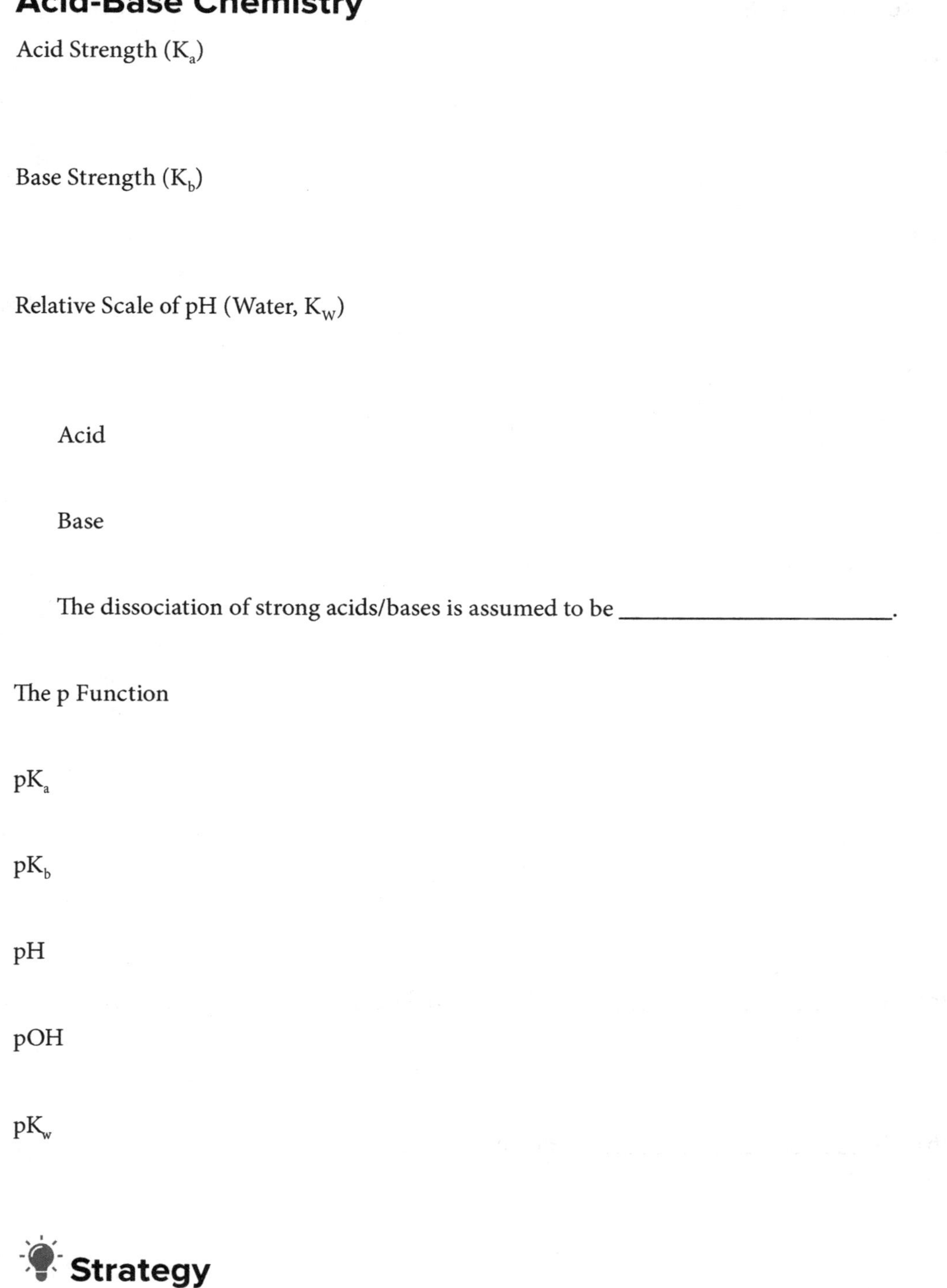

Acid Strength (K_a)

Base Strength (K_b)

Relative Scale of pH (Water, K_W)

Acid

Base

The dissociation of strong acids/bases is assumed to be ______________________.

The p Function

pK_a

pK_b

pH

pOH

pK_w

Strategy

Math Shortcut:

$[H^+] = 3.7 \times 10^{-7}$

$[OH^-] = 6.8 \times 10^{-4}$

$[K_a] = 8.1 \times 10^{-11}$

$pK_a = 9.1$

$pOH = 3.6$

Common Acid/Base Species

Strong	Acids	K_a	Bases	K_b

Weak

Weak

On the MCAT, if the acid/base is not ______________________, then it must be ______________________.

On the MCAT, if the acid/base is ______________________, then it must be ______________________.

Conjugate Pairs

Bronsted-Lowry vs. Lewis Definition

Type	Behavior	Example	Most Commonly Tested in
Bronsted-Lowry Acid			
Lewis Acid			
Bronsted-Lowry Base			
Lewis Base			

Amphoteric Species

Normality

Equivalents

Neutralization

Titrations

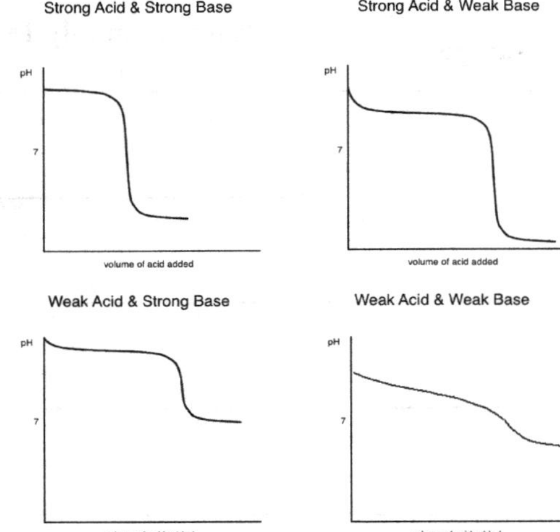

Titrant

Titrand

Equivalence Point

$$N_aV_a = N_bV_b$$

pH of Solution at Equivalence Point

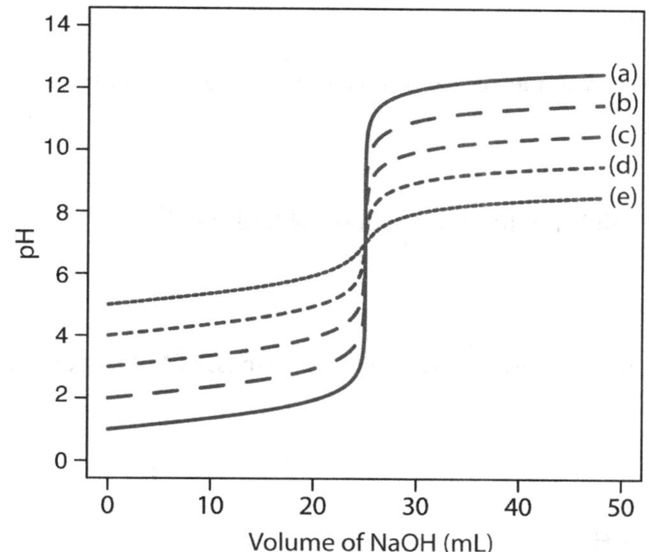

What is likely to have varied between curves a-e?

If a student accidentally adds excess water to the unknown titrand solution, what effect will this have on equivalence point?

Polyprotic Acid Titrations

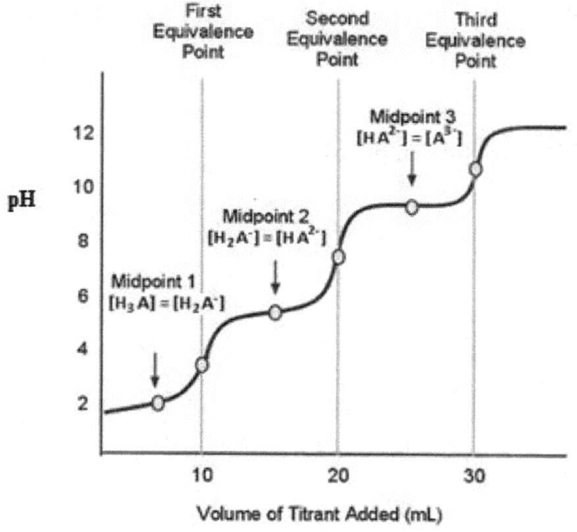

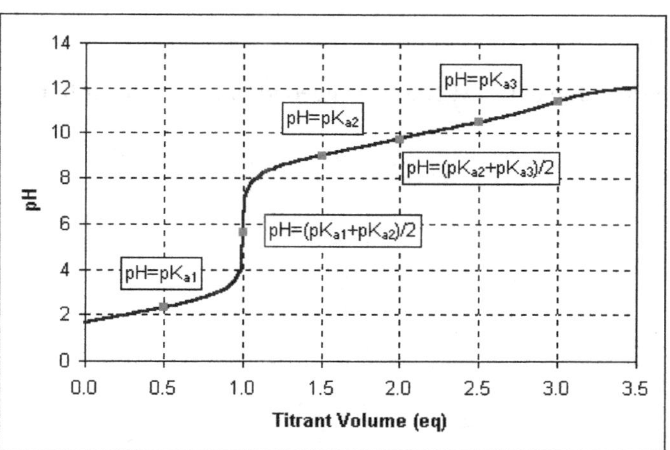

What type of species will we have at the first and second equivalence points?

What can we say about the concentration of each species at the equivalence points?

Practice Problems

What effect will the strength of the titrant/titrand have on the volume needed to reach the equivalence point?

How do we estimate the equivalence point if one species is solid and the other is aqueous? Both solid?

The gram-equivalent weight of acid A is 75 in neutralization reactions. If A has a molecular mass of 150 amu, what MUST be true of the acid?

How many g of KOH is needed to neutralize 50 mL of 0.1 M HF?

What volume of 0.03 M HCl is needed to neutralize 30 mL of a 0.1 N solution of $Mg(OH)_2$?

What volume of 0.03 M HCl is needed to neutralize 30 mL of a 0.1 M solution of $Mg(OH)_2$?

What volume of 0.4 M NaOH is needed to neutralize 100 mL 0.2 M HF? 100 mL of 0.2 M HCl?

Buffers

$$HA + H_2O \leftrightarrows H_3O^+ + A^-$$

$pH = pK_a + \log [A^-]/[HA]$

$$B + H^+ \leftrightarrows BH^+$$

$pOH = pK_b + \log [BH^+]/[B]$

What biological analysis technique utilizes this exact principle to identify proteins?

What is the pOH of a 0.01 M ammonia solution (pK_b ammonia = 9.89)?

What is the pH of a 0.001 M solution of ethanoic acid (pK_a = 4.75) at the half equivalence point when titrated with KOH?

What would be the pH at the equivalence point if 0.007 M HBr if titrated with sodium acetate?

If pH = pKa in a buffer solution, then [A-]/[HA] is equal to:

Timed MCAT Practice Passage

Mastery of the MCAT sciences is a two-part process. First you must study to understand (not just memorize!) the science content, and then you must study the content actively and challenge yourself within the context of the exam.

1. Complete your reading of the passage (3-4 minutes).
    - Write down what you believe to be the primary science content underlying the passage.
    - What facts or concepts do you anticipate to be tested? When you are done with the questions determine if you were correct. What passage clues were there to imply related topics that showed up in the questions?
    - Were there any key terms or important scientific relationships you missed?
    - Were you able to draw any conclusions from the data, if presented?

2. Complete the practice questions on your own (4-5 minutes)
    - Rephrase each question in your own mind after reading it to clarify the task.
    - Research the relevant area(s) of the passage or your own knowledge for information related to the task.
    - Respond to the question by choosing the answer that fits your research/calculations *and* satisfies the task.
    - If no answer seems obvious, eliminate answers that fail to have support in the passage or in the relevant science.

3. Analyze your wrong answer choices to the questions you missed.
    - Did you understand the task in the question?
    - What skill type was the question?
    - Did you know the science/formula/concept needed to answer the question?
    - Did you recognize the science being hinted at?
    - Were you able to find information in the passage quickly when you needed it?
    - Were there any necessary scientific concepts you failed to apply to the question?
        - If so, why?
    - If you made a mistake in calculations, have you identified your mistake?

This page left intentionally blank.

Maintenance of proper pH levels in various parts of the human body is vitally important for a number of different reasons, among them prevention of tissue degradation due to excessive acidity or basicity, and creation of an internal environment in which biochemical reactions can proceed at appropriate times and rates.

Systems and processes which can help to partially stabilize pH levels include respiratory feedback mechanisms, which can decrease the level of CO_2 in blood plasma and hence can avoid an excessive concentration of carbonic acid, H_2CO_3. Other mechanisms for doing so include a buffer system catalyzed by carbonic anhydrase enzymes and involving both carbonic acid (H_2CO_3) and bicarbonate (HCO_3^-). One such buffer system was replicated in vitro and a titration procedure was applied, measuring pH as a function of what percentage of buffer was in the form of bicarbonate. The measurements from this system are graphed in Figure 1.

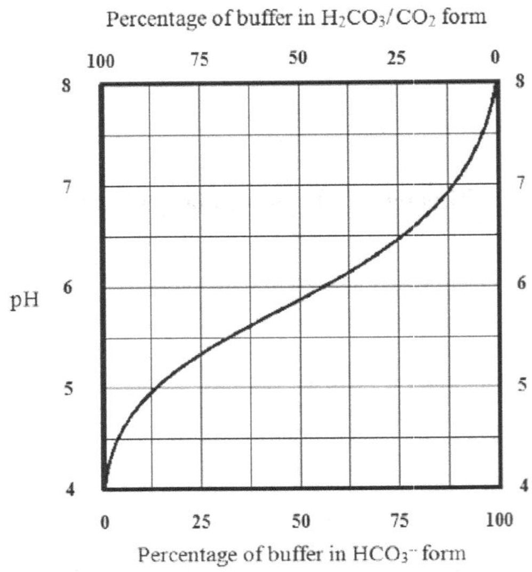

Figure 1 pH level as a function of buffer component percentage

Yet another system involves regulation of blood acidity by the kidneys, which can excrete either H^+ ions or bicarbonate ions, depending on which direction the chemical concentrations in the buffer system must shift to reach a safe blood plasma pH range. Excreting a substantial amount of bicarbonate will cause a significant number of the remaining carbonic acid molecules to separate into an H^+ ion and a bicarbonate ion.

Passage taken from the Next Step Chemistry review book, chapter 7

6. If respiratory function is interrupted at a time when excessive CO_2 is in the bloodstream, then the pH of the blood plasma will:

   A. increase, because increased CO_2 means increased acidity.
   B. decrease, because excessive CO_2 will cause elevated levels of carbonic acid.
   C. remain constant, because CO_2 will simply convert itself into H_2CO_3 by combining with water.
   D. remain constant, because CO_2 does not have a hydrogen atom and hence cannot affect pH level.

7. When pOH is equal to pH under conditions of 100°C and 1 atm, the number representing each value will be:

   A. 7, because the product of $[H^+]$ and $[OH^-]$ must match K_W.
   B. <7, because as temperature increases, more $[H^+]$ is produced.
   C. >7, because as temperature increases, more $[OH^-]$ is produced.
   D. pH and pOH cannot be quantified when $[H^+]$ equals $[OH^-]$.

8. Figure 1 indicates that the rate of change of pH level is high as a function of bicarbonate concentration between the pH ranges of 7 and 8. What might account for this?

   A. Increased HCO_3^- levels resulting in the donation of more $[OH^-]$ ions, causing a basic mixture of H_2O and OH^- to form
   B. Ionization of water
   C. The fact that titration occurred in the laboratory caused more inefficient functioning of the buffer system compared to how it would have operated in a living specimen
   D. Exhaustion of carbonic acid levels which could otherwise help to neutralize increased basicity

9. Titration of potassium acetate in solution was conducted in a further attempt to determine a superior buffer system. The equation describing the reactions preceding titration appears below:

$$KCH_3COO + H_2O \rightarrow K^+ + CH_3COO^- + H_2O \rightarrow CH_3COOH + OH^-$$

   What best describes what occurs in this process?

   A. An acidic salt is hydrolyzed
   B. A basic salt is hydrolyzed
   C. A weak acid is dissolved
   D. A strong acid is dissolved

Electrochemistry

$$2Al\ (s) + 3Mg^{2+}\ (aq) \rightarrow 2Al^{3+} + 3Mg\ (s)$$

OIL RIG

Reduced Species

Oxidized Species

Reducing Agent

Oxidizing Agent

Electrochemical Cells

Cathode

Anode

Current (movement of electrons)

Emf $E_{cell} = E_{cathode} - E_{anode}$

E < 0

E = 0

E > 0

$$\Delta G° = -nFE°_{cell} = -RTln(K_{eq})$$

Voltage as an Intensive Property

$Cu\ (s) \rightarrow Cu^{3+}\ (aq) + 3e^-$ E°= -1.83 $3Cu\ (s) \rightarrow 3Cu^{3+}\ (aq) + 9e^-$ E°=

Balancing Redox Reactions

Step 1—Assign oxidation number to each atom.
Step 2—Determine the net change in charge to determine the ratio of atoms
Step 3—Use the ratio to eliminate the net charge change
Step 4—Use the ratio as coefficients for the elements
Step 5—Add H^+ (acidic conditions), OH^- (basic conditions), and H_2O to balance charges.

Balance this reaction in an acidic aqueous solution:

$$TcO_4^- + H_2C_2O_4 \rightarrow Tc^{2+} + CO_2$$

Electrolytic Cells

Anode/Anode Reaction

$Zn^{2+} + 2e^- \rightarrow Zn(s)$ **E = 0.34 V**

$Cu^{2+} + 2e^- \rightarrow Cu(s)$ **E = 0.66 V**

- +

Zn

Cu

$ZnSO_4$

$CuSO_4$

Cathode/Cathode Reaction

Cell potential

Galvanic Cells

Anode/Anode Reaction

$Zn^{2+} + 2e^- \rightarrow Zn(s)$ **E = 0.34 V**

$Cu^{2+} + 2e^- \rightarrow Cu(s)$ **E = 0.66 V**

Voltmeter

V

salt bridge

KCl

Zn

Cu

$ZnSO_4$

$CuSO_4$

Cathode/Cathode Reaction

Cell Potential

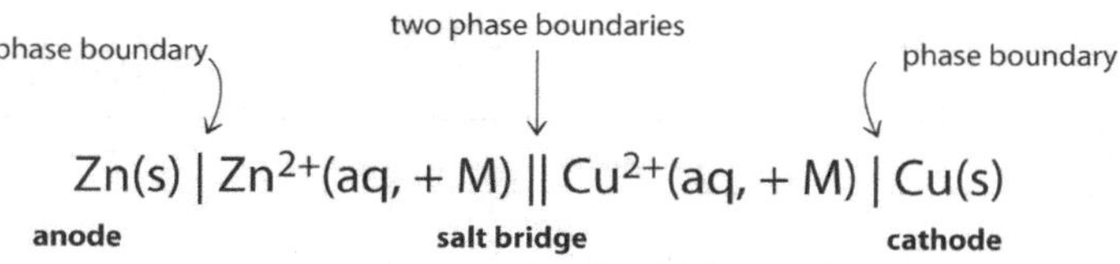

Salt Bridge

Nernst Equation

$$aA + bB \longleftrightarrow cC + dD$$

$E = E° - 0.06/n \log [Q]$ where $Q =$

What is the potential of a cell when $Q < K_{eq}$? $Q = K_{eq}$? $Q > K_{eq}$? $Q = 1$?

Nerve Tissue

Nernst Equation and Membrane Potential for a Given Ion

At equilibrium, $\Delta G_{Electrical}$ and $\Delta G_{Chemical}$ are equal:

$nFE = RT \ln [K_o/K_i]$

R is the gas constant, T is the absolute temperature (K),

F is the Faraday constant, E is the voltage, and n is the valence of K^+ (+1).

inside	MEMBRANE	outside
[K+] = Ki		[K+] = Ko

E(equilibrium voltage) = $RT/nF \ln [K_o/K_i]$

Species	Intracellular [X]	Extracellular [X]	Equilibrium Voltage
Sodium (Na^+)	15 mM	145 mM	V_{Na} = +60.60 mV
Potassium (K^+)	150 mM	4 mM	V_K = −96.81 mV
Chloride (Cl^-)	10 mM	110 mM	V_{Cl} = −64.05 mV

Given the values above, what explains why the resting membrane potential of a cell is -70 mV?

What active biological mechanism allows for the maintenance of the cell's resting membrane potential?

Timed MCAT Practice Passage

Mastery of the MCAT sciences is a two-part process. First you must study to understand (not just memorize!) the science content, and then you must study the content actively and challenge yourself within the context of the exam.

1. Complete your reading of the passage (3-4 minutes).
    - Write down what you believe to be the primary science content underlying the passage.
    - What facts or concepts do you anticipate to be tested? When you are done with the questions determine if you were correct. What passage clues were there to imply related topics that showed up in the questions?
    - Were there any key terms or important scientific relationships you missed?
    - Were you able to draw any conclusions from the data, if presented?

2. Complete the practice questions on your own (4-5 minutes)
    - Rephrase each question in your own mind after reading it to clarify the task.
    - Research the relevant area(s) of the passage or your own knowledge for information related to the task.
    - Respond to the question by choosing the answer that fits your research/calculations *and* satisfies the task.
    - If no answer seems obvious, eliminate answers that fail to have support in the passage or in the relevant science.

3. Analyze your wrong answer choices to the questions you missed.
    - Did you understand the task in the question?
    - What skill type was the question?
    - Did you know the science/formula/concept needed to answer the question?
    - Did you recognize the science being hinted at?
    - Were you able to find information in the passage quickly when you needed it?
    - Were there any necessary scientific concepts you failed to apply to the question?
        - If so, why?
    - If you made a mistake in calculations, have you identified your mistake?

There are two types of covalent bonds found in biologically important molecules, nonpolar and polar covalent bonds. In chemistry, the distinction between these types of bonds is based on differences in electronegativity between the nonmetal atoms involved in sharing pairs of electrons. If the difference in electronegativity between the two elements is less than 0.5, the bond is considered nonpolar and if the difference is greater than 0.5, but less than 2.0, the bond is considered polar. If the difference in electronegativity is greater than 2.0, the bond is no longer considered covalent. Listed in Table 1 are the electronegativity values for selected nonmetal elements.

Unequal sharing of electrons in a covalent bond, due to differences in electronegativity, imparts a degree of ionic character to the bond. The more electronegative atom will gain a partial negative charge (δ-) and the other atom in the bond will gain an equal amount of positive partial charge (δ+). These bond dipoles represent electric fields with vector properties. Having polar covalent bonds is a necessary requirement for a molecule to have a molecular dipole moment, but, if the bond dipole moments do not combine to give a net dipole moment, the molecule will be nonpolar. These molecular moments can increase the degree of intermolecular forces present. Table 2 lists the experimentally determined molecular dipole moments for selected compounds.

Formula	Name	Molecular Dipole (D)
CH_4	methane	0
NH_3	ammonia	1.47
H_2O	water	1.85
H_2CO	methanal	2.33
CO_2	carbon dioxide	0
CH_3COH	ethanal	2.7
$(CH_3)_2CO$	propanone	2.91
C_2H_6	ethane	0
N_2H_4	hydrazine	1.85
H_2O_2	hydrogen peroxide	2.26
CH_3NH_2	methyl amine	1.31
CH_3OH	methanol	1.69
$(CH_3)_2O$	dimethyl ether	1.30

Table 2 Molecular dipole moments, measured in Debyes (D)

Atomic Symbol	Electronegativity (Pauling scale)
H	2.2
C	2.6
N	3.0
O	3.4
F	4.0

Table 1 Electronegativity values for selected second period elements

Passage taken from the Next Step Chemistry review book, chapter 1

10. Which of the following is the best estimate of an O-H bond dipole moment in water? (Note: sin 104.5° = 0.95; sin 52° = 0.80; cos 104.5° = -0.33; and cos 52° = 0.55)

    A. 0.97 D
    B. 1.13 D
    C. 1.50 D
    D. 3.24 D

11. Which of the following compounds is expected to be the least soluble in water?

    A. Methanol
    B. Dimethyl ether
    C. Methyl amine
    D. Dimethyl amine

12. Shown below is drawing representing the most stable conformation of hydrogen peroxide. Which of the following vectors best represents the direction of electric field generated by the dipole moment of hydrogen peroxide based on this drawing?

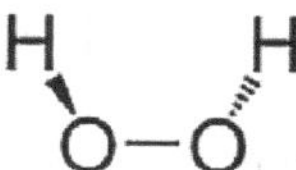

    A. ↓
    B. ↑
    C. ↘
    D. ↙

13. Which of the following compounds will have the highest boiling point?

    A. Methanal
    B. Propanone
    C. Hydrazine
    D. Methane

Problem-solving Cooldown

14. The operation of an electrochemical cell will be spontaneous if:

A. $E_{cell} = 0$
B. $E_{cell} < 0$
C. $K_{eq} = 1$
D. $K_{eq} > 1$

15. What is the standard free energy for the reaction below?

$$Mn_{(s)} + Cu^{+2}_{(aq)} = Mn^{+2}_{(aq)} + Cu_{(s)} \quad E° = +1.10 \text{ V}$$

A. –110 kJ/mol
B. –220 kJ/mol
C. +110 kJ/mol
D. +220 kJ/mol

16. When being recharged, a rechargeable battery acts as what type of electrochemical cell?

A. Galvanic
B. Electrolytic
C. Both galvanic and electrolytic
D. Neither galvanic nor electrolytic

17. Which of the metals CANNOT cathodically protect a sample of iron from oxidative corrosion?

Reaction	Potential (V)
Ag^{+} (*aq*) + e^{-} → Ag (*s*)	0.80
Cu^{2+} (*aq*) + 2 e^{-} → Cu (*s*)	0.34
Pb^{2+} (*aq*) + 2 e^{-} → Pb (*s*)	-0.13
Ni^{2+} (*aq*) + 2 e^{-} → Ni (*s*)	-0.26
Cd^{2+} (*aq*) + 2 e^{-} → Cd (*s*)	-0.40
Fe^{2+} (*aq*) + 2 e^{-} → Fe (*s*)	-0.45
Zn^{2+} (*aq*) + 2 e^{-} → Zn (*s*)	-0.76
2 H2O $^{2+}$ (*l*) + 2 e^{-} → H_2 (*g*) + 2 OH^{-} (*aq*)	-0.83
Al^{3+} (*aq*) + 3 e^{-} → Al (*s*)	-1.66
Mg^{2+} (*aq*) + 2 e^{-} → Mg (*s*)	-2.37

A. Al
B. Mg
C. Ni
D. Zn

18. In a cell can be represented with the notation: Cd (*s*) | Cd^{+2} (*aq*) || F^{-} (*aq*), F_2 (*g*) | Pt (*s*), which of the following must be true?

A. The battery has a cadmium cathode.
B. The battery has a fluorine anode.
C. cadmium will be oxidized.
D. The cell is galvanic.

This page left intentionally blank.

Test-like Thinking: CARS Practice Passage

Used both as a descriptor and as a pejorative term, "identity politics" began first as a set of mobilizing forces meant to advance the interests of certain disadvantaged groups (e.g. LGBT individuals, the disabled, feminist movements, etc.). While the successes of such movements cannot be denied, critics have focused more on the fracturing that identity politics has on the American electorate and the diversion of political energy and will away from fundamental underlying issues that affect nearly all Americans to more narrow concerns. For example, critics would assert for the average middle class gay American, the larger concerns of income inequality, lack of access to healthcare and affordable education, and environmental justice ought to predominate over more narrow concerns about marriage equality.

These critics often contrast identity politics with the politics of liberation. In *The Disuniting of America*, historian Arthur Schlesinger asserts that identity politics are inherently self-defeating. As such movements are so often focused on affirmations of the lives and identities of those who are marginalized by the mainstream , they ultimately further entrench such marginalization. This prevents any ability to push back against the political and economic power structures that would lock them out. Democracy itself, asserts Schlesinger, requires a common experience and a set of shared values and ideals. Thus the politics of liberation, in which marginalized groups are meant to "come out" (literally in the case of members of the LGBT community) and actively engage with mainstream culture and politics, create success in ways that identity politics, by their nature, cannot.

After the turn of the millennium, the term "identity politics" took on a new tone. Most notably during the 2008 Democratic Presidential Primary—in which the two major candidates were a white woman and a black man—some in the media began using the term as a catch-all for political pandering based on factors such as race, gender, sexual orientation, or nationality. Prior to 2008, only white men had ever been president of the US, so the 2008 primary season proved to be fertile ground for commentators and analysts. Any speech given by Hillary Clinton that addressed women's issues or any speech given by Barack Obama that addressed concerns of the black community were dismissed by many as "mere identity politics". In the face of such a twisting of the term, it is instructive to look to the history.

The phrase "identity politics" was coined by writers working as a part of the Combahee River Collective, an organization of black feminist lesbians active throughout the late 1970's. The group began as a small weekly gathering of like-minded individuals at the Cambridge, Massachusetts Women's Center. From 1977 to 1980, the group held a series of seven retreats gathering together a few dozen activists and writers. During these retreats, the women shared their life stories and examined how, as women of color and as lesbians, they were subjected not only to the oppressing effects of race, gender, and sexual identity, but to a marginalization that was more profound than even each of these three forces combined. Their exploration of the social and political issues that surrounded their lives eventually gave rise to the Combahee River Collective Statement. In just a few thousand words, this essay powerfully puts forth a vision of an inclusive politics.

The great irony at the heart of "identity politics" is that—as is so often the case with charged political terms—it came to be seen as representing the exact opposite of its true intent. As the Combahee River Collective developed it, identity politics is an expression of a political will identical to the politics of inclusion so often touted by others.

19. As described in the passage, Arthur Schlesinger would most likely *disapprove* of a political candidate who:

   A. wins office through a slim majority of votes, which were earned by appealing only to the interests of female voters at the expense of larger issues.
   B. neglects the needs of all of his constituents in order to focus solely on fundraising and advancing his own media profile.
   C. wins office by building a coalition of voters coming from several different demographic backgrounds.
   D. openly advocates for the politics of liberation while secretly pursuing an agenda that advances the interests of his large corporate donors.

20. According to the passage, which of the following was originally true of the term "identity politics"?

   A. It referred to an ideology in which people from various minority groups were to be included in the political life of mainstream America.
   B. It was a way for black and female voters to justify their electoral choices based solely on race or gender.
   C. It was only relevant to those who were subject to multiple, interlocking prejudices and marginalization.
   D. It emphasized a politics of inclusion that made moot larger concerns such as access to affordable healthcare and education.

21. The passage suggests that:

   A. those in the LGBT community are less concerned with income inequality than marriage equality.
   B. Arthur Schlesinger disapproves of the work of the Combahee River Collective.
   C. there can be synergistic effects in prejudice.
   D. every political term eventually has its meaning distorted.

22. A political commentator using the term "identity politics" in the dismissive sense described in the third paragraph would most likely apply this label to which of the following?

   A. A political TV ad narrated in Cantonese airing in a market with a large population of immigrants from Hong Kong
   B. A speech given by the first member of the Millennial generation to earn a major party nomination in a certain Congressional district in which the candidate advocates for legalizing recreational use of marijuana
   C. The Combahee River Collective Statement
   D. A speech given by a mayoral candidate in Spanish when addressing an audience that is over 90% Latino in which he advocates for immigration policies favorable to the Latino community

23. Which of the following describes a scenario that is analogous to "identity politics" as the author describes the history of this term?

   A. "Politically correct" was originally coined by public relations consultants working with political candidates to help them use language that would avoid offending voters but came to be used in the popular culture to mean an overzealous concern with language.
   B. "Right to work" was originally coined by labor advocates favoring strong labor unions to help workers earn a wage that would let them support a family but eventually came to be used by state legislatures to describe laws that made labor unions illegal.
   C. "Win-win" originally referred to a negotiation tactic in which one party attempts to frame a proposal as a benefit for both parties in the negotiation but later came to be replaced with "net-net" as shorthand for "net win for both parties".
   D. "Ministry of Peace" was used in George Orwell's *1984* as the name for the government ministry that was in charge of conducting the war effort.

To Do After Lesson 16

- ☐ Complete the Critical Analysis and Reasoning Skills section from the AAMC Online Official Guide at e-mcat.com
- ☐ Complete Chemistry QBank 2: Solutions, Acids, and Electrochemistry
- ☐ Complete Chemistry QBank 3: Bonding and Phases

Biochemistry 3 and Full Length 2 Review

LESSON 17

To Do Before Lesson 17

- ☐ Complete the Critical Analysis and Reasoning Skills section from the AAMC Online Official Guide at e-mcat.com
- ☐ Complete Chemistry QBank 2: Solutions, Acids, and Electrochemistry
- ☐ Complete Chemistry QBank 3: Bonding and Phases

In Lesson 17

Full Length 2 Review
Lessons Learned Journal
Pattern Analysis
What to Do Now
Problem-solving Warm-up
Biological Signaling
MCAT Practice Passage
Biochemical Lab Techniques
MCAT Practice Passage
Problem-solving Cooldown
Test-like Thinking: CARS Practice Passage

To Do After Lesson 17

- ☐ Complete Full Timed Section 4 from the Verbal Practice: 108 Passages book
- ☐ Complete the AAMC Chemical and Physical Foundations Section Bank (may be split over 2-3 days if needed)
- ☐ Complete Biochemistry QBank 2: Biotechnology and Analysis

Full Length 2 Review - Complete after taking Next Step FL#2

	Chem/Phys	CARS	Bio/Biochem	Psych/Soc
Did you finish the section on time?				
Did your score increase or decrease from FL1?				
How often did you look at the clock?				
Where did you spend most of your time (passages vs. Qs)?				
Did you eliminate choices but choose the wrong answer?				

The Plateau Effect: When doing more does not help your score

Habituation

Burnout

Wrong Diagnosis

Wrong Treatment

Short-term Thinking

Build your Lessons Learned Journal

Resource	Good For:
MCAT Review Books	
Content Questions	
Additional Practice Books	
Content Videos	
Full Length Exam	
Topic-specific Passages	

Test-like Simulation

Mouse/Trackpad

Non-dominant Hand

Test Location

Wrong Answer Analysis

Working Backwards

Content Weaknesses

Your Study Calendar

EXAMPLE

04	05	06	07	08	09	10
DAY 27 REQUIRED • Read Chem/Orgo CR Sections 8-10 • Read Psych/Soc SP Ch 1 and 2 OPTIONAL • Complete 2 CARS passages • Complete 20 questions from Psych/Soc Qbank	DAY 28 REQUIRED Day off! OPTIONAL	DAY 29 REQUIRED • Complete 35 questions from Chemistry section of Qbook OPTIONAL • Watch 2 Psych/Soc Content Review videos	DAY 30 REQUIRED • Session 6 • Complete 30 questions from Orgo Qbank OPTIONAL • Watch 2 Physics Content Review videos	No MCAT Work Today	DAY 31 REQUIRED • Complete every other question from Chem/Orgo CR Sections 8-10 OPTIONAL • Complete 20 questions from Biochem Qbank • Watch 2 Bio/Biochem Content Review videos	DAY 32 REQUIRED • Complete 30 questions from Chemistry section of Qbook OPTIONAL • Complete 2 CARS pasages • Watch 2 Psych/Soc Content Review videos
11 DAY 33 REQUIRED • Read Bio/Biochem CR Sections 6 and 9 OPTIONAL • Complete 2 CARS passages • Complete 30 questions from Psych/Soc Qbank	**12** DAY 34 REQUIRED • Session 7 OPTIONAL • Complete 2 CARS passages • Complete 20 questions from Chemistry Qbank	**13** No MCAT Work Today	**14** DAY 35 REQUIRED Day off! OPTIONAL	**15** DAY 36 REQUIRED • Complete every other question from Bio/Biochem CR Sections 6 and 9 OPTIONAL • Complete 30 questions from Psych/Soc Qbank	**16** DAY 37 REQUIRED • Read Psych/Soc CR Sections 1-3 OPTIONAL • Complete 2 CARS passages • Complete 20 questions from Psych/Soc Qbank	**17** DAY 38 REQUIRED • Complete Bio/Biochem section of FL #7 • Complete Psych/Soc section of FL #7 OPTIONAL • Watch 2 Chemistry Content Review videos
18 DAY 39 REQUIRED • Complete all questions from Graph Practice section of Qbook OPTIONAL • Watch 2 Physics Content Review videos	**19** DAY 40 REQUIRED • Session 8 • Watch 2 Chemistry Content Review videos OPTIONAL • ~~Complete 20 questions from Physics Qbank~~	**20** DAY 41 REQUIRED • Complete every other question from Psych/Soc CR Sections 1-3 • Read Bio/Biochem CR Sections 3-5 OPTIONAL • Complete 20 questions from Chemistry Qbank	**21** No MCAT Work Today	**22** DAY 42 REQUIRED Day off! OPTIONAL	**23** DAY 43 REQUIRED • Complete 45 questions from Biochem section of Qbook OPTIONAL • Watch 2 Orgo Content Review videos	**24** DAY 44 REQUIRED • Complete Chem/Phys section of FL #8 • Complete CARS section of FL #8 OPTIONAL • Complete 2 CARS passages

Full Length 2 Review: Chem/Phys Foundations Passage 6

Cefixime is a cephalosporin antibiotic, a class of antibiotics that contain a β-lactam ring fused to an unsaturated six-membered dihydrothiazine ring (Figure 1).

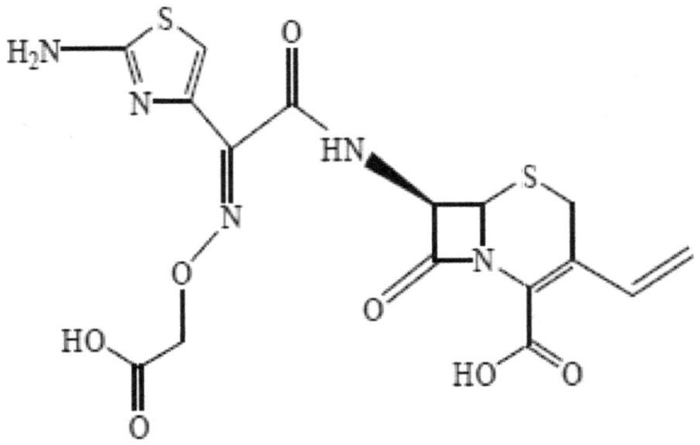

Figure 1 Cefixime

Cephalosporins function by inhibiting the bacterial enzyme PBP. The structural similarity between the core structure and D-alanyl-D-alanine, the terminal amino acid residue of the PBP substrates *N*-acetyl-glucosamine and *N*-acetyl-muramic acid, facilitates the irreversible binding of cephalosporin to the active site of PBP in a manner that is not competitive inhibition.

It was observed that certain metal complexes of cefixime can have greater activity than cefixime alone. To test these phenomena, scientists took metal salts of different transition metals and reacted them with the sodium salt of cefixime. They measured the bioactivity of the resultant metal-cefixime complexes (C1-C3. as inhibitors of enzymes other than PBP.

Structural characterization was performed using a UV/Vis spectrophotometer and infrared spectroscopy. First, the maximum absorbance (λ_{max}) was measured for cefixime and for each complex under study. The value of λ_{max} for a compound indicates the presence of a specific combination of chromophoric groups. Infrared studies of cefixime and C1-C3 show that each contained donor atoms that bind to metal ions, forming multinuclear chelates. After determining the metal-to-ligand ratio in the complexes, researchers proposed the hydrated complex structures shown in Figure 2.

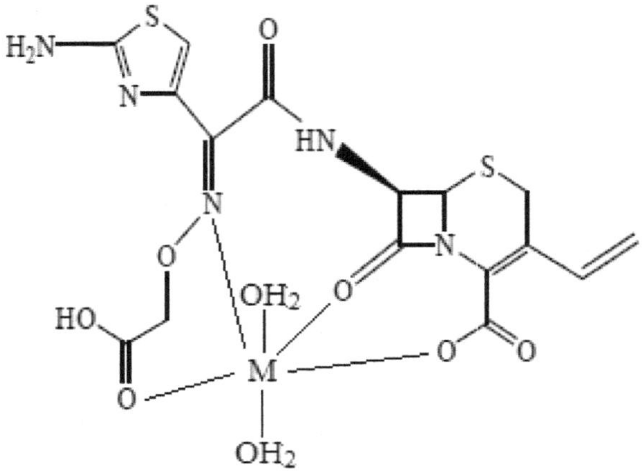

Figure 2 Proposed structure of cefixime transition metal complexes C1-C3 (C1: M = Cd^{+2}; C2: M = Cu^{+2}; C3: M = Fe^{+2}.

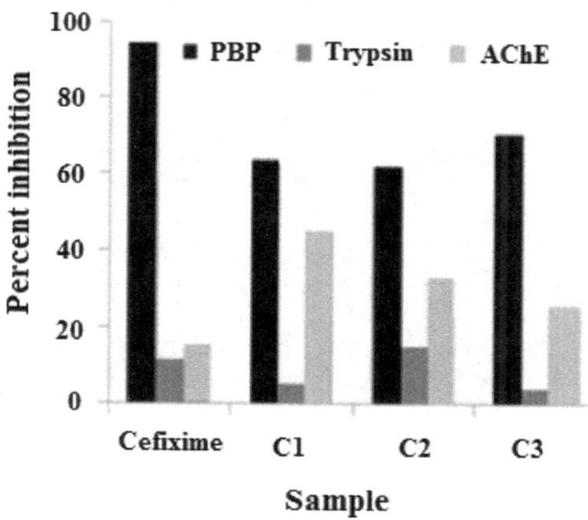

Figure 3 Inhibition of substrates

Following synthesis and characterization of C1-C3, inhibition assays of PBP and the human enzymes trypsin and acetylcholinesterase (AChE) were performed using cefixime and the complexes. Inhibitory activity was measured spectrophotometrically and reported as percent inhibition.

Were there any key terms you did not note? Did they appear in the questions?

____

____

Did you recognize the experimental goals?

____

____

Could you draw any conclusions from the presented results?

____

____

Did the passage offer any conclusions?

____

____

33. Cefixime displays what inhibitive behavior on PBP?

    A. Competitive inhibition
    B. Non-competitive inhibition
    C. Uncompetitive inhibition
    D. <u>Suicide inhibition</u>

Why is D correct?

A:

B:

C:

Wrong Answer Type Fallen for:

____

____

Content or Exam-related Mistake?

____

____

Lesson Learned

____

____

35. The close resemblance in the λ_{max} values of cefixime and the synthesized complexes best supports which theory?

A. **The chromophoric groups of cefixime and the complexes are similar.**
B. Complexation with metal ions does not affect λ_{max}.
C. The infrared spectrum of cefixime and the complexes are similar.
D. Synthesis of each complex from cefixime was carried out by a similar scheme.

Why is A correct?

B:

C:

D:

Wrong Answer Type Fallen for:

Content or Exam-Related Mistake?

Lesson Learned

Full Length 2 Review: CARS Passage 8

Altruism is doing something for the benefit of others without regards to the self. Altruism raises several issues within philosophy. Many philosophers suggest that altruism is actually enlightened self-interest, acting in a way that contributes to the quality of one's life, either materially or emotionally. At the most extreme, this definition denies that any action could be purely altruistic. These issues have been made more complex in recent years through examinations of biological altruism. Contrary to initial belief, it has been found that biological altruism is often not directed at kin, but that animals that participate in such actions regardless of the relationship to those they save ensure greater survival rates of their own kin. Other issues rise from consequentialist schools, including the necessity of self-denial if the action benefits the greater good (whether utilitarianism can be understood as altruistic), and the inquiry into the possibly corrosive personal effects of regarding others above self (an issue raised most thoroughly by Friedrich Nietzsche).

Practical altruism is a newly defined subset within this field. Based on the very simple idea that ethical behavior is defined by actively seeking to do the most good, its emphasis is on ascertaining that the maximum good is being reached. The accepted definition of ethical altruism is "a philosophy and social movement which applies evidence and reason to determining the most effective ways to improve the world." In practical altruism, taking a job on Wall Street and donating half of one's salary to a charity aimed at eradicating malaria is more ethical than devoting one's life to serving as a doctor treating patients with malaria if more cases of malaria could be prevented through the former actions. It matters not if the former altruist is living in comfort in a Manhattan apartment and not in Third World living conditions.

Under practical altruism, philanthropy that focuses on the individual is typically the most compelling form of charity for givers. However, this philanthropy fails the ethical test in comparison to other, more wide ranging, charities and raises several philosophical questions. Are we more driven by innate needs and emotions than our rational capacities? Can reason take a more prominent role in our decisions? Why are some people more apt to act in ways that look beyond their own interests and the interests of their kin? These are not new questions, but practical altruism newly inflects old philosophical questions about motive.

Practical altruism advocates like Mark Onion argue that it makes the world a better place. Onion argues that through it, "philosophy is returning to its Socratic role of challenging our ideas about what it is to live an ethical life," demonstrating "its ability to transform, sometimes quite dramatically, the lives of those who study it." Others, such as Stephanie Argueta, who specializes in the ethics of political science, posit that practical altruism effectively destroys community. "Paradigmatic practical altruists," she points out, tend to be "relatively well-off individuals who donate large amounts of money to organizations that aid impoverished strangers." By focusing on the good this does, she says, such donors tend to think of themselves as being heroes, "encouraging a savior complex and insularity among its members." Meanwhile, poor people who devote their time and resources to bettering the lives of their family and community are judged not as practical as the richer donors and democratic principles of inclusion are violated. In this manner, political efficacy is lessened by disenfranchising the very people practical altruism is meant to help. This continues despite abundant research demonstrating that lasting change is best effected by those living within a community.

42. Why would a practical altruist choose to work on Wall Street rather than as a doctor?

   A. The altruist's skill set is better suited to finance, meaning that he or she would be more successful in the field.
   B. The altruist would be able to have a larger impact on the greater good through donating a portion of his or her salary to charities with maximum impact.
   C. Through its emphasis on evidence and reason, a job in Wall Street would train the altruist in the most effective ways to better the world.
   D. The salary received on Wall Street would be significantly higher than that earned by a doctor, maximizing possible donations.

Why is B correct?

A:

___

___

C:

___

___

D:

___

___

Wrong Answer Type Fallen for:

___

___

43. Based on the passage, it can be inferred that utilitarianism:

   A. seeks to make rationalism the primary factor in motivating altruistic decisions.
   B. stresses the potentially corrosive effects of self-abnegation in shaping actions.
   C. requires that an action results in the greatest good for the doer of an action.
   D. focuses on consequences of actions without regards to the effect on the doer of an action.

Why is D correct?

A:

___

___

B:

___

___

C:

___

___

Wrong Answer Type Fallen for:

___

___

Full Length 2 Review: Bio/Biochem Foundations Passage 4

Fatty acid binding proteins (FABPs) are intracellular lipid carriers that, in addition to binding free fatty acids, interact with other endogenous lipids including the endocannabinoid *N*-arachidonoylethanolamine (AEA). AEA is synthesized in response to neuronal depolarization from a phospholipid precursor situated within the lipid bilayer of the neuronal membrane. Following reuptake into the postsynaptic neuron, it is acted upon by the catabolic enzyme fatty acid hydrolase (FAAH), yielding ethanolamine and a polyunsaturated fat, arachidonic acid (AA).

Figure 1 *N*-arachidonoylethanolamine

Previous research shows that endocannabinoids bind the pre-synaptic cannabinoid receptor 1 (CB1), producing pain-diminishing analgesic and anti-inflammatory effects. FABP5 and FABP7 bind to endocannabinoids with high affinity, mediating the intracellular trafficking of endocannabinoids to FAAH. Recently, it has been shown that pharmacological inhibition of FABPs elevates brain levels of AEA.

Research was performed to characterize the endocannabinoid system in knockout mice lacking both FABP5 and FABP7. Levels of AEA were found to be elevated in the brains of FABP5/7 knockout (KO) mice, while CB1 was normal. FAAH activity in brain homogenates of wild-type (WT) and KO mice was likewise measured (Figure 2).

To study changes in pain response in the test subjects, the tail immersion test was performed on 6 WT and 6 FABP5/7 KO mice. In the tail immersion test, an animal's tail is submerged in hot water, and the time required for the animal to withdrawal their tail, the latency, is measured. The same test was also performed 4 hours after injection of the mice with the inflammatory chemical carrageenan, an agent used to mimic human pain conditions in animal models of thermal hyperalgesia (Figure 3).

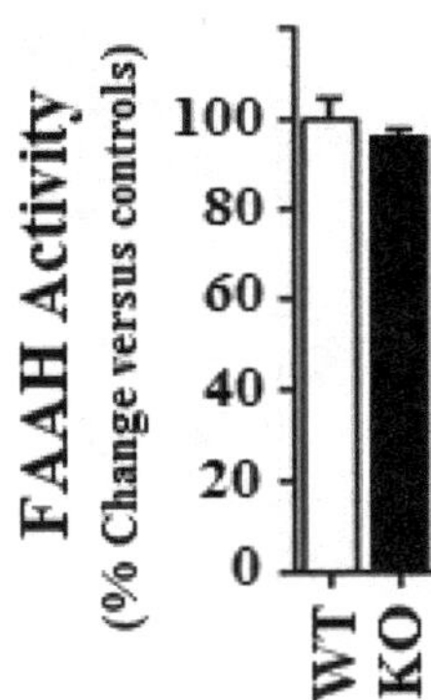

Figure 2 FAAH activity in brain homogenates of wild-type (WT) and FABP5/7 knockout (KO) mice

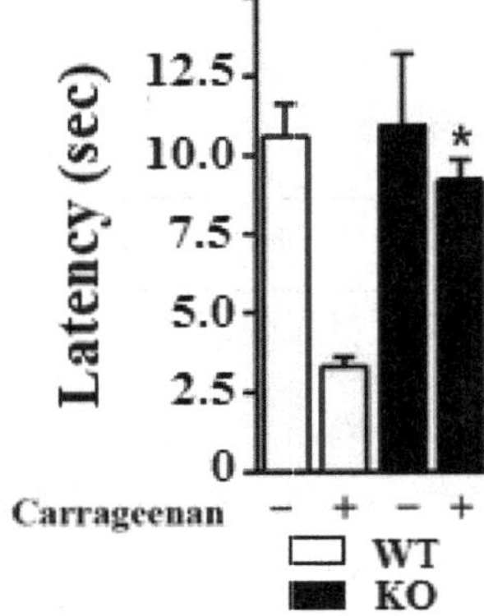

Figure 3 Latencies in the tail immersion test in wild-type and FABP5/7 knockout mice before and 4 h after carrageenan injection (note: *p < 0.01 versus carrageenan-injected WT mice)

Were there any key terms you did not note? Did they appear in the questions?

Did you recognize the experimental goals?

Could you draw any conclusions from the presented results?

Did the passage offer any conclusions?

18. Information in the passage indicates that signaling via CB1 in mice decreases the sensory response initiated by the activation of what receptor type?
    A. Chemoreceptors
    B. Nociceptors
    C. Baroreceptors
    D. Mechanoreceptors

Why is B correct?

A:

____

____

C:

____

____

D:

____

____

Wrong Answer Type Fallen for:

____

____

Content or Exam-Related Mistake?

____

____

Lesson Learned

____

____

21. Researchers likely measured FAAH activity in the brain in order to:
    A. exclude FABPs from playing a role in AEA metabolism.
    B. correlate FAAH activity with inflammatory markers in the brain.
    C. establish that FABPs directly regulate FAAH activity.
    D. determine if FAAH activity is modulated by FABPs.

Why is D correct?

A:

____

____

B:

____

____

C:

____

____

Wrong Answer Type Fallen for:

____

____

Content or Exam-Related Mistake?

____

____

Lesson Learned

____

____

This page left intentionally blank.

Full Length 2 Review: Psych/Soc Foundations Passage 3

The demographics of the United States are quickly becoming more diverse; ethnic minorities currently make up about 30 percent of the population, and that number grows each year. Each of these minority groups has its own customs, traditions, and values, which can affect their health beliefs and subsequent health behaviors. As such, there is increased need to make cultural competence a significant part of medical education, but little is known about the feasibility or effectiveness of cultural education programs.

An education researcher develops a vertically integrated curriculum, which involves developing cultural competency through interactive methods such as role-play, practice with standardized patients, journaling, and feedback from patients and supervisors. In this manner, students practice cultural competency while also studying basic sciences. This satisfies the necessary goal of developing the knowledge, attitudes, and clinical skills needed improve the health and well-being of their minority patients. The curriculum was disseminated to two hundred first year urban medical students, who were assessed at multiple points throughout their education on multiple measures of cultural competency. Based on these assessments, faculty members rated aspects of students' cultural competency on a scale of 1-10, with 10 indicating desired competency; the average faculty ratings of cultural competency at the initial (beginning first year) and final assessment points (end of fourth year) are outlined in Table 1.

Were there any key terms you did not note? Did they appear in the questions?

____

____

Did you recognize the experimental goals?

____

____

Could you draw any conclusions from the presented results?

____

____

Did the passage offer any conclusions?

____

____

Table 1 Faculty ratings of students' cultural competency

	Average Faculty Rating: Year 1	**Average Faculty Rating: Year 4**
Knowledge: overall culture	2.42	9.23
Knowledge: social determinants of health	2.23	9.42
Knowledge: variations in disease incidence and prevalence	2.84	8.97
Attitudes: cultural sensitivity	5.43	6.54
Attitudes: awareness of influence of cultural factors on values	4.32	7.45
Attitudes: awareness of influence of cultural factors on behaviors	4.57	6.23
Attitudes: awareness of influence of cultural factors on clinical outcomes	5.23	7.30
Skills: communicate with minority patients	1.21	5.43
Skills: understand patient beliefs about illness	2.52	5.66
Skills: use an interpreter or cultural liaison	1.22	4.33
Skills: negotiate patient participation in diagnosis and treatment	1.29	6.55

10. Which of the following is most likely to be increased as a result of the curriculum tested in the passage?

    A. Ethnocentrism
    B. Cultural relativism
    C. Altruism
    D. Health disparity

Why is B correct?

A:

C:

D:

Wrong Answer Type Fallen for:

Content or Exam-Related Mistake?

Lesson Learned

12. What type of research design was used in this study?

    A. Experimental design
    B. Retrospective cohort design
    C. Case control design
    D. Longitudinal cohort design

Why is D correct?

A:

B:

C:

Wrong Answer Type Fallen for:

Content or Exam-Related Mistake?

Lesson Learned

Science Analysis

In the sciences, which wrong answer type did you choose most often?

Opposite

Irrelevant detail

Distorted

Miscalculation

How was your pacing in the sciences?

What items did you do first?

How often did you check the clock?

CARS Analysis

In CARS, which wrong answer type did you choose most often?

Opposite

Irrelevant detail

Beyond main idea of passage

True but not supported by passage

How was your pacing in CARS? Where/did you find yourself behind on time?

How often did you check the clock?

Was there any 1 passage that hurt your score the most?

Was there any 1 question type more common in your missed questions?

Prioritizing questions

Max time for passage (Sci)

Max time for passage (CARS)

Max time per question (Sci)

Max time per question (CARS)

When to mark a question

When NOT to mark a question

Did you use	Chem/Phys	CARS	Bio/Biochem	Psych/Soc
Highlighting				
Note-taking				
Q-strategy				
Internal Pacing				
Review Button				
Mark Button				

What to Do Now

Examine your LLJ from the Full Length

Pattern Recognition

Useful Lessons

Useless Lessons

How Much Time Should I Spend?

1. Stick to your preferred reading/passage strategy as long as it works.
2. Each science passage should take ≈ 8 minutes, and for CARS passages you have 10 minutes. Check your timing every 2-3 passages.
3. Each discrete question should take ≈ 1 minute. Check your timing at the end of each discrete set.
4. If a question is taking too long (60+ seconds) or you are unsure of how to solve it, mark it and move on.

CARS Timing Method:

Item Complete	Time Remaining
Passages 1-2	70 minutes
Passages 3-4	50 minutes
Passages 5-6	30 minutes
Passages 7-8	10 minutes
Passages 9	0 minutes

Science Method (1)

Item Complete	Time Remaining
Discrete Qs	80 minutes
Passages 1-2	64 minutes
Passages 3-4	48 minutes
Passages 5-6	32 minutes
Passages 7-8	16 minutes
Passages 9-10	0 minutes

Must you do the discrete questions first?

How can you help keep track of your own pace in a section?

Your Next Step Syllabus

Should I use . . .	Yes, if you . . .
QBank	
MCAT Review Books	
Additional Practice Books	
Lesson Videos	
Content Videos	
Full Length Exams	

Revising Goals and Looking Ahead

Content Review Timeline

Passage Strategy Choice

Test-like Thinking

Timing/Pacing Method

Yes, Dr. ________________________________ you can do this!

Problem-solving Warm-up

1. Growth factor X acts to coordinate groups of local cells to elicit a fast but short response. Growth factor X most likely acts via:

   A. endocrine signaling.
   B. paracrine signaling.
   C. autocrine signaling.
   D. direct signaling.

2. A cell is infected with a virus. If the cell signals to undergo apoptosis in order to kill the virus, this is an example of:

   A. endocrine signaling.
   B. paracrine signaling.
   C. autocrine signaling.
   D. direct signaling.

3. Hormone response elements are bound to sequences in:

   A. DNA.
   B. rRNA.
   C. mRNA.
   D. tRNA.

4. Which of the following molecules is NOT a principal mediator in biological signal transduction in eukaryotic cells?

   A. IP_3
   B. cAMP
   C. NADH
   D. Fas

5. Inactive G protein is associated with the presence of:

   A. GTP.
   B. GDP.
   C. ATP.
   D. ADP.

Biological Signaling

Cells must be ready to respond to essential signals in their environment. These are often chemicals in the extracellular fluid.

Endocrine (hormones)

Paracrine (cytokines)

Autocrine

These signals may cause:

1

2

3

Intracellular vs. extracellular receptors (steroids, NO, peptides)

Steroid Receptors

Structure

Ligands

Mechanism

Nitric Oxide (NO) Receptors

Structure

Ligands

Mechanism

cGMP

G Protein-coupled Receptors

Structure

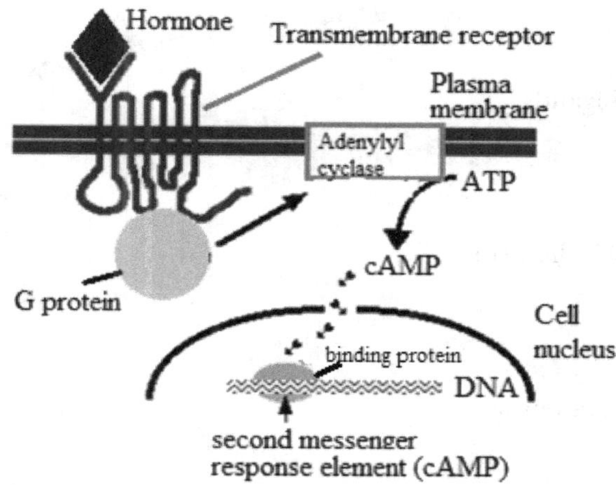

Transcription Factor activation

Ligands

Mechanism

cAMP

IP3

Examples

Turning GPCRs Off

Cytokine Receptors: Receptor Tyrosine Kinases

Structure

Ligands

Mechanism

Examples

Turning RTKs Off

Oncogenes

Examples:

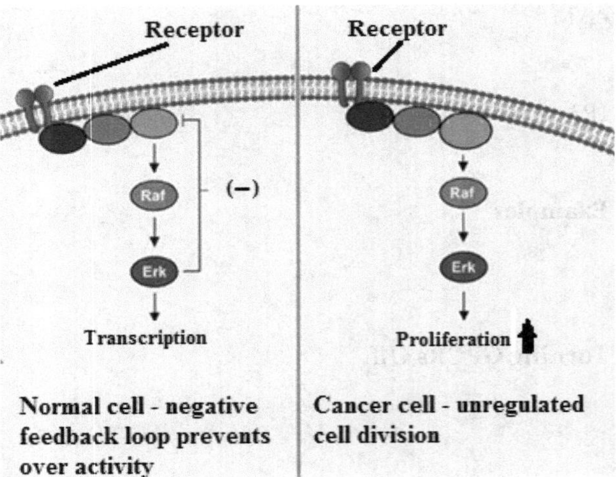

Anti-cancer Therapeutics:

The T-Cell Receptor for Antigen (TCR)

Structure

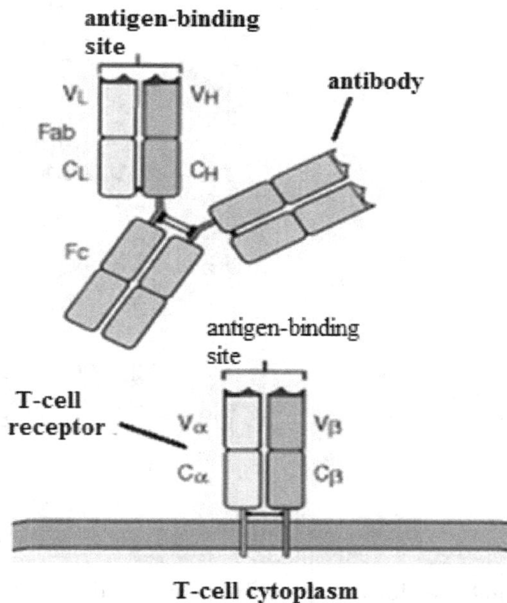

Ligands

Mechanism

Apoptosis

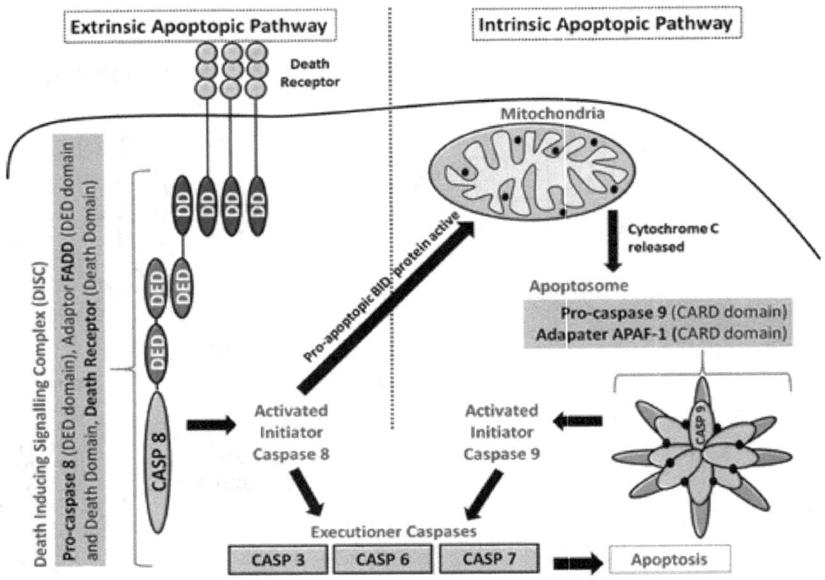

What role does apoptosis play in fetal development?

____

What pathologies can result from an imbalance of apoptotic signals?

____

Unlike cell necrosis, apoptosis produces cell fragments called ______________________ that phagocytic cells can remove before they can accumulate and cause damage.

The 2 common signal pathways involved in apoptosis are ________________ and ________________.

Timed MCAT Practice Passage

Mastery of the MCAT sciences is a two-part process. First you must study to understand (not just memorize!) the science content, and then you must study the content actively and challenge yourself within the context of the exam.

1. Complete your reading of the passage (3-4 minutes).
    - Write down what you believe to be the primary science content underlying the passage.
    - What facts or concepts do you anticipate to be tested? When you are done with the questions determine if you were correct. What passage clues were there to imply related topics that showed up in the questions?
    - Were there any key terms or important scientific relationships you missed?
    - Were you able to draw any conclusions from the data, if presented?

2. Complete the practice questions on your own (4-5 minutes)
    - Rephrase each question in your own mind after reading it to clarify the task.
    - Research the relevant area(s) of the passage or your own knowledge for information related to the task.
    - Respond to the question by choosing the answer that fits your research/calculations *and* satisfies the task.
    - If no answer seems obvious, eliminate answers that fail to have support in the passage or in the relevant science.

3. Analyze your wrong answer choices to the questions you missed.
    - Did you understand the task in the question?
    - What skill type was the question?
    - Did you know the science/formula/concept needed to answer the question?
    - Did you recognize the science being hinted at?
    - Were you able to find information in the passage quickly when you needed it?
    - Were there any necessary scientific concepts you failed to apply to the question?
        - If so, why?
    - If you made a mistake in calculations, have you identified your mistake?

Pseudomonas aeruginosa is one of the most common Gram-negative pathogens accounting for over 10% of all infections. With its increasing prevalence, multidrug-resistant strains are becoming increasingly common. The common complication resulting from *P. aeruginosa* is a lung infection associated with cystic fibrosis.

In an effort to further elucidate the difference between prokaryotic and eukaryotic protein synthesis, a study was conducted on the interactions between elongation factor Tu (EF-Tu) and elongation factor Ts (EF-Ts). The studies were conducted in hopes of developing new compounds that inhibit growth of the bacteria without adversely affecting the patient.

EF-Tu has an integral role in protein synthesis by bringing the aminoacyl-tRNA (aa-tRNA) to the A-site of the ribosome during the elongation phase of translation. EF-Tu forms a ternary complex with GTP and aa-tRNA in the cytoplasm, and this complex approaches the A-site of an actively translating ribosome. Once the ternary complex is bound to the ribosome and the codon-anticodon pairing is correct, GTP is hydrolyzed to GDP by activating the GTPase activity of EF-Tu. There is a conformational change in EF-Tu, and EF-Tu-GDP dissociates from the ribosome and recycled to the EF-Tu-TP complex in an exchange catalyzed by EF-Ts. Once EF-Tu-GDP is released, the aa-tRNA fully enters the A site.

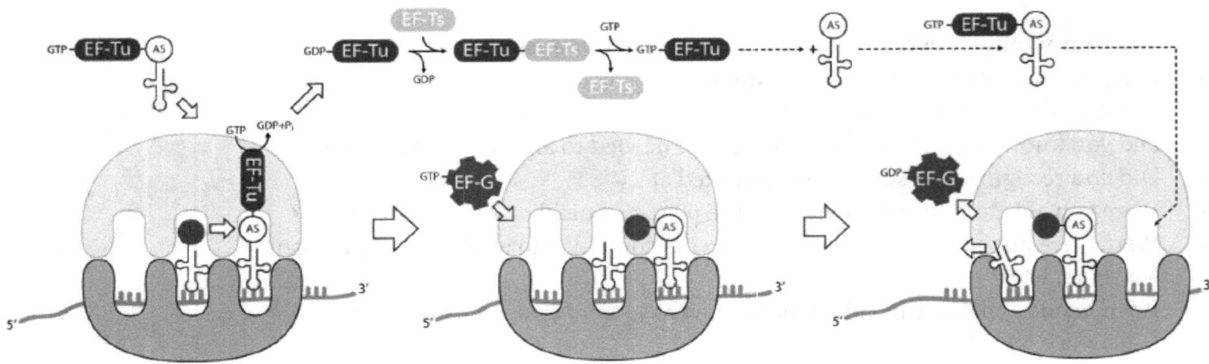

Figure 1 Elongation Phase of Translation in the Prokaryotic Cell

There are two delays offered by EF-Tu that helps to ensure translational accuracy. EF-Tu delays GTP hydrolysis if the anticodon in the A site does not match codon on the aa-tRNA and again when it frees itself from the tRNA to allow for an incorrectly paired tRNA to leave the A site.

Passage taken from the Next Step online QBank

6. Which of the following steps precedes the elongation steps described in the passage?
   A. The smaller subunit of the ribosome attaches to the cap at the 5' end of the mRNA and searches for an AUG codon by moving step-by-step in the 3' direction.
   B. With the initiating tRNA at the P site and the second aminoacyl-tRNA tightly bound at the A site, the α amino group of the second amino acid reacts with the "activated" methionine on the initiator tRNA, forming a peptide bond.
   C. RF1 recognizes UAG, and RF2 recognizes UGA; both these factors recognize UAA. RF3, a GTP-binding protein, acts in concert with the codon-recognizing factors to promote cleavage of the peptidyl-tRNA.
   D. The fMet-tRNA enters the P site, causing a conformational change which opens the A site for the new aminoacyl-tRNA to bind.

7. Which of the following has the greatest similarity when comparing prokaryotic and eukaryotic translation?
   A. Size of ribosomes
   B. Initiator tRNA
   C. Elongation factors
   D. Recognition sites for the smaller subunit of the ribosome

8. A molecule which does which of the following would be most effective in eliminating *Pseudomonas aeruginosa*?
   A. Inhibits the peptidyl transferase activity of the smaller subunit of the ribosome
   B. Binds to the Shine-Delgarno sequence to directly block binding of aminoacyl-tRNA at A site
   C. Binds to the 60S subunit to block translocation
   D. Binds to formylmethionyl-tRNA to prevent correct initiation

9. Which of the following laboratory procedures would be most effective in determining the concentration of GDP in EF-Tu preparation?
   A. Centrifugation
   B. Absorbance spectroscopy
   C. Extraction and filtration
   D. Fractional distillation

Biochemical Lab Techniques

- Lab techniques generally focus on one of two things: separating or identifying

- Separations and Purifications

  i. Focus on

  ii. What will be collected first? Second?

  iii. Watch for things that can't be separated with a given technique

  a. For example: azeotropes (95.6% ethanol, 4.4% water wt/wt)

  iv. Is it diagnostic or preparatory?

- Identification
  i. What **class of thing** does this technique identify?

  a. For example: IR is functional groups, NMR is for hydrogen arrangement

  ii. The MCAT will only expect you to memorize and identify certain common uses

Experimental Design

Controls: Positive vs. Negative

Accuracy vs. Precision

Independent vs. Dependent vs. Confounding Variables

Errors: Type I (false positive) vs. Type II (false negative)

Enzyme-linked Immunosorbent Assay (ELISA)

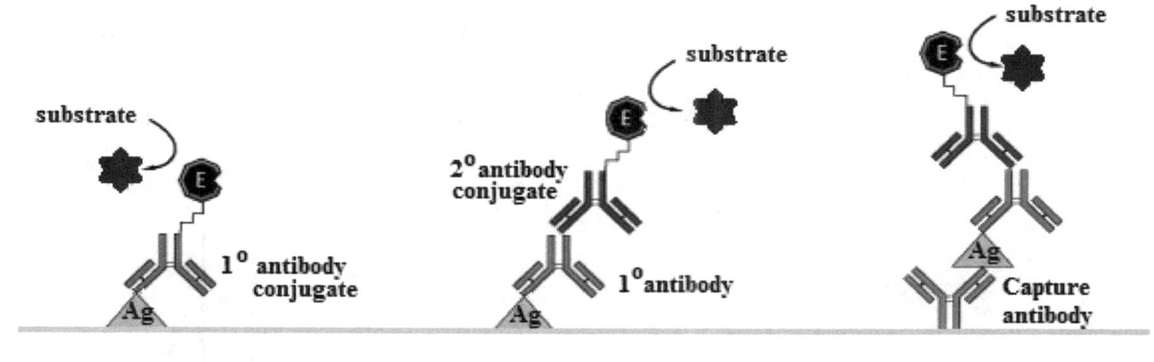

Method:

Bind

Wash

Label

Read

Good for detecting:

Radioimmunoassay (RIA)

Method:

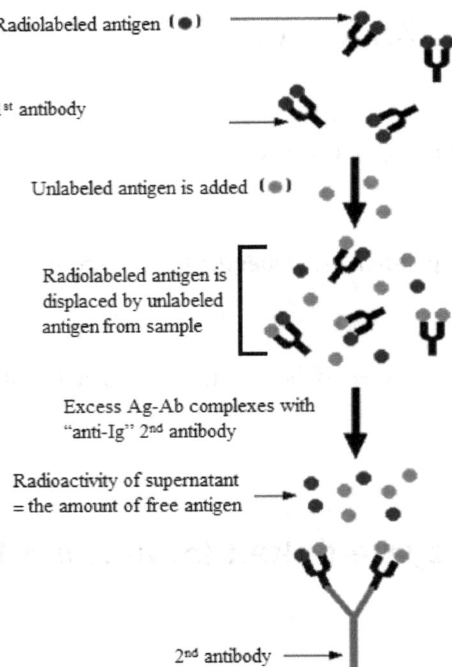

Good for detecting:

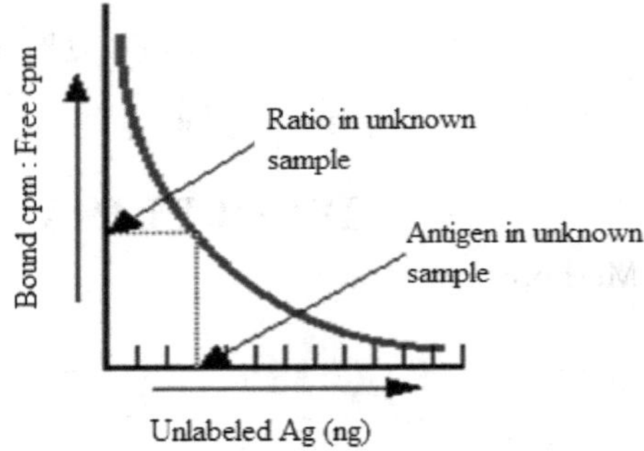

Blotting

	Southern	Northern	Western
What is separated by molecular weight?			
Probe			
What is learned from the test?			

Polymerase Chain Reaction (PCR)

Method:

Good for detecting:

After 7 rounds of PCR, how many copies of the DNA will be in the solution?

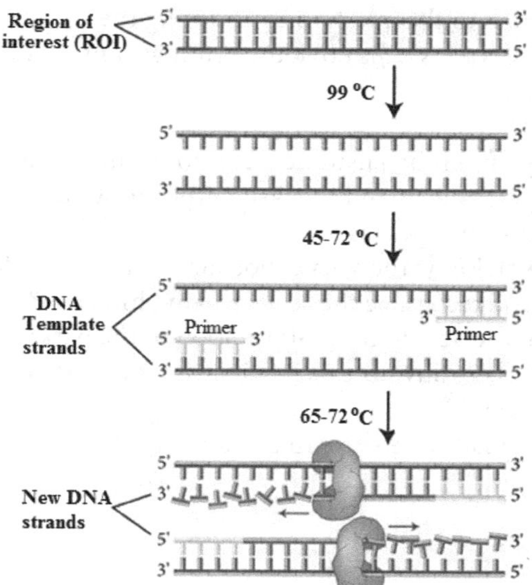

Timed MCAT Practice Passage

Mastery of the MCAT sciences is a two-part process. First you must study to understand (not just memorize!) the science content, and then you must study the content actively and challenge yourself within the context of the exam.

1. Complete your reading of the passage (3-4 minutes).
    - Write down what you believe to be the primary science content underlying the passage.
    - What facts or concepts do you anticipate to be tested? When you are done with the questions determine if you were correct. What passage clues were there to imply related topics that showed up in the questions?
    - Were there any key terms or important scientific relationships you missed?
    - Were you able to draw any conclusions from the data, if presented?

2. Complete the practice questions on your own (4-5 minutes)
    - Rephrase each question in your own mind after reading it to clarify the task.
    - Research the relevant area(s) of the passage or your own knowledge for information related to the task.
    - Respond to the question by choosing the answer that fits your research/calculations *and* satisfies the task.
    - If no answer seems obvious, eliminate answers that fail to have support in the passage or in the relevant science.

3. Analyze your wrong answer choices to the questions you missed.
    - Did you understand the task in the question?
    - What skill type was the question?
    - Did you know the science/formula/concept needed to answer the question?
    - Did you recognize the science being hinted at?
    - Were you able to find information in the passage quickly when you needed it?
    - Were there any necessary scientific concepts you failed to apply to the question?
    - If so, why?
    - If you made a mistake in calculations, have you identified your mistake?

This page left intentionally blank.

Huntington's disease (HD) is an inherited neurodegenerative disease caused by progressive neuronal loss istriatum region of the brain. The Huntingtin gene (*HTT*) is located on the short arm of chromosome 4 and codes for the Huntingtin protein, Htt. *HTT* contains a trinucleotide sequence of cytosine-adenine-guanine (CAG)—which is repeated multiple times. The trinucleotide repeat produces a chain known as a polyglutamine (polyQ) tract. The length of CAG repeat varies between individuals and dynamic mutations may increase its length between generations. When the length of this repeated section exceeds a certain threshold, it produces an altered form of Htt called mutant Huntingtin protein (mHtt), which is toxic to cells of the striatum.

Geneticists studying the inheritance pattern of HD found that it is rare for HD to be caused by a new mutation and suspected that the length of the repeated sequence influences the age of onset, progression of symptoms experienced by affected individuals and their affected offspring. Select findings are summarized in Table 1.

Table 1 Repeat count on *HTT* allele and resulting disease status (note probability of affected offspring in the case of one parent with a single expanded *HTT* allele containing the indicated repeat count and another parent with a repeat count < 26 on either *HTT* allele.)

Repeat Count	Disease Status	Age of onset	Probability of affected offspring
< 26	Not affected	N/A	0
27-35	Not affected	N/A	Non-zero, but much less than 50%
36-39	May be affected	40+ years	50%
40-49	Affected	26-39 years	50%
> 75	Affected	18-23 years	90%

The inheritance pattern of Huntington's disease in one family with an above average incidence of the disease revealed that of the 5 children had by the two parents suffering from HD, 4 out of 5 were proven to have at least one copy of the mutated gene.

Next the researchers wished to determine if zygosity for CAG mutation in Huntington disease is associated with a more severe clinical course as measured by disease staging. The results of their study are shown in Figure 1.

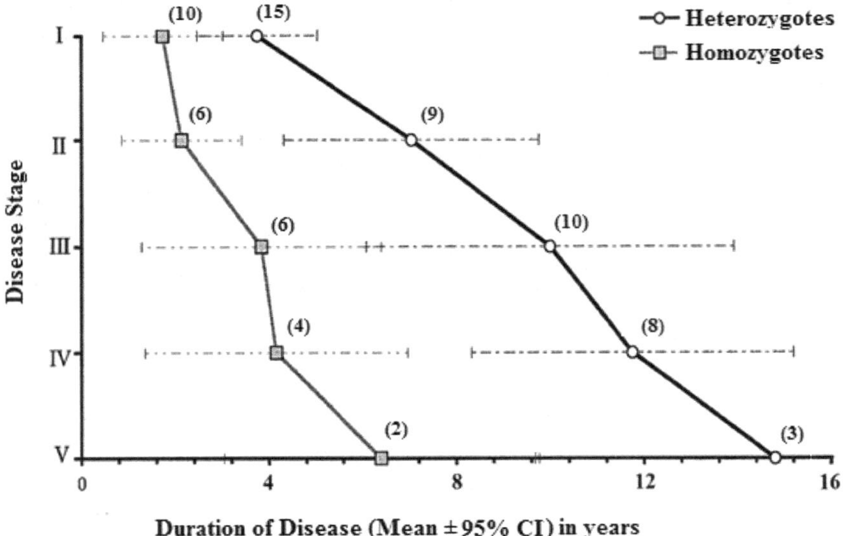

Figure 1 Zygosity effect on disease severity (note: the numbers in parentheses represent the total patients in each stage.)

Passage taken from the Next Step Biology review book, chapter 4

10. The passage best supports the conclusion that Huntington's disease displays what pattern of inheritance?

    A. Autosomal recessive; with more rapid progression in heterozygotes
    B. Autosomal dominant; with more rapid progression in heterozygotes
    C. Autosomal recessive; with more rapid progression in homozygotes
    D. Autosomal dominant; with more rapid progression in homozygotes

11. What is the maximum number of possible glutamine residues in the polyQ region of *htt* in a 37 year old man displaying a normal phenotype?

    A. 25
    B. 35
    C. 39
    D. 40

12. The geneticists concluded that the symptoms of HD generally become more severe and were diagnosed at an earlier age in affected offspring than in their affected parents. Is there a potential biological explanation for this phenomenon?

    A. No, the observation is due to heightened awareness of disease symptoms within affected families.
    B. No, regions of trinucleotide expansion, located on an autosome, occur only in somatic cells.
    C. Yes, mutant mHtt protein is synthesized by individuals containing CAG repeats.
    D. Yes, dynamic mutation results in expanded trinucleotides associated with a more severe disease phenotype.

13. According to the study results, at what stage of Huntington's disease does zygosity appear to have the strongest impact on survival?

    A. Stage I
    B. Stage III
    C. Stage IV
    D. Stage V

14. The observation that not all individuals containing between 36-39 CAG repeats display clinical symptoms of Huntington's disease can be explained in terms of what property of the disease's inheritance pattern?

    A. Incomplete penetrance
    B. Variable expressivity
    C. Pleiotropy
    D. Genetic anticipation

Problem-solving Cooldown

15. A researcher wishes to isolate and identify a signal protein thought to mediate neuronal transmission. Which method of detection would be most appropriate?

    A. Southern blot
    B. RT-PCR
    C. Western blot
    D. ELISA

16. Which of the following could NOT be a recognition site for restriction endonuclease?

    A. 5'-GAATTC-3'
    3'-CTTAAG-5'
    B. 5'-ATCGAT-3'
    3'-TAGCTA-5'
    C. 5'-CTGCAG-3'
    3'-GACGTC-5'
    D. 5'-GCTTGC-3'
    3'-CGAACG-5'

17. The smaller the nucleic acid fragment a student runs:

    A. the closer to the origin it will appear.
    B. the brighter color it produces with ethidium bromide.
    C. the faster it migrates during separation by electrophoresis.
    D. the slower it migrates during separation by electrophoresis.

18. What is the correct order for performing a Southern blot test prior to detection via x-ray film?

    1 = electrophoresis
    2 = digestion with restriction enzyme
    3 = ethidium bromide
    4 = radioactive probe

    A. 1,2,3,4
    B. 1,4,3,2
    C. 2,1,3,4
    D. 2,4,3,1

19. Restriction fragment length polymorphisms occur in the gene pool because individual some people have:

    A. DNA sequence differences in the pattern of restriction sites.
    B. DNA sequence differences that create different gene products.
    C. DNA sequence differences that make DNA more susceptible to denaturation.
    D. different mutations that alter the length of their mRNA.

20. In order to clone human DNA into bacterial cells, a lab must be sure to:

    A. use DNA with both exons and introns.
    B. add DNA without introns.
    C. use RNA with both exons and introns.
    D. remove any exons from the RNA.

This page left intentionally blank.

Test-like Thinking: CARS Practice Passage

"The Truman Show" is profoundly disturbing. On the surface, it centers on the worn out concept of the intermingling of life and media. This incestuous relationship abounds in America. Consider the cinematic president and presidential movie star, Ronald Reagan: in "The Philadelphia Experiment," a revived Rip Van Winkle sees Reagan on TV and exclaims, "This guy? He used to play cowboys in the movies!" From the White House to our own homes and certainly beyond, this phenomenon confidently extends into our Internet culture, with the "YouTube celebrity" providing a poignant example.

Specifically, "The Truman Show" is concerned with the blurring of the line between life and the representation of life in media. Truman lives in an artificial world, specially designed for him. Born and raised there, he knows nowhere and nothing else. Unbeknownst to him, the people around him are all actors; his life is recorded by 5,000 cameras and broadcast live, 24 hours a day. Because he is entirely unaware of this monstrosity that contains him, he is spontaneous and funny, a perfect television character, true in his playing because, to him, he's simply living.

The film's director, Peter Weir, takes a significant step further by perpetrating a massively immoral act on screen. Truman is lied to and deprived of free will. He is manipulated: every important person in his life, including his parents, are actors. Hundreds of millions of people regularly tune in to watch and therefore intrude upon what Truman sincerely believes to be his privacy. We see these viewers respond to the various dramatic or anti-climactic events of Truman's life: the realization that we are the moral equivalent of these viewers comes as a shock. We are live viewers and they are celluloid viewers. We both enjoy Truman's non-consenting exhibitionism. We know the truth, and so do they. Fortunately, we hold the privileged moral position of knowing it is a film.

But, moviegoers have willingly and insatiably participated in "Truman Shows" since Hollywood's early days. The lives of the famous studio stars (whether real or concocted) were aggressively exploited and built into their films. Jean Harlow, Barbara Stanwyck, and James Cagney, were all forced at some point to spill their guts in some cathartic act of filmed repentance, some not-so-symbolic humiliation. Arguably, "Truman Shows" are a common phenomenon.

Taking a step further, Weir raises the question of the director of the film as God and of God as the director of a film. The director of the show, Christoff, is obeyed blindly by his actors and crew. They suspend their moral judgment, succumbing to his sadistic whims. The torturer loves his victims: they define him and give his life meaning. Weir's film claims that, caught in a narrative, people act immorally.

Some psychological experiments support this: students have been led to administer what they thought were lethal electric shocks to colleagues, and to treat them horrifically in simulated prisons, all the while obeying orders. All the genocidal criminals of history did the same. Weir asks: should God be allowed to be immoral, or should he be bound by morality and ethics? Should we obey his commandments blindly, or should we exercise our own judgment?

21. According to the passage, which of the following statements is most accurate?

    A. "Celluloid viewers" are more morally upstanding than "live viewers"
    B. "Live viewers" are more morally upstanding than "celluloid viewers"
    C. "Celluloid viewers" hold a superior moral position to "live viewers"
    D. "Live viewers" hold a superior moral position to "celluloid viewers"

22. Which of the following arguments is LEAST significant within the context of the passage?

    A. The question of morality is vitally important
    B. Life and the media are inextricably linked
    C. Jean Harlow was symbolically humiliated by old Hollywood
    D. When they are caught in a narrative, people may act immorally

23. Suppose a film student wants to emulate Peter Weir's conceptual style. Based upon the passage, which of the following best describes what this student would do?

    A. Create films that question the status quo of American culture and media while exploring historical precedence
    B. Create films that represent the status quo of American culture while plumbing the depths of ethics and morality
    C. Create films that glorify the position of the innocent individual against an oppressive, morally decadent society
    D. Create films that reflect the values and concerns of American culture through the lens of popular philosophy

24. Based upon the passage, which of the following is most comparable to the figure of Christoff?

    A. A democratically elected president with questionable objectives
    B. A fascist dictator with genocidal aspirations
    C. An absolute monarch of questionable morality
    D. A master craftsman with uncontrollable ambition

25. Which of the following most likely accounts for why the author wrote the third paragraph?

    A. To emphasize the immorality of the circumstances first described in the second paragraph
    B. To setup the author's argument on the nature and morality of an authoritarian god
    C. To place the arguments of the first and second paragraphs within the specific context of America
    D. To illustrate and contextualize the superior quality of Peter Weir's filmmaking skills

To Do After Lesson 17

- ☐ Complete Full Timed Section 4 from the Verbal Practice: 108 Passages book
- ☐ Complete the AAMC Chemical and Physical Foundations Section Bank (may be split over 2-3 days if needed)
- ☐ Complete Biochemistry QBank 2: Biotechnology and Analysis

LESSON 18

Physics 3

To Do Before Lesson 18

- ☐ Complete Full Timed Section 4 from the Verbal Practice: 108 Passages book
- ☐ Complete the AAMC Chemical and Physical Foundations Section Bank (may be split over 2-3 days if needed)
- ☐ Complete Biochemistry QBank 2: Biotechnology and Analysis

In Lesson 18

Problem-solving Warm-up
Light and Electromagnetic Radiation
MCAT Practice Passage
Waves and Sound
MCAT Practice Passage
Geometric Optics
Atomic Phenomena
Problem-solving Cooldown
Test-like Thinking: CARS Practice Passage

To Do After Lesson 18

- ☐ Complete Full Timed Section 5 from the Verbal Practice: 108 Passages book
- ☐ Complete the AAMC Biological and Biochemical Foundations Section Bank (may be split over 2-3 days if needed)
- ☐ Complete Physics QBank 3: Sound and Light

Problem-solving Warm-up

1. A vertical spring stretches 9.93 m when a 5.11 kg mass is attached to it. The spring is moved to a horizontal position, attached to a 125 kg mass, stretched, and allowed to oscillate. What will be the period of its motion?

   A. $\pi\sqrt{(20)}$ s
   B. 5π s
   C. 10π s
   D. 25π s

2. For the majority of liquids, viscosity will:

   A. be inversely proportional to T.
   B. decrease as T decreases.
   C. be inversely related to the F required to move though the fluid.
   D. be directly proportional to the flow rate of the fluid.

3. Nancy is throwing coins into a fountain and notices the coins that rest at the bottom of the fountain appear to be closer to the surface than they actually are. Which phenomenon of light explains this illusion?

   A. Polarization
   B. Refraction
   C. Reflection
   D. Chromatic aberration

4. An object with a density of 4 g/cm^3 is fixed to the end of a vertical spring and allowed to sink into a box filled with liquid A (density = 2.4 g/cm^3) and reaches an equilibrium with the fluid 10 mm from the bottom of the box. If liquid A is replaced by liquid B (density = 3 g/cm^3) and all other factors remain unchanged, which of the following MUST be true?

   A. The length of the spring remains constant
   B. The k value will increase to compensate for the new liquid
   C. The spring is compressed
   D. The spring stretches

5. Resting on a table are two pipes, both closed at one end and both with variable lengths. Two tuning forks, both emitting identical waves (λ = 8 cm) are activated and held over the open end of each pipe. What must the lengths of the pipes be to facilitate resonance?

   A. 1.5 cm, 3 cm
   B. 2 cm, 6 cm
   C. 2.5 cm, 7.5 cm
   D. 6 cm, 9 cm

Light

Light exhibits properties of both waves and particles.

	Reflection	Refraction	Diffraction	Interference
Particle				
Wave				
Light				

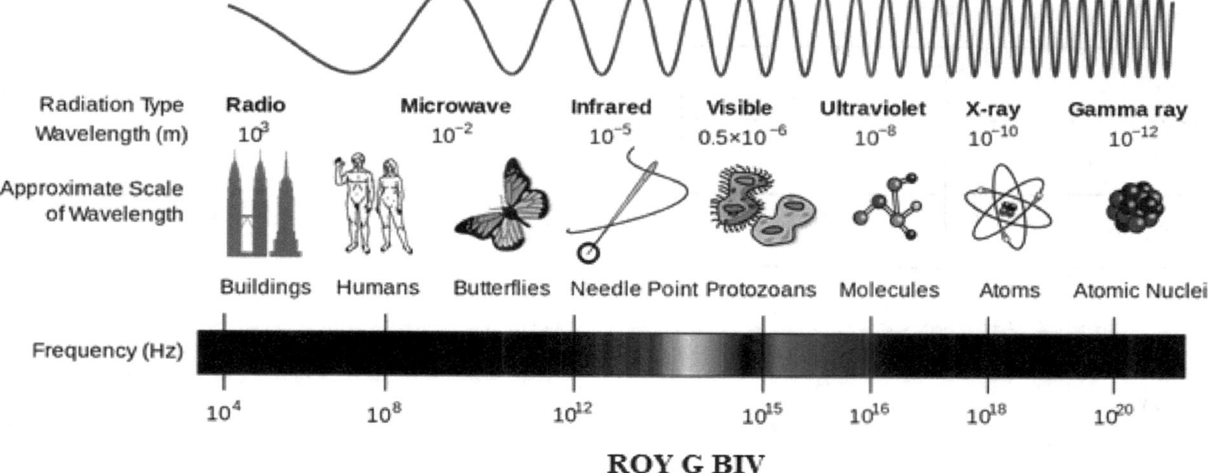

ROY G BIV

As you progress across the visual spectrum, frequency ______________________________ and wavelength ______________________________.

Energy = $hf = hc/\lambda$ velocity = $f\lambda$

Reflection & Refraction

The index of refraction, n, is a property of substance that determines by what ratio the speed of light will be slowed when is passes through the material.

$n = c/v$ where $c = 3 \times 10^8$ m/s

Snell's law ____________________________

As light enter a new medium with a new n, some light will be ___________________ at the boundary and the light that passes through may be ___________________.

Material	n
Vacuum	
Air	
Water	
Ethanol	
Diamond	

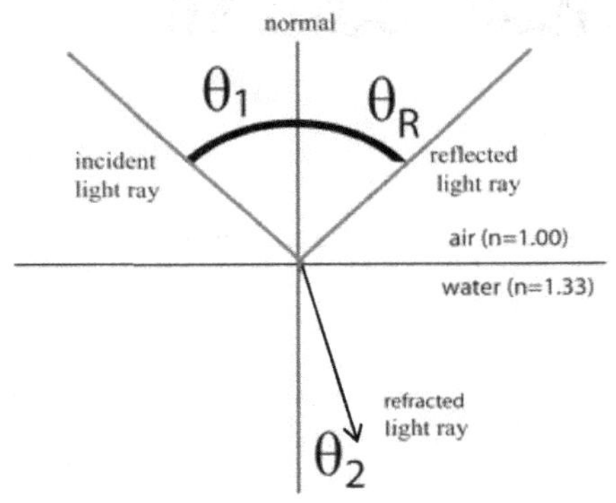

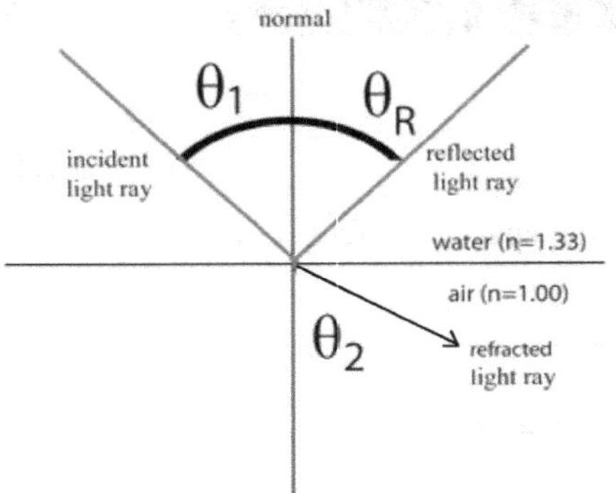

When $n_2 > n_1$

θ_1 θ_2

θ_1 θ_R

When $n_2 < n_1$

θ_1 θ_2

θ_1 θ_R

Total Internal Reflection

When light is incident upon a medium with a lower index of refraction, the ray is bent ____________________

the normal. At a critical angle of incidence, θ_C, the refraction angle θ_R will be ____________________.

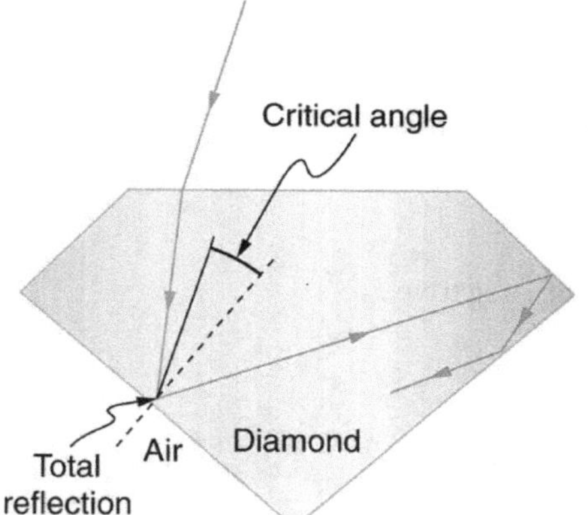

In TIR, Snell's Law can be re-written as:

Thus, a very large index of refraction will ____________________ the critical angle.

Total internal reflection contributes to the "sparkle" of diamonds

Dispersion

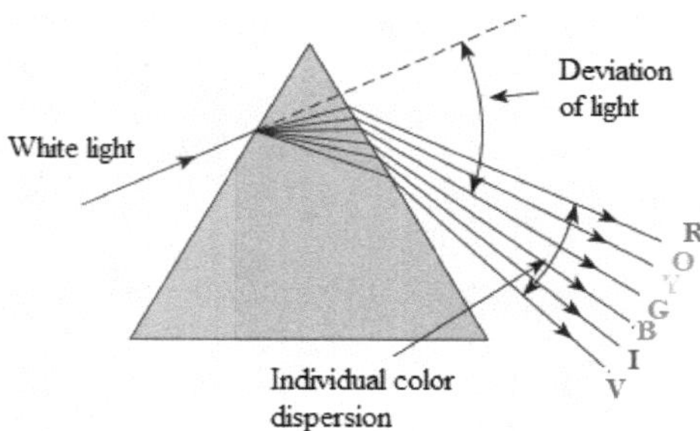

Dispersion is due to different colors of visible light having different ____________________.

As a result, each color will exit the prism at its own angle of refraction and its own ____________________.

If a green photon is split into 2 identical orange photons upon an elastic collision with a specialized crystal, how will the wavelengths of the orange photons (λ_O) compare to that of the original green photon (λ_G)?

Polarization

Lenses and Mirrors

Mirrors

Lenses

If the mirror surface is ___________________, the mirror is called "converging" or "positive."

If the mirror surface is ___________________, the mirror is called "diverging" or "negative."

In the example shown, the parallel rays converge at the ___________________.

The focal length of a spherical mirror, f =

Images can be one of two types:

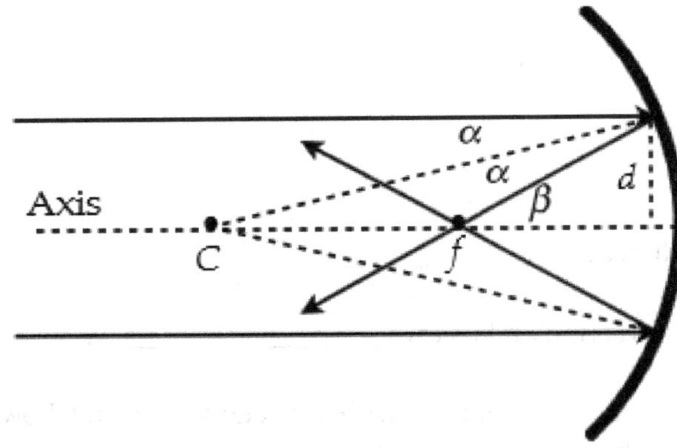

Virtual

Real

Obtaining Images—Mirrors

Principal rays are used to predict the images formed by lenses and mirrors.

1. A ray from the object point, passing through or toward the center of curvature. This ray strikes the mirror at normal incidence and is reflected straight back.
2. A ray parallel to the symmetry axis. For a positive mirror, this ray is reflected through the real focal point. For a negative mirror it is reflected away from the virtual focal point.
3. A ray passing through or toward the focal point, and emerging parallel to the axis.

What will be the resulting images for the scenarios below?

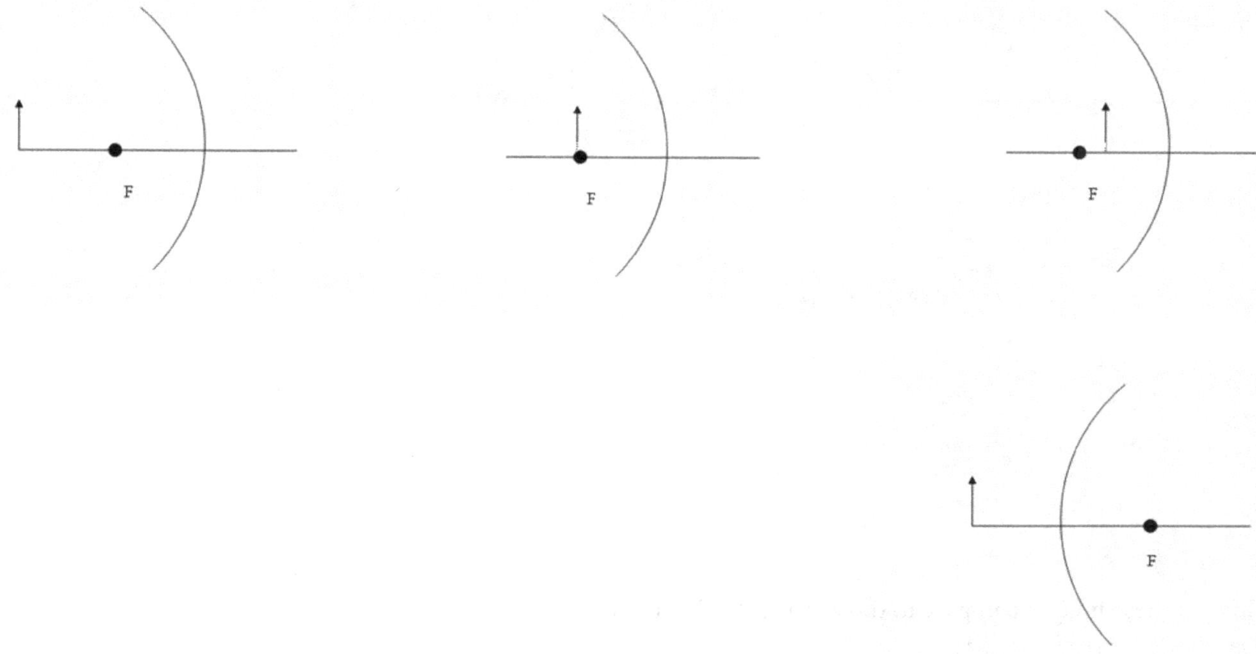

Obtaining Images—Lenses

Principal rays are used to predict the images formed by lenses and mirrors.

1. A ray from the object point to the center of the lens, where the two surfaces are parallel. This ray passes essentially straight through.
2. A ray from the object point parallel to the axis. This is refracted through the focal point for a positive lens, or away from it for a negative lens.
3. A ray passing through or toward a focal point emerges parallel to the axis.

What will be the resulting images for the scenarios below?

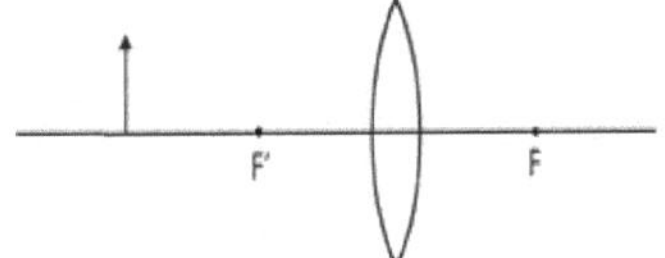

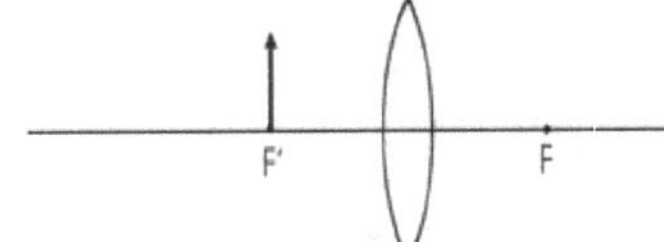

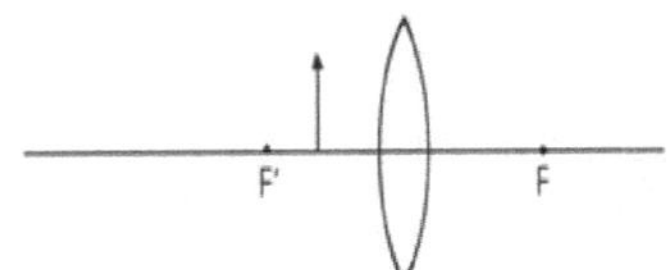

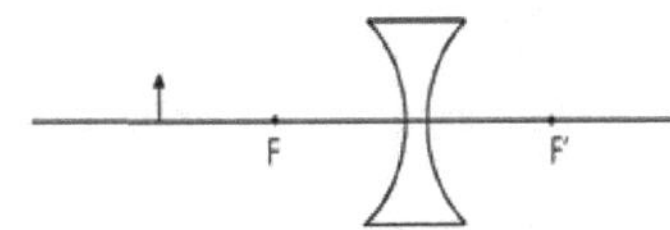

How do these images compare to those generated by mirrors?

	Converging	Diverging
Lens		
Mirror		

	Negative Value	Positive Value
f		
i		
o		
m		

Image Location Formula

1/f = 1/i + 1/o

Magnification Formula

m = -i/o

Lens Strength

Aberrations

Spherical

Astigmatism

Chromatic

The Eye as a Lens

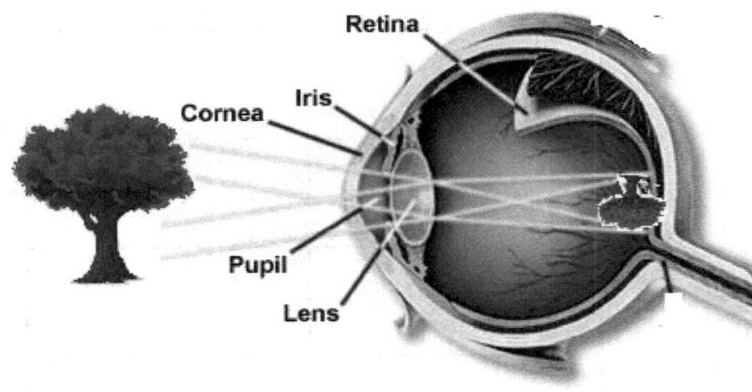

	Problem	Correction
Hyperopia		
Myopia		
Astigmatism		

Geometric Optics Worksheet Exercise

Object Distance	Ray Trace	Image	Image distance	Usually tested in
o = ∞	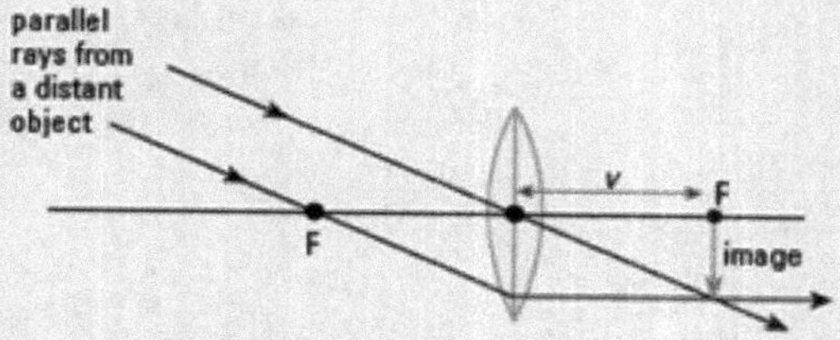 parallel rays from a distant object; v; F; F; image	- inverted - real - diminished	$v = f$ - opposite side of the lens	- object lens of a telescope
o > 2f	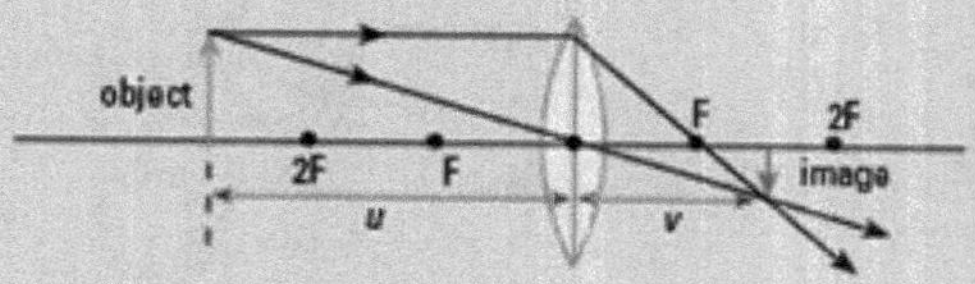 object; 2F; F; F; 2F; image; u; v	- inverted - real - diminished	$f < v < 2f$ - opposite side of the lens	- camera - eye
o = 2f	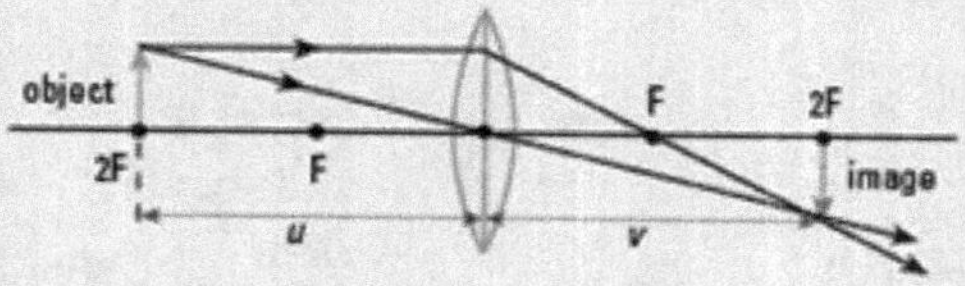 object; 2F; F; F; 2F; image; u; v	- inverted - real - same size	$v = 2f$ - opposite side of the lens	- photocopier making same-sized copy
f < o < 2f	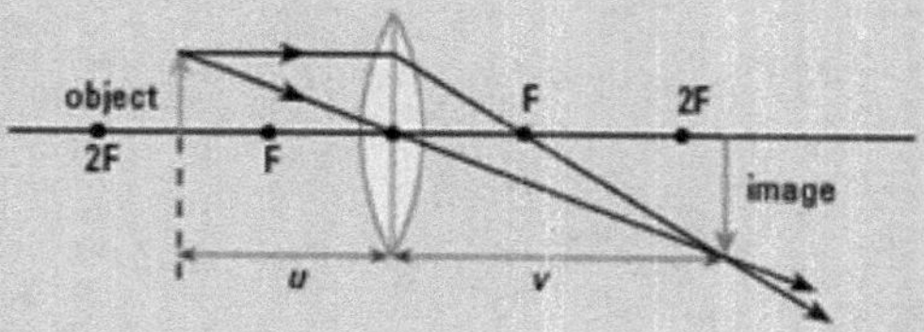 object; 2F; F; F; 2F; image; u; v	- inverted - real - magnified	$v > 2f$ - opposite side of the lens	- projector - photograph enlarger
o = f	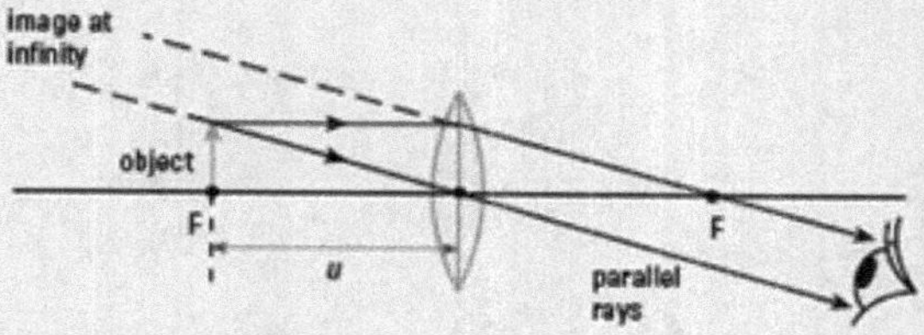 image at infinity; object; F; u; F; parallel rays	- upright - virtual - magnified	- image at infinity - same side of the lens	- to produce a parallel beam of light, e.g. a spotlight
o < f	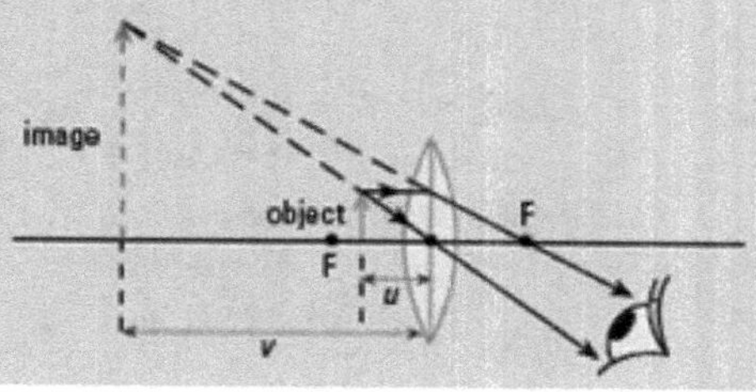 image; object; F; u; F; v	- upright - virtual - magnified	- image is behind the object - same side of the lens	- magnifying glass

Geometric Optics Worksheet Exercise Level 1

Object Distance	Ray Trace	Image	Image distance	Usually tested in
o = ∞	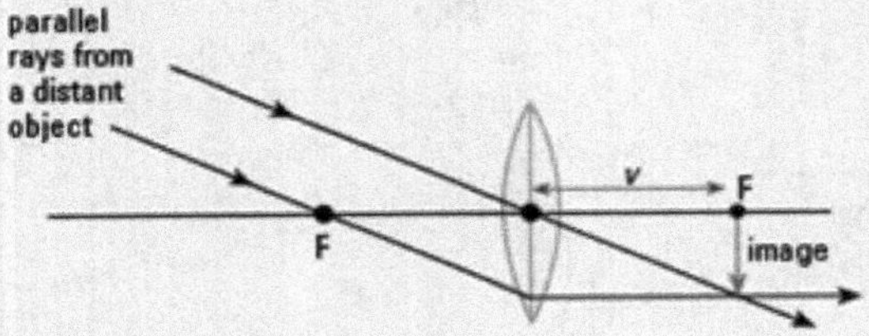 parallel rays from a distant object; F; v; F; image		$v = f$ - opposite side of the lens	- object lens of a telescope
o > 2*f*		- inverted - real - diminished	$f < v < 2f$ - opposite side of the lens	- camera - eye
o = 2*f*	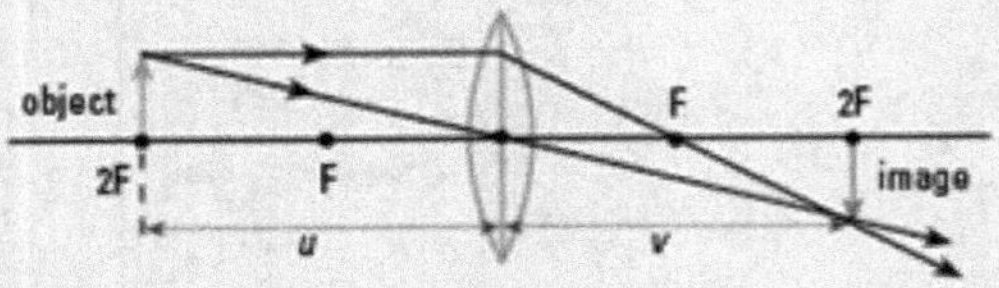 object; 2F; F; F; 2F; image; u; v		$v = 2f$ - opposite side of the lens	- photocopier making same-sized copy
f < o < 2*f*	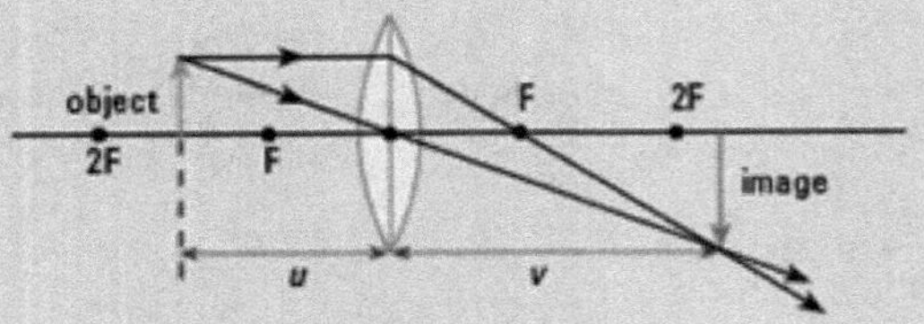 object; 2F; F; F; 2F; image; u; v	- inverted - real - magnified		- projector - photograph enlarger
o = *f*	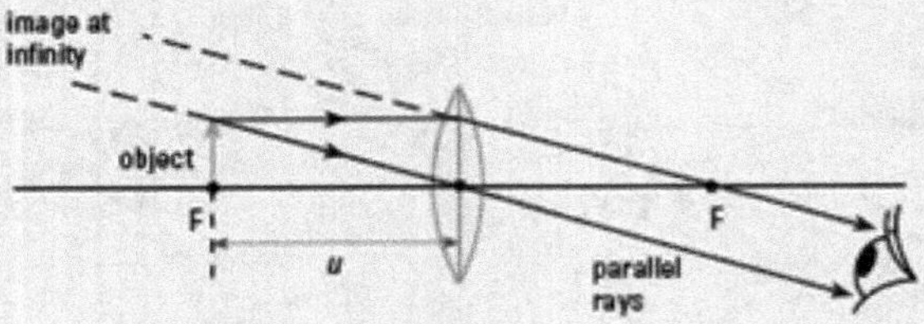 image at infinity; object; F; F; u; parallel rays	- upright - virtual - magnified	- image at infinity - same side of the lens	
	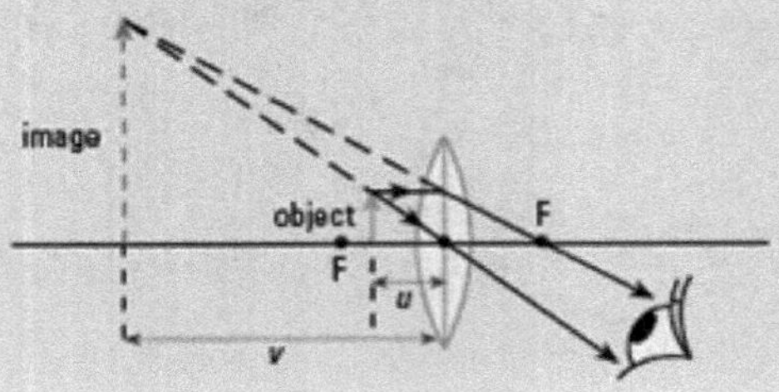 image; object; F; F; u; v	- upright - virtual - magnified	- image is behind the object - same side of the lens	- magnifying glass

Geometric Optics Worksheet Exercise Level 2

Object Distance	Ray Trace	Image	Image distance	Usually tested in
$o = \infty$			$v = f$ - opposite side of the lens	- object lens of a telescope
$o > 2f$		- inverted - real - diminished		- camera - eye
$o = 2f$	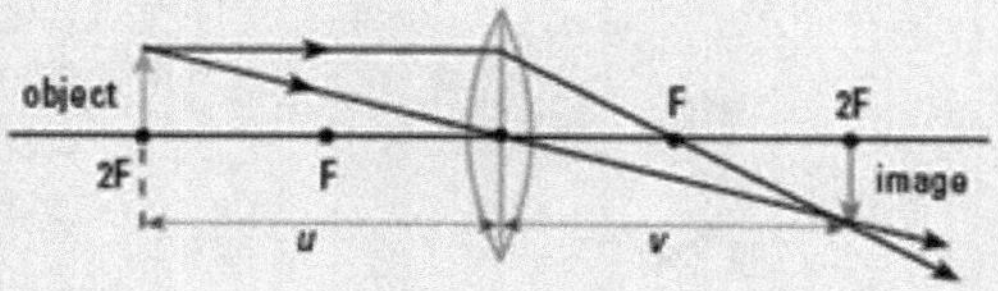			- photocopier making same-sized copy
$f < o < 2f$		- inverted - real - magnified		- projector - photograph enlarger
$o = f$	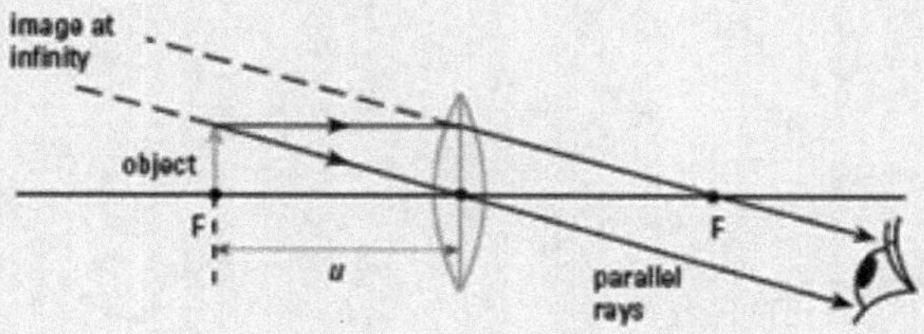		- image at infinity - same side of the lens	
		- upright - virtual - magnified	- image is behind the object - same side of the lens	- magnifying glass

Image adapted from Wikipedia under CCBY 3.0

Geometric Optics Worksheet Exercise Level 3

Object Distance	Ray Trace	Image	Image distance	Usually tested in
o = ∞				- object lens of a telescope
o > 2*f*		- inverted - real - diminished		
o = 2*f*				- photocopier making same-sized copy
f < o < 2*f*		- inverted - real - magnified		- projector - photograph enlarger
o = *f*				
		- upright - virtual - magnified		

Image adapted from Wikipedia under CCBY 3.0

Practice

Researchers are designing a new microscope for visualizing mitochondrial life cycles. It is decided the new scope will be based on a multiple lens system. In order to test the new design, two convex lenses and a concave lens are attached to a 10 m rod at mounting sites as shown in figure 1.

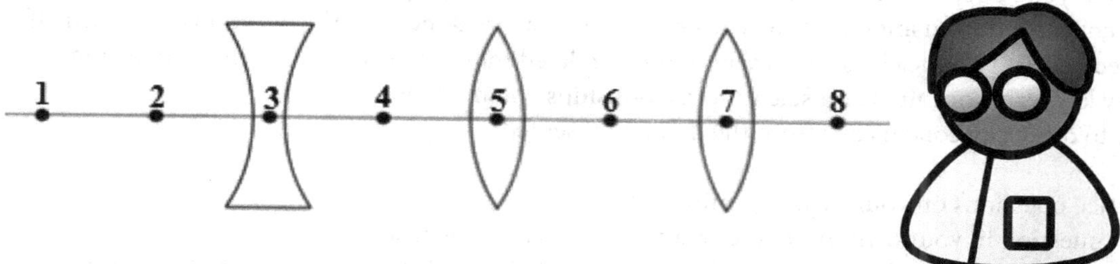

Figure 1 Microscope design setup

The lenses are shaped such that the converging lenses used have a focal length 20 cm while the diverging lenses used have a focal length of 15 cm. The mounting points, labeled 1-8, are each separated by 20 cm.

The researcher attaches an object to different points on the rod and stands as shown in the figure. Once the object is in place, the researcher looks through the lenses and observes the image created by the new design.

If the object is placed at the following points, where would the researcher see the image?

Point 2 Point 5 Point 6

If a 5 cm tall object is placed upright at point 2, what type of image will be created by the first lens? What will be the magnification?

If a new design is created where the magnification of each lens is 4x, what is the total magnification of the final image produced?

If an object is placed at point 7, what kind of image would be created and where will it be located?

What is the power, in diopters, of each lens?

Timed MCAT Practice Passage

Mastery of the MCAT sciences is a two-part process. First you must study to understand (not just memorize!) the science content, and then you must study the content actively and challenge yourself within the context of the exam.

1. Complete your reading of the passage (3-4 minutes).
    - Write down what you believe to be the primary science content underlying the passage.
    - What facts or concepts do you anticipate to be tested? When you are done with the questions determine if you were correct. What passage clues were there to imply related topics that showed up in the questions?
    - Were there any key terms or important scientific relationships you missed?
    - Were you able to draw any conclusions from the data, if presented?

2. Complete the practice questions on your own (4-5 minutes)
    - Rephrase each question in your own mind after reading it to clarify the task.
    - Research the relevant area(s) of the passage or your own knowledge for information related to the task.
    - Respond to the question by choosing the answer that fits your research/calculations *and* satisfies the task.
    - If no answer seems obvious, eliminate answers that fail to have support in the passage or in the relevant science.

3. Analyze your wrong answer choices to the questions you missed.
    - Did you understand the task in the question?
    - What skill type was the question?
    - Did you know the science/formula/concept needed to answer the question?
    - Did you recognize the science being hinted at?
    - Were you able to find information in the passage quickly when you needed it?
    - Were there any necessary scientific concepts you failed to apply to the question?
        - If so, why?
    - If you made a mistake in calculations, have you identified your mistake?

The Doppler effect, commonly used to describe frequency changes in sound waves, applies to all waves including electromagnetic radiation. One everyday application of these effects can be found in police radar guns, which use microwave signals in order to gauge the speed of drivers. In order to detect a target's speed, radar guns emit a microwave pulse in the direction of the target at a known frequency, and subsequently measure the frequency of the return microwave as it reflects off of the target vehicle. The frequency of this return wave—also known as the Doppler frequency—will be given by the Doppler equation. A graph displaying the observed frequency change of an electromagnetic wave versus target vehicle speed is shown below in Figure 1.

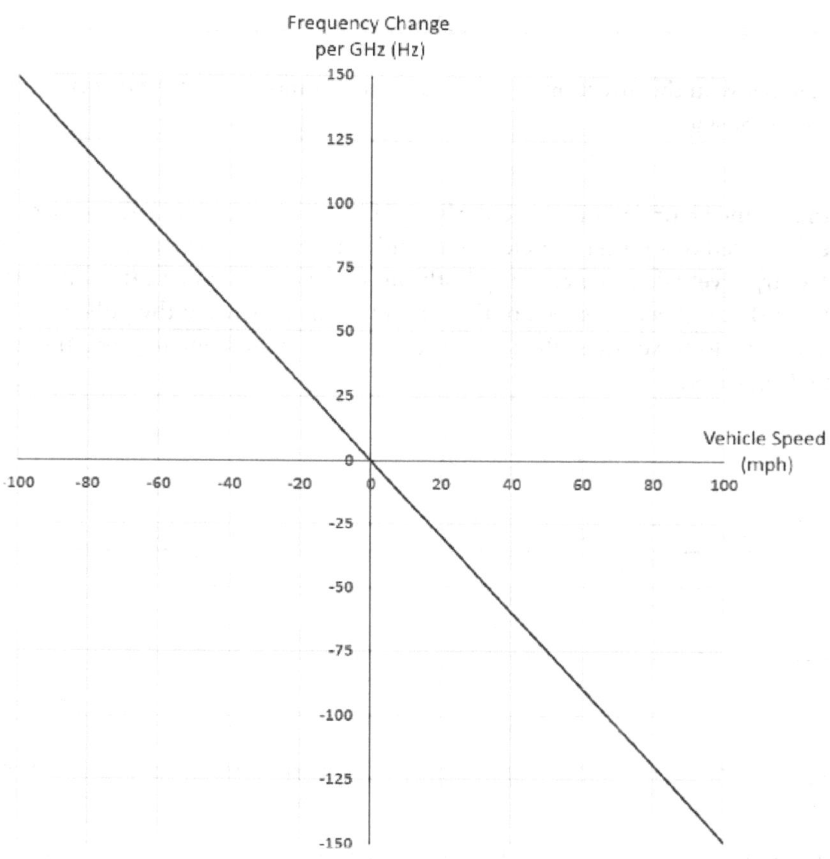

Figure 1 The frequency change per GHz (Hz) at a given target vehicle speed (mph). The frequency change is calculated as the difference between the Doppler frequency, f_D, and the emitted frequency, f. The results shown in the figure are for a 1 GHz microwave pulse.

In order to accurately measure a vehicle's speed using the Doppler effect, however, there are multiple complicating factors that must be taken into account. Perhaps the most important of these obstacles is referred to as the 'Cosine Error', which accounts for the fact that the Doppler effect is only observed for target motion in the same direction as the microwave pulse. The angle formed between the direction of the microwave pulse and the target vehicle's trajectory, therefore, will have a significant effect on the measured speed, with the observed speed given by Vt cos(β) , where ***Vt*** is the actual target's speed and β is the angle formed (Figure 2).

Passage taken from the Next Step Chemistry and Physics Strategy and Practice book, Chapter 1, Passage 1

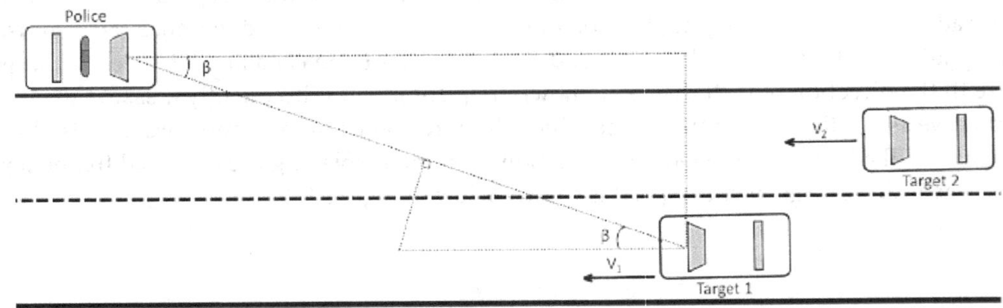

Figure 2 The angle formed between the direction of the target vehicle's motion and the direction of the microwave pulse, β, affects the measured target speed.

Discrepancies due to the cosine error can be particularly significant when radar guns are set to 'moving radar', a mode used to measure the speed of a target vehicle from inside of a moving police car. In moving mode the radar calculates the speed of a target vehicle by calculating both the speed of the police car itself (often using a nearby object as a reflective surface) as well as the speed of the target vehicle relative to the police car. Both measurements are subject to inaccuracies due to the cosine effect, and therefore can contribute to inaccuracies in the measured speed of a target vehicle (Figure 3).

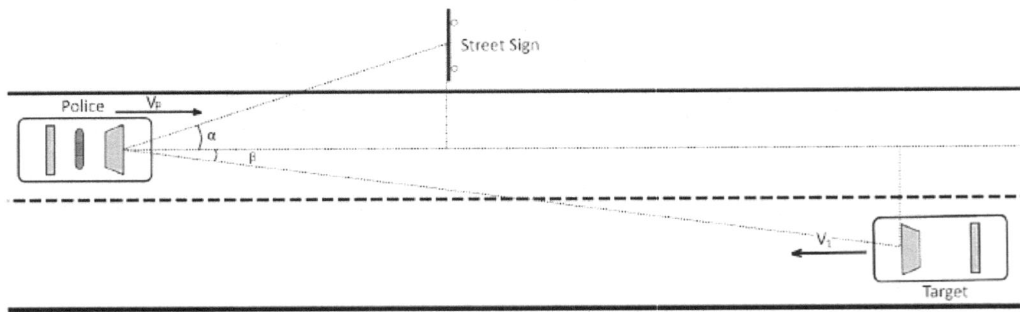

Figure 3 In moving radar mode, the measured speed of a target vehicle is dependent upon the angle α, which is based upon the direction of the police car's motion, as well as the angle β.

Passage taken from the Next Step online QBank

6. A stationary police officer directs his radar gun directly ahead at a target vehicle. The initial radar frequency is 0.5 GHz, and the observed frequency change is -60 Hz. Based on Figure 1, which of the following best approximates the speed of the target vehicle?

   A. 40 miles per hour toward the radar gun
   B. 80 miles per hour toward the radar gun
   C. 40 miles per hour away from the radar gun
   D. 80 miles per hour away from the radar gun

7. A radar gun within a police car travelling at 25 mph is pointed directly ahead at a target vehicle. The initial radar frequency is 1 GHz, and the observed frequency change is 75 Hz. Based on Figure 1, which of the following answers best approximates the speed and direction of the vehicle?

   A. 25 mph toward the police officer
   B. 50 mph toward the police officer
   C. 25 mph away from the police officer
   D. 50 mph away from the police officer

8. In the situation shown in Figure 2, how will the measured speed of target 1 compare to the measured speed of target 2, assuming both are moving at the same speed?

   A. Target 1's measured speed will be greater than Target 2's measured speed, and closer to the vehicle's actual speed.
   B. Target 1's measured speed will be greater than Target 2's measured speed, and further from the vehicle's actual speed.
   C. Target 1's measured speed will be smaller than Target 2's measured speed, and closer to the vehicle's actual speed.
   D. Target 1's measured speed will be smaller than Target 2's measured speed, and further from the vehicle's actual speed.

9. A stationary police officer directs his radar gun at a vehicle travelling away from him at 80 mph. When the angle between the vehicle's direction of motion and the direction of the microwave pulse is at 60°, which of the following would be closest to the observed vehicles frequency change? Assume the microwave pulse has a frequency of 1 GHz.

   A. -120 Hz
   B. -60 Hz
   C. 60 Hz
   D. 120 Hz

10. Instead of microwave radiation, a new form of radar is designed to use infrared radiation. Which of the following is NOT an accurate description of the differences between the two systems?

    A. The frequency shift per GHz would remain consistent between the infrared and microwave radar systems.
    B. The infrared system would require a more sensitive detection system for reflected waves.
    C. It would require more energy to emit the infrared radiation.
    D. Using infrared radiation would reduce the effectiveness of radar jamming devices that emit microwaves to interfere with police radar guns.

Leg Muscle as Spring

EXAMPLE

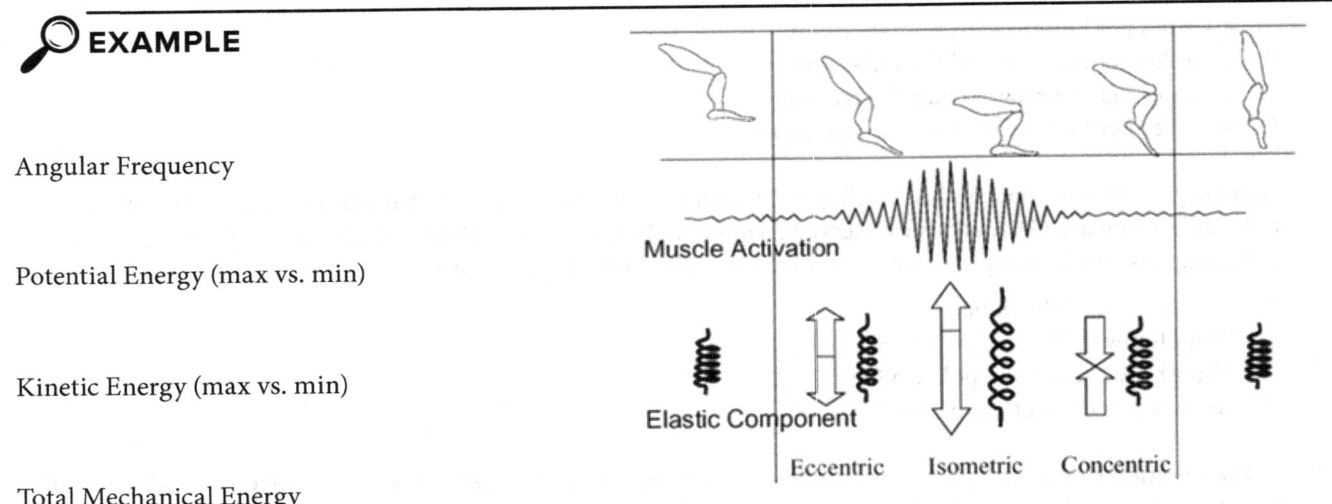

Angular Frequency

Potential Energy (max vs. min)

Kinetic Energy (max vs. min)

Total Mechanical Energy

Knee as a Pendulum

EXAMPLE

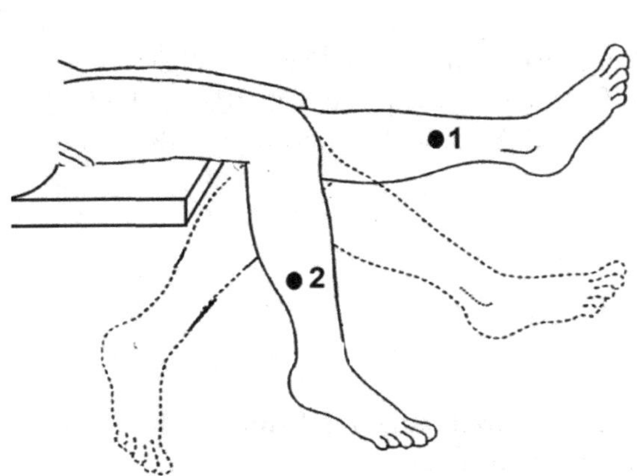

Angular Frequency

Potential Energy (max vs. min)

Kinetic Energy (max vs. min)

Total Mechanical Energy

Waves and Sound

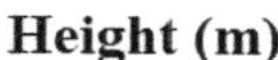

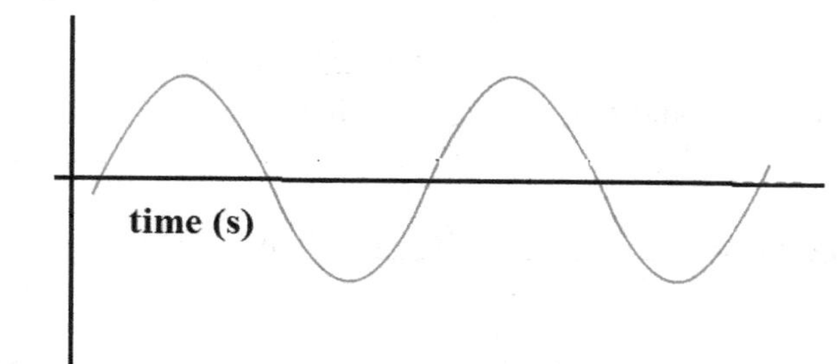

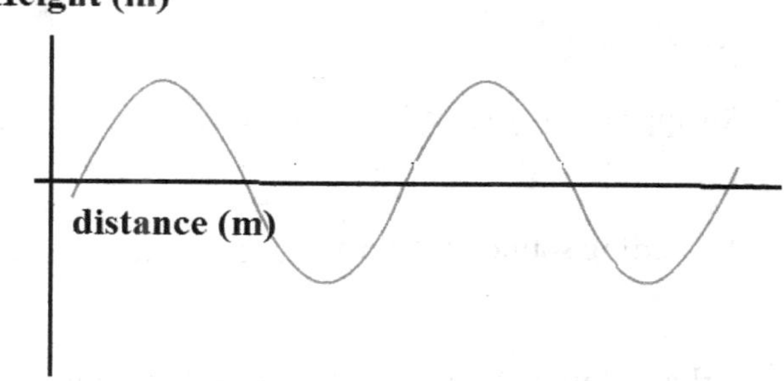

Frequency

Amplitude

Wavelength

Period

Intensity

$I(dB) = 10 \log [I/I_0]$

Power ~ Amplitude

Doppler Effect

$f_{observed} = f_{source}\left[\frac{v \pm vd}{v \mp vs}\right]$

An approaching sound will have a ______________ wavelength and a ______________ pitch.

A receding sound will have a ______________ wavelength and a ______________ pitch

If the ambulance above is moving left to right at 45 m/s emitting a 35 Hz siren, what will the stationary woman hear? What would happen if the woman were moving left to right at 100 m/s?

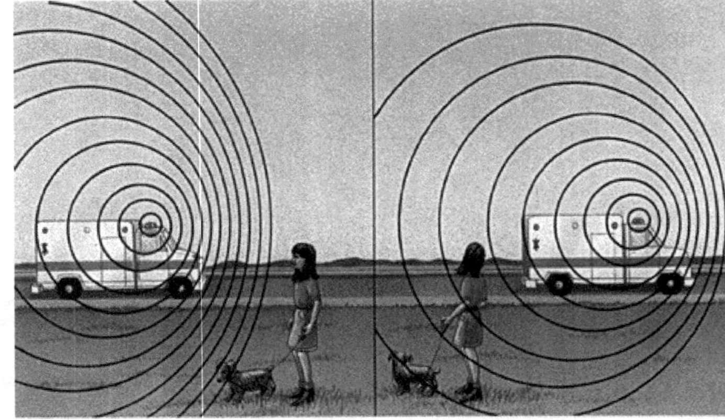

What situation between the ambulance and woman would result in no change in the siren's pitch?

Sound Interference

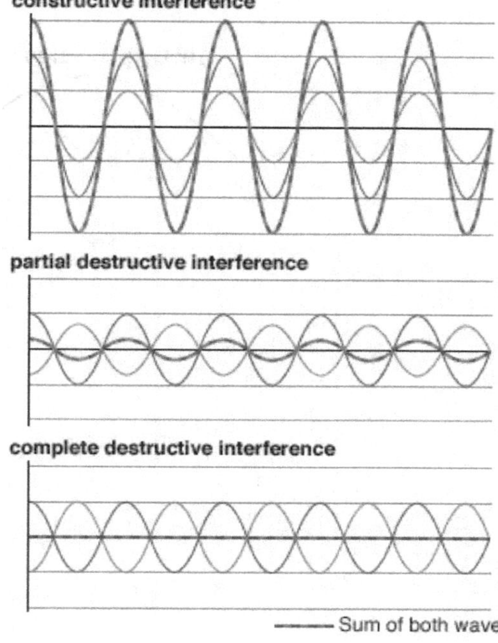

Wavelength Difference

Phase Difference

Resonance Frequency

Pushing a child on a swing will result in the child moving at the swing's resonant frequency. If you try to push harder, will you change the resonant frequency?

Standing Waves, Displacement, and Pressure

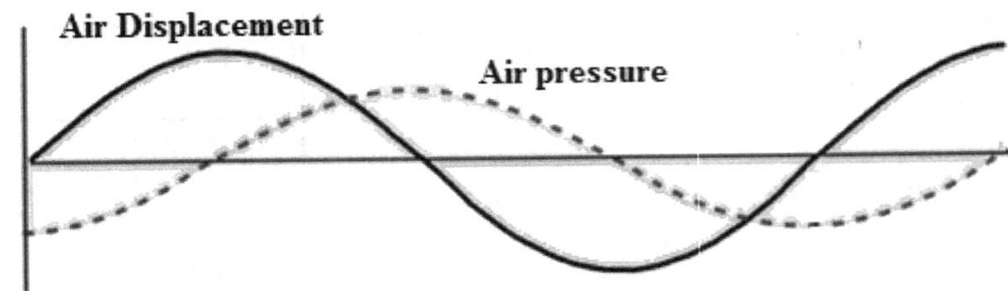

Open Pipe

Closed Pipe

Strings

$$v = \sqrt{\frac{T}{m/L}}$$

Strategy Discussion

Passage Strategy

Question Strategy

Timing/Pacing

What should you do if you come upon a question you do not know how to answer?

Science Content Review Strategies

Use the study strategies discussed throughout the course

As your test approaches, focus on a few weaker areas.

Science Passages

Core strategies

Preview the passage

- Skim to get a general sense of the passage
  - Info vs. experiment vs. study-based
  - General topic
- Does this look insanely hard? Is this my one "Skip It" passage?

Highlighting: ≈ 2-3 min to read, ≈ 5-6 min on questions

- Not just as you read along
- Highlight as a part of reflecting on the passage
- Contrast, Opinion, Cause and Effect

Note-taking: ≈ 3-4 min to read, ≈ 4-5 min on questions

- Complex relationships
- Key contrasts (esp. where lots of jargon is used to describe the two sides of the contrast)

Worst case scenario or "crunch time" strategy

- Skimming or questions-first: <1 min to read, ≈ 4 min on questions
- Always look at the pictures, even on questions-first approach

On the questions:

Atomic and Nuclear Decay

Atomic Mass =

Alpha

Beta +

Beta –

Gamma

Half-life

Exponential Decay

Mathematical Shortcut:

Timed MCAT Practice Passage

Mastery of the MCAT sciences is a two-part process. First you must study to understand (not just memorize!) the science content, and then you must study the content actively and challenge yourself within the context of the exam.

1. Complete your reading of the passage (3-4 minutes).
   - Write down what you believe to be the primary science content underlying the passage.
   - What facts or concepts do you anticipate to be tested? When you are done with the questions determine if you were correct. What passage clues were there to imply related topics that showed up in the questions?
   - Were there any key terms or important scientific relationships you missed?
   - Were you able to draw any conclusions from the data, if presented?

2. Complete the practice questions on your own (4-5 minutes)
   - Rephrase each question in your own mind after reading it to clarify the task.
   - Research the relevant area(s) of the passage or your own knowledge for information related to the task.
   - Respond to the question by choosing the answer that fits your research/calculations *and* satisfies the task.
   - If no answer seems obvious, eliminate answers that fail to have support in the passage or in the relevant science.

3. Analyze your wrong answer choices to the questions you missed.
   - Did you understand the task in the question?
   - What skill type was the question?
   - Did you know the science/formula/concept needed to answer the question?
   - Did you recognize the science being hinted at?
   - Were you able to find information in the passage quickly when you needed it?
   - Were there any necessary scientific concepts you failed to apply to the question?
     - If so, why?
   - If you made a mistake in calculations, have you identified your mistake?

Newton was able to demonstrate that when a thin beam of sunlight was passed through a prism, the light was dispersed due to refraction into the familiar colors of the rainbow (see Figure 1). He subsequently was able to reconstruct the white light by using a second prism. The corpuscular theory of light describes light in terms of discrete particles that pass through matter at different speeds due to collisions with atoms. Huygen's wave theory was useful in describing other aspects of light, such as diffraction, and interference. The angle (***q***) of refraction is dependent upon the index of refraction (***n***) for a particular material as shown in Equation 1.

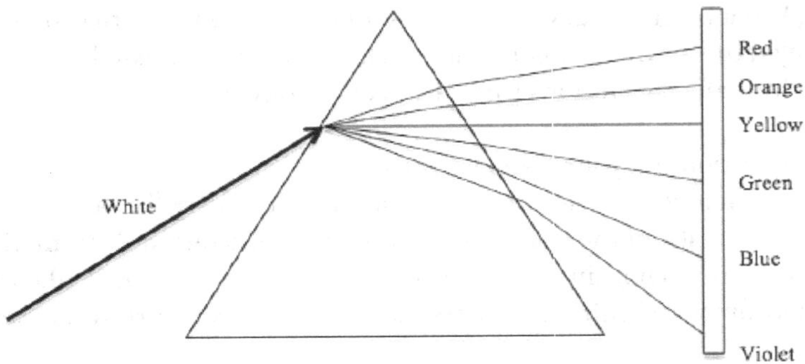

Figure 1 A schematic representation of a beam of white light passing through an equilateral triangular glass prism, resulting in the dispersion of the various color components of white light.

Equation 1 $$n_1 \sin \theta_1 = n_2 \sin \theta_2$$

Humans see colors based on perception of reflected, transmitted or emitted wavelengths of visible light. Two types of photosensitive cells, rods and cones are responsible for taking the light focused by the lens and producing an image. Rods are not significantly involved in the perception of color, but are important in the perception under conditions of low illumination. Cones can be subdivided into three basic types, blue, green and red, based on their wavelength of maximum sensitivity, though each cone has some sensitivity over a range of wavelengths. Materials that reflect multiple colors produce complex responses from cones, explaining the multitude of perceptions of colors. The most common color vision dysfunction is known as red-green color blindness, in which the red or green cones are either missing or function with diminished efficiencies. This abnormality is often associated with a recessive X chromosome mutation.

Passage taken from the Next Step online QBank

11. If a red laser pointer is focused on the surface of a rectangular piece of glass (n = 1.50) at an angle of 30°, what would be the value of the angle D?

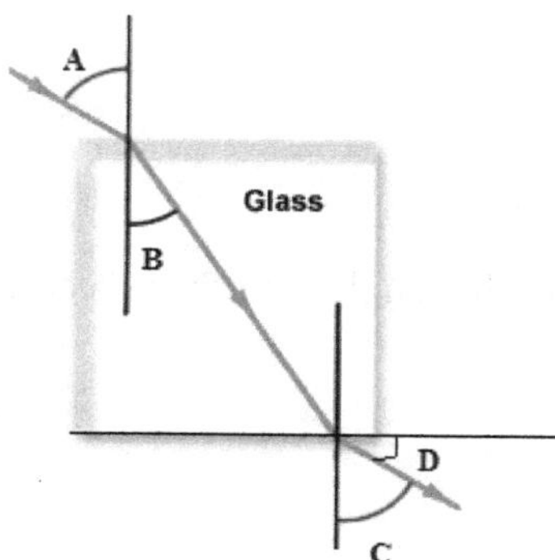

A. A°
B. (90-A)°
C. (B+C)°
D. (90-D)°

12. Which of the following monochromatic colors has the lowest velocity while passing through a glass prism?

A. Red
B. Yellow
C. Green
D. Blue

13. Which of the following best describes a discrete quantum of light?

A. Neutrino
B. Anti-neutrino
C. Proton
D. Photon

14. Which of the following best describes the image that is formed on the retina for an object that is more than one focal length away from the lens?

A. The image is real and inverted.
B. The image is real and erect.
C. The image is virtual and inverted.
D. The image is virtual and erect.

15. What is the speed of light in water if the index of refraction of water is 1.33?

A. 1.2×10^8 m/s
B. 2.3×10^8 m/s
C. 3.0×10^8 m/s
D. 4.0×10^8 m/s

16. Which of the following most likely represents the maximum wavelength sensitivity for red, green and blue cones, respectively?

I. 435 nm
II. 540 nm
III. 575 nm

A. I, II, and III
B. II, III, and I
C. III, I, and II
D. III, II, and I

Problem-solving Cooldown

17. What is the index of refraction for a medium in which light travels at 1.89×10^8 m/s?

    A. 0.8
    B. 1.0
    C. 1.6
    D. 1.9

18. A light ray has an angle of incidence of 44°. The reflected ray will make what angle with the reflecting surface?

    A. 22°
    B. 44°
    C. 46°
    D. 92°

19. If the critical angle of ruby (Al_2O_3) is 34°, which of the following incident angles would result in total internal reflection?

    A. 7°
    B. 17°
    C. 27°
    D. 37°

20. An object is placed between **f** and **2f** for a concave lens. The image formed will be located a distance:

    A. greater than 2f.
    B. between f and 2f.
    C. greater than f.
    D. between the lens and f.

21. A guitar string is 150 cm long and is vibrating at its first harmonic. The string vibrates up and down with 40 complete oscillations every 10 seconds. What is the speed of this wave?

    A. 3 m/s
    B. 6 m/s
    C. 9 m/s
    D. 12 m/s

This page left intentionally blank.

Test-like Thinking: CARS Practice Passage

The knight of faith, perhaps, is the concept that best encapsulates much of Kierkegaard's lengthy meditations on Christianity and how Christian ideals come to be contemplated by and instantiated in the life of each subjective individual.

While Kierkegaard himself would likely be aghast at the over-simplifications to which his work was subject by early American scholarship, with their distinctions between the three stages of human existence as described in Kierkegaard's work (that is, the aesthetic, the ethical, and the religious) being seen as the framework around which all of Kierkegaard's writings can be understood, these distinctions are directly relevant to the evolution of his ideas about the knight of faith. The religious is the stage at which a person, although still able to enjoy life's aesthetic pleasures and still able to act ethically in society, is primarily focused on his or her relationship with the infinite divine presence. Worldly logic, worldly concerns, and worldly relationships don't cease to exist when one develops to the religious stage, but rather they come to be of much less importance.

The knight of faith is one who has fully embraced the religious stage of individual existence. He or she is an individual whose faith in God is complete, and who is able to act with complete independence from the world. Kierkegaard leaves some ambiguity as to whether such a state requires independence and separation from the world, or merely allows for it. In his discussions about people who have actually been knights of faith, Kierkegaard presents only two clear examples: Abraham and Mary. In both cases, Kierkegaard speaks at length about the total isolation each experienced when voluntarily taking action on behalf of God.

Mary, when the angel came to her, voluntarily chose to bear Jesus. During that short communion between the angel and Mary, she was separated from all the world. Thereafter she carried Jesus and gave birth to him in the usual way (the Bible speaks of this as being done "after the manner of women"). It is not, then, birthing and raising the Christ that made Mary a knight of faith, but rather Kierkegaard holds that it was the moment of contact with the angel when she made the voluntary choice to accept God's son that she became a knight of faith.

Similarly, God's command to Abraham to sacrifice his firstborn son Isaac was one that was voluntarily accepted, even though it should have been rejected outright. Abraham could have told his wife or his son about God's command, but then he would have had to offer some explanation or justification for obeying this seemingly evil command. An accounting would be due, and this accounting could only be explained at the level or the aesthetic or ethical. But any such analysis would lead inevitably to the conclusion that God should be disobeyed. Instead, Abraham took Isaac on a three-day journey to the place of sacrifice and for those three days Abraham was alone with God. Each step was voluntarily taken. Isaac was at his side, but Abraham was alone with God during that trip. His acceptance made him a knight of faith, and at the moment he raised the knife, God sent an angel to intervene. For his obedience, Abraham was rewarded with a lifetime of faith and happiness.

22. Which of the following individuals would Kierkegaard most likely categorize as a knight of faith, as that concept is explained in the passage?
    A. A mother receives a command from God to sacrifice her infant twins, and she justifies her obedience to God's command by deciding that the rules of ethics place God's desires above her own.
    B. An army captain disobeys an order from his general to attack a village because people in the village have been welcoming to his troops in the past.
    C. A tribal priestess learns about Christianity from a traveling missionary and begins incorporating Christian symbols and beliefs into her own religion.
    D. A carpenter has a series of vivid dreams in which God commands him to give away all of his possessions and pray alone in a forest, and despite the protestations of friends and family, he does so.

23. The passage suggests that had Abraham tried to explain his obedience to God's command to his wife, his justification would have:
    A. provided adequate grounds for his subsequent behavior.
    B. made him change his mind about obedience to God.
    C. contradicted his subsequent behavior.
    D. persuaded his wife to join him on the three-day journey.

24. Which of the following statements, if made in one of Kierkegaard's later writings, would most *weaken* the author's thesis in the passage?
    A. "One cannot help but wonder whether Abraham was, perhaps, compelled by God to the edge of such a heinous action."
    B. "The transition between stages truly reveals the nature of each, for as an individual grows into the ethical he finds that the pleasures of the aesthetic are muted to the point of irrelevancy."
    C. "Indeed, Jesus himself was also the exemplary knight of faith, not in his Godhood, but rather in his voluntarily mounting the cross."
    D. "My notion of the knight of faith was no mere phantasm of youth, but was instead constructed to show the inevitability of God's command and the deep interconnection with the world one feels when the burden of choice is removed."

25. A person who in an accomplished musician and derives great pleasure from listening to Bach's organ concertos played in a large cathedral would be understood to be operating in which of Kierkegaard's three stages of human existence?
    A. The aesthetic
    B. The ethical
    C. The religious
    D. The ethical and the religious

26. The passage implies that:
    A. had Abraham disobeyed God's command, he would not have experienced a lifetime of faith and happiness.
    B. Mary's childbirth of Jesus was painful and difficult.
    C. the most popular understanding of Kierkegaard among American scholars today hinges on the tripartite distinctions of human existence.
    D. had Abraham explained to Isaac what he was about to do, Isaac would have resisted.

To Do After Lesson 18

- ☐ Complete Full Timed Section 5 from the Verbal Practice: 108 Passages book
- ☐ Complete the AAMC Biological and Biochemical Foundations Section Bank (may be split over 2-3 days if needed)
- ☐ Complete Physics QBank 3: Sound and Light

LESSON 19

Biology 4

To Do Before Lesson 19

- ☐ Complete Full Timed Section 5 from the Verbal Practice: 108 Passages book
- ☐ Complete the AAMC Biological and Biochemical Foundations Section Bank (may be split over 2-3 days if needed)
- ☐ Complete Physics QBank 3: Sound and Light

In Lesson 19

Problem-solving Warm-up
The Plasma Membrane
MCAT Practice Passage
Membrane-bound Organelles
MCAT Practice Passage
Bacterial Reproduction and Growth
Cell Development
Problem-solving Cooldown
Test-like Thinking: CARS Practice Passage

To Do After Lesson 19

- ☐ Complete the AAMC Psychological and Sociological Foundations Section Bank (may be split over 2-3 days if needed)
- ☐ Complete Biology QBank 4: Cell Cycle and Development
- ☐ Complete Biochemistry QBank 4: Metabolism

Problem-solving Warm-up

1. A biologist conducting experiments on cholesterol addition to the membrane (30°C) accidentally places the cell culture into the wrong refrigerator (5°C). Which of the following results is expected?

   A. Addition of cholesterol increases membrane fluidity by tightly packing the phospholipids.
   B. Addition of cholesterol increases membrane fluidity by inserting between phospholipids.
   C. Addition of cholesterol decreases membrane fluidity by inserting between phospholipids.
   D. Addition of cholesterol decreases membrane fluidity by tightly packing the phospholipids.

2. Which of the following molecules is expected to have the lowest diffusion rate though the cell membrane?

   A. Sucrose
   B. CO_2
   C. Ethene
   D. Ethanol

3. Which of the following is NOT necessarily involved in G-protein coupled receptor signaling?

   A. Release of neurotransmitter into synapse
   B. Acquisition of GTP by the G protein
   C. Dissociation of α subunit from β and γ subunits
   D. Intracellular phosphorylation cascade.

4. Testing of intracellular receptor mechanisms would be best carried out on:

   A. GH.
   B. NO.
   C. insulin.
   D. TSH.

5. A new drug is found to cause severe dehydration in infants. A physician suspects the drug is causing the dehydration via effects on chloride ion exporters in the large intestine. What is the most likely effect of this drug?

   A. The drug activates the transporter, which leads to water actively entering the intestinal lumen.
   B. The drug activates the transporter, which leads to water passively entering the intestinal lumen.
   C. The drug inactivates the transporter, so water cannot be exchanged for chloride.
   D. The drug inactivates the transporter, so the chloride ion repels water towards the intestinal lumen.

The Cell Membrane

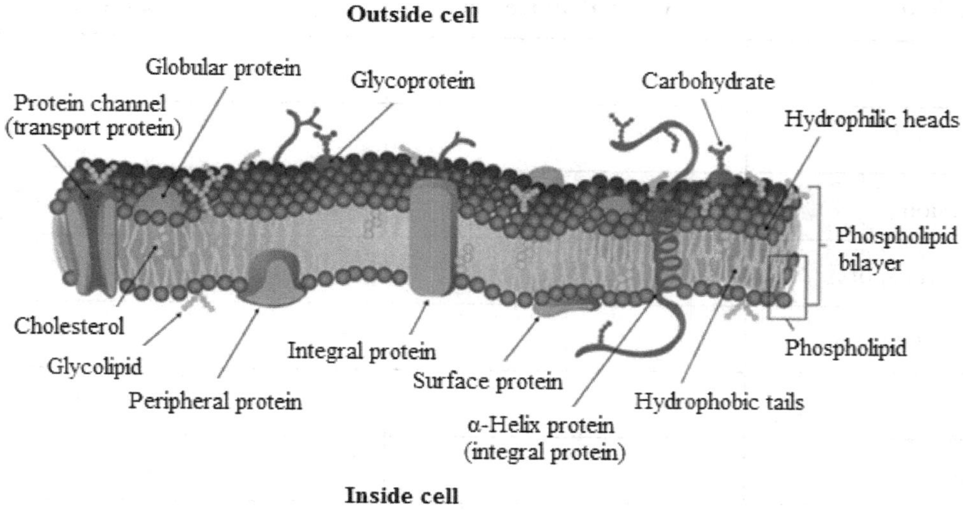

Hydrophobic vs Hydrophilic Components

Proteins

Glycoproteins

Carbohydrates

Glycolipids

Transport Mechanisms

Method	Energy Requirement	Examples
Diffusion		
Osmosis		
Facilitated Diffusion		
Primary Active Transport		
Secondary Active Transport		
Co-transport		
Endo/Exocytosis		

Under normal conditions, moving sodium ions outside of the cell means the ions move ________________ their concentration gradient and ________________ the membrane potential.

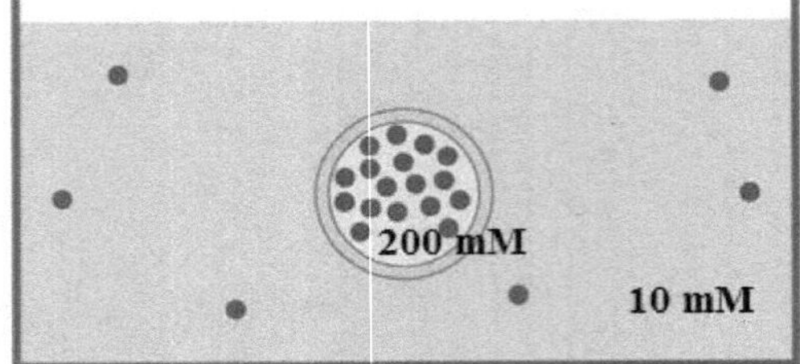

A single cell is injected with an unknown ion A and then placed into a solution of pure water. After a few minutes measurements show there is no net movement of ions in solution. If the figure below shows relative potentials and relative concentrations of A taken at the same time, which of the following must be true?

A. $|A| < 0$
B. $|A| > 0$
C. A requires ATP for transport
D. The membrane is impermeable to A

What will happen to the volume of the cell above if the membrane is permeable to water?

Is the solution inside the cell hypertonic or isotonic to the solution outside the cell?

At what intracellular solute concentration will water cease to be transported across the membrane?

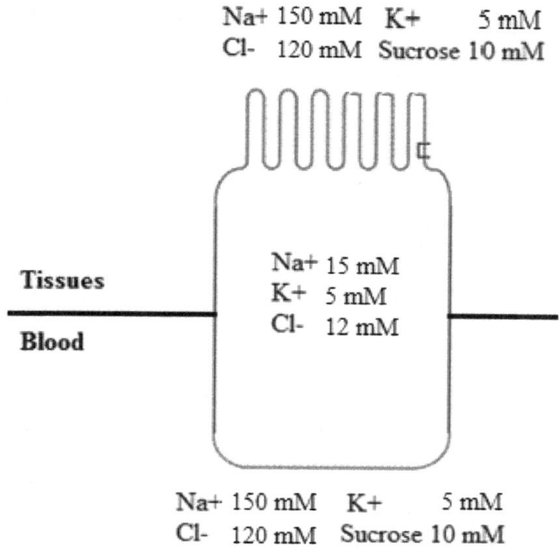

Which of the following transport configurations would increase blood [sucrose] and decrease tissue [sucrose]?

A. Basolateral: Na^+/K^+ pump and glucose channel; Apical: potassium/sucrose antiporters.
B. Basolateral: Na^+/K^+ pump and glucose channel; Apical: sodium/sucrose symporters.
C. Apical: sodium channel; Basolateral Na^+/K^+ pump and sodium/sucrose symporter
D. Apical: Na^+/K^+ pump and sucrose channel; Basolateral sodium/sucrose antiporter

Patients with pulmonary edema should be carefully monitored to prevent lung failure. How would the values of hydrostatic pressure and osmotic pressure at the pulmonary capillaries compare in patients who are at high risk for developing pulmonary edema?

Which of the following cells would consume ATP at the fastest rate?

A. A cell using a Na^+/K^+ antiporter
B. A cell using a symporter
C. A cell using phagocytosis
D. A cell using an open channel

Which class of cell junction would ensure that all permeable solutes must diffuse through the membrane when moving across a single-cell thick epithelial layer?

A. Gap junctions
B. Tight junctions
C. Desmosomes
D. Adherens junctions

ATP-driven Pumps

P-type (Na^+/K^+ ATPase)

Ca^{2+} ATPase

Sarcoplasmic

Plasma Membrane

Ion Channels

Cl^-

K^+

Voltage-gated Channel

Transmitter-gated Channel

Aquaporin Channels

Timed MCAT Practice Passage

Mastery of the MCAT sciences is a two-part process. First you must study to understand (not just memorize!) the science content, and then you must study the content actively and challenge yourself within the context of the exam.

1. Complete your reading of the passage (3-4 minutes).
   - Write down what you believe to be the primary science content underlying the passage.
   - What facts or concepts do you anticipate to be tested? When you are done with the questions determine if you were correct. What passage clues were there to imply related topics that showed up in the questions?
   - Were there any key terms or important scientific relationships you missed?
   - Were you able to draw any conclusions from the data, if presented?

2. Complete the practice questions on your own (4-5 minutes)
   - Rephrase each question in your own mind after reading it to clarify the task.
   - Research the relevant area(s) of the passage or your own knowledge for information related to the task.
   - Respond to the question by choosing the answer that fits your research/calculations *and* satisfies the task.
   - If no answer seems obvious, eliminate answers that fail to have support in the passage or in the relevant science.

3. Analyze your wrong answer choices to the questions you missed.
   - Did you understand the task in the question?
   - What skill type was the question?
   - Did you know the science/formula/concept needed to answer the question?
   - Did you recognize the science being hinted at?
   - Were you able to find information in the passage quickly when you needed it?
   - Were there any necessary scientific concepts you failed to apply to the question?
     - If so, why?
   - If you made a mistake in calculations, have you identified your mistake?

Alzheimer's disease (AD) is a common form of progressive dementia observed in both familial and non-familial forms. To evaluate the potential involvement of dysfunctional intracellular Ca^{2+} mobilization on AD-associated cognitive deficits, Ca^{2+} signaling was measured as fluorescence from human skin fibroblasts taken from healthy age-matched (AC) and healthy young (YC) donors, and from individuals with Alzheimer's disease (AD), where all cell lines were loaded with the calcium indicator fura-2. Fibroblasts were either untreated, treated with bombesin, an agent that upon binding its G protein-coupled receptor activates phospholipase C (PLC) to generate inositol 1,4,5-trisphosphate (IP_3 (which triggers release of calcium into the cytoplasm), or treated with Ca^{2+} channel blockers—agents that disrupt the movement of Ca^{2+} through calcium channels. Measurements were made under the extracellular Ca^{2+} conditions indicated, along with the results of the experiments, in Figures 1 and 2.

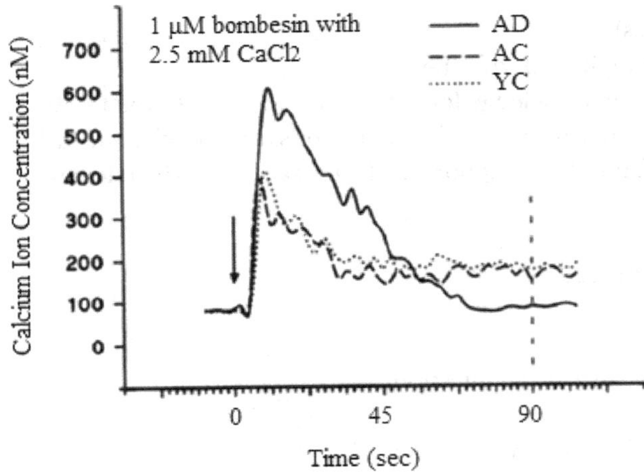

Figure 1 Ca^{2+} response induced by 1 μM bombesin (note the arrow indicates the time of bombesin application)

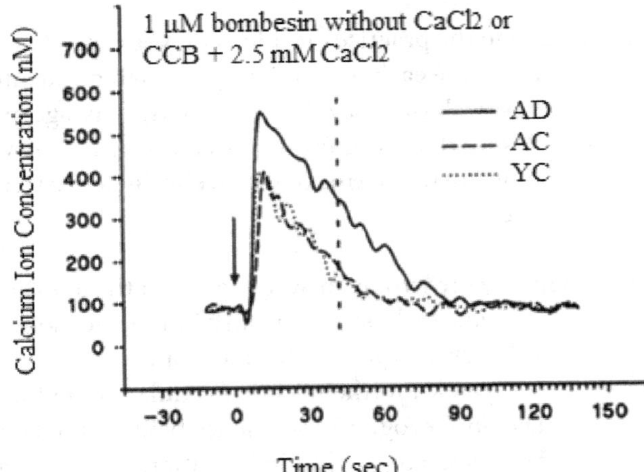

Figure 2 Ca^{2+} response induced by 1 μM bombesin without $CaCl_2$ present, and, when performed independently, Ca^{2+} response induced by 1 μM bombesin when 2.5 mM CaCl2 and divalent blockers of calcium channels (CCB) were present in the media (the Ca^{2+} response by cells under both treatment conditions was identical).

Further treatment of the cell lines with thapisgargin, an inhibitor of the Ca^{2+}-ATPase in the endoplasmic reticulum (ER) which acts to concentrate Ca^{2+} within the ER, elicited the same Ca^{2+} signals from AD, AC and YC cell lines.

Passage taken from the Next Step online QBank

6. Under several treatment conditions shown in Figures 1 and 2, tested fibroblasts displayed a sustained phase of constant Ca^{2+}signaling above baseline levels. Which of the following statements describing this sustained signaling is NOT supported by passage information?

   A. The sustained phase elicited by bombesin from AC and YC were eliminated by the removal of extracellular Ca^{2+}.
   B. Divalent cation Ca^{2+} channel blockers eliminated the sustained phase signals in all control cells.
   C. The sustained phases of fibroblast Ca^{2+} signaling do not depend on intracellularly stored calcium.
   D. The Ca^{2+} signal of AD fibroblasts showed no sustained phase.

7. The researchers concluded that AD-specific differences in initial bombesin-induced Ca^{2+} signaling in skin fibroblasts are due to dysfunction of an intracellular component of the PLC-IP_3 system. What additional findings would most *weaken* this conclusion?

   A. The thapisgargin-induced Ca^{2+} signal does not depend on extracellular Ca^{2+}.
   B. Bradykinin, another activator of PLC, elicited larger Ca^{2+} signals in AD than in YC cells.
   C. Radioligand binding revealed a greater number of bombesin binding sites in AD fibroblasts.
   D. Thapisgargin mobilized Ca^{2+} without a corresponding increase in inositol phosphates.

8. Which of the following steps in bombesin-induced Ca^{2+} signaling transduction depends on the availability of a high-energy bond?

   I. Binding of bombesin to its receptor
   II. G-protein activation
   III. Ca^{2+} reuptake into the ER
   IV. Protein kinase C kinase activity

   A. I and III only
   B. II and III only
   C. II, III, and IV only
   D. I, II, III, and IV

9. The researchers wish to relate AD-associated cognitive deficits to the AD-specific alterations of Ca^{2+} shown in the passage. What additional finding would best support this connection?

   A. Both familial and non-familial AD skin fibroblasts display AD-specific alterations.
   B. AD-specific differences in Ca^{2+} signaling have systemic expression in AD cells.
   C. Ca^{2+} signaling in AD-neurons increases with greater extracellular calcium concentration.
   D. AD-specific alterations are restricted to AD skin tissue fibroblasts.

10. Cleavage of phosphatidylinositol 4,5-bisphosphate (PIP_2) by PLC results in:

   A. retention of diacylglycerol (DAG) within the membrane and diffusion of IP_3 within the cell.
   B. retention of IP_3 within the membrane and diffusion of diacylglycerol (DAG) within the cell.
   C. retention of diacylglycerol (DAG) and IP_3 within the membrane.
   D. diffusion of diacylglycerol (DAG) and IP_3 within the cell.

Membrane-bound Organelles

Nucleus

Nucleolus

Nuclear envelope

Ribosomes

Endoplasmic reticulum

Golgi apparatus

Lysosomes

Peroxisomes

Mitochondria

Cell Structure

Cytoskeleton

Microfilaments

Microtubules

Intermediate filaments

Prokaryotic Reproduction and Growth

Archaea

Bacteria

Classification

Contrast with Eukaryotic Cells

Flagella and Cilia

Fission

Sexual Reproduction

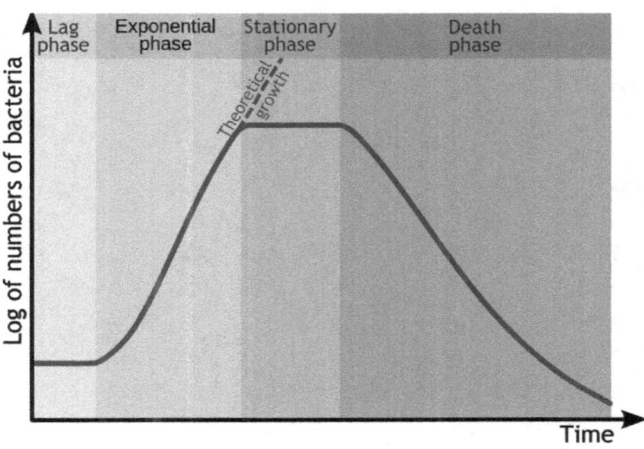

Bacterial Growth

Anaerobic vs. Aerobic Strains

Parasitic Life Cycle

Symbiotic Life Cycle

Chemotaxis

Prokaryote Genetics

Extragenomic DNA

Plasmids

Transformation

Conjugation

Transposons

Timed MCAT Practice Passage

Mastery of the MCAT sciences is a two-part process. First you must study to understand (not just memorize!) the science content, and then you must study the content actively and challenge yourself within the context of the exam.

1. Complete your reading of the passage (3-4 minutes).
   - Write down what you believe to be the primary science content underlying the passage.
   - What facts or concepts do you anticipate to be tested? When you are done with the questions determine if you were correct. What passage clues were there to imply related topics that showed up in the questions?
   - Were there any key terms or important scientific relationships you missed?
   - Were you able to draw any conclusions from the data, if presented?

2. Complete the practice questions on your own (4-5 minutes)
   - Rephrase each question in your own mind after reading it to clarify the task.
   - Research the relevant area(s) of the passage or your own knowledge for information related to the task.
   - Respond to the question by choosing the answer that fits your research/calculations *and* satisfies the task.
   - If no answer seems obvious, eliminate answers that fail to have support in the passage or in the relevant science.

3. Analyze your wrong answer choices to the questions you missed.
   - Did you understand the task in the question?
   - What skill type was the question?
   - Did you know the science/formula/concept needed to answer the question?
   - Did you recognize the science being hinted at?
   - Were you able to find information in the passage quickly when you needed it?
   - Were there any necessary scientific concepts you failed to apply to the question?
     - If so, why?
   - If you made a mistake in calculations, have you identified your mistake?

Pancreatic ductal adenocarcinoma (PDAC) is a lethal cancer with extremely poor prognosis. The role of micro RNA (miRNA) in other cancers has been elucidated, but due to high tissue heterogeneity of PDAC, studies have not revealed any particular pattern of miRNA dysregulation.

MiRNAs are small non-coding RNA molecules that direct post-transcriptional regulation of gene expression. Typically, miRNAs are produced either from their own transcriptional units or derived from the introns of coding genes. Both undergo different avenues of processing to produce a miRNA/miRNA* duplex. Only one strand is incorporated into the RNA-induced silencing complex (RISC), which interacts with the mRNA, while the other strand is degraded. For partially complementary miRNAs to recognize their targets, only nucleotides 2 through 8 in the 'seed region' have to be perfectly complementary, located in the 3' untranslated region (UTR). As a result of binding, the mRNA is silenced by translational repression or deadenylation. When there is perfect complementarity, the mRNA is silenced by endonucleolytic cleavage and degradation.

The epithelial-mesenchymal transition (EMT), in which cells lose their polarity and adhesion, is the initial step in tumor metastasis. Epithelial cells are highly ordered and display polarity by adhering to one another via tight junctions, while mesenchymal cells differ in shape and display the capacity for migration. Studies have demonstrated that the miR-200 family, a group of functionally related miRNAs, inhibits EMT by negatively regulating transcription factors ZEB1 and ZEB2. Studies have also shown that the tumor suppressor protein E-cadherin regulates EMT through its role in cell adhesion and maintenance of cell polarity. Experiments were conducted to assess whether miR-200 family expression correlates with the epithelial phenotype in PDAC cell lines, and the results are below:

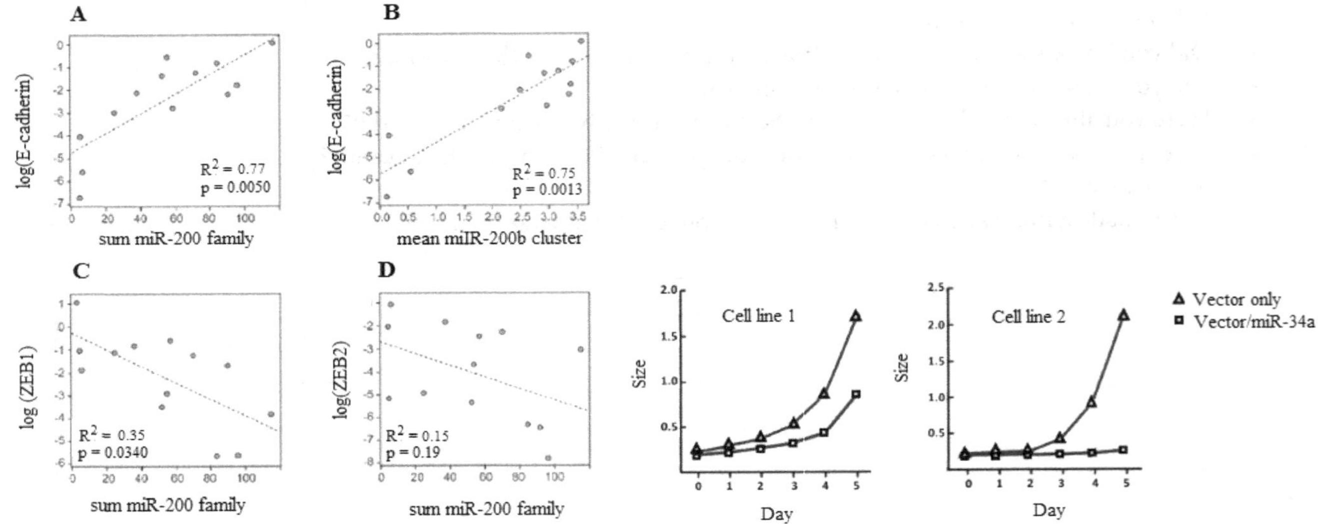

Figure 1 miR-200 family expression vs. E-cadherin, ZEB1, and ZEB2 levels

Figure 2 Growth rates of retrovirally-infected PDAC lines

In prostate cancer cell lines, miR-34a was found to be downregulated and suspected to have a role similar to E-cadherin. A vector was used to reintroduce expression of miR-34a into PDAC lines in order to elucidate its role, and some of the experimental data is shown in Figure 2.

Passage taken from the Next Step Biology and Biochemistry Strategy and Practice book, Timed Section 1, Passage 3

11. Anti-miRs are oligonucleotide analogs that have been used to correct defective miRNA-mRNA interactions. Based on the information given in the passage, which anti-miR would be most effective at silencing the miRNA for the following mRNA transcript?

5'-...CUAGAGUCCCCGGCGCGCCUUUCUGCUGCUGU...-3'

A. 5'-GCUGCUGC-3'
B. 5'-AAAGCAGC-3'
C. 5'-UCCCCGAU-3'
D. 5'-CGCGCCGG-3'

12. The 70 nucleotide hairpin structure of pre-miRNA is an example of secondary structure for nucleic acids. Which of the following structures would be similarly classified?

A. DNA-RNA hybrid
B. α-helix in transmembrane receptors
C. tRNA cloverleaf
D. Disulfide bond in IgG

13. There are certain elements on a plasmid vector that are essential for ensuring expression of a particular miRNA in the transfected cell. Which of the following is NOT an essential component?

A. Bacterial origin of replication
B. Reporter gene
C. Restriction enzyme sites
D. Host transcription initiating sequence

14. Based on the growth rate charts of the retrovirally infected PDAC cell lines, what of the following statements best describes the role of miR-34a?

A. miR-34a expression promotes extensive cell death and necrosis.
B. miR-34a is less effective at promoting cell death in cell line 1.
C. miR-34a exhibits potent antitumorigenic or anti-tumor forming properties in PDAC cell lines.
D. miR-34a is strongly downregulated in a majority of the PDAC cell lines.

15. As defined by the passage, what is necessary for the maintenance of the "epithelial" phenotype?

A. Low levels of miR-34a
B. High levels of ZEB-1 and ZEB-2
C. High levels of E-cadherin
D. Low levels of miR-200

Mechanisms of Development

Cell Specialization

Determination

Differentiation

Tissue Types

Cell Communication

Stem Cell Potency

Stem Cell Generation

Senescence and Aging

Hayflick Limit Theory

Problem-solving Cooldown

16. Researchers discover that as a result of their relative locations on chromosome 14, genes X and Y have much lower than expected recombination rates between them and appear in a similar order when compared to chromosome 16. This can best be explained by:

    A. transgenic genes.
    B. syntenic genes.
    C. chimeric genes.
    D. fusion genes.

17. The female ovum is imaged below after researchers discovered an especially thick matrix surrounding the ovum preventing entry of some of their vectors. This is most likely the:

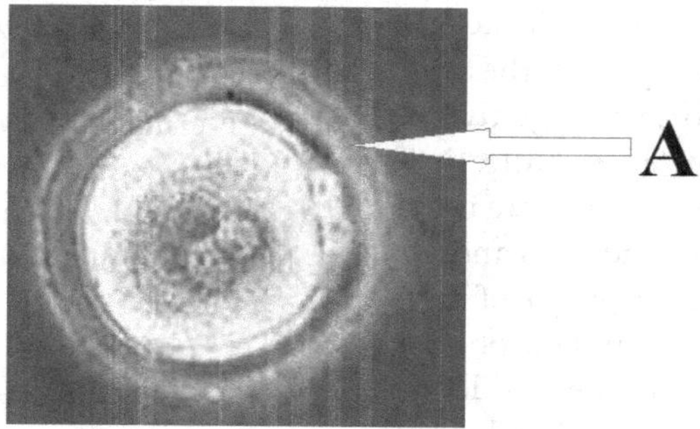

    A. acrosome.
    B. corpus luteum.
    C. zona pellucida.
    D. smooth endoplasmic reticulum.

18. The uptake of DNA materials by cellular transport is:

    A. transduction.
    B. transfection.
    C. conjugation.
    D. transamination.

19. Scientists successfully introduce a protein X-producing gene into a strep pyogenes bacterium. However, several days after successfully detecting protein X all traces of the protein are gone. Which of the following best explain this result?

    A. Stable transfection
    B. Transient transfection
    C. Electroporation
    D. Targeted mutagenesis

20. Which of the following cell types is most likely to line the innermost layer of the jejunum?

    A. Epithelial cells
    B. Adipocytes
    C. Glial cell
    D. Pericyte

Test-like Thinking: CARS Practice Passage

Thy soul was like a star and dwelt apart;
Thou hadst a voice whose sound was like the sea--
Pure as the naked heavens, majestic, free;
So didst thou travel on life's common way
In cheerful godliness: and yet thy heart
The lowliest duties on herself did lay.
[From Wordsworth's "Sonnet on Milton"]

Over the substantial fellowship of artists who have made our literature famous, Shakespeare and Milton tower conspicuously. Separately they represent the ages that produced them; together, they form a suggestive commentary on the two forces that rule humanity, that of impulse and that of fixed purpose. Shakespeare is the poet of impulse, of the loves and hates and fears and jealousies and ambitions that swayed the people of his time. Milton is the poet of steadfast will and purpose: he moves amid the changing impulses of the world, the hopes and fears, regarding them as trivial and momentary things that cannot force a great soul astray from its course.

It is helpful to keep such a comparison in mind while studying the literature of the Elizabethan and Puritan ages. As Shakespeare and Ben Jonson and their company of unrivaled wits made merry at the Mermaid Tavern, a young poet was growing up on the same London street, a poet who would take the Renaissance culture and love of beauty of the time and add to it the monumental moral earnestness of the Puritan. Such a poet, true to Puritan form, must have begun with his own soul, disciplining it, enlightening it, so he could express its beauty in literature. As Milton wrote himself, "He that would hope to write well hereafter in laudable things ought himself to be a true poem; that is, a composition and pattern of the best and most honorable things."

Here was a new proposition in art, suggesting the lofty ideal of Fra Angelico: that before one can write literature, which is itself the expression of the ideal, one must first develop in themselves the ideal human. Because Milton was human, he was compelled to know the best in humanity, and therefore, he studied prolifically, giving his life to music, art and literature, his nights to profound research and meditation. However, as he knew man is more than mortal, he also deeply engaged in, as he called it, "devout prayer to that Eternal Spirit who can enrich with all utterance and knowledge." In this way, Milton was in spirit far beyond the Renaissance, though he did live in the autumn of its glory, associating with its literary masters.

As the old Hebrew poet said, "There is a spirit in man, and the inspiration of the Almighty giveth him understanding." Here is the essential secret of Milton's life and work. It explains his long silences, his years passed without a word, and it explains how, when he did speak, it was like the voice of prophet who begins his speech with a sublime announcement: "The spirit of the Lord is upon me." It is this that helps to explain his style, so sublime and so marked for wonder by every historian of English literature. Essentially, his style was unconsciously sublime because he lived and thought, very consciously, in a sublime atmosphere.

21. Based upon the passage, which of the following statements would the author most likely agree with?

    A. Spiritually, Shakespeare and Milton were absolute equals
    B. Shakespeare and Milton may be equally considered the greatest artists of English literature
    C. Wordsworth would inarguably claim that Milton had a greater influence upon him than Shakespeare
    D. Shakespeare and Milton studied the liberal arts to a staggering and equal degree

22. Say a young woman wishes to master the piano. If this woman were to subscribe to the notions of Fra Angelico, which of the following best explains how she would approach her practice?

    A. She would need to study the great masters of the instrument, those that "towered conspicuously."
    B. She would need to develop the ideal of humanity in herself by vigorously pursuing the liberal arts.
    C. She would need to practice night and day, and not just on the piano, but on other instruments as well.
    D. She would need to identify what piano music expresses, and then develop that quality in herself.

23. Which of the following is the most likely reason why the author chose to include the poem at the beginning?

    A. To establish an image of a genius poet grounded in humility
    B. To demonstrate the breadth and significance of Milton's influence
    C. To suggest the superiority of Milton over Shakespeare
    D. To illustrate the pain and suffering Milton endured to make his work

24. Based upon the passage, which of the following best accounts for Milton's life and work?

    A. The lofty ideal of Fra Angelico
    B. The division of impulse and fixed purpose
    C. The saying of the old Hebrew poet
    D. Opposition to the Mermaid Tavern contingent

25. According to the passage, all of the following statements are true EXCEPT:

    A. Milton was as prolific a student as he was a writer.
    B. Milton was older than Shakespeare.
    C. Milton grew up on the same street as the Mermaid Tavern.
    D. Ben Jonson had a wit comparable to that of Shakespeare.

To Do After Lesson 19

- ☐ Complete the AAMC Psychological and Sociological Foundations Section Bank (may be split over 2-3 days if needed)
- ☐ Complete Biology QBank 4: Cell Cycle and Development
- ☐ Complete Biochemistry QBank 4: Metabolism

LESSON 20

The Road to Test Day

To Do Before Lesson 20

- ☐ Complete the AAMC Psychological and Sociological Foundations Section Bank (may be split over 2-3 days if needed)
- ☐ Complete Biology QBank 4: Cell Cycle and Development
- ☐ Complete Biochemistry QBank 4: Metabolism

In Lesson 20

Full Length Schedule Review
Using Your Next Step Score Report
Using Your Lessons Learned Journal
Pacing, Endurance and Timing
Test Friendly Habits
Worst-case Scenario CARS
Worst-case Scenario Science
Road to Your exam
Revising Your Schedule
Prioritizing Your Study Materials
Am I Ready?

To Do After Lesson 20

- ☐ Review Lessons Learned Journal, study sheets, and notes
- ☐ Complete Timed Section 6 from the Verbal Practice: 108 Passages book
- ☐ Complete Psychology and Sociology QBank 7: Social Inequality and Experimental Design

Full Length Schedule Review

How many?

How often?

In what order?

Using Your Next Step Score Report

Scaled scores

Results by section

Results by difficulty level

Results by reasoning skills

Results by concept category

Using Your Lessons Learned Journal

Why?

When?

How?

The tipping point

Pacing, Endurance, and Timing

Pacing

Endurance

Timing

Test-friendly Habits

Sleep/wake schedule

Time of practice test

Computer setup

Review time

Pacing guidelines

Meals

Drinks

Worst-case Scenario: CARS Passage 1

Tecumseh's Confederacy existed for less than a decade, but its conflicts with the United States set a pattern that would come to be repeated time again over the subsequent century. Starting with the Battle of Tippecanoe, in which a thousand US troops drove the Lenape and Shawnee from their homes and burned their winter food supplies, and ending with Tecumseh's death amidst the War of 1812, the Confederacy's opposition to the United States was both effective and ultimately futile.

The Confederacy originally began as a crystallization of several tribes around Tecumseh's brother, Tenskwatawa the Prophet. The Prophet had several visions as a young man, and began preaching that whites were children of the Great Serpent. From the very start, the Prophet's teachings defined a pattern for American Indian resistance and nativist movements that would reach its apogee with the Lakota interpretation of the Ghost Dance movement and ultimately the Wounded Knee massacre over 75 years later. These movements were defined by a demonization of whites and any elements of their culture and material goods, a call for a return to traditional lifestyles, and a pan-tribal syncretism. It is in this last point that Tenskwatawa's teachings also revealed the irony typically present in such movements; by having such an overwhelming common enemy in "the whites," American Indian nativist and revivalist movements pushed for a cross-tribal, cross-cultural, and multi-lingual Indian unity that would have previously been unthinkable anywhere in the New World outside the height of the Incan Empire and Aztec Triple Alliance.

The American response to this movement was swift, brutal and sadly all-too-often repeated over the coming century. On November 7, 1811, while Tecumseh and the majority of his warriors were away on a recruiting mission in the southern part of the Indiana territory, Governor (and later President) William Henry Harrison led a force of 1,000 infantry and cavalry to Prophetstown. In the ensuing battle, the US forces killed dozens and burned the settlement to the ground. Although the casualty numbers were relatively low for such conflicts, the loss of their homes and winter stores galvanized the response from the Lenape, Shawnee, Ottowa, Iroquois, and other smaller tribes.

Following the Battle of Tippecanoe, the slow-burning conflict that would later be called Tecumseh's War boiled over into a full conflict, with Tecumseh's Confederacy joining British forces in the War of 1812. The War of 1812 is often seen either as a minor theater in the larger Napoleonic Wars or as a historical oddity fought for unclear reasons that ended with little more than maintenance of the pre-war status quo. For Tecumseh's Confederacy, however, the War represented a fight against an existential threat and that resulted in an end to its existence.

. . . [T]hroughout the prosecution of its conflict with the US and in its resolution, the Confederacy continued to delineate patterns for relations between Indian tribes and US forces. Confederacy forces proved pivotal in several key conflicts throughout the Great Lakes region. The assistance of Confederacy troops provided essential support that allowed the British to capture Fort Detroit early in the war. Continual hit-and-run tactics and guerilla maneuvers just north of the St. Lawrence river pushed US forces into a defensive stance and halted progress into Canadian territory. Without the assistance of Tecumseh's fighters, the British may well have had to cede territory to the US at the end of the conflict. None of these successes, however, ended up mattering to the Indians when Tecumseh died at the Battle of Moraviantown late in 1813. Stripped of its charismatic leader, the Confederacy rapidly fell into disarray and dissolved shortly thereafter. Tecumseh's brother Tenskwatawa the Prophet lived until the late 1830's but was never again able to rally the support found under the Confederacy.

1. Suppose a chief leading a nation of dozens of allied tribes seeks to draw lessons from the history of Tecumseh's Confederacy. Such a chief would likely:
   A. entirely avoid conflict with US military forces and stick with negotiating treaties to protect tribal lands.
   B. seek allegiance with disaffected groups within the US military or larger US society.
   C. encourage individual tribes to always remain on the move and not invest in settlements like Prophetstown that could be attacked.
   D. work to ensure that many high-ranking and charismatic lieutenants are well known throughout the Confederacy and able to take command.

2. The passage implies which of the following about Tecumseh and Tenskwatawa the Prophet?
   A. Tecumseh himself was the only person needed to form and then maintain the Confederacy.
   B. Had Tenswatawa the Prophet been killed at Moraviantown instead of Tecumseh, the Confederacy would have fallen apart even faster.
   C. Both were needed to form and then maintain their Confederacy.
   D. Had Tecumseh been present during Harrison's attack on Prophetstown, the US forces would have been routed and Prophetstown preserved.

3. The author's attitude about the treatment that American Indian tribes saw from US military forces can best be described as:
   A. mildly disapproving but accepting of its necessity.
   B. strongly disapproving.
   C. neutral.
   D. enthusiastic about its efficacy if less so about its methods.

4. The passage implies that the greatest benefit coming from Tecumseh's Confederacy was felt by:
   A. the British.
   B. Tenskwatawa the Prophet.
   C. the US government.
   D. the Lakota tribes who practiced the Ghost Dance.

5. The most appropriate summary of the author's main idea is:
   A. Interactions between US government forces and Indian tribes were characterized by conflict, often with the Indians suffering greater losses and this pattern of interaction was typified by the history of Tecumseh's Confederacy.
   B. While Tecumseh was able to rally support against the US by uniting many different tribes, his movement ultimately failed because it relied on the existence of a single, charismatic leader.
   C. Given the huge disparity in numbers between any individual tribe and the US military, the only way for American Indians to successfully fight back was through cross-tribal unity.
   D. The War of 1812 may have been a less-important event in the history of the US, UK, and Canada, but to many American Indian tribes in the Great Lakes region, it was their defining conflict.

Worst-case Scenario CARS Passage 2

What a capital loses when it ceases to be the seat of sovereign power are those essential qualities that differentiated it from other urban forms. Underpinning any typology of capital cities will be their status as the primary spatial referent of sovereignty. Thus Mackenzie King, then Prime Minister of Canada, described Ottawa to the Parliament as "the focal point...to which all eyes of the Dominion are turned." As Daum and Mauch write, "all capitals share the fact that they are privileged vis-à-vis other cities within the same political system." They describe a capital as a "multiple hinge [that] mediates between its urban space, the surrounding society, and the nation, no less than between the nation-state and the international world." Linguistically, officially multilingual capitals like Ottawa act as a hinge between recognized language groups. They stand in also as synecdoche for their nations in news reports that say "Washington demands" such and such or "Ottawa announced" this or that.

As Piano observes above, a city is self-organizing as well as planned and it carries out its own message in a manner akin to a linguistic 'performative.' In a capital city, this is expressed in the pattern of government organization, architecture, urban planning, state pageantry, commemorations, religion, historiography, and even in protests and other expressions of popular culture. National capitals are special zones of national representation and, as argued above, they are monumental and legacy forming. On the other hand, the signature of a capital also is associated with its unconscious 'style' of civility, as expressed in various latent cultural forms that may or may not be reflected in the city's plan, national institutions and architecture. When abandonment occurs, and these distinctive qualities of a capital evaporate or are transferred to the new power center, one expects latencies to emerge.

Williamsburg's abandonment as Virginia's colonial capital had its precise hour. On June 8th, 1775, the last Royal Governor, the unpopular Lord Dunmore, vacated his official residence to join his family on board the HMS Fowey lying nearby in the York River. That morning of strange emptiness in the Governor's Palace effectively marked the end of Williamsburg's service as a capital of British imperial power. From 1699 onward it had been at once a nerve center of British rule in America as well as the intellectual cradle of revolutionary resistance, fostering the emergence of key founding figures such as Thomas Jefferson, Patrick Henry, and George Washington. By the end of the war, following Lord Cornwallis's surrender to Washington at nearby Yorktown in 1781, the victors had already moved the Virginian capital to its current location in Richmond and Williamsburg had begun its period of decay.

Its near miraculous resurrection as a town-sized historical museum in 1926 followed almost a century and half of obscurity and neglect. To visitors during the intervening period it seemed that the structures that marked it as a former capital had all but disappeared and that the town would be venerated only in the nation's written history. Restored to the halo of official Washington's grandeur by the fervor of a local cleric and the intense philanthropic interest of John D. Rockefeller Jr., it became both the living tomb of British gubernatorial power and the dead center of the founding of American democracy.

6. According to the passage, "Washington" in a news report that says "Washington arbitrates cease-fire in Sudan" refers to:

   A. Washington state.
   B. the President of the United States.
   C. the United States of America.
   D. Washington, DC.

7. Why does the author employ the oxymoron "living tomb" to describe Williamsburg, VA?

   A. To underscore the fact that it lost its capital status and was nearly lost to obscurity.
   B. To explain how it functions as a historical museum.
   C. To highlight the fact Williamsburg contains the tomb of the last Royal Governor, Lord Dunmore.
   D. To complete a metaphor about the death of colonial power in America.

8. The passage implies that all of the following are special roles of a capital city EXCEPT:

   A. to represent their country on the international stage.
   B. to serve as monuments to the legacy of their nation.
   C. to be the site of sovereign power.
   D. to be economic engines for their nation.

9. Which of the following is offered in the passage as support for the statement that "all capitals share the fact that they are privileged vis-à-vis other cities within the same political system"?

   I. A quotation from a politician
   II. The abandonment of Williamsburg at the end of British colonial rule
   III. A linguistic argument

   A. I only
   B. I and III only
   C. II and III only
   D. I, II, and III

10. Chichen Itza was once a Mayan regional capital in what is now Yucatán, Mexico. It was conquered by Spain in the 16th century and turned into a cattle ranch. It was rediscovered and excavated by a Mexican-American archeological partnership. Today the Mayan ruins attract more than 1.4 million tourists per year. How does this example affect the author's thesis?

    A. It weakens the author's thesis, because Chichen Itza was conquered rather than abandoned by a colonial power.
    B. It strengthens the author's thesis, because Chichen Itza is now a "living museum."
    C. It strengthens the author's thesis, because Chichen Itza's buildings no longer have administrative significance.
    D. It is irrelevant to the author's thesis, because Chichen Itza was founded a thousand years before Williamsburg, VA.

11. Suppose the federal government were to move today from Washington, DC to New York, NY. According to the author, which of the following scenarios would be LEAST likely to occur over the next 150 years?

    A. The White House is converted into a boutique hotel.
    B. The number of protests outside the Capitol decreases.
    C. The Supreme Court remains in Washington at 1 First St NE.
    D. The city undertakes a rebranding campaign to market its monuments and museums.

12. Which of the following is most analogous to Piano's characterization of the capital city as described in the 2nd paragraph?

    A. An artificial intelligence (AI) chatbot
    B. A town-sized historical museum
    C. Improvisational theatre
    D. A video game

Worst-case Scenario CARS Passage 3

Said Prof. Pfleiderer to the writer in the winter of 1897: "I am sorry to know that the Japanese are deficient in religious nature." In an elaborate article entitled, "Wanted, a Religion," a missionary describes the three so-called religions of Japan, Buddhism, Confucianism, and Shintoism, and shows to his satisfaction that none of these has the essential characteristics of religion.

The impression that the Japanese people are not religious is due to various facts. The first is that for about three hundred years the intelligence of the nation has been dominated by Confucian thought. tendency of Confucian ethics is to leave the gods severely alone, although their existence is not absolutely denied. When Confucianism became popular in Japan, the educated part of the nation broke away from Buddhism, which, for nearly a thousand years, had been universally dominant. To them Buddhism seemed superstitious in the extreme, which no true religion needs. It was not uncommon for them to criticize it severely. For this reason, beyond doubt, has Western agnosticism found so easy an entrance into Japan. Yet this statement implies that agnosticism is new to Japan.

And various other considerations demand our notice. Many Westerners have exceedingly shallow conceptions of the real nature of religion or the part it plays in the development of society and of the individual. But we do not pronounce the West irreligious because of ignorant or irreverent utterances. We must not judge the religious many by the irreligious few.

Particular beliefs and practices of religion have indeed changed and passed away, even in Christianity. But the essentially religious nature of man has re-asserted itself in every case. The outward expressions of that nature have thereby only become freer from elements of error and superstition. Exactly this is taking place in Japan to-day. The apparent irreligion of to-day is the groundwork of the purer religion of to-morrow.

If the Japanese are emotional and sentimental, we should expect them to be, perhaps more than most peoples, religious. This expectation is not disappointed by a study of their history. The universality of the respect and adoration, not to say love, bestowed throughout the ages of history on the "Kami" (the multitudinous Gods of Shintoism), is a standing witness to the depth of the religious feeling in the Japanese heart. True, it is associated with the sentiments of love of ancestors and country, with filial piety and loyalty; but these, so far from lowering the religion, make it more truly religious.

[Adapted from *Evolution of the Japanese: Social and Psychic*, by Sidney L. Gulic, 1903.]

Passage taken from the Next Step online QBank

13. Based on the passage, it can be assumed that one of the reasons Confucianism is not considered a religion is:

    A. that it fails to make a definite ruling on the status of the supernatural.
    B. its unfriendliness to established religions such as Buddhism.
    C. that it does not definitely accept the existence of gods.
    D. its interpretation of the Kami.

14. According to the passage, irreligiosity in Japan can be traced at least as far back as:

    A. the advent of Shintoism.
    B. the arrival of Western agnosticism.
    C. the first pushback against Christian missionaries.
    D. the arrival of Confucianism.

15. According to the passage, which of the following is a necessary element of true religion?

    A. Superstition
    B. Consistency in tradition and beliefs
    C. A strong consensus
    D. Love

16. The passage author likely would NOT agree with which of the following statements about religion?

    A. Religious convictions remain a constant anchor in a changing cultural landscape.
    B. Despite a sometimes vocal and ignorant minority, the West is by and large a religious bastion.
    C. The purest religions have shed their old superstitions.
    D. Religion is integral to the human spirit.

17. In China, a drop-off in religious belief coincided with political changes in the mid-20th century. According to the passage, this could be interpreted as:

    A. a natural progression towards agnosticism.
    B. a coincidental result of Confucianism's periodic return to Chinese fashion.
    C. due to the fundamentally irreligious nature of Asian societies reasserting itself.
    D. a transition period to a purer religion, free of outmoded beliefs.

18. Which of the following, if true, would most weaken the author's argument about the "essentially religious nature of man?"

    A. Those countries with the longest traditions of religious belief have the highest rates of religious identification.
    B. A longitudinal study finds that, without regular reinforcement, religious people lose their faith at markedly higher rate than agnostics or atheists spontaneously find faith.
    C. Over time, every day and household superstitions are found to become less prevalent.
    D. An increase in the worldwide percentage of people with religious faith can be attributed to the two fastest-growing religions.

19. The author would likely agree that, far in the future:

    A. religious conviction will be essentially universal.
    B. religion will have become effectively extinct.
    C. today's religious plurality will persist, though the relative frequencies are likely to shift.
    D. beliefs within nations will have homogenized, with blocks of both faithful and atheistic countries.

Review of Time Spent

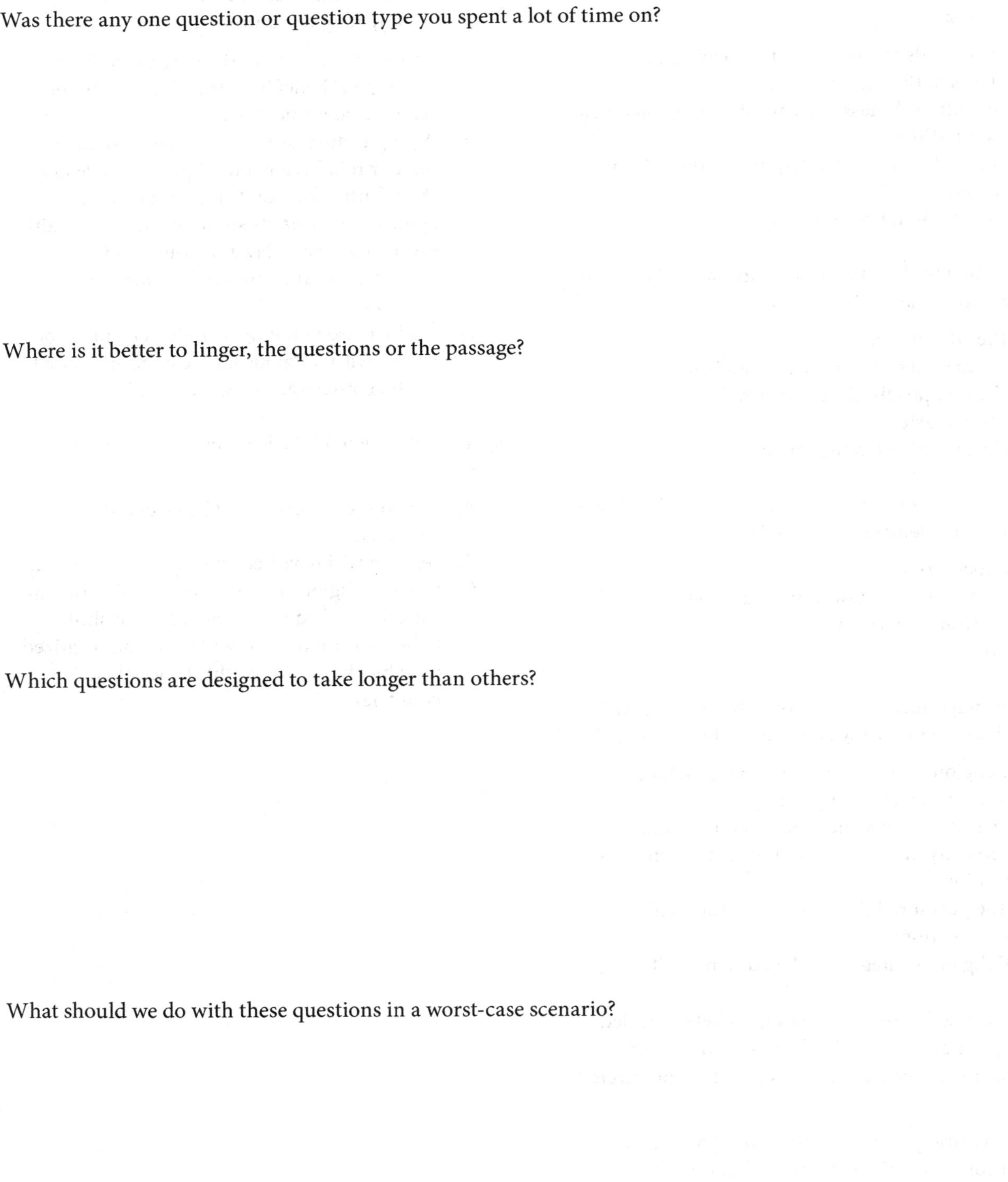

Was there any one question or question type you spent a lot of time on?

Where is it better to linger, the questions or the passage?

Which questions are designed to take longer than others?

What should we do with these questions in a worst-case scenario?

Worst-case Scenario: Science

You will now have the opportunity to take 3 passages, timed. But to simulate a real crisis scenario, you will only have 4 minutes for each passage (12 min total).

As you go through each passage, prioritize where you think your most efficient points will come from. Making tough decisions regarding priorities will be a big part of being both a medical student AND a physician.

After you are done, we will review the passage, questions, and see how we can prioritize quicker more efficient points when time is tight.

Typical Timing

Passage 3-4 minutes

Questions 4-5 minutes

Worst-case Scenario Timing

Passage 1 minute

Questions 3 minutes

Worst-case Scenario: Science Passage 1

Memory formation can be divided into four steps; encoding, consolidation, storage, and retrieval.

Encoding begins when a sensory perception is brought to attention; these sensations are integrated together in the hippocampus, where, if the stimuli is judged sufficiently important, it can be committed to long-term memory. This begins with the formation of a memory trace, a physiological change in brain physiology whose exact nature has yet to be observed. There are three sensory types of encoding: auditory, visual, and tactile. Semantic encoding is the process of encoding sensory input in association with a particular context. It has been observed that short-term memory encoding relies heaviest on acoustic encoding, while long-term memory is more dependent on visual encoding.

Consolidation stabilizes the memory trace once it has been created. It is thought to consist of two processes, synaptic and systemic consolidation. In synaptic consolidation, neurological rewiring occurs in the hippocampus to solidify the memory, while systemic consolidation refers to the process by which the memory, in time, becomes independent of the hippocampus. Consolidation occurs by the process of potentiation, whereby neurons that fire in concert become associated and more likely to fire together in the future. Sleep is thought to be key for this process, as sleeping patterns of activation of brain areas involved in learning frequently resemble those from the course of the previous day, suggesting a process of neurological reinforcement is taking place.

Experimental evidence has shown that long-term memory storage is widely distributed throughout the brain. Rats who have been trained to run a maze can still navigate it even with large portions of the brain removed. Karl Pribram observed that brain-damaged humans who had sections of brain removed did not suffer the loss of particular memories, but instead suffered increasing haziness of memory dependent on how much brain matter was lost. If potentiation of neurons during systemic consolidation is widespread, memory traces must be encoded in multiple cortical areas. This implies that memory is not actually "stored" like a file in a drawer, but is reconstructed as needed.

When retrieving memories, the brain is activated in a pattern similar to what occurred during the response to the original event, but awareness of the retriever's current conditions is now present. Thus, in memory retrieval, long-term memory is transformed into a short-term memory, where it can be accessed by the conscious mind, and subsequently it is re-encoded, re-consolidated and stored again in long-term memory, which further potentiates the neurons involved. This process by which memory is re-stored can result in modification of memories with information subsequently learned, and thus the content (and accuracy) of a memory can change over time.

1. Which neurotransmitter is LEAST likely to be involved in the process of potentiation for long-term memory storage?

   A. Dopamine
   B. Serotonin
   C. GABA
   D. Acetylcholine

2. A scientist is attempting to determine if interfering sensory stimuli can disrupt the process of short-term memory formation. What type of stimuli is likely to be most effective for this purpose?

   A. A series of rapidly flashing lights
   B. A noxious odor
   C. Repeated poking by a research assistant
   D. A recording of various loud noises

3. During REM sleep, motor cortex activation is significantly higher than during other stages of sleep. This suggests that REM sleep is key to the consolidation of:

   A. declarative memory.
   B. procedural memory.
   C. episodic memory.
   D. semantic memory.

4. Visual memory formation would be LEAST likely to be impaired if damage occurred to which of the following?

   A. Hippocampus
   B. Occipital lobe
   C. Thalamus
   D. Frontal lobe

5. Based on the passage's description of how memory works, learning which of the following is likely to be most difficult under the influence of alcohol?

   A. A new dance move
   B. A new acquaintance's name
   C. A new telephone number
   D. A new acquaintance's face

Worst-case Scenario: Science Passage 2

Stress management is a common issue for all hospital staff. In such a demanding work environment, physical, psychological, and social factors can all contribute to increased stress. One particular concern for the field of nursing in particular is the role of empathy in both care quality and stress management. The ability to empathize with patients and their struggles could be expected to motivate nursing staff to offer more dedicated and diligent care, resulting in a positive impact on job performance. At the same time, empathy for patients could be expected to increase the burden of negative emotions like worry and grief that nursing staff experience, contributing to stress and emotional burnout, with negative consequences for patient care.

A hospital was interested in discerning how empathy in nursing staff affected care in their wards. Patients were given a questionnaire to assess their opinion on the quality of their care. Nurses were given a questionnaire to assess their stress levels, as well as the nature of their empathetic response to patients. Their empathetic response to patients was assessed on three dimensions: emotional contagion (the tendency for nurses to sympathetically share what patients are feeling, such as pain or grief); emotional concern (the tendency for nurses to be concerned about a patient in a way that does not involve shared emotion, such as feeling concern for a suffering patient); and communicative responsiveness (the ability to communicate with patients about painful or sensitive topics effectively). These factors were measured using a series of statements that nurses or patients would rate from 1-5. The results are displayed below in Table 1.

Table 1 Correlation between scores on stress, patient care, and empathy measures. * denotes $p < .05$

	Emotional Contagion	Emotional Concern	Communicative Responsiveness
Patient's opinion of care quality	0.55*	0.62*	0.63*
Nurse's own stress level	0.46*	0.13	-0.27*

A follow-up analysis was then conducted to assess the effects of stress on various care quality measures. Data from the previous study was combined with administrative data provided by other departments of the hospital regarding individual patients and their nurses. These results are displayed in Table 2.

Table 2 Correlation between nurse's stress level and various patient care quality measures. All correlations resulted in $p < 0.05$

	Patient's Opinion of Care Quality	Patient Length of Stay	Nurse's Days Absent over Last Year
Nurse's own stress level	-0.36	0.31	0.33

6. Which of the following is a confounding variable that might directly affect the relationship between nurses' own stress levels and their patients' length of stay in the hospital?

   A. Stress coping strategies of nurse
   B. Emotional expressiveness of patient
   C. Severity of patient illness
   D. Nurse communicative responsiveness

7. Based on the data presented in the passage, what type of training might be most effective at improving patient outcomes?

   A. Training intended to improve nurses' ability to share patient emotions
   B. Training intended to improve nurses' ability to feel concern without sharing patient emotions
   C. Training intended to improve nurse's work-life balance
   D. Training intended to improve nurse's skills at discussing sensitive or emotional topics with patients

8. In a more biologically-oriented study, emotional contagion could be best operationalized by monitoring:

   A. cortisol levels in the blood.
   B. limbic system activation in the brain.
   C. oxytocin levels in the brain.
   D. sensory neuron activation.

9. Paragraph 1 states that "The ability to empathize with patients and their struggles could be expected to motivate nursing staff to offer more dedicated and diligent care." Another way to say this is that increased empathy might be expected to cause increased:

   A. self-efficacy.
   B. altruism.
   C. social facilitation.
   D. emotional concern.

10. A preliminary study at another hospital suggests that emotional contagion may work both ways: that patients may also share the emotions of nurses. What study would provide the strongest support for this theory?

    I. Patients of stressed nurses often have hypertension
    II. Patients of stressed nurses are found to experience lowered white blood cell counts compared to those of non-stressed nurses
    III. Patients of stressed nurses are found to experience trouble sleeping

    A. I only
    B. II only
    C. I and II only
    D. I, II, and III

Worst-case Scenario: Science Passage 3

In recent years there have been a series of findings in social science pointing to a greater role for biology in determining what have traditionally been considered "cultural" attitudes such as racial prejudice. In this case, the research is inextricably linked with the biology of emotion. People tend to rate socioeconomic groups along two dimensions: warmth (the degree of friendliness, sincerity, and trustworthiness they perceive in the group) and competence (the skillfulness and capability of the group). These judgments are tied to several emotions: disgust, fear, pity, pride, and envy. Any genetic differences that affect individuals' expression of these emotions might in turn be expected then to affect individual's expression of racial or cultural prejudice.

Other genetic factors may affect not the presence, but the expression of, racial or cultural prejudice. In recent years, open expression of prejudice has become subject to increasingly heavy social sanction. Individuals with prejudices who wish to be successful must disguise their opinions in social company in order to avoid this sanction. A study was conducted to determine the interactions of these variables on expressed racial prejudice.

Table 1 Correlation between emotional variables and prejudice expressed in the different discussion groups. $*p < 0.05$.

	Sensitivity of Fear Response	Sensitivity of Disgust Response
Prejudicial Statements Made	0.64*	0.57*

Subjects were exposed to situations in order to score the sensitivity of their fear and disgust responses in non-social contexts. Researchers also assessed their level of self-monitoring in social situations by asking how the subject would act in a given social situation. Finally, subjects participated in a discussion group ostensibly on politics, but was actually intended to measure the racial and cultural prejudice expressed by participants. Subjects were informed of some characteristics of their discussion group, such as their level of tolerance of racial and cultural diversity. Degree of prejudice was assessed by the number of statements judged to be prejudicial by a research confederate present in the discussions; the results are shown in Tables 1 and 2.

Table 2 Number of prejudicial statements in different discussion groups for high- and low-self-monitoring subjects.

	High Self-monitoring Capacity	Low Self-monitoring Capacity
Made in High-prejudice Group	3.3	3.5
Made in Low-prejudice Group	0.8	2.9

11. Which component of the limbic system would be likely to show increased activation in the people who made more prejudicial statements?

    A. Septal nuclei
    B. Hippocampus
    C. Amygdala
    D. Hypothalamus

12. The social sanctions faced upon displaying prejudice are most likely to be described as:

    A. stereotyping.
    B. stigmatization.
    C. deindividuation.
    D. reinforcement.

13. Based on the passage, which of the following individuals is most likely to voice prejudicial statements in an *unprejudiced* group?

    A. A subject who displays little response to images of slugs and spiders but is highly concerned with her public image
    B. A subject who displays little regard for the feelings of others and who is unfazed by pictures of snakes and insects
    C. A subject who is highly intimidated by wasps and scorpions but agrees with the statement "I always try to put my best foot forward."
    D. A subject who is extremely disgusted by worms and cockroaches and agrees with the statement "I'm not good at keeping up appearances."

14. Which of the following 'selves' is NOT being self-monitored in this experiment?

    A. Ideal self
    B. Tactical self
    C. Front-stage self
    D. Ought self

15. The subjects were not informed of the purpose of the discussion groups as this would likely harm the study's:

    A. internal validity.
    B. external validity.
    C. reliability.
    D. reproducibility.

Review of Time Spent

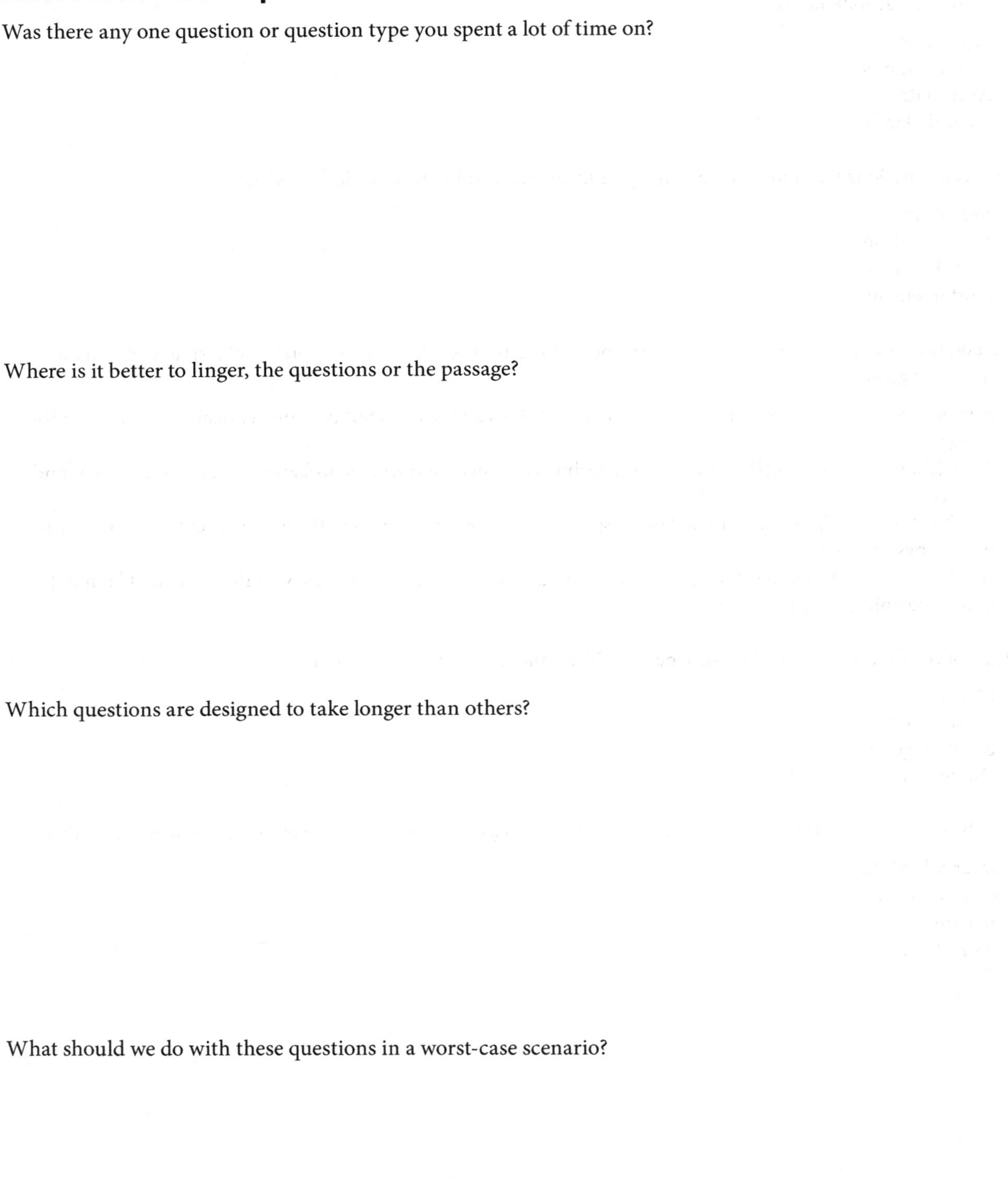

Was there any one question or question type you spent a lot of time on?

Where is it better to linger, the questions or the passage?

Which questions are designed to take longer than others?

What should we do with these questions in a worst-case scenario?

Prioritizing Your Study materials

Next Step Full Lengths

Next Step Timed Sections

Next Step QBank

Official Exams

Other Practice Materials

Content Materials

Am I Ready?

What should I look for....

3 Weeks Out

2 Weeks Out

1 Week Out

The Road to Your Exam

GET YOUR BODY ON TEST DAY RHYTHM!

SUNDAY	MONDAY	TUESDAY	WEDNESDAY	THURSDAY	FRIDAY	SATURDAY
					Test Day	

As soon as you possibly can:

Revise Your Study Schedule

If you have a month or more:

I.
II.
III.
IV.
V.

If you have only 2-3 weeks:

I.
II.
III.

The Final Week

Exactly one week before test day:

- Go visit the testing location
- Re-take the Next Step diagnostic test
- Pick your "I Hate It!!" topic for each section and practice that

The Day Before

- No MCAT!
- No MCAT!
- Really. Seriously. No MCAT.
- Have fun (but, you know, not TOO much fun)
- Double-check to make sure you have everything you need
- Get to bed on time

Test Day

MCAT checklist:

On Test Day:

During the test itself:

- Should I void my score?

After Test Day

To Do After Lesson 20

- ☐ Review Lessons Learned Journal, study sheets, and notes
- ☐ Complete Timed Section 6 from the Verbal Practice: 108 Passages book
- ☐ Complete Psychology and Sociology QBank 7: Social Inequality and Experimental Design

APPENDIX A: COURSE HOMEWORK LIST

To Do Before Lesson 1

- ☐ Watch the Orientation Video for your online syllabus
- ☐ Set up your online Study Plan (found by clicking the "Study Plan" tab at the top of your nextstepmcat.com home page)
- ☐ Take the MCAT Diagnostic half-length exam under TIMED conditions
- ☐ Visit the AAMC website to review MCAT procedures and timelines

To Do After Lesson 1

- ☐ Take the MCAT Diagnostic Exam under TIMED conditions (if not already done)
    - Review the Diagnostic Exam
- ☐ Read Verbal and Quantitative Chapters 1 and 2
- ☐ Read Chemistry and Organic Chemistry Chapter 1
    - Complete the practice passages in these chapters

To Do After Lesson 2

- ☐ Read and complete Verbal and Quantitative Reasoning Chapters 3 and 4
    - Determine the correct CARS reading strategy for you
- ☐ Read Physics Chapters 1 and 2
- ☐ Read Chemistry and Organic Chemistry Chapters 2 and 3
- ☐ Read Biology Chapters 1 and 2

To Do After Lesson 3

- ☐ Read Chemistry and Organic Chemistry Chapters 4 and 5
- ☐ Read Physics Chapters 3 and 4
- ☐ Read Verbal and Quantitative Reasoning Chapters 5 and 6
- ☐ Read Biology Chapters 3 and 4

To Do After Lesson 4

- ☐ Read Biochemistry Chapters 1 and 2
- ☐ Read General Chemistry and Organic Chemistry Chapter 6
- ☐ Read Physics Chapters 5 and 6
- ☐ Complete Biology QBank 3: Eukaryotic and Prokaryotic Cells

To Do After Lesson 5

- ☐ Read Physics Chapters 7 and 8
- ☐ Read Verbal and Quantitative Reasoning Chapters 7 and 8
- ☐ Read General Chemistry and Organic Chemistry Chapter 7
- ☐ Complete Physics QBank 1: Motion, Force, and Work

To Do After Lesson 6

- ☐ Read General Chemistry and Organic Chemistry Chapters 9 and 10
- ☐ Read Biology Chapters 5 and 6
- ☐ Read Biochemistry Chapters 3 and 4
- ☐ Complete Organic Chemistry QBank 1: Stereochemistry, Alkanes, and Alcohols

To Do After Lesson 7

- ☐ Read Biochemistry Chapters 5 and 6
- ☐ Read Psychology and Sociology Chapters 1, 2, and 3
- ☐ Complete Biochemistry QBank 3: Amino Acids and Bioenergetics

To Do After Lesson 8

- ☐ Read Psychology and Sociology Chapters 4, 5, and 6
- ☐ Read Biology Chapters 7 and 8
- ☐ Complete Psychology and Sociology QBank 1: Sensation and Consciousness

To Do After Lesson 9

- ☐ Read Biochemistry Chapters 7 and 8
- ☐ Read Chemistry and Organic Chemistry Chapters 11 and 12
- ☐ Complete Biology QBank 2: Gene Expression and Classical Genetics

To Do After Lesson 10

- [ ] Read General Chemistry and Organic Chemistry Chapter 8
- [ ] Read Psychology and Sociology Chapters 7 and 8
- [ ] Read Biology Chapters 9 and 10
- [ ] Complete Chemistry QBank 1: Atoms and Reactions

To Do After Lesson 11

- [ ] Read Psychology and Sociology Chapters 9 and 10
- [ ] Read Biochemistry Chapters 9 and 10
- [ ] Read Physics Chapter 9
- [ ] Complete Psychology and Sociology QBank 5: Sociological Approaches and Culture

To Do After Lesson 12

- [ ] Read Physics Chapter 10
- [ ] Read Biology Chapters 11 and 12
- [ ] Complete Physics QBank 2: Waves, Fluids, and Electrostatics

To Do After Lesson 13

- [ ] Read Psychology and Sociology Chapters 11 and 12
- [ ] Read Biochemistry Chapters 11 and 12
- [ ] Complete Timed Section 1 from the Verbal Practice: 108 Passages book
- [ ] Complete the Chemical and Physical Foundations section from the AAMC Online Official Guide at e-mcat.com

To Do After Lesson 14

- [ ] Complete Full Timed Section 2 from the Verbal Practice: 108 Passages book
- [ ] Complete the Biological and Biochemical Foundations section from the AAMC Online Official Guide at e-mcat.com
- [ ] Complete Psychology and Sociology QBank 4: Identity, Disorders, and Groups

To Do After Lesson 15

- [ ] Complete Full Timed Section 3 from the Verbal Practice: 108 Passages book
- [ ] Complete the Psychological and Sociological Foundations section from the AAMC Online Official Guide at e-mcat.com
- [ ] Complete Biology QBank 5: Nervous and Endocrine Systems

To Do After Lesson 16

- [ ] Complete the Critical Analysis and Reasoning Skills section from the AAMC Online Official Guide at e-mcat.com
- [ ] Complete Chemistry QBank 2: Solutions, Acids, and Electrochemistry
- [ ] Complete Chemistry QBank 3: Bonding and Phases

To Do After Lesson 17

- ☐ Complete Full Timed Section 4 from the Verbal Practice: 108 Passages book
- ☐ Complete the AAMC Chemical and Physical Foundations Section Bank (may be split over 2-3 days if needed)
- ☐ Complete Biochemistry QBank 2: Biotechnology and Analysis

To Do After Lesson 18

- ☐ Complete Full Timed Section 5 from the Verbal Practice: 108 Passages book
- ☐ Complete the AAMC Biological and Biochemical Foundations Section Bank (may be split over 2-3 days if needed)
- ☐ Complete Physics QBank 3: Sound and Light

To Do After Lesson 19

- ☐ Complete the AAMC Psychological and Sociological Foundations Section Bank (may be split over 2-3 days if needed)
- ☐ Complete Biology QBank 4: Cell Cycle and Development
- ☐ Complete Biochemistry QBank 4: Metabolism

To Do After Lesson 20

- ☐ Review Lessons Learned Journal, study sheets, and notes
- ☐ Complete Timed Section 6 from the Verbal Practice: 108 Passages book
- ☐ Complete Psychology and Sociology QBank 7: Social Inequality and Experimental Design

APPENDIX B: MCAT RESOURCE LIST

Next Step MCAT Review Book Series

MCAT Biochemistry

MCAT Biology

MCAT Chemistry and Organic Chemistry

MCAT Physics

MCAT Psychology and Sociology

MCAT Verbal, Quantitative, and Research Methods

Next Step Additional Practice Books

MCAT QBook

MCAT Verbal Practice: 108 passages for the new CARS Section

Next Step Online Practice Items

MCAT Science Diagnostic Exam

Half-Length MCAT Diagnostic Exam

MCAT Physics QBank

MCAT Biochemistry QBank

MCAT Biology QBank

MCAT Chemistry QBank

MCAT Psychology/Sociology QBank

MCAT Organic Chemistry QBank

Next Step MCAT Class Videos

Lesson 1 Video

Lesson 2 Video

Lesson 3 Video

Lesson 4 Video

Lesson 5 Video

Lesson 6 Video

Lesson 7 Video

Lesson 8 Video

Lesson 9 Video

Lesson 10 Video

Lesson 11 Video

Lesson 12 Video

Lesson 13 Video

Lesson 14 Video

Lesson 15 Video

Lesson 16 Video

Lesson 17 Video

Lesson 18 Video

Lesson 19 Video

Lesson 20 Video

Next Step Express Class Videos

Express Lesson Videos 1 - 15

Next Step MCAT Content Review Videos

Chemical and Physical Foundations

Acid-Base Chemistry

Alcohols and Phenols

Atomic and Nuclear Phenomena

Bonding and Intermolecular Forces

Buffers and Titrations

Carbohydrates

Carboxylic Acids and Derivatives

Circuits and Ohm's Law

Complex Circuits

Doppler Effect

Electrochemical Cells

Electron Configuration and Quantum Numbers

Electrostatics 1, 2

Equilibrium

Figure Interpretation in the Hard Sciences

Fluids 1, 2, 3

Formal Charge, Resonance, and VSEPR

Heat and Phase Changes

Ideal Gas Law

Isomers 1, 2

Lenses and Mirrors

Limiting Reagent and Stoichiometry

Magnetism

Math Skills 1

Math Skills 2

Mechanical Advantage

Organic Chem Lab Techniques

Periodic Motion

Periodic Trends

Redox Reactions

Reflection and Refraction

Resonance and Harmonics

Rotational Motion

Scientific Method and Data Interpretation

Solubility

Special Forces: Gravity, Friction, and Drag

Spectroscopy

Substitution and Elimination

Thermodynamics

Translational Motion

Waves

Work and Energy

Biological and Biochemical Foundations

Acid-Base Properties of Amino Acids

Amino Acid Structure and Properties

Amino Acid Titrations and Isoelectric Focusing

Bioenergetics

Bohr Effect in Hemoglobin

Chromosome Organization

Cofactors, Coenzymes, and Vitamins

Crossing Over and Linked Genes

Cytoskeleton

DNA Techniques

Electron Transport Chain

Electrophoresis and SDS-PAGE

Embryology

Enzyme Kinetics

Enzyme Types and Properties

G Protein-Coupled Receptors

Glycolysis

Gluconeogenesiss

Kidney Structure and Function

Kidney: Regulation of Water Balance

Krebs Cycle

Lipid Metabolism

Meiosis

Membrane Transport

Menstrual Cycle and Hormonal Control of Reproduction

Mitosis

Muscle

Nervous System Divisions

Neurons and Signal Transduction

Peptide and Steroid Hormones

Plasma Membrane Composition

Post-Transcriptional Modification

Prokaryotic Gene Regulation

Protein Stability

Protein Structure and Denaturation

Sex-Linked Genes and Inheritance

The Bicarbonate Buffer System

Types of Immunity

Types of Inheritance

Types of Mutations

Psycholgical and Sociological Foundations

Attitudes

Bias, Prejudice, and Discrimination

Central Nervous System

Cognition

Conditioning

Demographics

Emotion and Stress

Experimental Design 1, 2

Figure Interpretation in the Social Sciences

Group Psychology 1, 2

Memory 1, 2

Perception

Psychological Development

Psychological Disorders

Sleep

Social Change

Social Inequality

Status, Roles, and Groups

Theoretical Approaches to Sociology and Culture

Next Step Section Exams

Chemical and Physical Foundations

Full-Length Exam 6 Chemical and Physical Foundations Section Exam

Full-Length Exam 7 Chemical and Physical Foundations Section Exam

Full-Length Exam 8 Chemical and Physical Foundations Section Exam

Full-Length Exam 9 Chemical and Physical Foundations Section Exam

Full-Length Exam 10 Chemical and Physical Foundations Section Exam

Critical Analysis and Reasoning

Full-Length Exam 6 Critical Analysis and Reasoning Section Exam

Full-Length Exam 7 Critical Analysis and Reasoning Section Exam

Full-Length Exam 8 Critical Analysis and Reasoning Section Exam

Full-Length Exam 9 Critical Analysis and Reasoning Section Exam

Full-Length Exam 10 Critical Analysis and Reasoning Section Exam

Biological and Biochemical Foundations Foundations

Full-Length Exam 6 Biological and Biochemical Foundations Section Exam

Full-Length Exam 7 Biological and Biochemical Foundations Section Exam

Full-Length Exam 8 Biological and Biochemical Foundations Section Exam

Full-Length Exam 9 Biological and Biochemical Foundations Section Exam

Full-Length Exam 10 Biological and Biochemical Foundations Section Exam

Psychological and Sociological Foundations

Full-Length Exam 6 Psychological and Sociological Section Exam

Full-Length Exam 7 Psychological and Sociological Foundations Section Exam

Full-Length Exam Psychological and Sociological Foundations Section Exam

Full-Length Exam 9 Psychological and Sociological Foundations Section Exam

Full-Length Exam 10 Psychological and Sociological Foundations Section Exam

Next Step Online Full-Length Practice Exams

Full-Length Exam 1

Full-Length Exam 2

Full-Length Exam 3

Full-Length Exam 4

Full-Length Exam 5

Full-Length Exam 6

Full-Length Exam 7

Full-Length Exam 8

Full-Length Exam 9

Full-Length Exam 10

AAMC Practice Items

Sample Test (unscored)

Scored Practice Tests 1-3

Section Bank

Question Packs

Official Guide Practice Passages

APPENDIX C: LESSON PASSAGE CITATIONS

Lesson 2
Passage taken from the Next Step online QBank
Passage taken from the Next Step online QBank
Passage taken from the Next Step online QBank

Lesson 3
Passage taken from the Next Step MCAT Diagnostic Exam, Chemical and Physical Foundations, Passage 1
Passage taken from the Next Step online QBank
Passage taken from the Next Step online QBank

Lesson 4
Passage taken from the Next Step online QBank
Passage taken from the Next Step online QBank
Passage taken from the Next Step Biology review book, Chapter 3

Lesson 5
Passage taken from the Next Step Physics review book, Chapter 2
Passage taken from the Next Step online QBank

Lesson 6
Passage taken from the Next Step online QBank
Passage taken from the Next Step Biochemistry review book, Chapter 5

Lesson 7
Passage taken from the Next Step online QBank
Passage taken from the Next Step online QBank

Lesson 9
Passage taken from the Next Step online QBank
Passage taken from the Next Step online QBank

Lesson 10
Passage taken from the Next Step online QBank

Lesson 11
Passage taken from the Next Step online QBank
Passage taken from the Next Step online QBank

Lesson 13
Passage taken from the Next Step online QBank

Lesson 14

Passage taken from the Next Step Psychology and Sociology review book, Chapter 1

Passage taken from the Next Step online QBank

Lesson 15

Passage taken from the Next Step online QBank

Passage taken from the Next Step online QBank

Passage taken from the Next Step online QBank

Lesson 16

Passage taken from the Next Step Chemistry review book, chapter 7

Passage taken from the Next Step Chemistry review book, chapter 1

Lesson 17

Passage taken from the Next Step online QBank

Passage taken from the Next Step Biology review book, chapter 4

Lesson 18

Passage taken from the Next Step online QBank

Passage taken from the Next Step online QBank

Lesson 19

Passage taken from the Next Step online QBank

Passage taken from the Next Step online QBank

Lesson 20

Passage taken from the Next Step online QBank

APPENDIX D: LESSON IMAGE CITATIONS

Lesson 4

Glycolysis image adapted from Y. Mrabet via Wikipedia under CCBY-SA 3.0.

TCA image adapted from Y. Mrabet via Wikipedia under CCBY-SA 3.0.

Transcription image adapted from Dovelike via Wikimedia Commons under CCBY-SA 3.0 DNA replication image adapted from Dovelike via Wikimedia Commons under CCBY-SA 3.0

Lesson 5

Elbow image adapted from OpenStax via Wikipedia under CCBY 4.0

Ankle image adapted from OpenStax via Wikipedia under CCBY 4.0

Spine image adapted from OpenStax via Wikipedia under CCBY 4.0

Lesson 6

Isomer flowchart adapted from Vladsinger via Wikipedia under CCBY-SA 3.0

Phospholipid image adapted from OpenStax via Wikimedia under CCBY 4.0

Lesson 7

Peptide bond image adapted from OpenStax via Wikimedia under CCBY 3.0

Amino acid table adapted from D. Cojocari via Wikipedia under CCBY-SA 3.0

Ion channel image adapted from C. Neveu via Wikipedia under CCBY-SA 3.0

Antibody polymers image adapted from M. Brandli via Wikipedia under CCBY-SA 2.5

Motor protein image adapted from OpenStax A&P under CCBY 4.0

Sarcomere image adapted from Slashme via Wikimedia under CCBY-SA 3.0

Lesson 9

Neuron image adapted from Q. Jarosz via Wikipedia under CCBY-SA 3.0

Reflex arc image adapted from Federal Institute of Health and MartaAguayo via Wikipedia under CCBY-SA 3.0

Heart diagram image adapted from Drust-commonswiki via Wikipedia under CCBY-SA 3.0

Circulatory vessel image adapted from Adams999 via Flickr under CCBY-SA 2.0

EKG cycle image adapted from OpenStax via Wikipedia under CCBY 2.0

Lesson 10

Question 25 image adapted from Gonfer via Wikipedia under CCBY-SA 3.0

Lesson 11

Social class image adapted with artist permission from Qbark via Deviantart.com

Lesson 12

Alveolar image adapted from Slyavula Education via Flickr under CCBY 2.0

Lesson 13

Glycolysis Phase I image adapted from YMrabet via Wikimedia under CCBY-SA 3.0
Glycolysis Phase II image adapted from YMrabet via Wikimedia under CCBY-SA 3.0
Hormonal regulation of blood glucose adapted from M.Painter via Wikipedia under CC 3.0

Lesson 14

Maslow image used with permission from the artist by www.timvandevall.com
Pavlov image adapted from MagentaGreen via Wikimedia under CCBY-SA 3.0
Skinner box image adapted from Andreasl via Wikipedia under CCBY-SA 3.0
Bipolar image adapted from the Cleveland Center for Continuing Education via Wikimedia under CCBY 3.0
Bystander effect image adapted from Wikimedia Commons under CCBY-SA 3.0

Lesson 15

Menstrual cycle image adapted from Chris 73 via Wikimedia Commons under CCBY-SA 3.0
Nephron image adapted from Madhero88 via Wikipedia under CCBY 3.0
Renin-angiotensin system adapted from A.Rad via Wikipedia under CCBY-SA 3.0

Lesson 16

Galvanic and electrolytic cell images adapted from Gringer via Wikimedia under CCBY-SA 3.0

Lesson 17

T-cell receptor image adapted from OpenStax via Wikipedia under CCBY 3.0
Apoptosis image adapted from Tsgupta via Wikipedia under CCBY-SA 4.0

Lesson 18

Electromagnetic spectrum image adapted from NASA via Wikipedia under CCBY-SA 3.0
Ray diagram table adapted from EverybodyLovesRAYmond via Wikipedia under CCBY-SA 4.0
Doppler Effect image adapted from MGrundy via Wikimedia Commons under CCBY-SA 3.0
Scientist cartoon adapted from viktorvoigt via Wikipedia under CCBY-SA 3.0

Lesson 19

Cell membrane image adapted from NajedRabat via Wikimedia Commons under CCBY 4.0
Bacterial growth curve Image adapted from Michal Komorniczak via Wikimedia under CCBY-SA 3.0